DIGITAL SCHOLARLY EDITING

Digital Scholarly Editing

Theories and Practices

Edited by
Matthew James Driscoll and Elena Pierazzo

https://www.openbookpublishers.com

© 2016 Matthew James Driscoll and Elena Pierazzo. Copyright of each individual chapter is maintained by the authors.

This work is licensed under a Creative Commons Attribution 4.0 International license (CC BY 4.0). This license allows you to share, copy, distribute and transmit the text; to adapt the text and to make commercial use of the text providing attribution is made to the authors (but not in any way that suggests that they endorse you or your use of the work). Attribution should include the following information:

Matthew James Driscoll and Elena Pierazzo (eds.), *Digital Scholarly Editing: Theories and Practices*. Cambridge, UK: Open Book Publishers, 2016. http://dx.doi.org/10.11647/OBP.0095

In order to access detailed and updated information on the license, please visit https://www.openbookpublishers.com/isbn/9781783742387#copyright

Further details about CC BY licenses are available at https://creativecommons.org/licenses/by/4.0/

All external links were active on 26/7/2016 unless otherwise stated and have been archived via the Internet Archive Wayback Machine at https://archive.org/web

Updated digital material and resources associated with this volume are available at https://www.openbookpublishers.com/isbn/9781783742387#resources

Every effort has been made to identify and contact copyright holders and any omission or error will be corrected if notification is made to the publisher.

This book has been published with the generous support of the European Science Foundation.

This is the fourth volume of our Digital Humanities Series:

ISSN (Print): 2054-2410
ISSN (Online): 2054-2429

ISBN Paperback: 978-1-78374-238-7
ISBN Hardback: 978-1-78374-239-4
ISBN Digital (PDF): 978-1-78374-240-0
ISBN Digital ebook (epub): 978-1-78374-241-7
ISBN Digital ebook (mobi): 978-1-78374-242-4
DOI: 10.11647/OBP.0095

Cover photo: (Upper) *Edda Rhythmica seu Antiqvior, vulgo Sæmundina dicta*, vol. I (Copenhagen, 1787), p. 53 with comments by Gunnar Pálsson (1714–1791). Image © Suzanne Reitz, CC BY 4.0. (Lower) Clive Darra, 'Keyboard' (2009). © Clive Darra, CC BY-SA 2.0

Cover design: Heidi Coburn

All paper used by Open Book Publishers is SFI (Sustainable Forestry Initiative), PEFC (Programme for the Endorsement of Forest Certification Schemes) and Forest Stewardship Council(r)(FSC(r)) certified.

Printed in the United Kingdom, United States, and Australia
by Lightning Source for Open Book Publishers (Cambridge, UK)

Contents

Notes on Contributors   vii

Foreword   xiii
HANS WALTER GABLER

1. Introduction: Old Wine in New Bottles?   1
   MATTHEW JAMES DRISCOLL AND ELENA PIERAZZO

SECTION 1: THEORIES

2. What is a Scholarly Digital Edition?   19
   PATRICK SAHLE

3. Modelling Digital Scholarly Editing: From Plato to   41
   Heraclitus
   ELENA PIERAZZO

4. A Protocol for Scholarly Digital Editions? The Italian   59
   Point of View
   MARINA BUZZONI

5. Barely Beyond the Book?   83
   JORIS VAN ZUNDERT

6. Exogenetic Digital Editing and Enactive Cognition   107
   DIRK VAN HULLE

7. Reading or Using a Digital Edition? Reader Roles in   119
   Scholarly Editions
   KRISTA STINNE GREVE RASMUSSEN

SECTION 2: PRACTICES

8. Building *A Social Edition of the Devonshire Manuscript*   137
   RAY SIEMENS, CONSTANCE CROMPTON, DANIEL POWELL
   AND ALYSSA ARBUCKLE, WITH MAGGIE SHIRLEY
   AND THE DEVONSHIRE MANUSCRIPT EDITORIAL GROUP

9. A Catalogue of Digital Editions   161
   GRETA FRANZINI, MELISSA TERRAS AND SIMON MAHONY

10. Early Modern Correspondence: A New Challenge for Digital Editions   183
    CAMILLE DESENCLOS

11. Beyond Variants: Some Digital Desiderata for the Critical Apparatus of Ancient Greek and Latin Texts   201
    CYNTHIA DAMON

12. The Battle We Forgot to Fight: Should We Make a Case for Digital Editions?   219
    ROBERTO ROSSELLI DEL TURCO

Bibliography   239

Index   263

Notes on Contributors

Alyssa Arbuckle is the Assistant Director, Research Partnerships & Development, in the Electronics Textual Cultures Lab (ETCL) at the University of Victoria, B.C., in Canada, where she works with the Implementing New Knowledge Environments (INKE) group and the Digital Humanities Summer Institute (DHSI). Alyssa holds an MA in English from the University of Victoria and a BA Honours in English from the University of British Columbia. Her studies have centred on Digital Humanities, digital editions, new media and contemporary American literature. Her work has appeared in *Digital Studies, Digital Humanities Quarterly and Scholarly and Research Communication*, and she has given presentations, run workshops or coordinated events in Canada, Australia and the US.

Marina Buzzoni is Associate Professor of Germanic Philology and Historical Linguistics at Università Ca' Foscari in Venice, Italy. Her major scientific interests include Germanic diachronic linguistics, translation studies, textual criticism and digital editing—fields in which she has published numerous papers and scholarly contributions, as well as four monographic volumes. She has taken part in various national and international research projects, the latest of which focus on digital scholarly editing.

Constance Crompton is Assistant Professor of Digital Humanities and English, and Director of the Humanities Data Lab at the University of British Columbia's Okanagan Campus. She is a researcher with Implementing New Knowledge Environments (INKE) and, with Michelle Schwartz, co-directs Lesbian and Gay Liberation in Canada. She serves as the associate director of the Digital Humanities Summer

Institute and as a research collaborator with The Yellow Nineties Online. Her work has appeared in several edited collections as well as the *Victorian Review*, *Nineteenth-Century Gender Studies*, the *UBC Law Review*, *Digital Humanities Quarterly* and *Digital Studies/Champs Numerique*.

Cynthia Damon is Professor of Classical Studies at the University of Pennsylvania in Philadelphia. She is the author of *The Mask of the Parasite: A Pathology of Roman Patronage* (1997), a commentary on Tacitus' *Histories 1* (2003), a translation of Tacitus' *Annals* in the Penguin series (2013), and, with Will Batstone, of *Caesar's Civil War* (2006). She recently published an Oxford Classical Texts edition of Caesar's *Bellum civile* with a companion volume on the text (2015), as well as a new Loeb edition of the *Civil War* (2016). She is currently preparing a pilot edition of the *Bellum Alexandrinum* for the Library of Digital Latin Texts.

Camille Desenclos has since September 2015 been *Maître de conférences* (Associate Professor) at Université de Haute-Alsace. She gained her PhD in 2014 in early modern history with a thesis on 'The Words of Power: The Political Communication of France in the Holy Roman Empire (1617–1624)' at the École Nationale des Chartes under the supervision of Prof. Olivier Poncet. Her research interests focus on the history of diplomacy during the sixteenth and seventeenth centuries, in particular the relationship between France and the Holy Roman Empire, with special emphasis on diplomatic writing practices. She has produced two digital editions of correspondence: letters from the embassy of the Duke of Angoulême (1620–1621) and by Antoine du Bourg (1535–1538).

Matthew James Driscoll is Senior Lecturer in Old Norse philology at Nordisk Forskningsinstitut, a research institute within the Faculty of Humanities at the University of Copenhagen. His research interests include manuscript and textual studies, with special focus on popular manuscript culture in late pre-modern Iceland. He is also keenly interested in the description and transcription of primary sources, and has a long-standing involvement in the work of the Text Encoding Initiative, serving on the TEI's Technical Council from 2001 until 2010. From 2011 to 2015 he was involved in the research networking programme of NeDiMAH (Network for Digital Methods in the Arts and Humanities), funded by the European Science Foundation, and acted as chair of its working group on digital scholarly editions.

Greta Franzini is a PhD student at University College London's Centre for Digital Humanities, where she conducts interdisciplinary research in Latin philology, manuscript studies and digital editing. Her interests lie in the application of digital technologies to the study of Classical texts and in the interdisciplinary research opportunities offered by digital scholarly editions. Greta is also an early career researcher at the University of Göttingen, where she is involved in research pertaining to historical text reuse, natural language processing and text visualisation.

Hans Walter Gabler is Professor of English Literature (retired) at the University of Munich, Germany, and Senior Research Fellow of the Institute of English Studies, School of Advanced Study, London University. From 1996 to 2002 in Munich, he directed an interdisciplinary graduate programme on 'Textual Criticism as Foundation and Method of the Historical Disciplines'. He is editor-in-chief of the critical editions of James Joyce's *Ulysses* (1984/1986), *A Portrait of the Artist as a Young Man* and *Dubliners* (both 1993). His present research continues to be directed towards the writing processes in draft manuscripts and their representation in the digital medium. Editorial theory, digital editing and Genetic Criticism have become the main focus of his professional writing.

Simon Mahony is Associate Director for Teaching at University College London's Centre for Digital Humanities and Senior Teaching Fellow at the Department of Information Studies, where he is Programme Director for the MA/MSc in Digital Humanities. He has research interests in the application of new technologies to the study of the ancient world; using web-based mechanisms and digital resources to build and sustain learning communities, collaborative and innovative working; the development of education practice and the use of new tools and technologies to facilitate this. He is also an Associate Fellow at UCL's Institute of Classical Studies.

Elena Pierazzo is Professor of Italian Studies and Digital Humanities at Université Grenoble-Alpes; previous to that she was Lecturer at the Department of Digital Humanities at King's College London, where she was the coordinator of the MA in Digital Humanities. Her areas of special interest include Italian Renaissance texts, the editing of early-modern and modern draft manuscripts, digital editing and text encoding. She has been the Chair of the Text Encoding Initiative and involved in the TEI user-community, with particular focus on the transcription of modern and medieval manuscripts. She was co-chair of the working group on digital scholarly editions of NeDiMAH and one of the scientists-in-chief of the Digital Scholarly Editions Initial Training Network (DiXiT).

Daniel Powell is a Marie Skłowdowska-Curie Fellow in DiXiT. He is based in the Department of Digital Humanities at King's College London and affiliated with the Electronic Textual Cultures Lab and Department of English at the University of Victoria, with research interests in Scholarly Communication and Editing, the Digital Humanities and Early Modern Drama. He is Associate Director of the Renaissance Knowledge Network and serves on the Scholarly Advisory Committee for the Folger Shakespeare Library's *Digital Anthology of Early Modern English Drama*. From 2012 to 2015 he served as Assistant Editor for Digital Publication on the journal *Early Theatre*; since 2015 he has served as Editor for Digital Initiatives at *postmedieval: a journal of medieval cultural studies*. His work has appeared, among other places, in *Digital Studies/Le champ numérique, Renaissance and Reformation/Renaissance et Reforme, Scholarly and Research Communication* and *Religion and Literature*.

Krista Stinne Greve Rasmussen took her PhD at the University of Copenhagen in 2015. She has participated in the Velux-funded research project *Dansk editionshistorie* (History of Editing in Denmark) and has worked as a scholarly editor at The Works of Grundtvig project at the University of Aarhus (2010–2011). Her main research interests are scholarly editing, new media, the history of the book and literary criticism. She is a member of the governing bodies for the *Nordisk netværk for boghistorie* (Nordic Network for Book History) and the *Nordisk netværk for editionsfilologer* (Nordic Network for Textual Scholarship).

Roberto Rosselli Del Turco is Assistant Professor at the Università degli studi di Torino, where he teaches Germanic Philology, Old English language and literature and Digital Humanities. He is also Assistant Professor of Digital Humanities at the Università di Pisa. He has published widely in the Digital Humanities and Anglo-Saxon studies. He has recently edited and translated the Old English poem *The*

Battle of Maldon (2009) and is the editor of the Digital Vercelli Book, an ongoing project that aims at providing a full edition of this important manuscript. He is lead developer of Edition Visualization Technology (EVT), a software tool created at the University of Pisa to navigate and visualise digital editions based on the TEI XML encoding standard. He is also co-director of the Visionary Cross project, an international project whose aim is to produce an advanced multimedia edition of key Anglo-Saxon texts and monuments, in particular the *Dream of the Rood* and the Ruthwell and Bewcastle preaching crosses.

Patrick Sahle has studied History, Philosophy and Political Science in Cologne and Rome. He holds a PhD in Information Processing in the Humanities, based on his three-volume dissertation *Digitale Editionsformen (Digital Scholarly Editions)*. Currently he is Professor for Digital Humanities at Universität zu Köln, where he also acts as manager of the Cologne Center for eHumanities (CCeH), as Digital Humanities coordinator for the North Rhine-Westphalian Academy for Science (AWK), and as coordinator of the Data Center for the Humanities (DCH). He is also a founding member of the Institute for Documentology and Scholarly Editing (IDE).

Ray Siemens is Distinguished Professor of English and Computer Science in the Faculty of Humanities at the University of Victoria, B.C., and past Canada Research Chair in Humanities Computing (2004–2015). He is founding editor of the electronic scholarly journal *Early Modern Literary Studies*, and his publications include, among others, Blackwell's *Companion to Digital Humanities* (2004, 2015, with Susan Schreibman and John Unsworth), Blackwell's *Companion to Digital Literary Studies* (2008, with Susan Schreibman), *A Social Edition of the Devonshire MS* (2012, 2015, with Constance Crompton, Daniel Powell, Alyssa Arbuckle et al.), *Literary Studies in the Digital Age* (2014, with Kenneth Price) and *The Lyrics of the Henry VIII MS* (2016). He directs the Implementing New Knowledge Environments project, the Digital Humanities Summer Institute and the Electronic Textual Cultures Lab, recently serving also as Vice President/Director of the Canadian Federation of the Humanities and Social Sciences for Research Dissemination, Chair of the Modern Languages Association Committee on Scholarly Editions and Chair of the international Alliance of Digital Humanities Organisations.

Melissa Terras is Director of University College London's Centre for Digital Humanities, Professor of Digital Humanities at UCL's Department of Information Studies and Vice Dean of Research for the Faculty of Arts and Humanities. Her publications include *Image to Interpretation: Intelligent Systems to Aid Historians in the Reading of the Vindolanda Texts* (2006) and *Digital Images for the Information Professional* (2008), and she has co-edited various volumes, such as *Digital Humanities in Practice* (2012) and *Defining Digital Humanities: A Reader* (2013). She is currently serving on the Board of Curators of the University of Oxford Libraries and the Board of the National Library of Scotland, and is a Fellow of the Chartered Institute of Library and Information Professionals and Fellow of the British Computer Society. Her research focuses on the use of computational techniques to enable research in the arts and humanities that would otherwise be impossible.

Dirk Van Hulle is Professor of English Literature at the University of Antwerp and director of the Centre for Manuscript Genetics and recently edited the new *Cambridge Companion to Samuel Beckett* (2015). With Mark Nixon, he is co-director of the *Beckett Digital Manuscript Project* and editor-in-chief of the *Journal of Beckett Studies*. His publications include *Textual Awareness* (2004), *Modern Manuscripts* (2014), *Samuel Beckett's Library* (2013, with Mark Nixon), *James Joyce's Work in Progress* (2016) and several genetic editions in the *Beckett Digital Manuscript Project*, including *Krapp's Last Tape/La Dernière Bande, L'Innommable/The Unnamable* (with Shane Weller) and the *Beckett Digital Library*.

Joris J. van Zundert is a Researcher and Developer in Humanities Computing and Digital Humanities in the Department of Literary Studies at the Huygens Institute for the History of The Netherlands, a research institute of the Netherlands Royal Academy of Arts and Sciences (KNAW). As a researcher and developer his main interest lies with the possibilities of computational algorithms for the analysis of literary and historic texts and the nature and properties of humanities information and data modelling. His current research focuses on computer science and humanities interaction and the tensions between hermeneutics and 'big data' approaches.

Foreword

Hans Walter Gabler

The NeDiMAH Experts' Seminar on Digital Scholarly Editions, held at the Huygens Institute for the History of the Netherlands in The Hague in November 2012, was one of the most substantial and concentrated gatherings around a given subject I have ever, I think, attended. Nor is this an idealised memory: it is now fully borne out by the essays deriving from that Seminar assembled in the present volume, each of which is a fresh and much deepened take on the topics addressed in The Hague.

To explore the subject 'Digital Scholarly Editing: Theories and Practices', as this volume is now titled, is to map out the range of demands that digitality makes on textual criticism and editing today. It is also to envisage fresh conceptualisations for the future of these twin disciplines foundational to the humanities. The 'scholarly edition' lives in our present time, and will in the future live more uncompromisingly yet, in the digital medium. In consequence, the systemic triplet on which it relies, the hop, step and jump of textual criticism, editing and edition, needs in important respects to be reconceived. It needs to be re-comprehended in terms of the medium. While the scholarly edition will remain, as it has been, the fruit of state-of-the-art investigative and critical text-focused scholarship, its form and mode of presentation will cease to be the book. As a digital scholarly edition, it is, and will increasingly be, established through text-critical methodology and editorial execution rendered digitally operative in a technically fully digital environment. So, too, the digital scholarly edition will be used: it will be studied and explored, mined and enriched wholly in the digital medium. By no means, though, will this end the symbiosis of text and book. Yet in the digital age, great potentials of innovation lie in the separation of the material medium of the transmission of texts, and the digital medium of the use of editions. Texts as texts depend for readability, and indeed enjoyment, on their presence and simple, since culturally ingrained, availability in the materiality of the book. But texts as texts are not the be-all and end-all of scholarly editions.

An edited text is by its nature a dialogue staged and conducted by an editor (or editorial team) with 'the text' of a work as it has commonly been transmitted in variant material texts. The edited text that an edition offers is thus the product of concordant labours of criticism, textual criticism and editing. Comprehensively, these constitute the scholarly edition's concurrent discourses, which are traditionally understood to be oriented towards the texts of the given work and its transmission, on the one hand, and towards the mediation and elucidation of the work on the other. In terms of the text orientation, the edition's pivotal discourse is commonly the edited text, towards which are correlated (to give them their traditional names): the textual apparatus, formalised and with its specific information abbreviated into symbols, the textual notes, phrased in natural language, and collations from preceding editions of the given work, usually recorded in lists. The argument, or rationale, for the edition is given in the Editorial Introduction. This whole aggregate of discourses is held together by a common reference grid. To facilitate the mediation and elucidation of the work, moreover, the edition's reference system equally allows the linking-in of all manner of commentary substance into the edition.

A scholarly edition, then, is relationally coordinated throughout. The medium which in our time allows modelling the relational structure of editions is the digital medium. The task ahead is therefore to realise the scholarly edition as a digital scholarly edition. This demands exploring the medium's potentials to their full extent. At present, editions realised in a digital environment still tend to remain largely imitative of scholarly editions in print. What the medial shift requires however is a thorough re-conception, and in consequence re-modelling. The scholarly edition used to be an end product, going public when all textual and critical scholarship was done. The digital scholarly edition, by contrast, may from the moment it is technically stable be opened up as a shared enterprise. It may so already in its still ongoing process of content enrichment become generally accessible as a dynamically interactive knowledge and research site. A digital scholarly edition conceived as a research site will thus, from within the Digital Humanities, set an example for what computer science presently strives for: HCI—human computer interaction.

This, in all prefatory brevity, is the conceptual background to the essays assembled in this volume. In their range of reflection on theory and practice, they substantially advance the maturing of digital scholarly editing into the innovative cultural technique that, from out of the humanities, it is already well on its way to becoming.

1. Introduction:
Old Wine in New Bottles?

Matthew James Driscoll and Elena Pierazzo

In the past few years we have succeeded in raising the profile of digital editing; networks, conferences, events, training, journals and publications—nothing seems able to stop the stream of scholarly contributions within the field of textual scholarship around the world. The present book is part of this development, and highlights some of the work done between 2011 and 2015 under the auspices of NeDiMAH, the Network for Digital Methods in the Arts and Humanities, which has been funded by the European Science Foundation with the aim to reflect on and provide guidance in a wide range of fields within the Humanities at the time of their conversion to the digital medium. One of the workgroups within NeDiMAH, chaired by the editors of the present publication, has been devoted to digital scholarly editing. During the lifetime of the workgroup we have organised three dedicated events and a panel within the 2013 annual conference of the Text Encoding Initiative (TEI), held at the Università La Sapienza in Rome, as well as sponsoring the participation of young scholars in relevant workshops and trainings. This book represents an enriched version of the second of these events, which was held on 21 November 2012 at the Huygens Institute in The Hague.[1] We called the one-day event an 'expert seminar',

---

1 See the outline of the event on the website: http://nedimah.eu/reports/experts-seminar-report-hague-21-nov-2012.

© M. J. Driscoll and E. Pierazzo, CC BY 4.0   http://dx.doi.org/10.11647/OBP.0095.01

as it was attended by some of the most authoritative voices in the field; but an emerging field needs new voices too, and so we also invited a number of early career researchers. The current publication reflects the same richness, authoritativeness and openness to the future, featuring contributions by established and emerging scholars in roughly equal measure.

The experience of the NeDiMAH workgroup has been extremely positive, and we have now passed the baton to another network, namely the DiXiT, funded by the European Commission via a Marie Curie Action.[2] In fact, DiXiT not only sees the participation of many of the people present in this publication, but was built on that very experience; DiXiT provides training for early career researchers and organises events on digital scholarly editing, the impact of which will be assessed in the next few years, but promises to be considerable.[3] As for training, in the past few years many initiatives have characterised the textual scholarship scene, particularly in Europe. For instance, since 2009 the graduate training programme Medieval/Modern Manuscript Studies in the Digital Age (MMSDA) has provided foundational training in digital methods to graduate students;[4] the MMSDA experience has been repurposed in a condensed version as a tutorial during the preliminary phases of the Digital Humanities conference in Sydney (2015). More recently, the Erasmus Plus network on DEMM (Digital Editing of Medieval Manuscripts)[5] has started to provide advanced training for MA and PhD students. On the publication side, one cannot but make

---

2   See the DiXiT website at http://dixit.uni-koeln.de

3   Elena Pierazzo, 'Disciplinary Impact: The Effect of Digital Editing', *Digital Humanities 2015*, University of West Sydney, Sydney 29 June–3 July, http://dh2015.org/abstracts/xml/PIERAZZO_Elena_Disciplinary_Impact__The_Effect_of/PIERAZZO_Elena_Disciplinary_Impact__The_Effect_of_Digit.html

4   See Peter A. Stokes, 'Teaching Manuscripts in the "Digital Age"', in *Kodikologie und Paläographie im Digitalen Zeitalter 2 — Codicology and Palaeography in the Digital Age 2*, ed. by Franz Fischer, Christiane Fritze and Georg Vogeler, in collaboration with Bernhard Assmann, Malte Rehbein and Patrick Sahle, Schriften des Instituts für Dokumentologie und Editorik 3 (Norderstedt: BOD, 2010), pp. 229–45; Simon Mahony and Elena Pierazzo, 'Teaching Skills or Teaching Methodology', in *Digital Humanities Pedagogy: Practices, Principles and Politics*, ed. by Brett D. Hirsch (Cambridge: Open Book Publishers, 2013), pp. 215–25, http://dx.doi.org/10.11647/OBP.0024

5   See http://www.digitalmanuscripts.eu

a reference to the online journal *Scholarly Editing*, the content of which is not exclusively on digital topics, but its provision of digital editions as part of its content represents an innovative and exciting approach to some of the issues of support and sustainability discussed in this book.

In addition, large numbers of articles and monographs are appearing, demonstrating on the one hand the dynamicity within the field and on the other the compelling need of the community to discuss the changes and the implications brought by computers. It is evident that something is radically changing in the scholarly editing world: the way we work, the tools we use to do such work and the research questions to which we try to give answers—all of these have changed, in some case beyond recognition, with respect to the older print-based workflow.

These changes have produced a compelling need to reflect on the implications of such changes from a theoretical and practical point of view, assessing if the changes in the way we work (the heuristics of editing) are determining also changes in the understanding of scholarly editing and of the texts we edit (the hermeneutics of editing). We know how there has always been an intimate relationship between what instruments make it possible to observe and measure and what sort of research scientists undertake: 'we shape our tools, and thereafter our tools shape us', in the words attributed to Marshall McLuhan.[6]

What seems even more compelling, however, is to understand what digital scholarly editing actually is: is it a new discipline or a new methodology? Are we simply putting 'old wine in new bottles', or are we doing something which has never been done—indeed, never been doable—before?

Several years ago a series of conferences devoted to 'Supporting Digital Humanities' were held under the auspices of the two big European Humanities research infrastructure projects DARIAH (Digital Research Infrastructure for the Arts and the Humanities) and CLARIN (Common

---

6   This quotation, widely attributed to McLuhan, does not actually feature in any of his books; it does however appear in an article *about* McLuhan by John M. Culkin, SJ: 'A Schoolman's Guide to Marshall McLuhan', *Saturday Review* (18 March 1967), pp. 51–53, 71–72, and according to the authors of the *McLuhan Galaxy* blog (i.e. the McLuhan estate), it is an idea 'entirely consistent with McLuhan's thinking on technology in general'; see https://mcluhangalaxy.wordpress.com/2013/04/01/we-shape-our-tools-and-thereafter-our-tools-shape-us

Language Resources and Technology Infrastructure). The theme for the second of these, held in Copenhagen in 2011, was 'Answering the unaskable', the idea being that digital technologies have the potential to transform the types of research questions that we ask in the Humanities, allowing us not only to address traditional questions in new and exciting ways, but ultimately also to formulate research questions we would never have been able to ask without access to large quantities of digital data and sophisticated tools for their analysis.

This assertion has been questioned, but research questions change constantly, and always have, even as our perception of the world changes, in keeping with our ability to perceive it.

In order to respond to this question it is perhaps worth examining what has actually changed for textual scholars owing to the introduction of computers, the first revolution being access.

Locating primary sources

For the textual scholar the availability of online catalogues principally means the ability to locate manuscripts and other primary sources more easily and quickly than has hitherto been the case. This was the dream underlying the MASTER project (1999–2001) and many similar attempts at union catalogues of (European medieval) manuscripts: being able to search in all repositories everywhere at the same time. The CERL (Consortium of European Research Libraries) portal, ENRICH (European Networking Resources and Information Concerning Cultural Heritage), the Schoenberg database, *Manuscriptorium* in Prague, *Digital scriptorium* in the US, *eCodices* in Switzerland, *TRAME* in Italy—not to mention the online catalogues of major libraries such as the British Library, Bibliothèque Nationale de France, Harvard University Library and so on—have all improved access to primary and secondary sources and have therefore had a huge impact on the day-to-day work of scholars and editors. Most of these efforts have been made possible by the conscious use of established standards and protocols, since it is only the quality and interoperability of the metadata which make it possible to query multiple databases simultaneously.

Digital images

Once you have found your primary sources you can, in many cases, now view digital images of them, sometimes high-resolution images which are (some would say) better than the originals. One cannot really overestimate the impact that such digital images have had on editorial work: the ready availability of digital facsimiles represents such a huge leap forward that some scholars have even been tempted to say that 'we need never see the document itself'.[7] An animated debate surrounds and questions the pervasive use of digital images in manuscript studies, however, lamenting their lack of embodiment and the possibility of misunderstanding or overlooking some crucial codicological feature;[8] but it is undeniable that digital images have changed greatly the way many manuscript scholars work—even if too many online digital libraries still have far too little in terms of navigational aids to be of any great use to scholars. The uneven quality of the digital images, as well as, in many cases, the lack of a systematic programme of digitisation, give more the impression of a patchwork quilt than of a reliable research tool; there is still room for improvement in this area.

The availability of digital images has also encouraged the development of digital palaeography and quantitative codicology,[9] as well as research on automatic handwriting recognition and OCR for manuscripts and early printed books.[10] This research has not yet

---

7   Meg Twycross, 'Virtual Restoration and Manuscript Archaeology', in *The Virtual Representation of the Past*, ed. by Mark Greengrass and Lorna Hughes (Farnham: Ashgate, 2008), pp. 23–47 (p. 23).

8   Elena Pierazzo, *Digital Scholarly Editing: Theories, Models and Methods* (Farnham: Ashgate, 2015), pp. 97–98.

9   See the three volumes published by the IDE (Institut für Dokumentologie und Editorik) *Kodikologie und Paläographie im Digitalen Zeitalter — Codicology and Palaeography in the Digital Age* published between 2009 and 2015; in particular see Peter A. Stokes, 'Computer-Aided Palaeography, Present and Future', in *Kodikologie und Paläographie im Digitalen Zeitalter — Codicology and Palaeography in the Digital Age*, pp. 313–42.

10 See Tal Hassner, Malte Rehbein, Peter A. Stokes and Lior Wolf, 'Computation and Palaeography: Potentials and Limits: Manifesto from Dagstuhl Perspectives Workshop 12382', *Dagstuhl Manifestos*, 2 (2013), 14–35; Lior Wolf et al., 'Identifying Join Candidates in the Cairo Genizah', *International Journal of Computer Vision*, 94 (2011), 118–35; Lambert Schomaker, 'Writer Identification and Verification', in *Advances in Biometrics: Sensors, Algorithms and Systems*, ed. by N. K. Ratha and Venu Govindaraju (London: Springer, 2008), pp. 247–64.

produced reliably working products, but much more is to be expected in the coming years.

Transcribed texts

There is a vast number of electronic versions of cultural heritage texts freely available on the Internet. Many of them, unfortunately, are all but unusable, for a variety of reasons. They may be the result of uncorrected ('dirty') OCR taken from old, out of copyright editions, and may therefore bear little resemblance to their originals; or they may be totally missing the critical apparatus, which copyright status and the difficulty of representation on a scrollable page are the main reasons for its rare appearance alongside the main text (see the chapter by Cynthia Damon in the present volume, pp. 201–18). The result is that without the apparatus the reader cannot have any real idea what he or she is actually reading. One could—and people regularly do—argue that the availability of these mutilated texts is better than nothing, but in many ways these texts are actually worse than nothing, since they are misleading and fuel the idea that texts exist outside the dialectic between documents and editors, and that editions *can* possibly establish texts once and for all, undermining in this way the very survival of textual scholarship itself, as argued by Elena Pierazzo in this volume (pp. 41–58).

Proper digital editions, although certainly on the increase, are unfortunately still few and far between.

Crunching the data

But none of this, arguably, is fundamentally different from what we as textual scholars have always done, the only difference being that we can now process much larger amounts of data more quickly than has previously been possible for one person. What is new in these approaches is that we are now able to process these huge amounts of data in new ways, collating, for example, the socio-economic status of the scribes and/or commissioners of manuscripts with the format and the layout of the page, density of the text and the nature/genre of the work being copied, as it develops over time and geographical area. This is the approach chosen by the SfarData project, which aims to locate, classify and identify all extant dated Hebrew manuscripts from the Middle Ages.[11] It is also the approach of Jesse Hurlbut, who has developed a method for analysing the overall layout of manuscript pages, which he calls 'the manuscript average'.[12]

But, as with the creation of large catalogues and meta-catalogues of manuscripts, unleashing the potential of this approach depends on the interoperability of data, which means using a common standard.

Automatic collation, stemmatology and cladistic methods

Computers have been used since their inception to try to relieve what Peter Shillingsburg has called the 'idiot work' of textual editing.[13] Automatic collation and the automatic generation of stemmata are still in their infancy — or at least not as far advanced as one might have wished — but as interest increases and more sophisticated applications are being developed there is hope for significant breakthroughs in the foreseeable future; and here too, much depends on the use of accepted standards. The cladistic (or phylogenetic) method is perhaps the only born-digital method available in textual scholarship, since it is based on heavy computational techniques and has arisen through interdisciplinary collaboration between textual scholars, computer scientists and bio-geneticists.[14]

Standards

The necessity of using accepted standards has been mentioned in connection with most of the previous items, and indeed it is hard to overestimate the importance of the establishment of common standards

---

11   See the project website: http://sfardata.nli.org.il
12   See the description of this method from the scholar's blog: http://jessehurlbut.net/wp/mssart/?page_id=2097
13   Peter L. Shillingsburg, *Scholarly Editing in the Computer Age: Theory and Practice* (Ann Arbor: University of Michigan Press, 1996), p. 139.
14   Caroline Macé and Philippe V. Baret, 'Why Phylogenetic Method Work: The Theory of Evolution and Textual Criticism', in *The Evolution of Texts: Confronting Stemmatological and Genetical Methods*, ed. by Caroline Macé et al. (Pisa and Rome: Istituti Editoriali e Poligrafici Internazionali, 2006), pp. 89–108; Matthew Spencer, Elizabeth A. Davidson, Adrian C. Barbrook and Christopher J. Howe, 'Phylogenetics of Artificial Manuscripts', *Journal of Theoretical Biology*, 227 (2004), 503–11.

for metadata, transcription of texts and the description of events, people and dates. In fact, the development of tools and software able to 'crunch' data that can lighten editorial work and guide scholars into new territories requires the establishment of a shared vocabulary and baseline understanding of the most common features of such editorial work. This is perhaps the area where research has advanced the most: the early establishment of the Text Encoding Initiative—in 1986, before the development of the World Wide Web—has been fundamental to the development of the very idea of digital scholarly editing. But in spite of early and widespread use of the TEI in all stages of editing, much is still to be done. The 'problem' with the TEI is that its comprehensiveness and flexibility make it hard for developers to create meaningful tools that can serve more than one project at a time. Nonetheless, the effort toward standardisation has made it possible to develop an international, trans-disciplinary community that is interested in digital editing. Furthermore the existence of the TEI as a standard for many aspects of editorial work is now helping to highlight areas where standardisation is yet to be found—or there are too many competing standards; in other words, the standardisation operated by the TEI has whetted our appetite for more. In fact, in spite of the influential models offered by the TEI and by the various standards promoted by the Library of Congress, comprehensive authority files of titles, authors, persons and places are still to come. Standard mechanisms for dating would also be helpful—when, exactly, was 'the beginning of the 14th century'?[15]

Social editing

From the evolution of the digital society and from the ubiquity of social networks derives a new take on the idea of teamwork in editing (social editing). The idea that one can indeed put a text 'out there' and invite people (either other editors or the lay public, depending on the project) to transcribe, collate, correct and collaboratively edit it has

---

15 See, for instance, the paper presented by Peter A. Stokes at the *Digital Humanities* conference (Sydney, 29 June–3 July 2015): 'The Problem of Digital Dating: A Model for Uncertainty in Medieval Documents', in *Digital Humanities 2015 Book of Abstracts* (Sydney, 2015), http://dh2015.org/abstracts/xml/STOKES_Peter_Anthony_The_ Problem_of_Digital_Datin/STOKES_Peter_Anthony_The_Problem_of_Digital_ Dating__A_M.html

caused a bit of a stir in the editorial community, raising questions about authoritativeness, the role of editors and what is needed for an edition to be labelled as 'scholarly'; the chapter by Siemens et al. in this book will certainly contribute to the debate.

This sketch of the innovations introduced to textual scholarship by computer technology, although brief, is perhaps enough to allow us to declare that doing things digitally is not simply doing the same old thing in a new medium. In addition, it seems that not only have the methods changed, but this new medium requires a fair bit of theoretical re-thinking and reflection on the significance of what we are doing and its impact on the discipline and on our notions of textuality. The present publication aims to do precisely this: on the one hand to provide an overview of opinions on what is actually changing in scholarly editing from a theoretical point of view, and on the other hand to provide a sample of case studies where such reflections are tested against manuscripts and works from different areas and times.

The book is thus divided in two main sections: Theories and Practices. This division does not mean that theoretical and broad-reaching considerations will only be found on the first section, however: on the contrary, the division is only to manifest how the second group of contributions tends to focus on specific cases and draw from them more general statements, while the chapters in the first group have more methodological aims, but without neglecting the occasional reference to concrete case studies. And it seems only natural that this should be the case: textual scholarship is a 'field' discipline, and theories and methods only emerge in practice.

The first section opens with Patrick Sahle's attempt to answer a very basic question: what is a scholarly digital edition (pp. 19–40)? The chapter presents in condensed form the most important points from his monumental *Digitale Editionsformen*, published in 2013.[16] In his contribution he determines that it is the following of a digital paradigm which distinguishes digital editions from digitised editions, where the latter are found to follow a page paradigm instead. In other words, it

---

16 Patrick Sahle, *Digitale Editionsformen: Zum Umgang mit der Überlieferung unter den Bedingungen des Medienwandels*, 3 vols., Schriften des Instituts für Dokumentologie und Editorik 7–9 (Norderstedt: BOD, 2013).

is the capability of digital editions to 'transmedialise', to move from medium to medium, that gives them the possibility of transcending boundaries and establishing a new field of enquiry.

The second contribution, by Elena Pierazzo, focuses on the fluidity and changeability of texts in general and of digital texts in particular. Texts change over time and across media, and in spite of the early conviction of editors that the uncovering of the lost original (the *Urtext*) was an achievable goal, the reality of texts demonstrates how this belief cannot be supported: texts are never perfect (in the philosophical sense), but can always be perfected. Electronic texts have an even larger degree of changeability, and digital editing therefore forces editors finally to embrace textual variation as a defining feature of textuality.

Marina Buzzoni (pp. 59–82) discusses the pros and cons of building a protocol for the creation of digital scholarly editions, claiming how the accountability of editorial work, which has been claimed to be the requirement for defining an edition as scholarly, can be only fulfilled digitally. She then proceeds to analyse the defining characteristics of scholarly editions in the light of the Italian school of textual scholarship, reflecting on how these transpose into the digital medium. Her attention focuses in particular on the most striking feature of a scholarly edition, namely the critical apparatus, and she discusses the way this can be formalised, remediated and made more usable and ultimately scholarly in a digital framework, lamenting the current limitations offered by the Critical Apparatus module of the TEI.

Joris van Zundert (pp. 83–106) claims that the so-called novelty promised by digital editions is actually held back by the pervasiveness of the most powerful model: the book. Starting from a software development point of view, van Zundert examines the drawbacks of most current digital editions, and investigates ways and possibilities for a methodological breakthrough. In examining the shortcomings of some current editions, he singles out the communication gap that exists between textual scholars and software developers and the tension between the model of the book championed by the former group and the new born-digital knowledge models proposed by the latter. In order to analyse the impact of this tension (or trading zone), he employs sociolinguistic terminology to show how a creole language develops between the two groups, providing mechanisms through which collaboration and new kinds of scholarship can be built. He calls this retention of the physical book as a model for digital editions a regression, with respect to the early theoretical framing of hypertexts as the new digital paradigm. He then calls for a renewed interest in a dialog between textual scholarship and computer science and the elaboration of a more effective inter-linguistic creole.

Dirk Van Hulle (pp. 107–18) adopts a cognitive approach for his examination of the personal libraries of modernist authors. He claims that genetic digital editing may be the key to creating a bridge and a bi-directional exchange between literary studies and cognitive science, supporting his claim with examples gathered from the *Beckett Digital Manuscript Project*. The case study shows how Samuel Beckett's marginalia in his private books bears witness to a creative process that extends over decades, and gives an example of how intertextuality functions as a model of the extended mind. The integration of the digital editions of the manuscripts with the digital editions of the personal library of Beckett, as well as the modelling of the type of marginalia and annotation, are the key ingredients to opening new research perspectives into the editing of modern literary drafts, raising the question of what constitutes the interest of the editor and where we should place our intellectual boundaries now that the digital medium allows us to include entire libraries in digital editions as well as all the surviving witnesses of any given work.

The chapter by Krista Stinne Greve Rasmussen (pp. 119–34) shifts the focus from editorial work to the users of digital editions or, more precisely, readers and types of readers. In fact, she distinguishes between readers who are primarily interested in accessing a reliable text, users who engage with the interpretation of the text and with the editorial work itself, and co-workers, who contribute to the editions themselves with commentaries, annotations and even editorial intervention. More than defining types of people, these categories tend to define attitudes and roles, which can change in time and moments. In her analysis, she examines differences in perceptions of texts, works and documents in print and in digital form. The open-endedness of digital knowledge sites (as defined by Shillingsburg) represents a threat to the reader (as defined by Rasmussen), who is distracted by the urge to click and fails to appreciate the text as a full aesthetic object. The author claims that digital scholarly editions can (and should) also take the shape of information sites, i.e. places where a reliable text can simply be read, top to bottom, with no or only minimal paratextual and editorial paraphernalia. This separation between text and editorial statement may not always be necessary, though: for the establishment of the essential relationship between text and readers, it may be sufficient for readers to have the impression that an edition, a digital one, is actually a finished product, a challenge big enough, given the intrinsic variability of digital products.

The section on Practices opens with the contribution by Ray Siemens (pp. 137–60) and his team on their ground-breaking edition of the Devonshire manuscript. The chapter contains an account of the key decisions behind the creation of a digital edition of this important Tudor period manuscript on an open, social platform such as Wikibooks. This 'social' edition is social in two ways: on the one hand, it makes reference to the theory of the so-called social text championed by D. F. McKenzie and Jerome McGann; on the other hand it uses a social platform like a Wiki, where knowledge is crowdsourced. But it is also the text that is edited that is social to begin with: it is in fact the product of the multiple hands at the court of Henry VIII, who over the space of a few years composed and assembled the collection as we know it now. It is therefore the nature of the text, in a sense, that pushes toward a different editorial solution, open to the contribution of unforeseen editors, as the manuscript itself was open to unforeseen contributions. This editorial solution of course has repercussions well beyond this specific case and opens a series of questions about the future of scholarly editions and the role of the editor: if editors will no longer be the textual gatekeepers, what will they become? But perhaps this is not the right question to ask, the authors of the contribution preferring to look at the meaning of scholarship in the new web 2.0 context, where the (academic) work can be exposed to scrutiny and improvement of the users (the textual stakeholders), and what is changing in the perceptions of their work and their outcomes.

Before asking questions about the scholarship of digital editions and the role of digital editors, however, it is perhaps worth asking what digital editions look like, how are they built and what they offer to their users. This is what the chapter by Franzini, Terras and Mahony (pp. 161–82) attempts, namely by investigating the many different shapes of digital editions in the form of a collaborative, online catalogue of editions. The catalogue's pragmatic approach to the definition of digital edition is then able to provide scholars with interesting insights into what in practice it means to produce a scholarly edition, accounting for disciplinary (classics vs. modern texts) and methodological (TEI or non-TEI) divides.

The following two contributions both focus on one of the most keenly felt shortcomings of the TEI schema and modelling, namely the uneven support provided for the encoding of correspondence and of the critical apparatus. The text of Camille Desenclos (pp. 183–200) reports on the progress made on the modelling of early modern correspondence within a project at the École Nationale des Chartes over a large corpus of correspondence of diplomats, in particular French, writing from many European courts over several centuries. The chapter reflects on the specificity of correspondence and on the complication of separating data from metadata in letters, considered as data-rich devices. Desenclos points out a traditionally grey area of digital modelling of documents, as demonstrated by the TEI's only partial support for the encoding of letters. In recent years, however, a large community has gathered around this issue, with substantial improvements already reaching the community of scholars.[17] But while the work within the TEI community has so far produced a better understanding of the kind of human and social interactions that are witnessed by correspondence, Desenclos is more interested in the modelling of the actual document, its various parts and components, and what we can learn from their presence, absence and layout. In her chapter (pp. 201–18), Cynthia Damon focuses her attention on the modelling of the critical apparatus of ancient texts and on the patchy support given to scholars by the TEI in this field. She claims that the critical apparatus needs to be seen as much more than a simple list of variant readings; rather, it is the vault where all the understanding and scholarship of the editors is kept and showcased. At present the TEI only provides a mechanism for recording the actual variants, but not the

---

17 Sabine Seifert, Marcel Illetschko and Peter Stadler, 'Towards a Model for Encoding Correspondence in the TEI', *Journal of the Text Encoding Initiative*, 9 (forthcoming); Peter Stadler, 'Interoperabilität von digitalen Briefeditionen', in *Fontanes Briefe ediert*, ed. by Hanna Delf von Wolzogen and Rainer Falk (Würzburg: Königshausen & Neumann, 2014), pp. 278–87.

arguments that explain why they have been rejected, or for documenting the long tradition of editorial arguments which characterises classical texts. It is questionable whether editors, in order to take full advantage of digital methods, should 'start from scratch', namely by transcribing all extant witnesses, collating them automatically and then using the results of such a collation to build a stemma and textual apparatus using computational methods. Damon protests that this approach tends to forget that classical texts have been edited for centuries, and that a good edition should also take into account previous scholarship in the form of earlier discussions and conjectures, all aspects that cannot easily be included in a 'simple' computational workflow; she concludes by calling for a new approach where the digital edition takes into account the complexity of the editorial work and its tradition.

The concluding chapter, by Roberto Rosselli Del Turco (pp. 219–38), laments the relatively marginal status still held by digital editions with respect to printed ones, despite more than twenty years of activity in the digital field. In many cases, clearly, print is still the medium of choice for the publication of the fruits of editorial endeavour, and digital editions have not yet been accepted among the scholarly community; they may well be used behind the curtains, but when it comes to citations and referencing it is the printed edition that takes centre stage, thereby depriving the producer of the digital edition of legitimate acknowledgment. A first major obstacle, in Rosselli Del Turco's eyes, lies on the production side: we do not produce enough digital editions because of a general lack of easy-to-use, out-of-the-box tools and publication infrastructure. Another problem is a result of fragmentary and conflicting user-interfaces, which prevent users from truly enjoying them. The biggest obstacle to the general diffusion and acceptance of digital scholarly editions, however, is the failure of digital editors convincingly to demonstrate the superiority of digital editions with respect to printed ones. Ultimately, then, it is on the metaphorical shoulders of the digital editors to show what is so special about their work and the advantages of producing and using them. Yet the editors cannot do all the work on their own: more far-reaching problems such as the need for the long-term sustainability of digital products require a synergy of effort from all the digital 'workers'. The future of digital editions, in other words, depends on the capability of editors to collaborate with others and to promote the results of their collaborative efforts.

This book aims at contributing to the larger debate on the impact of the digital in scholarship, in particular for scholarship in the Humanities. We trust that the quality of the chapters, the combination of topics and approaches, as well as scholars at different stages of their career, will make this collection a point of reference for the digital editorial discourse. What is the future of digital editing? What is in store for editing in the digital age? We are now starting to see glimpses of a future that looks more confusing than ever, with a resurgence of print publications aimed at the general public, and a strong push toward Open Access publication for academic endeavours. This publication positions itself at the crossing of these tendencies, by choosing a hybrid form of publication, digital and print, as well as marrying the Open Access cause without compromises. With our choices we hope to ensure a long life to what we think it is a very valuable and rich contribution to a discipline that is profoundly renewing its heuristics. There is certainly a lot of old wine in our new bottles, but there is new wine too and the combination of the two is a product that is strongly grounded in its roots but certainly looks toward the future.

SECTION 1: THEORIES

2. What is a Scholarly Digital Edition?

Patrick Sahle

Introduction: Why do we need a definition?

Humanities research is focused on cultural artefacts such as texts, images or physical objects. Usually they are kept in libraries, archives and museums and are thus not encountered as original material objects; rather, scholars work with surrogates of them created especially to make them more accessible and to facilitate research. Over the last centuries, the desire to uncover the cultural treasures of the past and to reconstitute important documents, texts and works in the most reliable way possible has led to the development of the concept of the critical edition in the modern sense. This implies the application of wide knowledge, ranging from material and bibliographic criticism to historical understanding and textual criticism, and can lead to very complex forms of publications. Editions are created by the best experts in a field. They establish reliable sources for research, authorise and canonise certain readings, and thus channel and frame our perception of history, literature, art, thinking, language etc.

Accordingly, critical editing is a central field in the humanities, spanning nearly all disciplines and subjects. Over time, it has evolved into an independent research area offering a large corpus of theorising literature, sophisticated methodologies, learned associations and societies, dedicated conferences and journals and even specialised study programmes at the postgraduate level. In continental Europe at least, the discipline bears the distinct label *Editorik* or *Editionswissenschaft* in German and *ecdotica, ecdotique* or *ecdotics* in Italian, French and English respectively. Despite—or perhaps even because of—its relevance for many different subjects, there is no comprehensive definition for critical editions that would extend its validity beyond single genres, types of documents, transmission settings or methodological approaches. The idea of critical editing originates and has been most developed in literary studies of classical and medieval texts. Here, the attempt either to reconstruct a lost 'original version' (*Urtext*) from antiquity, or to realise the author's will and intention for texts that have been contaminated and altered in the processes of transmission is central. Obviously, these ideas are bound to very specific settings of the creation and transmission of texts. They depend on particular theoretical assumptions and have been questioned in their goals ever since. The most prominent interpretation of critical editing as *textual criticism* thus seems rather narrow in a more global perspective.[1]

Scholarly digital editions (or SDEs) offer the opportunity to overcome the limitations of print technology. The new possibilities have a fundamental impact on the theory and methodology of critical editing in general. The large corpus of research literature on digital scholarly editing is full of discussion about new features, functions, properties and characteristics of this kind of scholarly endeavour and how this changes our practices, our theoretical grounds and our goals. Among the pioneers of digital editing, Peter Robinson in particular has proposed a clear and condensed set of central aspects which come close to a definition.[2] Yet, this erudite characterisation *describes* core properties

---

[1] Characteristically, *critical edition* in the English Wikipedia is only a redirection to the article on *textual criticism*. In the German Wikipedia, *Edition* already reflects the concept of a 'critical edition' — in addition there are further articles on *Historisch-kritische Ausgabe* (historical critical edition; *Kritische Ausgabe*/critical edition redirects here), *Quellenedition* (source edition), *Editionswissenschaft* (editorial science), *Editionsrichtlinie* (editorial guideline) and, of course, *Textkritik* (textual criticism). The Italian Wikipedia, besides *Ecdotica* (to which *critica del testo* redirects), has an article on *Edizione critica*.

[2] Peter Robinson, 'What is a Critical Digital Edition?', *Variants: The Journal of the European Society for Textual Scholarship*, 1 (2002), 43–62, names six essential aspects: (1) a critical digital edition is anchored in a historical analysis of the materials; (2) a critical digital edition presents hypotheses about creation and change; (3) a critical digital edition supplies a record and classification over time, in many dimensions

rather than defining what a SDE actually *is*. When Robinson claims, for example, that a scholarly digital edition must 'enrich reading', then this names one of the most important goals of such an edition but does not yield sufficient criteria to distinguish the digital edition from other things.

We still lack a clear definition to help us identify and label things as SDEs. So the question remains: how do you recognise a digital scholarly edition when you see one? As an important tool in our common methodology, we need a sharper knife here: what are we talking about when we talk about SDEs? What is part of the population and what not? Are we talking about the same things and the same set of objects? Or are we talking at cross-purposes? To develop our theories and methodologies further, we need to know more precisely where our empirical basis lies and what the population is. This has both theoretical and practical relevance. In my own work over the last twenty years I have used a working definition to collect and catalogue SDEs.[3] This definition now seems sufficiently well tested to be ripe for presentation and further discussion. If it has been functional for classification and cataloguing, it can serve as a tool in further empirical and systematic research. And this, in turn, is essential in building the new methodology and theory of scholarly editing in the twenty-first century.

Premises and goals

In the attempt to give a definition, we have to be clear about our scope. Digital editions are created in many different disciplines. Beyond the most formative impact of philology and literary studies, disciplines such as historical linguistics, history, art history, philosophy, musicology or

---

and in appropriate detail; (4) a critical digital edition may present an edited text, among all the texts it offers; (5) a critical digital edition allows space and tools for readers to develop their own hypotheses and ways of reading; (6) a critical digital edition must offer all this in a manner that enriches reading. I have discussed this set in 'Digitales Archiv und Digitale Edition: Anmerkungen zur Begriffsklärung', *Literatur und Literaturwissenschaft auf dem Weg zu den neuen Medien*, ed. by Michael Stolz (Zürich: germanistik.ch, 2007), pp. 64–84, chapter 10.2, and in Patrick Sahle, *Digitale Editionsformen: Zum Umgang mit der Überlieferung unter den Bedingungen des Medienwandels* I–III, Schriften des Instituts für Dokumentologie und Editorik 7–9 (Norderstedt: BOD, 2013), II, 150–51.

3   See the latest catalogue, active since 2006, at http://www.digitale-edition.de

archaeology have their own requirements and traditions. In the past, methods from philological disciplines have most often been adapted to other fields, although some have also developed their own approaches. Sophisticated editions require large amounts of time and money, making it unlikely that a subject, once dealt with, will be tackled again soon. Moreover, foundational work such as digital representation and basic transcriptions may be created only once. For this reason, editions should be as useful across disciplinary boundaries as possible. While this already suggests a common methodology, the demand for a shared definition increases with digital media and online editions that should be as widely accessible and usable as possible for all interested disciplines. The same holds true for the various textual genres, types of documents and materials. The notion of *scholarly editing* should not be restricted to literary texts but has to cover all cultural artefacts from the past that need critical examination in order to become useful sources for research in the humanities.[4] Undoubtedly, the idea of critical editing according to the Lachmannian paradigm—that is the application of the highly developed techniques of textual criticism for the reconstruction of a lost *Urtext* or an author's intention—is the most influential and most highly developed approach within the field. There have, however, always been dissenting approaches and other schools of thought.[5] The construction of a reading text beyond the actual document witnesses as *the* main goal of editing, for example, has been questioned right from the start. In the study of history, textual criticism had been adopted but was flanked by historical criticism, accounting for the properties of the material documents as well as explaining the textual information by summarising, annotating or indexing them. For a broad understanding of the field, further schools such as critical bibliography, diplomatic or documentary editing, genetic editing or documentary editing have to be considered. None of these areas should be neglected in the attempt

---

[4] The edition of the *Bayeux Tapestry* [CD-ROM], ed. by Martin K. Foys (Woodbridge: Scholarly Digital Editions, 2002), is a good example of a subject that cannot be reduced to carriers of text but which — as mainly pictorial and material objects — is subject to the same editorial methodology.

[5] For a first overview see my 'Die disziplinierte Edition — eine kleine Wissenschaftsgeschichte', *Editionswissenschaftliche Kolloquien 2005/2007. Methodik — Amtsbücher — Digitale Edition — Projekte*, ed. by Matthias Thumser and Janusz Tandecki (Toruń: Deutsch-Polnischer Gesprächskreis für Quellenedition, 2008), pp. 35–52.

to come to a comprehensive definition. This may, in a first step, delineate what scholarly editions are, before we then move on to *digital* scholarly editions. In addition, building upon the editions that we know already should help us to keep the tradition and to save the scholarly achievements of the past. An adequate and productive definition should integrate all editorial schools, address all humanities disciplines, cover all textual genres and every kind of object. And, no less important, a good definition should be short and simple.

A simple definition for scholarly editions?

As previously mentioned, in collecting and cataloguing scholarly editions to serve as an empirical basis for deeper analysis, I have been working with my own definition for many years now. This definition simply reads:

> *Edition ist die erschließende Wiedergabe historischer Dokumente.*

In German, this works quite well. Unfortunately, however, it relies on the central, yet untranslatable, term *erschließen*, which encompasses any activity that increases the amount of information concerning a specific object and thus enhances its accessibility and usability. Depending on context, words such as *develop, open up, deduce* or *infer* may be used to render this concept in English. They do not cover the wider notion intended here, however. To capture the basic idea that all of these processes involve making thoughtful, reflective and reasonable judgments about the objects of study, the word *critical* may not only be an approximation but an even better label for the concept. Thus, I propose the following definition:

> *A scholarly edition is the critical representation of historic documents.*

This surely fulfils the requirement for a short and simple statement, but it also contains four fundamental points that need to be discussed and explained further.

First: representation. Representation means the recoding of a document or an abstract work and its transformation in the same or another kind of media. This is usually done on the visual layer by image reproduction or on the more abstract textual layer by transcription. Representation spans a wide scale between materially oriented reproductions of documents and the constitution of new readings of a text—e.g. in the attempt to reconstruct and realise a lost original or an author's intention. Representations try to capture objects in their entirety and can be further transformed into publications. This already indicates a possible distinction between representation and presentation which will be discussed later. For the moment it is important that representation is a necessity for an edition. Critical engagement without representation is not an edition—but an examination, a catalogue or a description.

Second: critical. To achieve a broad understanding of all kinds of scholarly editions, those that are out there now or which could possibly be created in the future, we have to start with an open and wide notion of *critical*. We cannot constrain our understanding to the most prominent exponent of criticism, which is *textual criticism*. Regarding editions, we have to take into account that there exist as well historic criticism, bibliographic criticism, material criticism, visual criticism and other forms of criticism. In short, criticism must stand for all processes that engage in a critical or reflective way—that is, on the basis of a scholarly agenda—with the material in question and help in 'opening it up'.

Criticism as a practice and a process may take different forms. Think of the rules that are applied in the transcription of a document. While the transcription itself is a representation, the specification of rules and their application make this a critical process. Identifying structures, named entities or other objects of interest and making them explicit, e.g. by annotation, is yet another form of criticism. Judgments about punctuation, orthography, wording, corrections and emendations are typical tasks of textual criticism and are sometimes seen as the highest form of philology. In addition, free or formalised descriptions of the documents, their texts and their treatment within an edition are the backbones for the edition's authority and reliability for its further scholarly usage. Finally, a critical attitude is required to decide with which additional material, to what extent and in what form an edited text should be contextualised in order to make it more understandable and accessible. To sum up, we may take the word *critical* as a container for all those activities that apply scholarly knowledge and reasoning to the process of reproducing documents and transforming a document or text into an edition. The critical handling of the material is a second necessary condition for an edition. A representation without such treatment or the addition of information is not an edition—but a facsimile, a reproduction or—nowadays—a digital archive or library. *Critical representation* as a compound notion of editing aims at the reconstruction and reproduction of texts and as such addresses their material and visual dimension as well as their abstract and intentional dimension.[6]

Third: documents. Most editions focus on *texts* or even *works*. I prefer the term *documents* here for two reasons. On the one hand, not all editions have works or texts as their primary goal. Some material simply does not have textual content, or the textual content or the notion of an abstract work behind its physical embodiments is not central to the edition. At the same time, there are disciplines, schools and theoretical approaches where the material document itself lies at the heart of the editorial interest. However, every non-abstract object that is the subject of an edition can be called a document. On the other hand, text can be described as a *function* of documents.[7] In the real world, the document is always the antecedent. Even if an edition is built upon an abstract notion of text or work, it always starts with material documents. Even if an edition tries to establish a certain text reading or version, beyond the evidence of textual witnesses reconstructing a lost *Urtext* or constituting from all witnesses as the best text a 'text that never was',[8] this is based upon documentary evidence.[9] Accordingly, *document* can—at least functionally—completely cover the notion of text.

Fourth: historic. Editions are created for all disciplines. Historic does not mean *for history* here. Editions are the groundwork for further research and for reliable, authoritative texts that can be used

---

6   For a discussion of this characterisation, see Mats Dahlström, 'How Reproductive is a Scholarly Edition?', *Literary and Linguistic Computing*, 19.1 (2004), 17–33, http://dx.doi.org/10.1093/llc/19.1.17

7   See Hans Walter Gabler, 'Das wissenschaftliche Edieren als Funktion der Dokumente', *Jahrbuch für Computerphilologie*, 8 (2006), 55–62, http://computerphilologie.tu-darmstadt.de/jg06/gabler.html

8   This famous phrase goes back to David Greetham; see, for example, 'Editorial and Critical Theory: From Modernism to Postmodernism', in *Palimpsest: Editorial Theory in the Humanities*, ed. by George Bornstein and Ralph G. Williams (Ann Arbor: University of Michigan Press, 1993), pp. 9–28 (p. 18).

9   See Hans Walter Gabler, 'The Primacy of the Document in Editing', *Ecdotica*, 4 (2007), 197–207.

in humanities scholarship and teaching. They explore the uncharted circumstances of documents, texts and their transmission. They may correct errors introduced by the conditions of production, copying and publishing. They explain what is not evident to the present-day reader. In short, they bridge a distance in time, a historical difference. Texts that are created today do not need to be critically edited. They can speak for themselves. Only historic documents and texts need an editor to make them speak clearly.

What is a scholarly *digital* edition?

A scholarly edition is the critical representation of historic documents that often stand for a certain text or work. But what then is a *digital* scholarly edition? It has been said that digital editions are essentially different from printed editions in their content, structure and role. Yet, they share the same subject and have the same goals. Because of that, we can stick to the same general definition. The difference is not so much between *editions* and *digital editions*, but between the various forms of editions. The scholarly edition as we know it from the last several centuries is the printed edition, but the changes in our technological and media environment make us aware of the fact that there is an alternative to the print edition. The print edition is no longer *the edition* but becomes recognisable as a particular form. Therefore, the basic definition of the scholarly edition is valid for both varieties and we have only to discuss the difference between the printed and the digital edition. To do so, we could name the distinct contents and features of them. Or, we could describe in detail how they deal with the representation and critical treatment of their material. Digital editions already at first glance display additional, specific, characteristic aspects. Some of them can be gained by transforming printed editions into electronic texts and digital publications. Here we may talk about accessibility, searchability, usability and computability. But there are other, more essential aspects of digital editions that stem from a change in the praxis of preparation, in the methods applied and in the underlying theoretical assumptions. It can be said that digital editions follow a *digital paradigm*, just as printed editions have been following a paradigm that was shaped by the technical limitations and cultural practices of typography and book printing. With the mere digitisation of printed material, the implications of a truly digital paradigm cannot be realised. Digital imaging of source documents and the potential of digitally encoded text can be named as two examples of this phenomenon. As for the former: while printed editions, due to economic restrictions, usually come without facsimiles as a visual counterpart to the typographic text, digital editions usually start with visual representations, are indeed expected to provide this evidence, and where they do not, they need to justify the absence of this feature. As for the latter: while printed editions normally give exactly one version of a text, the deeply marked up textual code of the digital edition theoretically covers several views of the text and may lead to various presentations generated by specific algorithms. This fundamental difference in paradigm and its consequences for the reality of editions in our digital media landscape lead to the following important conclusion:

A digitised edition is not a digital edition.

As long as the contents and functionalities of a typographically born and typographically envisioned edition do not really change with the conversion to digital data, we should not call these derivate editions 'digital'. It is the conceptual framework that makes the thing—not the method of storage of the information either on paper or as bits and bytes. We can make this more productive in a more definitional manner by stating that:

A digital edition cannot be given in print without significant loss of content and functionality.

Of course, the content of digital editions can—in theory—be printed out. And, of course, the text of digital editions could still be read on paper. However, a main characteristic of a digital edition is its representation of a potentially large number of documents in a potentially limitless number of different views, such as facsimile, diplomatic transcription and reading versions. All are generated from the same electronic code according to certain, sometimes even user controlled, modulations. The same holds true for functionality: there is no simple search, no advanced search, no real interactivity, no control over behaviour and appearance, and no source code download in printed editions. There are fewer browsing paths, no real hyperlinks, and no integrated technical tools. That is why digitisation may change the accessibility of a printed edition and may add at least some basic functionalities such as searching—but digitisation does not make a printed edition a digital edition. There is still the difference in the general framework of the whole task. For the moment, this difference may be described rather vaguely as such:

> Scholarly digital editions are scholarly editions that are guided by a digital paradigm in their theory, method and practice.

We will have to see how this paradigm can be further described and concretised.

Aspects of the *digital paradigm* in editing

Markup languages, digital media and the web have been with us for some decades now. The changes in technology and media and their repercussions on our understanding of publication, text and authorship have been under discussion from the earliest days on. We already have a large corpus of theoretical literature and well established hypotheses on the new—or not so new anymore—media environment.[10] As regards scholarly editions, I have tried to give a rough conspectus of these issues elsewhere.[11] Only some characteristics of our digital data and media that are important for the methodology and practice shall be mentioned here very briefly. *Multimedia* has been among the buzzwords of the

---

10 To name but a few: *Beyond the Book: Theory, Culture, and the Politics of Cyberspace*, ed. by Warren L. Chernaik, Marilyn Deegan and Andrew Gibson (Oxford: Office for Humanities Communication, 1996); *Electronic Text: Investigations in Method and Theory*, ed. by Kathryn Sutherland (Oxford: Oxford University Press, 1997); James J. O'Donnell, *Avatars of the Word: From Papyrus to Cyberspace* (Cambridge, MA: Harvard University Press, 1998); *Reimagining Textuality: Textual Studies in the Late Age of Print*, ed. by Elizabeth Bergmann Loizeaux and Neil Fraistat (Madison: University of Wisconsin Press, 2002); *Rethinking Media Change: The Aesthetics of Transition*, ed. by David Thorburn and Henry Jenkins (Cambridge, MA: MIT Press, 2003); Peter L. Shillingsburg, *From Gutenberg to Google: Electronic Representations of Literary Texts* (Cambridge: Cambridge University Press, 2006); *Text and Genre in Reconstruction: Effects of Digitalization on Ideas, Behaviours, Products and Institutions*, ed. by Willard McCarty (Cambridge: Open Book Publishers, 2010), http://dx.doi.org/10.11647/OBP.0008

11 Sahle, 'Ausgewählte Aspekte der Edition im Medienwandel', in *Digitale Editionsformen*, II, 157–280.

early years but still denotes the changing relationship between *text* and visual forms of representing documents. In the world of printed books, it has always been easier to give a transcription than a facsimile, and accordingly text was seen as the primary form of representation, with images of documents as mere illustrations. Nowadays, even if only for the practical process of editing, projects start with digital facsimiles and subsequently create transcriptions and edited versions of the text. As for the publication, the present day user tends to expect the visual evidence as a matter of course and might be vexed by its absence. *Hypertext* is another buzzword from the dawn of electronic textuality. With the World Wide Web and its underlying technologies, the complex and advanced theory of hypertextuality has been reduced to the practice of simple links. However, even these *hyperlinks* are very momentous and mark an important difference between printed and digital texts. While the former always included rather *implicit* links and references, the hyperlinks of the latter restructure the contents of editions, open up new and manifold paths of reception and blur the boundaries between an edition and its contexts. The pervasive linkage between different contents and parts promote a *modularised* structure and a module-oriented vision of scholarly editions. Instead of concentrating on one authoritative reading as the primary goal and content, digital editions connect various forms of representation with editorial knowledge and contextual material. This is brought to the public in the process of a *fluid publication* in a double sense. What we see on the screen is often generated in real time from the current state of data, representing the current state of the editorial knowledge in a project. This is one aspect of fluidity. The other is the loss of a distinct moment of publication. Release early—release often! The edition loses its recognisability as an authoritative, final statement. Instead, it becomes a permanent but potentially always changing documentation of an ongoing examination and processing of the objects in question. In this way, the edition as a publication is a *process rather than a product*. It grows incrementally not only before its final release, but also during its availability to the public. The edition as data driven fluid publication is, at least in principle, always *open* to change and amendments. Thus, the edition is seen as an open enterprise. In theory, it never closes down and never reaches a final state. There is always something left to do. The edition invites the team of editors and *collaborators* to add more material and more knowledge. As regards the people involved and the roles they play, the road leads from the single omniscient editor of the printed edition to the team of specialists with differentiated roles in the conceptually and technically complex digital edition. It leads to a social edition, where input comes from within the team and from outside. Contributions are made by external institutions such as libraries and archives but some editions also try to attract and activate the communities of the scholarly or even wider interested public. In the end, the practice of crowdsourcing makes everybody a potential editor or at least a contributor to a fundamentally collaborative endeavour.

Amplification and change of functionalities is one of the most obvious aspects in comparing traditional to digital editions. The book is a perfect device for the passive consumption of a limited amount of one-dimensional static information. Digital media, with its complex, multimedia, networked content, is in principle interactive and adaptive. It asks for more sophisticated browse and search functions to access all the material and information of an edition. A printed edition can be read. A digital edition is more like a workplace or a laboratory where the user is invited to work with the texts and documents more actively. Accordingly, in recent years we have even seen the integration of new features and tools into the edition, allowing for customisation, personalisation, manipulation and contribution. In the idea of virtual research environments, the border between primary material, its usage for interpretation and analysis, and the publication of findings is finally obliterated.

At the heart of the edition there is still *the text*. But what is that text which the edition presents? In contrast to the one-text paradigm of the print edition, the digital edition shows a strong tendency towards multiple texts. As has been said, the digital facsimile, which is a representation of the text, is already a common starting point nowadays. But even the text as a linguistic entity represented by transcription is manifold. Often, editions offer a diplomatic version *and* a critically treated constituted edited or reading text. Sometimes texts are additionally given in translation and semantic information is pulled out and organised in a database or presented by indices. From a systematic point of view, it can be said that the representation of text is locatable on a scale of possible treatments and steps of processing of a document and its transcription. This spectrum reaches from positions that are close to the document (like image) to positions that are close to the user (like reading text), since they apply and add ever more interpretative and processing steps to the text.

Behind the presentation of text as taking different positions in a range of all possible renditions, there lies not only the idea of incremental informational and critical digestion. Varying forms of text are not just teleologically moving toward one final goal. Rather, this conveys and embodies a pluralistic *notion of text*, where different information channels of documents and texts are perceived and can be represented on the level of encoded data. These textual dimensions are the subject of a pluralistic theory of text and include, to give just a few examples, the visual, the material, the scriptographic/typographic, the linguistic, the work-related and the semantic channel of information.[12] It is clear that different forms of textual presentation in scholarly editions address these notions of what text actually is in different but complementary ways. As regards the *digital paradigm*, the expansion of the textual representation comes with the inversion of the role of the *critically edited text*. Within the typographic paradigm, the edited text is by far the most important feature, the core and the exclusive centre of the edition. All other forms of evidence, such as illustrative images, bibliographic information, details of script and typesetting, variant readings or semantic interpretations, are just substrata to or fortifications of it. Within the digital paradigm, the process is reversed: the editor does not *write* the edited text. Rather, it is developed gradually from the material documents, from visual evidence through the transcription and through the application of critical, historical, stylistic and philological knowledge. In the digital edition there is little reason to hide these other layers of textual representation from the user. But as one effect of this change in methodology, the edited text is relativised and the multiple text is facilitated.

---

12 For a first sketch of the 'pluralistic theory of text' and the changes in our 'notion of text' see Sahle, 'Textverständnis und Textbegriff', in *Digitale Editionsformen*, III, 1–98.

From a technical point of view, basic concepts of electronic texts, descriptive markup and current publishing architectures have led to what is called the *single source principle*. All knowledge about a text is united in a single information resource from which the publication and all textual forms within are generated algorithmically. From a conceptual point of view, these developments in the creation of digital scholarly resources can be called 'transmedialisation'[13]—because today information resources are being created without primarily thinking of them in terms of publication. We are less looking forward to the layout and functionality of the presentation, but start with the decoding and encoding of what is actually there. We create information resources that are guided by abstract models and abstract descriptions of the objects at hand. The dogma of our current markup strategies is the separation or rather translation from form to content. Thus, we do not just transform our textual witnesses from one (material) media and form into another (digital) media and form. Rather, we try to encode structures and meaning of documents and texts beyond their mediality. And from this data we may or we may not create, and from time to time recreate, arbitrary forms of presentation in one media or another. If asked what is really the gist of the matter in our still ongoing change from analogue to digital media—what 'the real revolution' is—my answer, at least, would be *transmedialisation*. The shift from media orientation to data orientation with its focus on abstraction, modelling and multi-purpose representations can be shown particularly clearly for the field of scholarly editions. Here we see a transition from the edition as a media product to the edition as a modelled information resource that can be presented in media but is about the abstract representation of knowledge in the first place.

This has consequences when it comes to the desirable transfer of editorial knowledge from the past. When printed editions are digitised, they are transformed into electronic text and digital code. As digital (re-)

---

13 See in particular Sahle, 'Inhalt und Form: Medienwandel als Transmedialisierung', in *Digitale Editionsformen*, II, 157–65, and Sahle, 'Zwischen Mediengebundenheit und Transmedialisierung. Anmerkungen zum Verhältnis von Edition und Medien', *editio — International Yearbook of Scholarly Editing*, 24 (2010), 23–36.

publications they become more easily and widely accessible, searchable and reusable. Yet, what does not change is their paradigm. The edited text does not get closer to the documents, there is still no visual evidence, no making explicit of textual structures or semantic information, limited potential for multiple views on the text. This is why a digitised edition is not a digital edition.

Truly digital editions show some or most of the above mentioned characteristics of the digital paradigm. However, while the definition given so far helps to identify scholarly digital editions and to distinguish them from other things, there are still some open ends to discuss and some possible problems in finding the exact borderline.

Open ends?

All answers seem to lead to new questions. Every definition needs words to explain its subjects, and these words in turn need to be discussed and specified. For a start, five aspects are rather arbitrarily taken up, shedding some light on open questions and areas where further thinking may be needed.

SDE vs. DSE. Labels are important when we try to come to a common understanding of the subjects we are talking about. Some talk about *Scholarly Digital Editions (SDE)*, others *Digital Scholarly Editions (DSE)*. Should we use two different labels, describe two different notions, identify two different concepts and thereby construct two different things here? Maybe there are indeed two different paths in the development and creation of critical editions. A *Scholarly Digital Edition* would emphasise that there is the phenomenon of digital publication and now is the time to care for its scholarly quality. This would mean to add the critical dimension to otherwise potentially uncritical publications. On the other hand, the *Digital Scholarly Edition* would refer to the tradition and methodologies of the scholarly edition and reflect its transformation into the digital realm. Since both should lead to the same result, they do not necessarily denote different things and, beyond the detailed discussion about approaches and perceptions, both may be used as synonyms. This may hold as well for another pair of labels. As has been argued earlier, the term critical can be taken as the central *definiens* for what we talk about. Thus, *Digital Critical Edition* and *Critical Digital Edition* work equally well and can be used as further synonyms.

Digital Edition vs. Digital Archive.[14] Words refer to concepts. Within the current changes, even concepts seem to be in motion. Editions widen their content. When they aim at including ever more documents and finally at *completeness*, and when the first level of representation may be just a digital facsimile with some metadata, then the edition looks more and more like an archive. In fact, some projects that started by calling themselves *editions* have later changed their name to *archive*. On the other hand, digital archives are already critical on the bibliographic level and imply the possibility to incrementally add further critical information, other forms of representation (such as transcription) and may finally even present an edited text.[15] In fact, some projects that started by calling themselves *archives* have later changed their name to *edition*.[16] If we take the critical engagement and the application of scholarly knowledge as the defining characteristics of an edition, then we can say that from a certain point on, an archive starts to be an edition. However, the disparate handling of the content in a project may as well lead to the observation that some parts have the character of an edition while others resemble an archive.

Questions of quality and thresholds. A thing can be called a scholarly edition when it is based on scholarly knowledge and critical engagement. Editions have to conform to academic standards to be accepted as the basis for further academic research. An edition gives a complete representation of its subject. Both conditions, for content and quality,

---

14 For a dedicated discussion of this topic, see Sahle, *Digitales Archiv*, 2007. On the delineation of different labels, particularly 'archive' and 'digital thematic research collections', see Kenneth M. Price, 'Edition, Project, Database, Archive, Thematic Research Collection: What's in a Name?', *Digital Humanities Quarterly*, 3.3 (2009), http://www.digitalhumanities.org/dhq/vol/3/3/000053/000053.html

15 Mats Dahlström, 'Critical Editing and Critical Digitization', in *Text Comparison and Digital Creativity: The Production of Presence and Meaning in Digital Text Scholarship*, ed. by Ernst Thoutenhoofd, Adrian van der Weel and Willem Th. van Peursen (Amsterdam: Brill, 2010), pp. 79–97, has recently coined the notion of 'critical digitization' to convey that there is a critical stance towards the documents at any stage of the process of creating digital surrogates.

16 For projects that call themselves *archives* or *editions* see the catalogue at http://digitale-edition.de. Among those which constantly manoeuvre between the terms are the *Dante Gabriel Rossetti Archive*, the *Walt Whitman Archive*, the *William Blake Archive* and the *Shelley-Godwin Archive*.

raise the question from what point on something is a scholarly edition. In both cases there would be something like a threshold. And that is hard to define precisely. According to the 'release early' principle of web projects, an edition would be presented as soon as possible to activate its potential audience and to encourage participation and feedback. But:

An edition project is not an edition.

Over the past decades we have seen many attempts to create editions on high levels of methodology, aiming at covering large amounts of material but eventually just fizzling out and remaining as sketches, drafts and prototypes. So where can the line be drawn between the preliminary publication and the edition? The criteria here must be content and usability. As soon as the publication makes a substantial amount or percentage of the intended documents or texts available so that it can be fruitfully used in research, we may call it an edition. The question of quality is even harder to answer, particularly in times of upcoming public, social, crowdsourced editions. Obviously, a scholarly edition comes with the promise of reliability and high standards. Digital images, transcription, textual criticism, comments, annotations and contextual texts have to substantiate the claim that this is the best possible representation of the editorial subject and that the best experts have assiduously and painstakingly applied all existing knowledge in a rigorous method. In theory, the scholarly edition is always the 'best realisation possible'. Obviously these qualities are very hard to measure objectively. There are, however, other aspects that can be checked and verified in the evaluation of scholarly editions.[17] Some of them are more functional, like accessing the edition by means of browsing and searching or the provision of registers and indices. Others are more concerned with the edition as an academic venture. They regard the editorial essentials: can the edition be cited and referenced? Is it determinable bibliographically because responsible editors and place and time of creation and publication are indicated? Are the basic assumptions, the

---

17 See the 'Kriterien für die Besprechung digitaler Editionen, Version 1.1', Institute for Documentology and Scholarly Editing 2014, http://www.i-d-e.de/publikationen/weitereschriften/kriterien-version-1-1. English version 'Criteria for Reviewing Scholarly Digital Editions', http://www.i-d-e.de/publikationen/weitereschriften/criteria-version-1-1

theory behind the edition, the methods and procedures of transcription and criticism of the text stated clearly and applied transparently? The most basic exigency in traditional editing—*State your rules and follow them!*—is as well the central law and starting point of all digital editing. As for the quality of these rules and their application, again the question of usefulness is crucial. Does the edition provide a reliable proxy for the documents? Can scholarly research be trustworthily based on the edition without the need to go back to the originals?

What is one *digital edition?* Talking about editions, evaluating editions and cataloguing editions requires their identification by external boundaries and internal constituents. This was not a problem in the world of books. The edition was limited and identified by binding, covers, bibliographic description and as a stabilised product. The digital edition claims to be a process rather than a product, and is thus unstable as regards publication and changing content. Furthermore, the editor as fixed point is weakened by the larger teams of specialists, collaborators or even the public contributors in the social and crowdsourced edition. The publication, as algorithmically generated from separated underlying data, becomes arbitrary. Data, even from distributed sources may fuel various editions, differing in scope and distributed over place and time. Editorial content is transformed into modules or even more fine granular sets or particles of addressable, linkable and integratable objects. Editorial projects serve as platforms and portals featuring single works that are processed and annotated in depth and presented with particular functionalities. All of these phenomena make it hard to decide what forms *a* or *one* digital edition in the end. It seems that a solution can only come from the editors themselves. They set the framework and define the subject. If they declare something to be *the edition* we may follow them. As in the old world, the edition can then be defined as a bibliographical object that should clearly be identified and described.

Publication vs. data. If the edition is arbitrarily created from abstract data and may be recreated by others in different forms at any time—is the edition still the publication or is it rather the data behind the publication? It seems that the data is the place where the editorial content is stored, where the editorial processes are recorded and the editorial knowledge is kept. The most important task for the editor is the creation of information as rich, accurate and reliable data. The creation of online publications or print spin-offs from this data may be left to other specialists such as publishing houses, web agencies or media designers. In fact, editions are produced in this manner. Nevertheless, it may still be the editor who is responsible for the edition as a publication as well and thus identified as the creator of it. This is surely true for, but may be restricted to, those cases where the editor is the head of the publishing process deciding on the selection of material, its presentation as well as features and functions for browsing, searching and using the edition. The situation will be more complicated when another publication is created by somebody else. Decisions on the arrangement of a new presentation may be called *editorial* as well, and perhaps we have to differentiate at least two layers of editorial activities: creating data and creating an edition as publication. And there is even a layer in between. Following the idea of edition as mere data, it would best be provided via formalised web services for harvesting or direct integration into more presentational forms with graphical user interfaces.[18] Such services would be another, and perhaps the most adequate, form of publication.

Conclusion

There is nothing as practical as a good theory. An attempt has been made here to propose a broad, but hopefully clear, short and simple definition. It should be interdisciplinary, embracing all scholarly approaches, schools and materials. Most of all, it should be functional: it should give us clear guidance in how to distinguish scholarly digital editions from other entities such as retrospectively digitised editions, electronic texts, textual corpora, digital facsimiles, editorial projects, digital archives, digital libraries etc. The simple word *edition*, especially in the English language, can mean any kind of publication. Yet, *scholarly edition* refers to something else that may lead to a publication but is framed by very specific activities and is guided by a particular set of theoretical assumptions and methodologies. The scholarly edition undergoes a fundamental change that is triggered by the new possibilities of digital

---

18 See Peter Boot and Joris van Zundert, 'The Digital Edition 2.0 and The Digital Library: Services, not Resources', *Digitale Edition und Forschungsbibliothek, Bibliothek und Wissenschaft*, 44 (2011), 141–52, http://peterboot.nl/pub/vanzundert-boot-services-not-resources-2011.pdf

technologies of description, encoding and publication. Nevertheless, it takes up and takes further the basic ideas of critical editing that have been with us for some centuries now. Others may emphasise that our whole concept of editing is changing so completely that it may dissolve and be replaced by other labels. In my work, however, I see the continuity in the basic goals of providing reliable, trustworthy and useful representations of our textual and documentary heritage as the basis for further research in the humanities. My own catalogue of scholarly digital editions is an attempt to supply some empirical data for the ongoing methodological debate. To do so, I have to draw a rather sharp line between scholarly editions in a quite narrow sense and other phenomena that are also related to the manifold activities in making our cultural heritage accessible.

When it comes to integrating a certain item into the catalogue of scholarly digital editions, I apply the definition given above by simply asking four questions:

1. Is there a full representation of the subject in question? This may be an edited text or at least a very accurate transcription. Sometimes, although this is rather an exception than the rule and depends on the specific characteristics of the material, a digital facsimile may suffice. Sometimes even a structured database can be a complete representation.[19]

2. Is it *critical*? Have rules for the processing of the material been stated and substantiated? Have these rules been applied in the light of the relevant scholarly knowledge on the material, its genesis, its contexts and its reception? Does the edition add information to the representation making it more accessible, understandable and usable?

3. Is the edition of academic quality? Have the rules been applied rigorously and in a transparent manner? Are the responsibilities stated clearly? Does the edition suffice as a substitute for the previous editions or primary documents making it unnecessary to go back to them in most cases? Does it enable further scholarly research on a reliable and trustworthy basis?

4. Does the edition follow a digital paradigm? Does it make use of the possibilities of digital technology and media? Is it not printable without a major loss of content and functionality?

---

19   Think here of serial historical sources, such as account books.

Of course, this is only one possible view on editing in the digital age. It is subjective and surely based on some biographic and geographic preconditions, but it tries to respect and embrace the different disciplines, editorial schools, materials and genres and to build a bridge between the tradition and the current changes. And, at least, it has been under permanent practical application for ten years so that it now seems ripe for further discussion and development.

3. Modelling Digital Scholarly Editing: From Plato to Heraclitus

Elena Pierazzo

Editing is without doubt one of the oldest scholarly activities within the Humanities. David Greetham traces its origin to the decision of Peisistratus (560–527 BC) to establish an 'official' text of Homer. It was this 'suspicion' about the authenticity of a text, he stresses, a mistrust of variants, which led to the birth of textual awareness, which in turn has developed over the last millennium and a half into the many theories and practices of what we can now call textual scholarship.[1]

Texts come in different versions, and variation in texts is inevitable; or, as John Bryant puts it, 'the fluid text is a fact, not a theory'.[2] In antiquity, before the invention of print, variation was mostly due to the fact that the manual act of copying resulted in the insertion of involuntary errors and innovation in the text while copying.[3] The invention of print has

---

[1] David Greetham, 'A History of Textual Scholarship', in *The Cambridge Companion to Textual Scholarship*, ed. by Neil Fraistat and Julia Flanders (Cambridge: Cambridge University Press, 2013), pp. 16–41 (p. 18).

[2] John Bryant, *The Fluid Text: A Theory of Revision and Editing for Book and Screen* (Ann Arbor: University of Michigan Press, 2002), p. 1. A similar concept can be derived from Peter Shillingsburg, 'Text as Matter, Concept, and Action', *Studies in Bibliography*, 44 (1991), 31–83 (in particular pp. 47–51).

[3] To these one must, of course, add authorial revisions which may not be as common as in the case of modern authors but are by no means absent. Even more important are re-elaborations of texts which are particularly common in certain genres, such as epic, sermons, commentaries and so on, on which see further below.

given the impression that this problem was resolved, since all copies coming from the press were supposed to be identical; this belief has been shaken by two sets of research, however. The first considers the actual process of printing and all the possible 'mishaps' that characterise such a process (correcting errors, introducing errors, recomposing forms, substituting gatherings etc.).[4] The second concentrates on the text itself and the editorial activity within the publishing houses, where manuscripts provided by authors were corrected, standardised and manipulated for publication.[5] Another line of research concentrates on the analysis of surviving authorial drafts; for this approach the object of study is the process of writing and of authoring. The 'final' text is therefore considered as just one stage along the textual journey, as it is 'final' only until the author decides to alter it or it becomes 'final' with the death of the author.[6] Finally, born-digital texts are versioned by definition, since a new version is created every time the 'Save' command is (virtually) pressed. Yet, in spite of the multiformity of texts, the editorial and, perhaps more importantly, publishing framework is in most cases the *reductio ad unum*, namely the conflation of variation and version into a single, authoritative text. The example mentioned of Peisistratus aiming to establish the 'official' version of Homer is typical: ever since antiquity the purpose of editorial work has been the production of the one, true, 'official' version of the text from the many that are available.

The obligation to provide a reliable text to the reader has been at once embraced and required by publishers. In fifteenth-century Italy, the first publishers consorted with leading intellectuals in order to

---

[4] See, among others, Fredson Bowers, *Principles of Bibliographical Description* (Princeton: Princeton University Press, 1949), and Ronald B. McKerrow, *An Introduction to Bibliography for Literary Students* (Winchester: St Paul's Bibliographies, 1994).

[5] See, for instance, the studies over the so-called 'accidentals' produced following the seminal work of W. W. Greg ('The Rationale of Copy-Text', *Studies in Bibliography*, 3 (1950–1951), 19–36), a brief account of which can be found in David Greetham, *Textual Scholarship: An Introduction* (New York: Garland, 1994), pp. 333–35. More recently Kathryn Sutherland has studied the normalising role of publishers for Austen's works; see *Jane Austen's Textual Lives: From Aeschylus to Bollywood* (Oxford: Oxford University Press, 2005).

[6] This is the approach pursued by *critique génétique* or Genetic Criticism, for which see Almuth Grésillon, *Eléments de critique génétique: lire les manuscrits modernes* (Paris: Presses universitaires de France, 1994).

publish the most correct text. Publishing technology in fact enabled the simultaneous production of hundreds of copies of the same text, and therefore the importance of printing a good text became paramount. In the early stages of print, the time and resources that were saved in mechanically producing many more-or-less identical copies of the same text (as opposed to hand copying them) made it sustainable to invest in the quality of texts, giving an impulse to textual scholarship, which became a commodity with a commercial value. On the other hand, one could also say that the philological skills championed by Humanists such as Lorenzo Valla or Agnolo Poliziano had found the technology able to showcase such skills and knowledge. This convergence of scholarship and technological innovation had a huge impact on the culture of the early modern period and became the vehicle for the diffusion of new religious ideas developed alongside Biblical philology.[7] The publishing industry has for centuries used philological arguments to promote their products with labels such as 'newly corrected', 'accurately checked against the oldest manuscripts', 'improved' and 'purged' used as advertising, establishing a strong and long-lasting partnership with scholars. Some of these scholars became resident editors, with famous collaborations such as the one between Pietro Bembo and Aldus Manutius in sixteenth-century Venice, but also with the work of much less glamorous people (such the ones superbly described by Anthony Grafton),[8] the role of which can be located in between publishers and authors. The early modern period saw a significant increase of literacy, which, in a virtuous circle, at once made print commercially viable and was fuelled and augmented by print. The new religious climate also called for a centrally controlled and established text as it was crucial for religious reformers that their followers were handed the same version of the Bible or of the prayer book. In Protestant countries the push towards direct access to the reading of the Bible also gave a strong impulse to

---

7   See, for instance, Elizabeth Eisenstein, *The Printing Press as an Agent of Change* (Cambridge: Cambridge University Press, 1982), where the author argues for an extraordinary push towards fixation and standardisation produced by print, but also the impulse towards the democratisation of knowledge that partially made possible the establishment of the Reformation, where individual access to the Scriptures became fundamental.

8   Anthony Grafton, *The Culture of Correction in Renaissance Europe (Panizzi Lectures)* (London: British Library, 2011).

literacy. The requirement to teach a growing number of people how to read also favoured the introduction of what Christian Vandendorpe calls the 'standards of readability', which include the simplification and standardisation of page layout, the unification of spelling and punctuation and the regularisation of syntax.[9] Textual variation gradually became unacceptable both theoretically and culturally; and even if the unification of texts was only attained in principle—since, inevitably, textual transmission determines variation—the provision and the delivery of the one authoritative and authentic text became a goal actively pursued by publishers and scholars for different but convergent reasons.

This culture, which aimed at the establishment of the one text, contrasts with the much more varied medieval practices of textual transmission. While for some religious and legal texts there was a need to be identical to their antecedent (a necessity that still made allowance for correction and contamination), for vernacular literature it was custom to 'acclimatise' the text to the linguistic environment where the copied text was to be read. For example, with highly elaborative traditions such as epic or sermons alteration and therefore the creation of new versions was considered normal practice, at least for some types of texts. The textual variety of medieval texts has been seen (and in some cases is still seen) by many scholars as a problem to fix in the quest for the original text. This point of view has started to shows some cracks, starting in the beginning of the twentieth century with Joseph Bédier's famous criticism of the Lachmannian method, and then with even more strength by the mid-1980s, with the concurrent works of Bernard Cerquiglini, D. F. McKenzie and Jerome McGann.[10] In the case of Cerquiglini, in his seminal work *Éloge de la variante* (1989) translated into English ten years later as *In Praise of the Variant*, attention was drawn to variation as a testimony to the cultural environment that produced a specific copy.[11] In his vision, manuscripts are no longer simply witnesses to works but

---

9   Christian Vandendorpe, *From Papyrus to Hypertext: Toward the Universal Digital Library* (Urbana and Chicago: University of Illinois Press, 2009), pp. 15–21.

10 This movement was anticipated by the work of Paul Zumthor, who theorised variance (*mouvance*) in medieval texts (*Essai de poétique médiévale*, Paris: Seuil, 1972); his influence has been rather limited outside the field of medieval studies, however.

11 Bernard Cerquiglini, *Éloge de la variante: Histoire critique de la philologie* (Paris: Seuil, 1989); English translation by Betsy Wing, *In Praise of the Variant: A Critical History of Philology* (Baltimore: The Johns Hopkins University Press, 1999).

witnesses to culture, and ought therefore to be studied in their own right. The work of Cerquiglini was deeply influential and lay at the base of subsequent theoretical elaborations such as 'New' or 'Material' Philology,[12] with profound influences also on Genetic Criticism. In the same span of years, with a focus on modern and printed texts, McKenzie and McGann started to investigate the various agencies and social constraints surrounding textual production. Both reached the conclusion, seemingly independently, that texts cannot be seen as the intellectual product of one agent (the author), but as the often-unstable result of the dialectic interaction among several entities, with each instance of a text to be considered as a carrier of meanings of its own.

The new theories of text based on the recognition of textual variation soon found a natural medium where variation can be presented to the readers: the digital environment. Print technology (and the infrastructure around it) has developed a way of dealing with textual variation that has been considered by many as deeply unsatisfactory: the critical apparatus. The contributions of Cynthia Damon and Marina Buzzoni in this volume show that considering the critical apparatus as a way of recording textual variation is highly reductive, since it encompasses sophisticated and specialised scholarship. However, the criticism of the apparatus still stands: its highly condensed and abbreviated formalism, elaborated for a technology where space is limited, constitutes a cultural threshold only accessible by people with the highest level of education in the very specific field that has produced such a product. The indecipherability (for most) of the critical apparatus has made it easy for readers to ignore them and so for publishers to omit them in so-called 'reading editions' or 'editions for the general public'; the same omission is noticeable for many digital libraries,[13] the consequences of which will be discussed further below. To be fair, there are print editions that try to

---

[12] The launch of 'New Philology' is traditionally related to the special issue of *Speculum* published in 1990, edited by Stephen G. Nichols, whose introductory essay 'Philology in a Manuscript Culture' has a programmatic role. For a summary of the issues, see M. J. Driscoll, 'The Words on the Page: Thoughts on Philology, Old and New', in *Creating the Medieval Saga: Versions, Variability and Editorial Interpretations of Old Norse Saga Literature*, ed. by Judy Quinn and Emily Lethbridge (Odense: University Press of Southern Denmark, 2010), pp. 85–102.

[13] This absence is particularly noticeable for classical texts; see for instance the Perseus Project (http://www.perseus.tufts.edu/hopper) and the *(Abridged) Thesaurus Linguae Grecae* (http://www.tlg.uci.edu/demoinfo/demoauthors.php).

account for textual variation in different ways with different grades of success. John Lavagnino for instance, presents the case of the variorum edition of S. T. Coleridge's poems edited by J. C. C. Mays, but then he agrees that such an edition is not easy to use, as it takes 'six volumes for what a conventional presentation could easily fit into one'.[14] The question here is whether editions such as this one are difficult to use because we are not accustomed to using them, or because the medium is not suitable.

The one-text culture is then the result of several convergent social, cultural and scholarly forces: the necessity of trusting texts for worship and legality, the necessity of simplifying the access to texts for people with different levels of literacy and education, the commercial viability of the delivery of texts as printed books, the scholarly engagement with textual transmission and modern readership. In particular, it is worth focusing attention on scholarly critical editions as cultural products of all the aforementioned forces. Critical editions in particular are very sophisticated forms of publication. Their purpose is to provide a reliable and citable text which is often comprised of the combinations of readings attested by different witnesses. Critical editions are often difficult and time-consuming to produce and, in the case of very complex textual traditions, can become lifelong projects, representing the culmination of the intellectual career of a scholar. As stated above, texts come in versions, and in most cases such versions are the consequence of, to use Peter Shillingsburg's words, 'infelicities in transmission'.[15] If we consider text transmission as a form of communication, the classic Shannon-Weaver theory can be helpful in explaining this particular aspect. According to this model, a communication act is represented by the transmission of a message produced by a source from a sender to a receiver via a specific channel until it reaches its destination, using a shared code. Such communication is never perfect, however, as it can be affected by 'noise' on the chosen channel and by the fact that the code of the sender and the receiver can never fully coincide. So every time a text is transmitted, whether by copying it by hand or by typesetting it, something about the text changes, either because the sender (scribe,

---

14 John Lavagnino, 'Access', *Literary and Linguistic Computing*, 24 (2009), 63–76 (p. 74), http://dx.doi.org/10.1093/llc/fqn038

15 Shillingsburg, *Text as Matter*, p. 51.

printer) more or less knowingly alters it because the medium imposes certain changes (format, types, material, commercial constraints etc.), or because the receiver (the reader, who in turn can become the next scribe of the transmission chain) misunderstands it.[16] The detection and correction of these infelicities in transmission are the objects of classical textual criticism theory. Critical editors try to make sense of textual transmission and consequent variation, and critical editions are the vehicles chosen to present their understanding to the readers. Such vehicles have been elaborated and refined along several centuries and are based on a theory of the text that aspires to the reconstruction of the author's intention, and such intention is understood to be only one. It should however be possible in theory to separate the critical activity of the editors who investigate the phases of textual transmission from the format in which such investigations are delivered. Nevertheless it is also true that scholarship, and in particular textual scholarship and critical editing, has been deeply shaped by its own delivery format, becoming in practice almost inseparable from it.

The implications of the one-text culture are widespread and profoundly shape our understanding of and expectations about the nature of texts and the way they should be presented. The provision of 'clean' reading texts, where almost no traces of the underlying editorial work are visible, have contributed to giving readers a false impression that stability, a 'trueness' of the texts, is an achievable goal, and that texts exist in a sort of pure, Neo-Platonic state, which should not be stained by editorial marks or doubts. It is reputed that Michelangelo was able to 'see' the finished sculptures that were hidden inside the blocks of marble, and that he thought his role as a sculptor was to free the perfect shape that was at the heart of the block, liberating it from the inert material. This poetic image, deeply influenced by the Neo-Platonism that dominated a great part of the intellectual life of the Italian Renaissance, is perfectly exemplified by some of the most extraordinary works he sculpted, namely the series of six sculptures that go under the title of *I Prigioni* [The Prisoners], four of which are preserved at the

---

16 It is arguable that in the digital word the message can indeed be transmitted without alteration; the varying contexts of manifestation — laptop, tablet, phone, desktop, web browser, downloaded file, etc., all with different settings and aspects to them — do however still result in a certain amount of variation, and in spite of all effort, the level of 'noise' can never be reduced to zero.

Galleries of Academia in Florence, while two are in Paris, at the Louvre. All these statues represent 'slaves' in the act of freeing themselves from the rock that imprisons them. These sculptures can be used as a metaphor for the editorial work that aspires to free the text from the debris of transmission. The underlying concepts of a text freed from impurity can even lead to the belief that, once that the editorial work has been done, it may become so authoritative as to become unquestionable. Edward Vanhoutte cites the case of Fredson Bowers, who, in a lecture delivered in 1958, objected to the suggestion that an editor should give an account of his own workings in order to allow a reader to reproduce and verify the editorial work, since 'bibliographical research is an essential part of the scholarly editor's tasks and thus completed at the moment of the publication of the edition'.[17] Bowers then concluded that: 'It is an anomaly for an editor proposing to establish a text to expect wiser heads to carry forward and then to apply the basic bibliographical examination of the document on which the very details of the establishment should have rested. "Every reader his own bibliographer" is an absurdity'.[18] The case of Bowers can perhaps be considered an extreme, rather than the norm. In the Italian tradition, for instance, the belief that an editor can attain such a self-assured confidence in his or her work is almost inconceivable. Generations of scholars have been formed in the belief that any edition is only a working hypothesis and that the original can only ever be approximated but never attained.[19] The same awareness is present in contemporary American textual theory; Peter Shillingsburg

---

17 Edward Vanhoutte, 'Every Reader his own Bibliographer — An Absurdity?', in *Text Editing, Print and the Digital World*, ed. by Marilyn Deegan and Kathryn Sutherland (Farnham: Ashgate, 2009), pp. 99–110 (p. 99, n. 1).

18 Fredson Bowers, 'Principle and Practice in the Editing of Early Dramatic Texts', in *Textual and Literary Criticisms: The Sandars Lectures in Bibliography 1957–1958* (Cambridge: Cambridge University Press, 1966), pp. 117–50 (p. 146).

19 See for instance the following quotation from Alfredo Stussi, which is also cited by Marina Buzzoni in the present publication: 'l'edizione critica [...] è un'ipotesi di lavoro e quindi il lettore deve essere messo in grado di verificarla punto per punto ed eventualmente di dissentire' [a critical edition [...] is, in fact, a working hypothesis and therefore the reader should be able to verify it point-by-point, and possibly disagree], *Fondamenti di critica testuale*, ed. by Alfredo Stussi (Bologna: il Mulino, 2nd ed. 2006), pp. 20–21 [my translation]. It is believed that the first formulation of such a principle is to be traced to Gianfranco Contini in *Breviario di Ecdotica* (Turin: Einaudi, 1986).

declares: 'No edition was ever or will ever represent a work adequately. Full stop. The positive. The hopeful. The perfection. The adequacy. The triumph of scholarship. They will not occur'.[20] However, even if mitigated by theoretical and methodological concerns about the effectiveness of the editorial work, the duty of the editor seems to be the production of one authoritative text (or at least aspiring to). Once the apparatus and the critical analysis of the tradition are stripped out and the naked text is proposed as a reading text, this text inevitably presents itself as The Text. This is also lamented by John Bryant: 'the smoothness of the reading text, a hallmark of critical editing, in effect denies us an immediate awareness of the actual roughness of the textual record, and textuality itself'.[21]

The digital environment knows none or little of the space limitation of print. The absence of this limitation has made possible the provision of texts in versions and texts as versions in a way that is much simpler, more intuitive and dynamic than corresponding print attempts. The *Samuel Beckett Digital Manuscript Project*[22] demonstrates this principle, as it includes all the documents that compose the *dossier génétique* of each of the works included, providing several visualisations for each of them and tools for exploring their differences. Another example is offered by the digital edition of *De trein der traagheid*, edited by Xavier Roelens, Edward Vanhoutte and Ron Van der Branden,[23] where each of the nineteen witnesses that compose the tradition of this work is available on its own or in comparison with others; in addition a reading edition is also provided. Some of these digital endeavours have been labelled 'archives' instead of editions since they present all the witnesses of a work with or without the support of digital facsimiles. This is the case,

---

20 Peter Shillingsburg, *From Gutenberg to Google* (Cambridge: Cambridge University Press, 2006), p. 154.
21 Bryant, *The Fluid Text*, p. 27.
22 *Samuel Beckett Digital Manuscript Project*, ed. by Dirk Van Hulle et al. (Antwerp: University Press Anwerp, 2013), http://www.beckettarchive.org; see Dirk Van Hulle's contribution in this volume.
23 Johan Daisne, *De trein der traagheid*, ed. by Xavier Roelens, Edward Vanhoutte and Ron Van der Branden (Gent: Centrum voor Teksteditie en Bronnenstudie, 2012), http://edities.ctb.kantl.be/daisne/index.htm

for instance, with the *Rossetti Archive* or the *Whitman Archive*.²⁴ The choice of labelling them 'archives' has generated a large amount of discussion on their scholarly nature (are they 'critical' enough?) and their alleged lack of textual focus.²⁵

These editions have been accompanied by fierce discussions, with scholars arguing in particular that offering readers too many choices will only cause disorientation rather than engendering in them an appreciation of the complexity of textual variety. As stated by Robinson 'it appears that rather few readers (indeed, rather often, only editors) actually want to see all the images, all the transcripts, all the collations', and while 'printed editions acted as filters',²⁶ the digital medium provides readers with an overload of unregulated data that struggles to become information, since 'value [...] is added through [a] chain of literary agents, specialist readers, editors and publishers'.²⁷ Others have reminded editors of their responsibilities as providers of critical texts, rather than simply of witnesses.²⁸ Yet it is likely that some of these critiques are connected with the uneasiness of a new textual model that is endemic in digital texts, a model based on variation and plurality of manifestations and representations.²⁹

Digital texts can be defined as inherently variable; in fact the variance of digital texts occurs in several contexts and can assume several shapes. The first and most basic form of variation arises from the fact that each

---

24 *The Complete Writing and Pictures of Dante Gabriel Rossetti: A Hypermedia Archive*, ed. by Jerome McGann (Charlottesville: IATH, 2008), http://www.rossettiarchive.org; *The Walt Whitman Archive*, ed. by Ed Folsom and Kenneth M. Price (University of Nebraska-Lincoln: Center for Digital Research in the Humanities, 1995–), http://www.whitmanarchive.org

25 Kenneth M. Price, 'Edition, Project, Database, Archive, Thematic Research Collection: What's in a Name?', *Digital Humanities Quarterly*, 3.3 (2009), http://digitalhumanities.org/dhq/vol/3/3/000053/000053.html; Jerome McGann, 'Electronic Archives and Critical Editing', *Literature Compass*, 7.2 (2010), 37–42.

26 Peter Robinson, 'Electronic Editions for Everyone', in *Text and Genre in Reconstruction: Effects of Digitalization on Ideas, Behaviours, Products and Institutions*, ed. by Willard McCarty (Cambridge: Open Book Publishers, 2010), pp. 145–63 (p. 150), http://dx.doi.org/10.11647/OBP.0008

27 Marilyn Deegan and Kathryn Sutherland, *Transferred Illusions: Digital Technology and the Forms of Print* (Farnham: Ashgate, 2009), p. 115.

28 Alfredo Stussi, *Introduzione agli studi di filologia italiana* (Bologna: il Mulino, 2007), pp. 245–46; Peter Robinson, 'Towards a Theory of Digital Editions', *Variants*, 10 (2013), 105–32.

29 See Patrick Sahle's contribution in this volume.

digital reader (or user) will access the text from different devices, the shape and dimension of which cannot be controlled by the editor and can vary dramatically. The experience of reading a text on the screen of a mobile phone can be radically different from that of a tablet or a laptop; the same applies to texts read from a web browser or downloaded within an eReader application or even printed out on A4 paper. All of these manifestations present the same text, yet the reading experience (and ultimately the message) can vary greatly. This is even more the case for digital scholarly editions that are offered from within a web-based user interface and often rely on specific software, the availability of which may not be possible in different environments such as the one offered by mobile devices. The second form of variation stems from the fact that many digital texts actually change. Since the digital medium allows for easy modifications, even after their first publication, many people take this opportunity and edit the texts as they go along. This 'work-in-progress' type of publication has become quite common if not the norm for digital scholarly editions. Many editions are in fact published quite early and in their elaboration stage in order to collect feedback and maintain the interest of the readers throughout the lifespan of the project.[30] This new mode of publication offers a strident contrast to the traditional print-based publication system, which sees long delays and frantic checking before the texts are actually printed, as once one has 'pressed the print button' nothing can be done to fix errors that inevitably escape the most thorough of controls. This change is bound to have profound consequences for the production and consumption of scholarship.

The third form of variation of digital texts is deliberately offered as a feature of many digital editions: the possibility of displaying the same text in different ways. In fact, by the application of different sets of rules contained in the so-called stylesheets, if the text has been produced by the means of text encoding, it is possible to visualise it in any number of different formats, for instance as a critical, diplomatic, variorum or as a reading text. These visualisations can be generated dynamically

---

[30] Just one of many examples is the Henry III Fine Rolls project that had a rolling publication of the edited text during the lifespan of the project: *Henry III Fine Rolls Project*, ed. by David Carpenter et al. (London: King's College London, 2009–2013), http://www.finerollshenry3.org.uk/home.html

on-demand by the users and form the staple of what has been defined as a paradigmatic edition,[31] where paradigmatic variation lies at the heart of the theoretical set up of both the edition and its publication.

The digital medium with its inherent variability presents itself as the ideal environment to deal with text variation in ways that go beyond the possibilities offered by the print medium. Since space is not an issue, and hypertextuality simplifies navigation from one version to the next, editors have embraced the new medium in order to explore different types of scholarship able to take advantage of such variability. Coping with and exploiting this digital variability requires a rethinking of most of the heuristics of textual scholarship, as well as its editorial products. This necessity is clearly present in Michael Sperberg-McQueen's reflection:

> Editors may justly feel that electronic editions have translated them from a stable environment with difficult but well-known problems into a river of Heraclitean flux, in which everything is changing from moment to moment, and the editor and edition are expected to adapt actively to those changes from moment to moment, without being able to rely on many of the principles which used to be stable guides to editorial thinking.[32]

Editors and editions then have to learn how to swim in this sea of mutability, which requires:

> endowing an edition not only with a store of factual *knowledge* concerning the work presented, but also with the *capability* of dealing gracefully with the mutability of the electronic medium, by exploiting the possibilities for reader-controlled changes to the edition's presentation and by adapting successfully to rapid changes in the hardware and software environment.[33]

The change from a Neo-Platonic view of the text—which only needs to be freed from the errors of the transmission to present itself in its pristine status—to a Heralictean view—according to which texts are mutable by nature—has several consequences in terms of the purpose

---

31 Elena Pierazzo, 'Digital Documentary Editions and the Others', *Scholarly Editing*, 35 (2014), http://www.scholarlyediting.org/2014/essays/essay.pierazzo.html

32 C. M. Sperberg-McQueen, 'How to Teach your Edition how to Swim', *Literary and Linguistic Computing*, 24 (2009), 27–52 (p. 30), http://dx.doi.org/10.1093/llc/fqn034

33 *Ibid.* [italics in the original].

of editing, the role of the editor, the role of the reader, the workflow of editing and the types of products that we aim to publish. First of all, the purpose of editing needs to change from the provision of a stable and quotable text to the provision of an accountable reconstruction of some of the various states of the text—some, since an exhaustive account is impossible by definition in a Heraclitean framework. This does not mean that the editors do not have to provide a reading version of the text, but that this should not be the main or only focus of editing. Cesare Segre has described scholarly editions as diasystems: the system of the text and the one of the transmission of the text, or the real image of the text (the one of the author) and the historical perceived image of it.[34] Traditionally, scholarly editions that present the system of the text have become predominant: the font, the layout, the distribution of text and variants on the page clearly denote a hierarchical dependency between the text and the account of the text's transmission. A theoretical framework that recognises the intrinsic mutability of texts needs to reverse this hierarchy, however, so that the representation of the historical perception of the text occupies the centre stage of the editorial discourse.[35]

This change of focus of the editorial endeavour is at once fuelled and determined by the change of medium, in the sense that while a digital environment has made it possible to exploit the variability of texts, it has also invited scholars to consider doing so. Richard J. Finneran notes that

---

34 Cesare Segre, *Semiotica filologica: Testo e modelli culturali* (Turin: Einaudi, 1979).

35 Cf. the passage, cited and translated by Marina Buzzoni in the present volume, from Cesare Segre, 'La critica testuale', in *XIV Congresso Internazionale di Linguistica e Filologia romanza (Napoli, 15–20 Apr. 1974)*, I–V (Naples and Amsterdam: Macchiaroli-Benjamins, 1977–1981), I, pp. 493–99 (p. 497): 'Occorre [...] capovolgere i rapporti gerarchici fra testo e apparato, dare la maggiore enfasi all'apparato e considerare il testo come una superficie neutra [...] su cui il filologo ha innestato le lezioni da lui considerate sicure, fra le tante considerate. Ma l'edizione si merita l'attributo di *critica* molto di più attraverso l'apparato, se discorsivamente problematico: perché esso sintetizza il diasistema della tradizione, e perché svolge un vaglio completo, anche se non sempre conclusivo, delle lezioni'. [There needs to be a turnaround [...] in the hierarchical relationships between the text and the apparatus, give greater emphasis to the apparatus and consider the text as a neutral surface [...] on which the philologist has grafted the readings which he deemed certain among the many considered. However, the edition deserves the attribute of being 'critical' through the apparatus, if discursively problematic: because it summarises the diasystem of the tradition, and because it carries out a full assessment, even if not always conclusive, of the readings].

the advent of new technologies 'coincided with a fundamental shift in textual theory, away from the notion of a single-text "definitive edition"' remarking that while 'a traditional print edition is able to accommodate this new thinking in textual theory either awkwardly or not at all, digital technology is its necessary and inevitable realization'.[36] On a similar line are Marilyn Deegan and Kathryn Sutherland, with the caveat that they describe the renewed interest in more complex considerations of textual transmission, consumption and dissemination as not being 'computer-dependent' but 'computer-convergent'.[37]

What are the consequences for the consumption of texts? What is the impact of a dynamic, Heraclitean view of texts on their readers and users? From the perspective of the readers, this approach may represent a striking novelty which may or may not be received as a good thing. For readers who are educated by the traditional format of text delivery (the one-text edition), a digital resource that presents many versions and that showcases the transmission over the reading text may result in an unwelcomed approach; others may instead find the new format more engaging as it affords other types of reading beside the linear top-to-bottom one. Reading is an activity that takes various shapes, from the linear reading of novels and essays to the fragmentary reading of newspapers, to the information-seeking reading of dictionaries, to the intensive re-reading of objects of study. Governed by economic constraints, the publication of texts has aimed at satisfying many if not all types of reading with a single product, but as the same constraints do not apply for the digital environment, it is conceivable to produce editions that aim at only one type of reading (and readers) or editions that provide different outputs for different readers, where textual variation is not hidden away in the fear that this may ruin the aesthetic pleasure, but presented in an accessible and engaging way. Textual variation does not need to be presented as a hyper-specialised and cryptic critical apparatus, nor as a series of texts put side by side; texts and textual scholarship can be made accessible and interesting. For example, an innovative publishing house, Touch Press, has since 2010 published several apps for iPads in the field of science and literature

---

36   *The Literary Text in the Digital Age*, ed. by Richard Finneran (Ann Arbor: University of Michigan Press, 1996), p. x.
37   Deegan and Sutherland, *Transferred Illusions*, p. 64.

outreach which allows for textual variation. Beside very successful apps about the periodic table of elements and the galaxy, they have produced an edition of *The Waste Land* by T. S. Elliot and of the *Sonnets* of Shakespeare.[38] These apps present the texts in different ways, as video, audio, written words and any combinations of the above; they also include multimedia commentaries, facsimiles of first editions and, in the case of *The Waste Land*, of the typeset text as corrected by the author. It is probably not a coincidence that such an approach is pursued by a publishing house that specialises in science outreach. In the sciences there is an established tradition of encouraging the general public to engage with scientific discovery, resulting in a rapid growth in the science communication industry as demonstrated by a number of teaching programmes that have recently emerged.[39] This interest in the sciences is usually created by publications written by high profile scientists aimed at the lay public[40] and various initiatives that encourage a large section of the interested public into understanding science. We could also consider here science and natural history museums, for instance, where, especially in English-speaking countries, it is customary to offer science-oriented entertainment and learning activities. Such activities are also present in certain areas of the humanities, such as art and art history, as well as in history where books aimed at the non-specialist public are quite common. Other than reading editions and editions with commentaries for students, not many of these activities have involved textual scholars and scholarship, especially since in these cases the focus is usually more on understanding and interpreting the text itself rather than on a variation or transmission. The digital environment in its various embodiments may well be a more flexible space in which to seek public engagement with editorial endeavours, if indeed editors are willing to do it.

---

38   See http://www.touchpress.com/#our-apps
39   See, for instance, the MA programmes offered by the Imperial College London, University of Sheffield, University of Edinburgh, University of Cardiff, to name only a few examples in the UK.
40   See, for instance, Stephen Hawking's *A Brief History of Time: From the Big Bang to Black Holes* (New York: Bantam, 1988), published many times since its first edition; according to current estimation (2016) the book has sold about ten million copies worldwide.

The effect of moving away from the one-text paradigm may have consequences far beyond the public of readers. Corpus linguistics, computational linguistics, stylometry, authorship attribution, data mining and many other scholarly disciplines and methodologies that approach texts from a quantitative point of view are based on the assumption that we can query the one text, and that not only does the one text exist, but also that we know what it is. For quantitative approaches the fact that texts only exist as versions is irrelevant, since the large amount of data used for such approaches normally offsets small differences and minutiae such as those that one could consider informing different text versions. For most of these approaches the one text is all that is needed, and more than one will actually only produce noise and falsify the results. This, of course, is a simplification, since we are seeing more complex approaches to textuality and textual variation being adopted by some scholars of corpus linguistics, in particular those working with historical corpora,[41] but in spite of this crude generalisation it is not far from the truth that most data mining, distant reading and NLP methods assume texts to be stable, uncontroversial entities. What will the consequence of a paradigmatic change be on these methodologies? Probably none at first, since it is very likely that in most cases a cultural change such as the one invoked here will go unnoticed for a while at least. Even then—since these methodologies willingly ignore any textual complexity, adopting in most cases a positivistic view of the text—acknowledging text mutability would require a profound change in such methods, a change that seems unlikely to happen. Each discipline selects its own level of simplification and abstraction of its object of study; the simplification level that is conveyed by the one and plain text may look a step too far for textual scholars but may perfectly serve the needs of other research approaches. Furthermore, if editors do not emphasise the importance of textual variation it is hard to imagine that others will do it on their behalf.

One obvious problem is the increased difficulty in citing texts. To affirm that all academic culture is based on citations may be an exaggeration, yet the possibility of tracing and attributing a certain

---

41 See, for instance, the *Syntactic Reference Corpus of Medieval French* (http://srcmf.org) and the TXM tool developed at École Normale Supérieure of Lyon by Serge Heiden (http://textometrie.ens-lyon.fr).

portion of text to a specific source is a fundamental requirement for any publication wanting to be defined as scholarly. This is not an exclusive problem of mutable texts, but a problem that concerns all scholarship delivered in digital form, including editions based on the one-text paradigm. As maintained by Christine L. Borgman 'notions of fixity are problematic in a digital, distributed world'; yet, she continues, 'it must remain possible to cite publications, data, and other sources in persistent ways, so that others can evaluate the evidence on which a scholarly work rests. Dynamic objects, however, will be increasingly common in scholarly work'.[42] The task of coherently preserving fixed versions of online resources seems out of reach for the moment, with scholars and producers of digital resources relying on institutional repositories and on libraries and infrastructures,[43] yet considerable investment and raising awareness may help in changing this situation. What is more likely to happen, however, is that scholars will learn how to cope with ephemeral objects, with innovation becoming increasingly more important than longevity. This change is indeed already taking place. The web has educated its users to check the 'last updated' date and to use this date as an indicator of quality and the fact that the resource is well looked after.[44] Therefore when accessing completed resources such as the *Rossetti Archive*, completed in 2008,[45] one cannot fail to feel a sense of mistrust of a resource which has seemingly been 'abandoned' for eight years, at the time of writing—which is, on the face of it, somewhat paradoxical, given the fundamental requirement of scholarship to be immutably and indefinitely preserved.

We are in a phase of cultural re-mediation, where most of our cultural artefacts are adapted to the new medium or substituted with digital equivalents, or allegedly so; texts and editions of texts are no exception: the examples of apps of *The Waste Land* and the *Sonnets* shows this, as

---

42   Christine Borgman, *Scholarship in the Digital Age: Information, Infrastructure, and the Internet* (Cambridge, MA: MIT Press, 2007), p. 232.
43   See Elena Pierazzo, *Digital Scholarly Editing* (Farnham: Ashgate, 2015), chapter 8.
44   See, for instance, the Guidelines to evaluate digital resources issued by the University of Berkeley, which advises students to check if the resource is 'stale' since recent updates demonstrates that 'the page author is still maintaining an interest in the page, or has abandoned it' (*Evaluating Web Pages: Techniques to Apply & Questions to Ask*, UC Berkeley Library, 2012, http://www.lib.berkeley.edu/TeachingLib/Guides/Internet/Evaluate.html).
45   McGann, The Rossetti Archive.

well as the rapid diffusion of eBooks and tablets. Re-mediation is not a simple transposition since the medium shapes the messages in profound and unexpected ways.[46] But while we will probably understand some of the long-term consequences only in the course of the next generations, we are also offered the opportunity to lead some of these changes by engaging at once with texts, the medium and the readers, to try to produce different and more complex representations of the text and text culture. Digital mutability may respond well to textual mutability but only if the latter is recognised and embraced, and if we make a feature of it rather than considering it a bug.

---

46   'The medium is the message', as famously said by Marshall McLuhan; the phrase first appeared in his *Understanding Media: The Extensions of Man* (New York: McGraw-Hill, 1964), p. 7.

4. A Protocol for Scholarly Digital Editions? The Italian Point of View

Marina Buzzoni

Preliminary remarks

This chapter discusses whether it is desirable to establish a *protocol* that would provide, if not a standard, at least some guidance on how to structure the core elements that one should expect to find in a scholarly electronic edition.

A preliminary examination is thus needed to determine which features should be defined as fundamental. Though the debate on the issue is still intense, many scholars in the field of digital philology[1] now agree that there are at least five domains in which scholarly digital editions may offer important advantages over paper editions, namely:[2]

1. the possibility to present and manage *quantities of data* that are not normally publishable in a paper book;

---

[1] Digital philology encompasses the field of textual criticism and editorial scholarship in the electronic medium. More precisely, it engages with the interaction between Information and Communication Technology (ICT) systems and the philological study of documents/texts which have been converted into digital format. See, for example, the section titled 'The Digital Philology', in *Digital Critical Editions*, ed. by Daniel Apollon and Claire Belisle (Urbana-Champaign: University of Illinois Press, 2014), pp. 50–55.

[2] On these topics see *Digital Philology and Medieval Texts*, ed. by Arianna Ciula and Francesco Stella (Pisa: Pacini Editore, 2006), pp. vii–xiii and 232–36.

2. the *relationability* of the data provided, i.e. the possibility of making connections between data and processing them at a speed, precision and complexity otherwise unattainable;

3. their *interoperability*, i.e. broadly speaking, the ability to share information in computing environments and — in principle — between different computer systems, thus enhancing the possibility of interaction within the scientific community in time and extension which a traditional book does not allow for;[3]

4. their *multimediality* and *multimodality*, which allow for the organisation of data into hierarchically structured hypertexts, as well as the inclusion of non-textual data in the edition (e.g. audio and video files);

5. and, last but not least, *user interaction*.

More specifically, these domains represent what can be considered the added value of scholarly digital editions, not in terms of mere application but rather in terms of theoretical and/or methodological improvement. For example, the availability of space offered by the digital edition, together with the relationability of the data provided, are prerequisites which allow users to *account for* the choices made by the editor more easily and economically than in printed form;[4] and *accountability* is a necessary component of scientific reliability. Paradoxically, the 'new' digital medium goes in the direction indicated by thoroughly traditional philologists like the Italianist Domenico De Robertis, according to whom an edition can be called critical in a strict sense only if it furnishes the reader with all the documentation necessary to evaluate it and to produce another, maybe different edition that is nevertheless based on the same material.[5] More recently, Alfredo Stussi — among many others — has called attention to a closely related issue:

---

3 It has recently been argued that *interoperability* in a strict sense is very difficult to achieve (cf. Fotis Jannidis, 'Digital editions in the Net: Perspectives for Scholarly Editing in a Digital World', in *Beyond the Screen: Transformations of Literary Structures, Interfaces and Genre*, ed. by Jörgen Schäfer and Peter Gendolla (Bielefeld: Transcript Verlag, 2010), pp. 543–60, in particular: 'Interoperability of Programs', pp. 551–56); therefore *exchangeability* would seem a more appropriate term to apply in this case. A discussion of this thorny issue, however interesting it may be from the theoretical point of view, is beyond the scope of the present chapter.

4 It is not a question of having just *more* data at our disposal, but rather of having more *network-related* data.

5 De Robertis states that, in order to be considered excellent ('eccellente'), a critical edition should provide '[i] materiali necessari e sufficienti per un'altra edizione critica della stessa opera condotta secondo differenti criteri di utilizzazione dei

Once the textual-critical problems regarding both content and form have been resolved, however many witnesses there may be, the manner in which this information is presented to the potential user of the critical edition is highly important. A critical edition is, in fact, a working hypothesis, and hence the reader must be able to verify it point by point, and, indeed, to disagree [with the editorial choices made].[6]

Digital editions as 'editions-in-time'

In principle, a Scholarly Digital Edition should present the five features listed under section 1 regardless of the subtype to which it belongs.[7] Furthermore, these same features should be fulfilled in every single module that makes up an edition, otherwise the potential of the digital environment would not be fully exploited. As recently claimed by Dino Buzzetti: 'One might be tempted to say that present-day digital editions, for all their merits, are not yet fully digital, since they do not fully exploit the distinctive features of the digital form of textual representation *to obtain better critical and analytical results*'.[8] And further on: '[...] the means

---

    medesimi testi'. [The necessary and sufficient materials for another critical edition of the same work produced according to different criteria of use of the same texts (my translation)].
    Domenico De Robertis, 'Problemi di filologia delle strutture', in *La critica del testo: Problemi di metodo ed esperienze di lavoro*, Atti del Convegno di Lecce 1984 (Rome: Salerno editrice, 1985), pp. 383–404.

6   *Fondamenti di critica testuale*, ed. by Alfredo Stussi, 2nd ed. (Bologna: il Mulino, 2006), pp. 20–21: 'Una volta risolti i problemi critico-testuali di sostanza e di forma, quale che sia il numero dei testimoni, molto conta il modo in cui i risultati vengono presentati al pubblico che utilizzerà l'edizione critica. Quest'ultima è un'ipotesi di lavoro e quindi il lettore deve essere messo in grado di verificarla punto per punto ed eventualmente di dissentire'.

7   Among the many edition types produced in the field of scholarly digital editing (e.g. image-based editions, text archives, collections of multiple versions, diplomatic editions of witnesses—to mention but a few) a broad distinction can be drawn between the 'archival' and the 'reconstructive/interpretative' type (see, among others, Patrick Sahle, 'Digitales Archiv—Digital Edition: Anmerkungen zur Begriffsklärung', in *Literatur und Literaturwissenschaft auf dem Weg zu den neuen Medien: Eine Standortbestimmung*, ed. by Michael Stolz et al. (Zürich: germanistik.ch, 2007), pp. 64–84; Francesco Stella, 'Tipologie di edizione digitale per i testi medievali', in *Poesía medieval: Historia literaria y transmisión de textos*, ed. by Vitalino Valcárcel Martinez and Carlos Pérez González (Burgos: Fundación Instituto Castellano y Leonés de la Lengua, 2005), pp. 327–62. See also Patrick Sahle's chapter 'What is a Scholarly Digital Edition?' in the present volume.

8   Dino Buzzetti, 'Digital Edition and Text Processing', in *Text Editing, Print, and the Digital World*, ed. by Marilyn Deegan and Kathryn Sutherland (Farmham: Ashgate, 2009), pp. 45–62 (p. 45) [my italics].

of rendering a text—spoken, written, printed, digital—affords a different and distinctive approach to seizing it. In this respect, an "image", or representation of the text in digital form, *can considerably enhance our opportunities of penetrating deeply into its discourse'*.[9] A major advantage of a digital edition is its potential to provide a model capable of embodying the *edition-in-time* ('edizione-nel-tempo') as a result of *text-in-time* ('testo-nel-tempo') postulated by Gianfranco Contini.[10] A text can be considered as a dynamic entity that originates from the tension between the initial, multi-faceted creative process and the subsequent re-elaborations and modifications which it inevitably undergoes. According to Contini, the edition too should be '*in time*, opening up in the "pragma" and making the editorial choices subject to a variable teleology'.[11] In fact, in order to convey more precisely the mobility of the text, an edition cannot carry the connotations of a rigidly defined structure; rather, it should aim at injecting history into the critically reconstructed text by taking into account the different synchronic stages that make up its diachronic dimension, namely the evolutionary line of the textual tradition.[12] In this perspective, Contini's view of *edition-in-time* represents an antidote to Bédier's radical scepticism towards any kind of reconstruction. The inherent risk of Bédier's well-known argumentations against the so-called 'Lachmannian method' is to open the path to editions which, in the name of the dogma of the witness as vehicle for an alleged historical text, result instead in

---

9   *Ibid.*, p. 46 [my italics].
10 Gianfranco Contini, 'Filologia', in *Enciclopedia del Novecento* (Rome: Istituto della Enciclopedia Italiana, 1977), II, pp. 954–72 (p. 955); Gianfranco Contini, 'La critica testuale come studio di strutture', in *La critica del testo: Atti del II Congresso Internazionale della Società Italiana di Storia del Diritto* (Florence: Olschki, 1971), I, pp. 11–23 (p. 12).
11 Gianfranco Contini, *Breviario di ecdotica* (Turin: Einaudi, 1990), p. 14: 'l'edizione è pure *nel tempo*, aprendosi nel pragma e facendo sottostare le sue decisioni a una teleologia variabile' [the edition is also *in time*, opening itself in practice and subjecting its decisions to a variable teleology (my translation)].
12 *Ibid.*, p. 45: '[lo stato dinamico del testo] è tanto più da affermare in quanto è da riconoscere la necessità, in contraddizione o piuttosto composizione con essa, di piattaforme dove sostare lungo la linea evolutiva: sincronie intermedie che si oppongono alla sincronia originaria come limite di un processo diacronico'.
    [(the dynamic state of the text) must be affirmed all the more insofar as we recognise the necessity, in contradiction or rather in accordance with it, of platforms on which to pause along the evolutionary line: intermediate synchronies which stand in opposition to the originary synchrony as a limit to a diachronic process (my translation)].

an inactive and almost frozen object, suffocated within the borders of its own materiality, fixed once for all. Broadly speaking, this is what happens with his critical edition of the *Chanson de Roland* based solely on the Oxford manuscript.[13] In order to give new life to a paralysed text, the Italian philologist Cesare Segre, on the pattern laid down by Contini, opens it up again to the diachronic dimension —both in the direction of a rehabilitation of the reconstructive process based on a thorough *recensio*, and simultaneously by representing the after-life of the text, as well as its dynamicity, which reaches the highest peaks in two families of witnesses (labelled as γ and δ, respectively).[14]

In order to grasp the dynamic nature of a text (its inherent *mouvance*, as defined by Paul Zumthor[15]), not so much the witness itself but rather the 'critical apparatus' acquires a crucial role, as underlined on several occasions by the Italian philological school.[16] It is no coincidence that back in 1974 Cesare Segre argued that the apparatus should be the location where the tension between respect for the antigraph and the innovative thrust of the copyist is brought to the fore:

> There needs to be a turnaround [...] in the hierarchical relationships between the text and the apparatus, give greater emphasis to the apparatus and consider the text as a neutral surface [...] on which the philologist has grafted the readings which he deemed certain among the many considered. However, the edition deserves the attribute of being 'critical' through the apparatus, if discursively problematic: because it summarizes the diasystem of the tradition, and because it carries out a full assessment, even if not always conclusive, of the readings.[17]

---

13 *La Chanson de Roland*, ed. by Joseph Bédier (Paris: L'édition d'art, 1921).
14 *La Chanson de Roland*, ed. by Cesare Segre (Milan and Naples: Ricciardi, 1971).
15 Paul Zumthor, *Essai de poétique médiévale* (Paris: Seuil, 1972); Paul Zumthor, *La lettre et la voix* (Paris: Seuil, 1987).
16 See, for example, Paola Pugliatti, 'Textual Perspectives in Italy: From Pasquali's Historicism to the Challenge of "Variantistica" (and Beyond)', in *Text: An Interdisciplinary Annual of Textual Studies*, ed. by W. Speed Hill, Edward M. Burns and Peter Shillingsburg (Ann Arbor: University of Michigan Press, 1998), XI, pp. 155–88; Marina Buzzoni and Eugenio Burgio, 'The Italian "Third Way" of Editing Between Globalization and Localization', in *Internationalität und Interdisziplinarität der Editionswissenschaft*, Beihefte zu *Editio* 38, ed. by Michael Stolz and Yen-Chun Chen (Berlin: Walter de Gruyter, 2014), pp. 171–80.
17 Cesare Segre, 'La critica testuale', in *XIV congresso internazionale di Linguistica e Filologia romanza (Napoli, 15–20 Apr. 1974)* (Naples and Amsterdam: Macchiaroli-Benjamins, 1978), I, pp. 493–99 (p. 497).

It is therefore in the apparatus that the diasystem[18] of the tradition is best highlighted, and its *historicity* fully appreciated.[19] Since an edition is always a working hypothesis (see above, footnote 6),[20] the critical apparatus is the key that allows the reader to understand the choices made by the editor to present the text in that particular shape. It is in the apparatus that the reader finds information about the editorial process that resulted in the text he or she is reading—thus enabling her/him to evaluate the editor's decisions—as well as the different shapes assumed by the text itself in the period in which it was composed and committed to posterity.[21] A crucial problem which arises when dealing with the apparatus in the digital medium is how to make it respond to modern scholarly needs,[22] without either drastically reducing or completely concealing its critical nature.[23]

The 'digital' apparatus and quantity

In most of the digital edition projects developed so far, a specific form of apparatus—when provided—seems to have gained particular success,

---

18   A term applied to textual criticism by Cesare Segre, 'Critique textuelle, théorie des ensembles et diasystèmes', *Académie royale de Belgique: Bulletin de la classe des lettre set des sciences morale set politiques*, 62 (1976), 279–92, to express the idea that the text transmitted in a given manuscript represents the contact between the linguistic system of the author and those of the copyists who filter the exemplar through their own code. A diasystem can thus be seen as a sort of compromise between two or more semiotic systems coming into contact with one another. Segre operates a semantic redefinition of the linguistic notion of diasystem coined by the dialectologist Uriel Weinreich in 1954 (Uriel Weinreich, 'Is a Structural Dialectology Possible?', *Word*, 10 (1954), 388–400).
19   Cf. also *Storicità del testo, Storicità dell'edizione*, ed. by Fulvio Ferrari and Massimiliano Bampi (Trento: Dipartimento di Studi Letterari, Linguistici e Filologici, 2009).
20   *Fondamenti di critica testuale*, p. 20.
21   On these topics see also Paolo Trovato, *Everything You Always Wanted to Know about Lachmann's Method: A Non-Standard Handbook of Genealogical Textual Criticism in the Age of Post-Structuralism, Cladistics, and Copy-Text* (Padua: libreriauniversitaria.it edizioni, 2014).
22   Cf. Elena Pierazzo, *Digital Scholarly Editing: Theories, Models and Methods* (Farnham: Ashgate, 2015), in particular p. 157.
23   For example, the complete list of both formal and substantial variants provided by Nila Vázquez in a separate section of her 2009 edition of *The Tale of Gamelyn*, oddly titled '*Apparatus criticus* of the Edition' (pp. 336–79), can indeed be useful for the reader; this apparatus records the raw results of the collation, however (see note 200, p. 332), to which the critical process has still to be applied. See Nila Vázquez, *The Tale of Gamelyn of the Canterbury Tales: An Annotated Edition* (Lewiston: The Edwin Mellen Press, 2009). For a more detailed discussion of the critical nature of the apparatus see below.

namely the so-called 'horizontale Kollationspartitur'[24] exemplified by the famous edition of Chrétien de Troyes' *Lancelot* (= *Le Chevalier de la Charrette*, ca. 1180), which was produced at Princeton by a team of romance scholars between 1997 and 2010.[25]

Yet, from a theoretical point of view this 'horizontale Kollationspartitur' is too dependent on categories that still stick to a linear representation of the object *text*, not completely fulfilling the digital features mentioned above. For example, in order to meet the requirement of quantity (see above, section 1, point 1), a critical apparatus should drop its traditional focus on single words in favour of a sentence-oriented or even text-oriented approach. In other words, it should be centred on dimensions that would allow one to go beyond the 'chopped' variants with which readers are usually presented in paper editions (see Fig. 4.1) and which make it extremely difficult to identify the potential relationships between them:

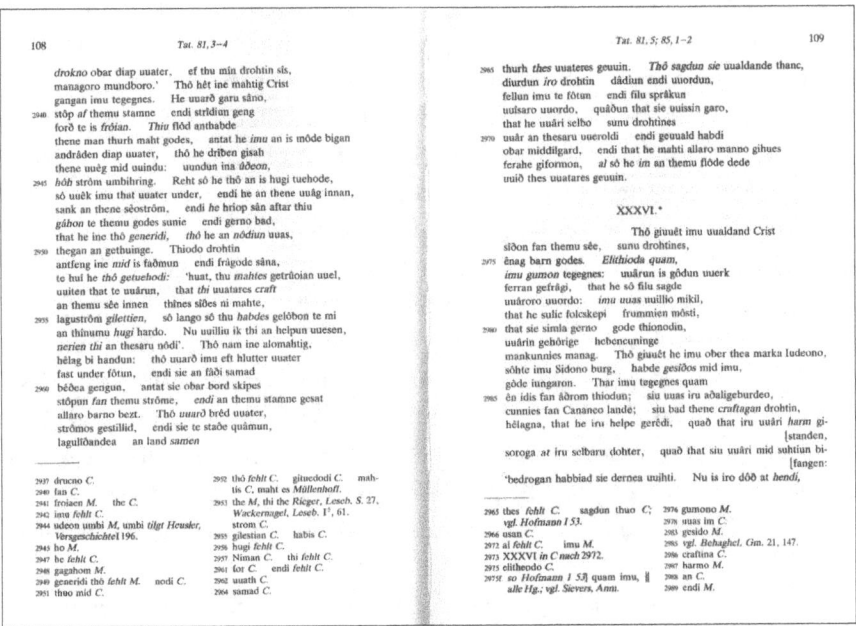

Fig. 4.1 A page taken from Taeger's 1996 edition of the *Heliand*, showing a linear critical apparatus focused on single words.

---

24 Peter Stahl, 'Kollation und Satztechnik als Vorbereitung für eine kritische Edition', in *Maschinelle Verarbeitung altdeutscher Texte* IV, ed. by Kurt Gärtner et al. (Tübingen: Max Niemeyer Verlag, 1991), pp. 142–47.

25 *The Princeton Charrette Project*, http://www.princeton.edu/~lancelot/ss

To overcome this word-oriented perspective would be to increase the number of potential users, in particular, though not exclusively, among scholars. A linguist, for example, might be interested in features attesting intra- and inter-linguistic variation for the representation of sentence-level syntax, semantics and discourse. This is the kind of information that is generally not present—or at the very least rare—in a traditional linear apparatus.

A brief example taken from the text currently being edited by the present writer—the ninth-century Old Saxon alliterative reworking of the Gospel titled *Heliand*—illustrates this point. The poem, about 6000 lines long, has come down to us in a nearly complete form in two manuscripts: a continental MS M (München, cgm. 25, preserved at the Bavarian *Staatsbibliothek*) and an English MS C (Cotton Caligula A.vii, preserved in the British Library). A further four fragments transmit short passages of the text: i.e. V (Codex Palatinus Lat. 1447, discovered by Karl Zangemeister in 1894 and now housed at the Vatican Library in Rome; ll. 1279–1358); P (formerly preserved at the University Library of Prague, now in Berlin, Bibliothek des Deutschen Historischen Museums, R 56/2537; ll. 958b–1006a), S (the Straubing fragment, currently held in München, Bavarian *Staatsbibliothek*, cgm. 8840; ll. 351–722), and—last but not least—L, the newly discovered Leipzig fragment, found in 2006 (Leipzig, Universitätsbibliothek, MS Thomas 4073; ll. 5823–5870a).[26] Since the major editions produced so far[27] are based on M—which has always been considered the guide-manuscript in editorial practice — many sentence-level linguistic phenomena that only C displays have been completely neglected. A word-oriented linear apparatus has contributed considerably to these phenomena being left out, and they have become so difficult to detect that even trained experts have serious trouble discerning them. A paradigmatic example is represented by the so-called *attractio relativi* (or 'case attraction'),[28] frequently attested

---

26   For a general overview, see the essays contained in the anthology *Perspectives on the Old Saxon Heliand: Introductory and Critical Essays, with an Edition of the Leipzig Fragment*, ed. by Valentine A. Pakis (Morgantown: West Virginia University Press, 2010).

27   For example: *Heliand und Genesis*, ed. by Otto Behaghel, 10th ed. by Burkhard Taeger (Tübingen: Max Niemeyer Verlag, 1996).

28   In a relative structure, the relative pronoun can bear the case required by the matrix clause — instead of that required by the subordinate — if that case is more marked (where 'more marked' means further right in the following hierarchy: nominative > accusative > other).

in early Germanic languages such as Gothic, Old English, Old High German, as shown by the following sentence taken from the Old High German *Liber evangeliorum* (Otfrid, I.17, 38):[29]

mit	uuórtun	[then Ø	[ér	thie	áltun	fórasagon	___	záltun]]
with	words$_{DAT}$	which$_{DAT}$	before	the	old	prophets		told
"with	(the) words,	which	previously	the	old	prophets	had	told"

Here the relative pronoun (*then*) features the dative case in agreement with its antecedent (*uuórtun*), even though the subordinate clause would have required the accusative.

Not surprisingly, Old Saxon relative clauses may also display case attraction. However, the phenomenon is not recorded in any of the most common and widely used Old Saxon grammars. The reason for this omission can be traced to the very nature of the available editions. *Attractio relativi* occurs almost only in the C-text, therefore the variant readings that should confirm the phenomenon are relegated to the apparatus. Since the latter is built as to focus on single words, it only accounts for the variation of the pronominal form rather than of the whole sentence, making it very difficult to pinpoint the structure. In a nutshell: a traditional linear apparatus risks concealing most of the complex linguistic and textual features that a thorough scrutiny of the manuscripts has brought to the fore. An interactive hypertextual apparatus would instead make them (more) visible.

The 'digital' apparatus and relationability

As regards relationability (see above, section 1, point 2): a scholarly electronic edition permits the presentation in the hypertext of all the evidence which the reader requires to grasp both intertextual and intratextual connections.[30] In principle, a scholarly electronic edition

---

29 The OHG text is quoted from *Althochdeutsches Lesebuch*, ed. by Wilhelm Braune and Karl Helm, 17th ed. by Ernst A. Ebbinghaus (Tübingen: Max Niemeyer Verlag, 1994), p. 107.

30 As Huygens claims 'even if you try to reconstruct the oldest attainable stage of the manuscript tradition, which should be your aim, you must nevertheless be aware of the fact that [...] the original itself played much less important a role [...] than its often defective descendants'. R. B. C. Huygens, *Ars edendi: A Practical Introduction to Editing Medieval Latin Texts* (Turnhout: Brepols, 2000), p. 39.

should allow the editor to present the critically reconstructed text, as well as the different versions and the many forms the text assumes when it becomes part of a historical transmission chain.[31] The interesting point is that, contrary to what is too often assumed, these two perspectives (the genetic/reconstructive and the historical/material) are frequently complementary, rather than mutually exclusive. In most cases, in fact, they do not preclude one another. The digital environment proves totally adequate for representing *both* the reconstructed interpretative text (when considered necessary by the editor) *and* its chronological dimension. The conventional paper edition, on the other hand, tends to privilege either a single stage or a few stages of the tradition.[32] Furthermore, conventional paper editions hardly ever allow for cross-checking of the data since, if it is true that most of the times the apparatus accounts for the choices made by the editor, it is equally true that the elaboration of an alternative proposal by the reader remains a chimera, due to the paucity of information, and to the fact that the data provided are usually unstructured. Thus, the historically transmitted texts become almost unrecognisable in the apparatus of variant readings.[33] In some textual traditions, especially those belonging to the Middle Ages, the aforementioned diachronic issue comes on top of other crucial editorial problems, such as how to represent the stratification of intertextual relationships within the same work.[34] In a traditional paper apparatus, these features find their place in additional registers (e.g. the *apparatus fontium*) that accompany the *lectio variorum*. Similarly, Francesco Stella's

---

31 Cf. Anna Maria Luiselli Fadda, 'Quale edizione-nel-tempo (Contini) per i documenti e i testi germanici nel ventunesimo secolo?', in *Storicità del testo, Storicità dell'edizione*, pp. 11–22; Marina Buzzoni, '*Uuarth thuo the hêlago gêst that barn an ira bôsma*: Towards a Scholarly Electronic Edition of the *Hêliand*', in *Medieval Texts — Contemporary Media: The Art and Science of Editing in the Digital Age*, ed. by Maria Grazia Saibene and Marina Buzzoni (Pavia: Ibis, 2009), pp. 35–55; Marina Buzzoni, 'The "Electronic *Heliand* Project": Theoretical and Practical Updates', in *Linguistica e filologia digitale: Aspetti e progetti*, ed. by Paola Cotticelli Kurras (Alessandria: Edizioni dell'Orso, 2011), pp. 55–68.
32 An example is the case of synoptic editions.
33 Cf. also the discussion above on the limits of a linear apparatus.
34 A definition of 'intertextuality' that better suits our purpose is perhaps that given by Gérard Genette: 'in a more restrictive sense, [it is] a relationship of co-presence between two texts or among several texts: that is to say, eidetically and typically as the actual presence of one text within another'. Gérard Genette, *Palimpsests: Literature in the Second Degree*, trans. by Channa Newman and Claude Doubinsky (Lincoln: University of Nebraska Press, 1997), pp. 1–2.

digital edition of the Latin *Corpus rhythmorum* provides a multi-layered apparatus which accommodates *Loci vetustiores*, *Loci coaevi* and *Loci seriores*, along with the *lectio variorum* given in the right upper part of the box, as shown in Fig. 4.2:[35]

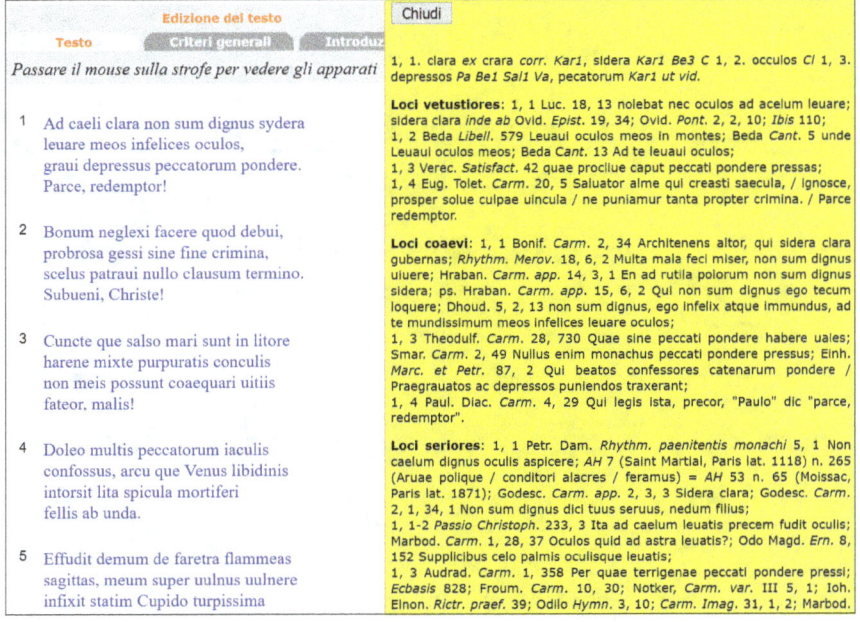

Fig. 4.2 *Corpus Rhythmorum*: multi-layered apparatus.

This modality of representing intertextual features is undoubtedly an improvement over printed editions, especially if one considers that the apparatus can be accessed in different ways, and can point both to a synoptic view of different redactions (Fig. 4.3), as well as to one specific redaction (Fig. 4.4).[36]

---

35 http://www.corimu.unisi.it; see also *Corpus rhythmorum musicum saec. IV–IX*, ed. by Francesco Stella (Florence: SISMEL-Edizioni del Galluzzo, 2007).

36 The editor argues that '[t]he edition presents the texts in seven different forms: manuscript reproduction, diplomatic transcription of the verbal text, diplomatic musical transcription of the neumes, alphanumeric musical transcription of the notation, "historical" transcript on staff of the medieval melody, vocal execution of the "historical" transcription, critical edition in the traditional sense'. This is undoubtedly true, but the degree of relationability between the data provided remains quite low. Francesco Stella, 'Digital Philology, Medieval Texts, and the *Corpus* of Latin Rhythms: A Digital Edition of Music and Poems', in *Digital Philology and Medieval Texts*, pp. 223–49.

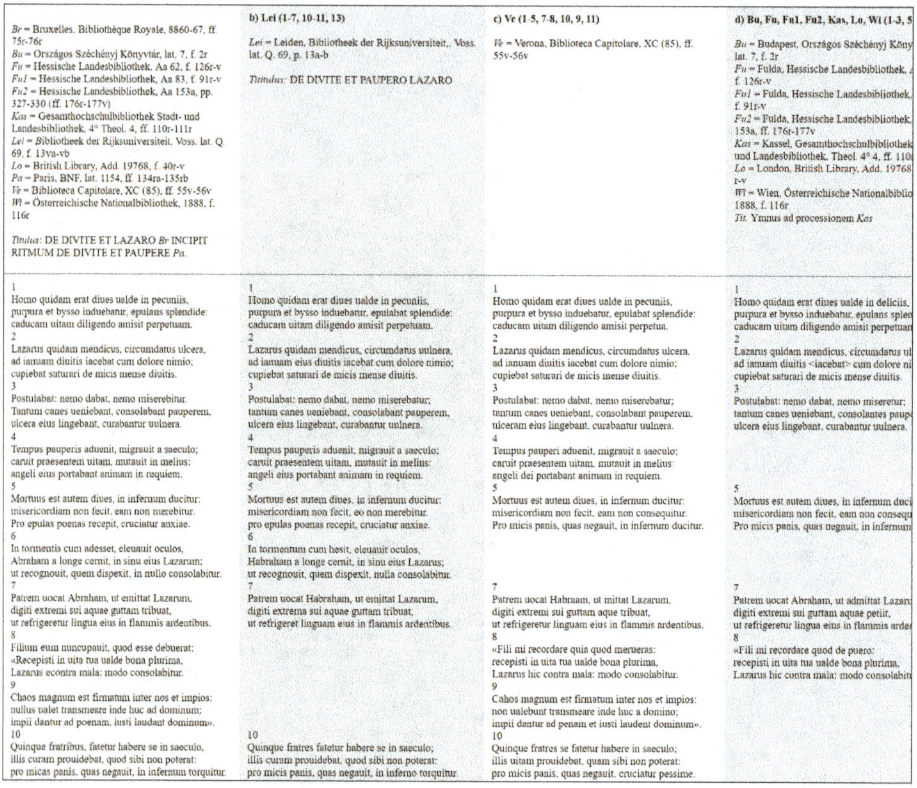

b) Lei (1-7, 10-11, 13)	c) Ve (1-5, 7-8, 10, 9, 11)	d) Bu, Fu, Fu1, Fu2, Kas, Lo, Wi (1-3, 5
Br = Bruxelles, Bibliothèque Royale, 8860-67, ff. 75r-76r *Bu* = Országos Széchényi Könyvtár, lat. 7, f. 2r *Fu* = Hessische Landesbibliothek, Aa 62, f. 126r-v *Fu1* = Hessische Landesbibliothek, Aa 83, f. 91r-v *Fu2* = Hessische Landesbibliothek, Aa 153a, pp. 327-330 (ff. 176r-177v) *Kas* = Gesamthochschulbibliothek Stadt- und Landesbibliothek, 4° Theol. 4, ff. 110r-111r *Lei* = Bibliotheek der Rijksuniversiteit, Voss. lat. Q. 69, f. 13va-vb *Lo* = British Library, Add. 19768, f. 40r-v *Pa* = Paris, BNF, lat. 1154, ff. 134ra-135rb *Ve* = Biblioteca Capitolare, XC (85), ff. 55v-56v *Wi* = Österreichische Nationalbibliothek, 1888, f. 116r *Titulus*: DE DIVITE ET LAZARO *Br* INCIPIT RITMUM DE DIVITE ET PAUPERE *Pa*.	*Lei* = Leiden, Bibliotheek der Rijksuniversiteit,, Voss. lat. Q. 69, p. 13a-b *Titulus*: DE DIVITE ET PAUPERO LAZARO	*Ve* = Verona, Biblioteca Capitolare, XC (85), ff. 55v-56v	*Bu* = Budapest, Országos Széchényi Köny lat. 7, f. 2r *Fu* = Fulda, Hessische Landesbibliothek, f. 126r-v *Fu1* = Fulda, Hessische Landesbibliothek, f. 91r-v *Fu2* = Fulda, Hessische Landesbibliothek, 153a, ff. 176r-177v *Kas* = Kassel, Gesamthochschulbibliothek und Landesbibliothek, Theol. 4° 4, ff. 110 *Lo* = London, British Library, Add. 19768 r-v *Wi* = Wien, Österreichische Nationalbiblio 1888, f. 116r *Tit*. Ymnus ad processionem *Kas*

(Parallel columns of text, each beginning:)

1
Homo quidam erat diues ualde in pecuniis, purpura et bysso induebatur, epulans splendide: caducam uitam diligendo amisit perpetuam.

2
Lazarus quidam mendicus, circumdatus ulcera, ad ianuam diuitis iacebat cum dolore nimio; cupiebat saturari de micis mense diuitis.

3
Postulabat: nemo dabat, nemo miserebitur. Tantum canes ueniebant, consolabant pauperem, ulcera eius lingebant, curabantur uulnera.

4
Tempus pauperis aduenit, migrauit a saeculo: caruit praesentem uitam, mutauit in melius: angeli eius portabant animam in requiem.

5
Mortuus est autem diues, in infernum ducitur: misericordiam non fecit, eam non merebitur. Pro epulas poenas recepit, cruciatur anxiae.

6
In tormentis cum adesset, eleuauit oculos, Abraham a longe cernit, in sinu eius Lazarum; ut recognouit, quem dispexit, in nullo consolabitur.

7
Patrem uocat Abraham, ut emittat Lazarum, digiti extremi sui aquae guttam tribuat, ut refrigeret lingua eius in flammis ardentibus.

8
Filium eum nuncupauit, quod esse debuerat: «Recepisti in uita tua ualde bona plurima, Lazarus econtra mala: modo consolabitur.

9
Chaos magnum est firmatum inter nos et impios; nullus ualet transmeare inde huc ad dominum; impii dantur ad poenam, iusti laudant dominum».

10
Quinque fratribus, fatetur habere se in saeculo, illis curam prouidebat, quod sibi non poterat: pro micas panis, quas negauit, in infernum torquitur.

Fig. 4.3 *Corpus Rhythmorum*: synopsis.

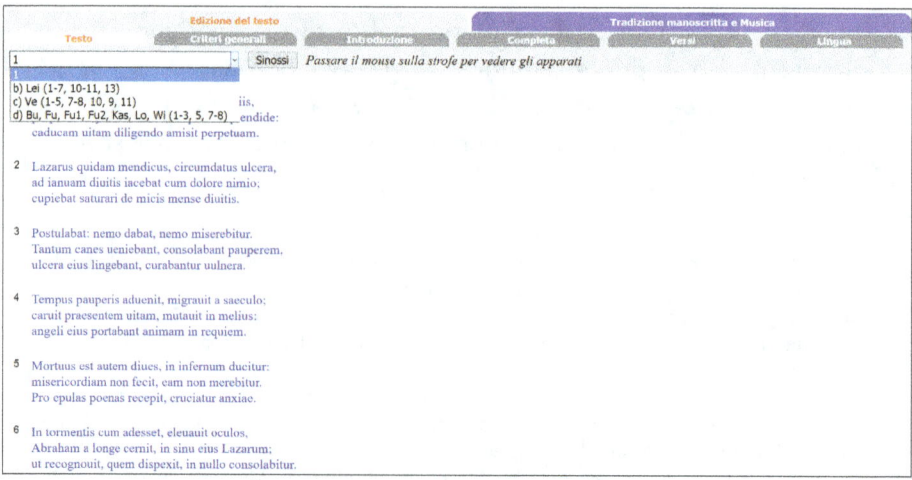

Fig. 4.4 *Corpus Rhythmorum*: single redaction.

Yet, one cannot fail to notice that the apparatus is linearly structured—which means that it mimics what may also be found in book form. In fact, the boxes that accommodate the various kinds of information are not mutually interconnected, which opens the path to the discussion of the next feature, i.e. multimediality/multimodality (see above, section 1, point 4).

The 'digital' apparatus and multimediality/multimodality

Multimediality and—when relevant—multimodality are the most important requirements the critical apparatus module should meet, since these two features subsume the previous ones and make them fully available to the readers. The improvement offered by these options should therefore be a major theoretical concern and perhaps also a priority in the critical debate. The possibility of connecting the apparatus with other windows showing, for example, the transcriptions of a single witness or the manuscript images is not simply a question of providing more information; rather, it allows the contextualisation of each variant reading, which can thus be studied *in vivo*, rather than *in vitro*. The apparatus gains new life and is hopefully used by more readers in a variety of different ways in the hyper-textual environment. The possibility of giving more context, as well as more 'paratextual elements'—both epitextual and peritextual[37]—is a major improvement from the scholarly point of view, since it provides the tools to better interpret the text, and 'enhance[s] our opportunities of penetrating deeply into its discourse', just as envisaged by Dino Buzzetti.[38]

An ongoing project that meets the requirements of multimediality is the *Parzival-Projekt*, in which three research teams (based at Bern, Berlin and Erlangen), under the guidance of Michael Stolz of the University of Bern, are preparing the ground for a new electronic edition of Wolfram's *Parzival*. Their theoretical assumption is that

> A new critical edition of *Parzival* will have to come to terms with the abundance of variant readings and the not inconsiderable problems of

---

37 Gérard Genette, *Paratexts: Thresholds of Interpretation*, trans. by Jane E. Lewin (Cambridge: Cambridge University Press, 1997).
38 See above, footnote 8.

establishing a text against the methodological background of the polarity of New Philology and New Phylogeny.[39] A challenge that was voiced in the *Parzival* scholarship of the 1960s now seems more relevant than ever before. It was then argued that it was necessary 'to publish all the material that was collected for critical assessment before the question of manuscript interrelation could be clarified' (E. Nellmann). Perhaps the idea, when it was voiced in 1968, had a Utopian ring. Today, however, it can be put into practice, step by step, with the aid of computer technology, and at reasonable expense. A critical electronic edition will constitute a work-base that would be an indispensable prerequisite for any new edition of *Parzival*.[40]

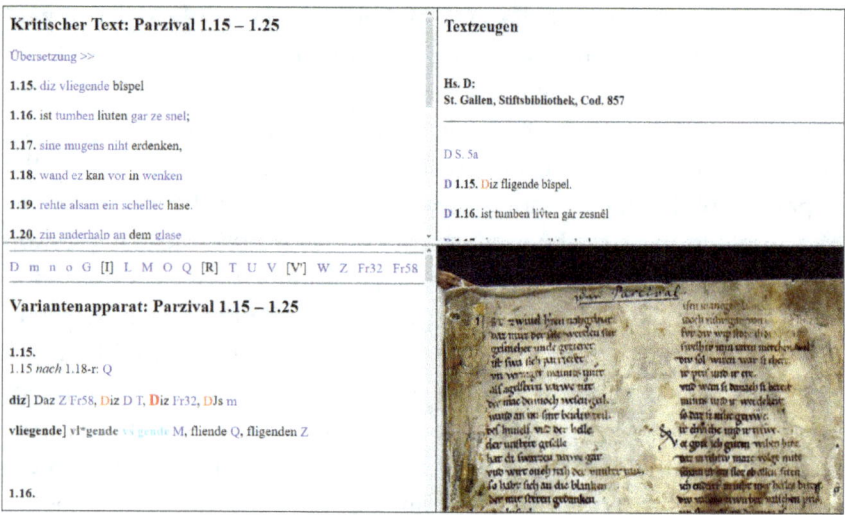

Fig. 4.5 The *Parzival-Projekt* template.

---

39 Although the monographic number of *Speculum* edited by Stephen Nichols in 1990 is considered to be the *manifesto* of the so-called 'New Philology', in Italy the debate about 'reconstruction' *versus* 'documentation' has pervaded textual criticism studies since their very beginning. In 1934, for example, Giorgio Pasquali published a volume titled *Storia della tradizione e critica del testo* in which he supported the need to integrate the reconstruction of a stemma with the study of the history of tradition, and suggested that certain ambiguities and aporias in the transmission of Latin and vernacular texts could be explained by assuming *ab origine* the existence of either authorial or scribal changes (Giorgio Pasquali, *Storia della tradizione e critica del testo* (Florence: Le Monnier, 1934)). It is interesting to note that at about the same time as Pasquali wrote his book, the Italianist Michele Barbi explicitly transferred his methodology to various Italian classics including Dante, Foscolo and Manzoni, publishing a book specifically focused on what he called 'the new philology' (Michele Barbi, *La nuova filologia e l'edizioni dei nostri scrittori da Dante a Manzoni* (Florence: Le Monnier, 1938)).

40 http://www.parzival.unibe.ch/englishpresentation.html

Indeed, what the research teams claim to be their programme is embodied in the fourfold interface chosen to present the reader with their 'edition' (see Fig. 4.5).

In the upper left window a normalised critical text is given—based on manuscript D, which scholars have always considered as the guide-witness. The lower left window accommodates the apparatus of variant readings, while the windows on the right contain the transcriptions and facsimiles of each single witness. All the windows are interconnected by hypertext-links, and permit users an interactive interchange between base-text, apparatus of variants, transcriptions and facsimiles. On the screen, every variant is fully contextualised.

Similar theoretical concerns have inspired the 'Electronic *Heliand* Project', started at the University of Venice in 2006 under the guidance of the present writer. The template used in this project is based on a series of click-and-drag resizable windows,[41] which can be activated or deactivated by the user, so that he or she can freely choose the material to view and in which order, according to his or her own interests.[42] The windows are not isolated items; they are connected by hyperlinks. Thus, by clicking on a word in the main window (at the top-left of the screen) the user can activate other windows, such as, for example, one containing the image of a manuscript, or one providing its transcription (see Fig. 4.6 and Fig. 4.7).

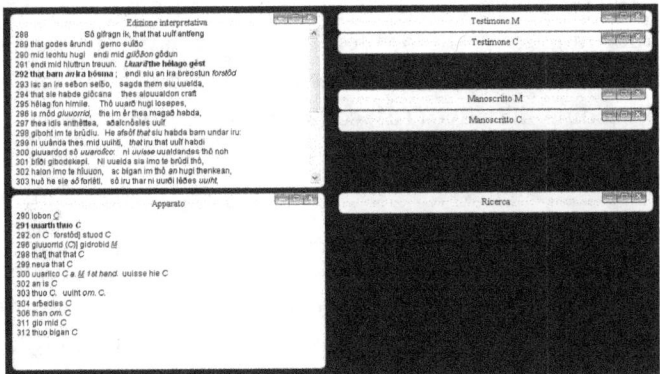

Fig. 4.6 The 'Electronic *Heliand* Project' template: flexibility of text representations.

---

41 We took inspiration from the template used by the editors of the *Parzival-Projekt*, and then we developed a new application.

42 Technically, the modal windows were developed using a Java/Ajax Open Source Framework, which can build up a multi-layered structure.

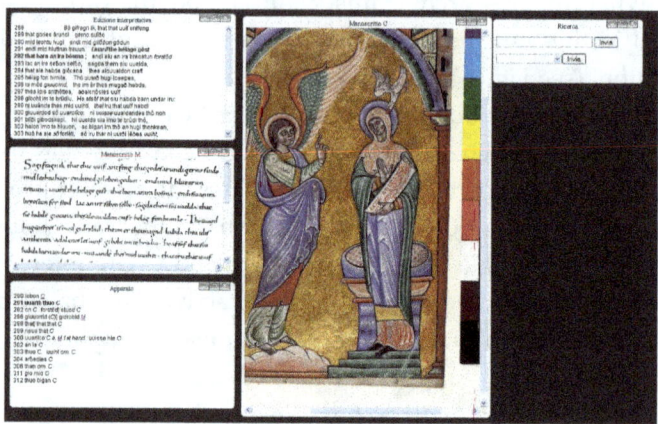

Fig. 4.7 The 'Electronic *Heliand* Project' template: text and manuscript images.

What is relevant for the present analysis is that all the hyperlinks are centred on the apparatus (in that they proceed from it and return to it); therefore, the latter is only apparently shaped in a linear fashion, since each variant reading included in it by the editor and selected by the user can be contextualised at different levels: e.g. word, phrase, sentence, text and paratext,[43] material document.[44] The centrality of the apparatus module is perfectly in line with the view of the edition as a *working hypothesis* discussed above. Its hypertext structure greatly enhances the possibility of deriving information from the data provided, while conforming to a standard for the representation of the apparatus in digital form, in particular the standard developed and maintained by the Text Encoding Initiative (TEI) consortium that favours—among other things—interoperability and hopefully improves survival over time.

TEI encoding scheme: Main issues and future perspectives

Two of the most crucial issues related to the application of the TEI encoding scheme to the critical apparatus are, on the one hand, the 'method' followed to link the apparatus to the text and, on the other hand, certain specific encoding procedures. As for the former, the

---

[43] The texts given are: the critically reconstructed text, a single redaction (which groups together two or more manuscripts) and the witnesses.

[44] High resolution images are provided for each manuscript.

preferential adoption of the 'parallel segmentation method' to the detriment of the other two ('location-referenced method' and 'double end-point attachment method'[45]) seems to be common to many born-digital projects that are TEI-conformant.[46] This might depend on a series of variables, including the lack of easy-to-use tools supporting the encoding process, which can be difficult to carry out manually, especially in the case of double end-point attachment.[47] Yet, parallel segmentation also has an evident theoretical advantage over the other two since the much-disputed concept of 'base-text' remains in the background: 'the texts compared are divided into matching segments all synchronised with one another. This permits direct comparison of any span of text in any witness with that in any other witness'.[48] Further on in the same section one reads that the parallel segmentation method 'will also be useful where editors do not wish to privilege a text as the "base" or when editors wish to present parallel texts'.[49] Note, however, that even when no base-text is postulated, no philologist would consider the critical apparatus simply as a 'repository of variants'. The apparatus is indeed different from the descriptive *lectio variorum* one can get by, say, applying any collation software to the transcription of the witnesses. The apparatus is critical—i.e. interpretative—in that it accommodates certain variant readings, and excludes some others, according to the

---

45 On the three methods see the TEI Guidelines, Chapter 12 (Critical Apparatus), and in particular section 12.2 (Linking the Apparatus to the Text), http://www.tei-c.org/release/doc/tei-p5-doc/en/html/TC.html#TCAPLK. On the actual priority of parallel segmentation over the other two methods, see http://wiki.tei-c.org/index.php/Critical_Apparatus_Workgroup: 'most of the issues raised here are connected with the parallel segmentation method, not because it is the more flawed, but because it is the more used by the members of this group [*sc.* Marjorie Burghart, James Cummings, Fotis Jannidis, Gregor Middell, Daniel O'Donnell, Matija Ogrin, Espen Ore, Elena Pierazzo, Roberto Rosselli Del Turco and Christian Wittern]'.

46 The parallel segmentation method is often preferred despite its well-known drawbacks, e.g. encoding complexity and considerable overlapping especially with rich traditions, which may generate problems of scalability.

47 'While location-referenced and double end-point attachment might be useful for mass conversion of printed material (for the former) and/or when using a piece of software handling the encoding (for the latter), the parallel segmentation method seems to be the easiest and more powerful way to encode the critical apparatus 'by hand', http://wiki.tei-c.org/index.php/Critical_Apparatus_Workgroup

48 See section 12.2.3 (The Parallel Segmentation Method) of the TEI Guidelines, http://www.tei-c.org/release/doc/tei-p5-doc/en/html/TC.html#TCAPLK

49 *Ibid.*

editorial principles to which the philologist conforms.[50] A (Neo-) Lachmannian editor might want to include solely the readings which bear a stemmatic value, thus eliminating those of the *codices descripti* and the *lectiones singulares*. If the editor is, instead, more interested in highlighting the linguistic features displayed by a text, or the history of its transmission, he or she might want to include formal variants too, thus accepting for example the *lectiones singulares* in the apparatus. In both cases, the editor's task is to discriminate between variants and/or groups of variants, and this can be done electronically only by structuring them through encoding.[51]

Coming now to specific issues related to TEI recommendations, a positive feature is undoubtedly represented by encoding flexibility. The fact, for example, that readings may be encoded either individually, or grouped for perspicuity using the <rdgGrp> element helps philologists to discriminate between variants and, if this is the case, to create a hierarchical order. The most problematic areas, instead, are constituted by specific phenomena like transpositions (which cannot be marked up explicitly), the handling of punctuation (of which no encoding examples

---

50 It goes without saying that a traditional critical apparatus (1) accommodates either all the variant (substantial) readings (in which case it is called 'positive') or those rejected by the editor (in which case it is called 'negative'); (2) gives a record of the choices made by previous editors; (3) provides palaeographic information, as well as information about the cruces. When needed, further registers may be added. Note that, in order to fully understand the choices operated by the editor, the apparatus is to be read together with the prefatory note (and the stemma, if provided). Cf. Anna Maria Luiselli Fadda, T*radizioni manoscritte e critica del testo nel Medioevo germanico* (Rome and Bari: Laterza, 1994), in particular pp. 247–48 ('L'apparato critico'). See also Cynthia Damon's chapter 'Beyond Variants: Some Digital Desiderata for the Critical Apparatus of Ancient Greek and Latin Texts' in this volume.

51 For the reasons discussed so far, I remain sceptical about the proposal raised at the TEI Critical Apparatus Workgroup to rename the 'critical apparatus' as either 'textual variance' or 'textual variants', since one does not have to be critical in providing the raw results of *collation*. About the proposal: 'The very name of the chapter, 'Critical apparatus', is felt by some to be a problem: the *critical apparatus* is just inherited from the printed world and one of the possible physical embodiments of *textual variance*. E[lena] P[ierazzo] therefore proposes to use this new name, moving from 'critical apparatus' to textual variance [...] M[arjorie] B[urghart] proposes to use *textual variants* instead, since it focuses more on actual elements in the edition, when 'variance' is nothing concrete but a phenomenon'. http://wiki.tei-c.org/index.php/Critical_Apparatus_Workgroup

are provided),[52] as well as of omissions/additions or *lacunae*. Generally speaking, even the representation of the palaeographic features of the witnesses in the apparatus module can be quite problematic.[53] Encoding a long ('verbose') apparatus entry is most of the times extremely time consuming, very tricky and often frustrating, especially when information needs to be suppressed because of the lack of elements and/or attributes, or even because it is not always possible to break up the information into consistent base-units in order to keep all witnesses synchronised. In those cases, adding a note (in the <rdg>?) would help — though not always; yet, it seems like avoiding the problem rather than facing it.

Apart from these difficulties, a major issue until recently has been represented by the 'status' of the <app> element itself, which seems to have been considered as a phrase- or word-level only element. Editors of texts whose length varies considerably between the witnesses (for example: poems showing a different number of stanzas, or both poetic and prose texts with many omissions) have found the <app> element, for example, nested in the <l> element, as prescribed by the Guidelines, somewhat awkward.

```
<l n="1">
  <app>
    <rdg wit= "#C"> Manega uuâron, the sia iro môd gespôn </rdg>
    <rdg wit= "#M"/>
  </app>
</l>
```

The editor was forced to repeat the encoding of the <app> string for every varying line (in this case, for example, from line 1 to line 84, which are attested only in the C-redaction of the *Heliand*). Clearly the time was ripe for a revision that would lead not only to a more economic encoding practice, but also to a practice more respectful of the actual hierarchy of textual content. Fortunately, the TEI has now (October 2015) accepted a proposal to make <app> a block-level element so that <rdg> can now

---

52 'Metrical punctuation' could also be included as a further problematic field.
53 As already stated, this is a requirement that a well-structured apparatus should fulfil (see above, note 42).

contain <p> and <l> elements, which means that its content is no longer restricted by any line or sentence border.

An experiment in the wake of Lavagnino (2009)

The issue of the drawbacks of apparatuses that fail to serve their purpose regularly comes up in the scholarly debate. In an essay devoted to a critical rethinking of the idea of access to data, John Lavagnino argues that editors should represent their work as providing not simply data but rather critical points of view on the texts they are offering.[54] Though the argument that by focusing on the 'activity of the editor', rather than that of the 'user', too many editions 'offered access to the wrong thing'[55] is not entirely convincing, I do share the opinion that an edition—and all the more its critical apparatus—should suit different audiences, as well as present 'ways of filtering' the data provided by the editor that could enable readers to interrogate also the text's transmission history.[56] The integration of textual scholarship and textual criticism that Lavagnino seems to call for in his article may offer a useful model for a more discursive critical apparatus, which would record the relevant information traditionally included in separate sections, for example in the introduction. An experiment in this approach is represented by the *Digital Ramusio* project, sustained by Ca' Foscari University of Venice and coordinated by Eugenio Burgio, Antonella Ghersetti and the present writer. The project, whose main aim was to provide a hypertext edition of Giovanni Battista Ramusio's *Dei Viaggi di Messer Marco Polo gentiluomo veneziano* (1559) capable of representing Ramusio's own 'desk' in a virtual environment, was launched in February 2015 and is now available Open Access at the following website: http://virgo.unive.it/ecf-workflow/books/Ramusio/main/index.html. In the *Digital Ramusio*, the modal windows allow the user to visualise a chapter of the main text (R) in parallel with its major sources (Z, V, VB, L, P and VA, F), three of which are given in new born-digital editions. Each chapter and chapter section of R is accompanied by a philological commentary

---

54 John Lavagnino, 'Access', *Literary and Linguistic Computing*, 24.1 (2009), 63–76.
55 Ibid., p. 66.
56 Ibid., p. 72.

made accessible through pop-up windows which present the relevant interface to the user. The philological commentary—containing the identified sources and their variant readings against R, the analysis of their manipulation by Ramusio, as well as some informative notes—serves the purpose envisaged by Lavagnino, namely that of filtering the data provided by the editor through the provision of a narrative able to explain and make sense of them, as shown in Fig. 4.8.[57]

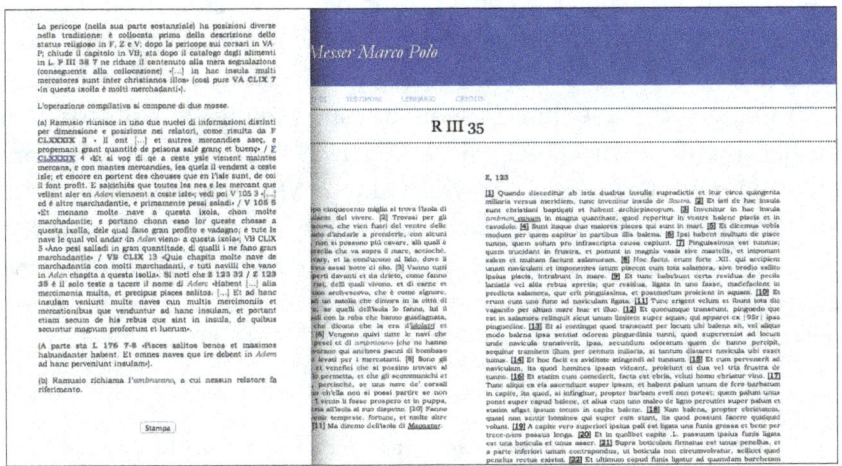

Fig. 4.8 Ramusio's *Dei Viaggi di Messer Marco Polo*: the philological commentary by chapters and sections.

It goes perhaps without saying that this editorially radical choice was made possible by the peculiarity of both Ramusio's text itself and the Polian tradition to which that text belongs, whose intrinsic *mouvance* is well recognised by scholars in the field.[58]

---

[57] The edition offers more options to the user, e.g. the possibility to display (and superimpose) the entire text of the *Milione* redactions transmitted by the source witnesses, and access the records containing the information on the Eastern *realia* both through the 'Lemmario' button in the main Menu and through the internal page links. Cf. 'Istruzioni per l'uso', http://virgo.unive.it/ecf-workflow/books/Ramusio/main/istruzioni.html

[58] See, for example, *Giovanni Battista Ramusio 'editor' del 'Milione': Trattamento del testo e manipolazione dei modelli*, Atti del Seminario di ricerca, Venezia, 9–10 settembre 2010 (Rome and Padua: Antenore, 2011).

The 'digital' apparatus and user interaction

After this brief digression on encoding procedures and experimental apparatuses, let us return to our main path and discuss the last core feature that the apparatus module should display, i.e. user interaction (see above, section 1, point 5). The idea of setting up a shared virtual environment, which would facilitate a dialogue between the editorial team and the (critical) reader, is indeed tempting. This, in principle, would enhance scholarly debate, promote new research and allow quicker updates of the edition. In fact, many questions are still open, among which: how can a 'social/collaborative edition'[59] be reconciled with the idea of the editor's scientific responsibility? Should we plan on filtering the information, and how? In a 'social edition', what are the valid indicators of real user interaction? What can we use to create an accurate model for evaluating socially enhanced editions? With the exception of some essays that focus on the first of these issues (i.e. the editor(s)' scientific responsibility), to my knowledge there exists no detailed study of user interactions in the field of ecdotics.[60] A study of

---

59   Ray Siemens, Meagan Timney, Cara Leitch, Corina Koolen and Alex Garnett, with the ETCL, INKE and PKP Research Groups, 'Toward Modeling the Social Edition: An Approach to Understanding the Electronic Scholarly Edition in the Context of New and Emerging Social Media', *Literary and Linguistic Computing*, 27 (2012), 445–61. Elena Pierazzo draws a line between 'collaborative editions' seen as the output of the work carried out by a team of selected scholars, and 'social editions' in the proper sense. The latter are based on the idea that the text should be offered to the community 'not only for contributions such as annotation, comments, and translations, but also for the editing of existing texts or the addition of new texts'. Pierazzo, *Digital Scholarly Editing*, p. 18. Other scholars use the two expressions interchangeably. See, for example, *A Companion to Digital Literary Studies*, ed. by Ray Siemens and Susan Schreibman (Oxford: Blackwell, 2008).

60   A learned term from the Greek *ékdosis* 'edition'; in its French form (*ecdotique*), it was first used by Henri Quentin in a seminal work titled *Essais de critique textuelle* (Paris: Picard, 1926) to indicate the methodology of manuscript edition. See also Sebastiano Timpanaro, *The Genesis of Lachmann's Method*, ed. and trans. by Glenn W. Most (Chicago: University of Chicago Press, 2005), originally published in Italian as *La genesi del metodo del Lachmann* (Florence: Le Monnier, 1963). User interaction has been well studied in social networks (see, for example, Christo Wilson, Bryce Boe, Alessandra Sala, Krishna P. N. Puttaswamy and Ben Y. Zhao, 'User Interactions in Social Networks and their Implications' (2009), https://www.cs.ucsb.edu/~ravenben/publications/pdf/interaction-eurosys09.pdf. Different models of social editions are briefly discussed in Pierazzo, *Digital Scholarly Editing*, pp. 18–21, but the general impression one gets is that it is still too early to be able to evaluate the 'added value' of such models in editorial practices (see, in particular, p. 21).

this kind would be most welcome, since it would prepare the ground for the philologist to make operative choices on the basis of objective data, rather than of subjective points of view.

Final remarks

In lieu of a conclusion, I would like to provide a provisional answer to the question posed in the title and at the beginning of this chapter: is a 'protocol' for scholarly digital editions desirable? As shown by the discussion on the apparatus module, the answer seems to be yes, provided that the protocol encompasses the domains in which scholarly digital editions may offer important advantages over paper editions, without being too strict as to orient the editor to follow a specific ecdotic praxis. The philologist should take full responsibility for his or her choices, which depend both on the theoretical framework to which he or she conforms, and on the peculiarities of the manuscript tradition he or she is dealing with. Nonetheless, the adoption of a (shared) protocol would have positive repercussions both on the products (i.e. the editions) and on the core features themselves, the former acting as material to test the reliability of the latter when deemed necessary. This study has also shown that the critical apparatus is the site where the dynamic nature of a text can be conveyed better by the editor(s) and grasped more easily by the readers:

> Anyone who uses a critical edition should be able to grasp with ease the criteria followed and the decisions made at each level. A critical apparatus serves this purpose no less than a detailed introduction. [...] the apparatus allows convenient comparison of the readings accepted in the text with those discarded.[61]

---

61 Alfredo Stussi, *Introduzione agli studi di filologia italiana*, 4th ed. (Bologna: il Mulino, 2011), pp. 143–44: 'Chi utilizza un'edizione critica deve poter conoscere senza difficoltà i criteri seguiti e le scelte operate ai vari livelli. Non meno di un'accurata introduzione, serve a tal scopo l'apparato critico che [...] consente, con rapidi controlli, di confrontare la lezione messa a testo con quella o quelle scartate'. The debate on this as well as similar issues can also be found in Peter L. Shillingsburg, *Scholarly Editing in the Computer Age: Theory and Practice* (Ann Arbor: University of Michigan Press, 1996). Shillingsburg's text, however, is mainly dedicated to 'authorial philology'.

Particular attention to the representation of that module—often dismissed as too technical—in digital form should perhaps be the major concern of anyone who intends to produce an edition that truly deserves to be called 'scholarly'. In this respect, a revision of the section of the TEI Guidelines dealing with the Critical Apparatus to make it meet the theoretical needs of the philologist would not only help enhance the value of the apparatus itself, freeing it from being considered simply as a 'repository of variants', but would also enhance the digital edition as a whole.

5. Barely Beyond the Book?

Joris van Zundert

'There is nothing deterministic about the Internet'[1]

Of methodological interaction and paradigmatic regression

This is a story about the methodological interaction between two scientific fields, that of textual scholarship and that of computer science. The names of the fields, however, only imprecisely delineate the permeable boundaries between research domains where methodologies interact—for obviously the world is much more fluid than such nouns suggest.[2] The interactions of interests are much more complex than the simplified image of a dynamic whereby one field donates a methodology to another. Rather than trying to reflect on the current state and the future potential of the digital scholarly edition from well inside the field of textual scholarship, let us approach the topic from the perspective of the multidisciplinary methodological interaction that has arisen to support the theoretical and practical development of the digital scholarly edition over the recent years. Textual scholarship in its digital fashion belongs to the broader field of Digital Humanities, itself

---

1   David Lowery, frontman of Camper Van Beethoven and lecturer at Terry College of Business, University of Georgia, http://www.salon.com/2013/12/04/david_lowery_silicon_valley_must_be_stopped_or_creativity_will_be_destroyed
2   Herbert A. Simon, 'Technology Is not the Problem', in *Speaking Minds: Interviews with Twenty Eminent Cognitive Scientists*, ed. by Peter Baumgarter and Sabine Payr (Princeton: Princeton University Press, 1995), pp. 232–48.

© Joris van Zundert, CC BY 4.0   http://dx.doi.org/10.11647/OBP.0095.05

a field built on interdisciplinarity, where many skills and theories of the realms of computer technology and those of scholarship intersect, and thus where many new interfaces and interactions arise between those skills and the fields they are tied to.[3] This is where Digital Humanities acquires its innovative power, or at least the promise of that power.

That innovative power, however, can be both exciting and confusing. The point where disciplines intersect is not a space for the calm, cool and collected exchange of technical and methodological knowledge. Rather, it is a place where the inherent social aspects of science and research are brought markedly into the foreground.[4] Take for example Jan Christoph Meister's description of the 'lamented conflict between "computationalists" and "humanists"'. This conflict, Meister states,

> arises as soon as we become afraid of our own courage and shy away from jumping across these two fault lines. Let's cut through that fear. The task remains [...] to 'become capable of both—the metaphor and the formula, the verse and the calculus [...]'. That's a borderline experience, no doubt, and those who prefer to pitch their tent in the comfortable centre of either laager don't run the risk of questioning their own philosophical, epistemological and ethical identity as easily.[5]

Meister's word use is notably emotive ('afraid', 'fear', 'courage') and at the same time vividly touches on the impact of the social dimension ('conflict', 'borderline experience', 'risk') of the epistemological interaction that is expressed. As Christine Borgman has suggested this is a situation where it can be useful, with respect to the design of scholarly infrastructure, to take these interactions and the behaviour connected to them as the objects of study.[6] Let us do exactly that here. Taking the digital scholarly edition as a part of the scholarly infrastructure for

---

3   Susan Hockey, 'The History of Humanities Computing', in *A Companion to Digital Humanities*, ed. by Susan Schreibman, Ray Siemens and John Unsworth (Oxford: Blackwell, 2004), pp. 3–19, http://www.digitalhumanities.org/companion/view?docId=blackwell/9781405103213/9781405103213.xml&chunk.id=ss1-2-1&toc.depth=1&toc.id=ss1-2-1&brand=default

4   Bruno Latour, *Science in Action: How to Follow Scientists and Engineers through Society* (Cambridge, MA: Harvard University Press, 1988).

5   Jan Christoph Meister, 'Computationalists and Humanists', *Humanist Discussion Group*, 2013, http://lists.digitalhumanities.org/pipermail/humanist/2013-June/011053.html

6   Christine Borgman, 'The Digital Future Is Now: A Call to Action for the Humanities', *Digital Humanities Quarterly*, 3.4 (2009), http://www.digitalhumanities.org/dhq/vol/3/4/000077/000077.html

textual scholarship, we can try to infer what the historical interactions between textual scholarship and computer science tell us about the current state and development of the digital scholarly edition.

The field of science and technology studies (STS) offers a useful frame for critical study and reflection on what occurs at the interfaces of the various research fields within digital scholarship. When these fields intersect, it is not simply a question of objective interactions concerning technology and methodology; rather, these interfaces are also the site of social processes that guide and steer the methodological interaction. Within STS such processes are often referred to as the social shaping of technology—that is, the mutual interplay between technology, its developers or champions and the users of that technology. It is this interplay that changes properties and application of the technology at hand. For example, such interplay is very prominent in software development, in which development iterations and lifecycles are a clear expression of the interaction between builders and users as they shape software until the users' requirements are satisfied.[7]

I have previously argued that social shaping of technology can lead to 'paradigmatic regression'.[8] These are acts of shaping that translate an expression of the paradigm of the new technology into an expression of a paradigm that is already known to the user. Resistance to new technologies, where the use or sophistication of the new technology is denied, can of course be a motivator of paradigmatic regression.[9] Not all regressions are necessarily motivated by conservatism or resistance, however. But even when users do embrace a new technology, the act of its social shaping may create a paradigmatic regression effect. An example of this effect can often be found when a metaphor is used in a graphical user interface (GUI). GUI metaphors are used to convey the

---

7 Cf. e.g. Gwanhoo Lee and Weidong Xia, 'Toward Agile: An Integrated Analysis of Quantitative and Qualitative Field Data on Software Development Agility', *MIS Quarterly*, 34 (2010), 87–114.

8 Joris van Zundert, 'The Case of the Bold Button: Social Shaping of Technology and the Digital Scholarly Edition', *Digital Scholarship in the Humanities* (8 March 2015), http://dx.doi.org/10.1093/llc/fqw012

9 Clement Levallois, Stephanie Steinmetz and Paul Wouters, 'Sloppy Data Floods or Precise Methodologies? Dilemmas in the Transition to Data-Intensive Research in Sociology and Economics', in *Virtual Knowledge: Experimenting in the Humanities and the Social Sciences*, ed. by Paul Wouters, Anne Beaulieu, Andrea Scharnhorst and Sally Wyatt (Cambridge, MA: MIT Press, 2013), pp. 151–82.

processes or data underlying a particular piece of software in a manner that is meaningful or intelligible for human users. In order to help the user understand a new target domain or a new paradigm, it is expressed by way of a conceptual domain or a paradigm that is already known to the user. An obvious example is the metaphor of the desktop, which was used to communicate the functions of a PC to as broad an audience as possible.[10] The only trouble is that such metaphors are necessarily incomplete as they conceal both the good and the bad of the deeper computational model. Inconsistencies in the model are hidden by a metaphor that suggests completeness to the user. Equally, metaphors hide useful functions and possibilities of the model that are not covered by the metaphor's originating paradigm.[11] In our example, the desktop metaphor does nothing to reveal the power of automation that a PC delivers to its user. GUI metaphors are probably best viewed as the expression of the assumptions that software developers hold about the user's interaction with the underlying model—but not, in any case, as a transparent and effective way of allowing the user to engage with the computer's raw power. Metaphors are in this respect paradoxical: what is meant to be a transparent means of interaction with new possibilities of a computational model is in fact an opaque barrier confining the user to a well-rehearsed collection of concepts and processes.

What happens at the intersection?

Paradigmatic regression is not only to be found in graphical user interfaces, we can observe similar dynamics at the level of methodological interaction between or even within research domains. To understand how paradigmatic regression can also occur as a result of the interaction between computer science and textual scholarship, it is useful to view this interaction through the lens of an existing analytical metaphor for such interaction: the trading zone.

---

10 Cf. *Readings in Human-Computer Interaction: Toward the Year 2000*, ed. by Ronald M. Baecker et al., 2nd ed. (San Mateo: Morgan Kaufmann, 1995).

11 Pamela Ravasio and Vincent Tscherter, 'Users' Theories on the Desktop Metaphor — or Why We Should Seek Metaphor-Free Interfaces', in *Beyond the Desktop Metaphor: Designing Integrated Digital Work Environments*, ed. by Victor Kaptelinin and Mary Czerwinski (Cambridge, MA: MIT Press, 2004), pp. 265–94.

The processes at the intersection of research domains (such as textual scholarship and computer science) have been compared to those in trading zones.[12] Whether they are zones of economic activity or those where methodologies of different fields are amalgamated, pidgins commonly arise in such places. As Peter Galison says: 'A reduced common language, which begins with participants in a zone agreeing on shared meanings for certain terms, then progresses to a kind of pidgin and eventually to a creole, which is a new language born out of old ones'.[13] Galison also draws attention to the possible existence of visual and mathematical creoles. Indeed, these are not hard to identify in Digital Humanities: a good example can be seen in the works of Franco Moretti, who has methodologically integrated quantification and visualisation methods such as graphs, maps and tree heuristics into comparative literature studies.[14] Nor is it very hard to identify current Digital Humanities as a whole with a new expert community as, according to Galison, they may take shape during the 'creole stage' at the intersection of domains. It has been argued that, in creoles of natural language, it is the subordinate group that provides most of the syntactic structure for the creole, whereas the dominant group provides lexical items and concepts. Though Galison provides some empirical observations, it remains an open question whether the same patterns hold for the emergence of methodological pidgins at the interface of different research domains.

What interests us here is whether we can indeed observe the formation of a methodological creole in the emerging vocabulary of Digital Humanities, and whether hints can be found in that vocabulary of a similar regressive dynamic to that observed on the graphical user interface level. It may be that Matthew Kirschenbaum provides us with some—admittedly still anecdotal—evidence of precisely such a dynamic. In a recent article, Kirschenbaum attempts

---

12 Peter Galison, 'Trading with the Enemy', in *Trading Zones and Interactional Expertise: Creating New Kinds of Collaboration*, ed. by Michael E. Gorman (Cambridge, MA: MIT Press, 2010), pp. 39–40.

13 Michael E. Gorman, Lekelia D. Jenkins and Raina K. Plowright, 'Human Interactions and Sustainability', in *Sustainability: Multi-Disciplinary Perspectives* (Sharjah, UAE: Bentham Science Publishers, 2012), pp. 88–111.

14 Franco Moretti, *Graphs, Maps, Trees: Abstract Models for Literary History* (London: Verso, 2007).

to trace the origin of the label 'Digital Humanities'. He identifies a key moment, reported to him by John Unsworth, which seems to have been the tipping point that would propel this label towards its current status of de facto denominator of what then was and still is a non-homogeneous research domain. Unsworth relates the choice of 'Digital Humanities' to a discussion surrounding the title of the Blackwell 2004 *Companion to Digital Humanities*: 'Ray [Siemens] wanted "A Companion to Humanities Computing", as that was the term commonly used at that point; the editorial and marketing folks at Blackwell wanted "Companion to Digitized Humanities". I suggested "Companion to Digital Humanities" to shift the emphasis away from simple digitization'.[15] Of course we cannot take this as a *pars pro toto* for the social shaping of the dynamics for a whole field, but it is suggestive. Ray Siemens by no means stands alone in his preference for 'Humanities Computing'. Susan Hockey, for instance, titled her contribution to this very companion 'The History of Humanities Computing'.[16] Significantly, it is the prominent authorities in the field, veritable Nestors, who consistently speak of 'Humanities Computing'—people like Dino Buzzetti: 'humanities computing—I still prefer this designation to digital humanities'.[17] According to Siemens, the term was 'commonly used at that point', yet the publishers preferred the new term in order to broaden the appeal of the concept by choosing a metaphor that felt less challenging. This was a small but pivotal event in the history of the field, which simultaneously points to the state of Digital Humanities as a methodological pidgin and to an act of paradigmatic regression. The vocabulary juxtapositions in both terms are constructs of a methodological pidgin. Where 'Humanities Computing' suggests an equal interaction or relation between two fields with a stress on computational activity, the term 'Digital Humanities' (purposefully or not) pushes the balance back toward

---

15 Matthew Kirschenbaum, 'What Is Digital Humanities and What's it Doing in English Departments?', in *Debates in the Digital Humanities*, ed. by Matthew K. Gold (Minneapolis: University of Minnesota Press, 2012), pp. 3–11, http://dhdebates.gc.cuny.edu/debates/text/38

16 Hockey, 'The History of Humanities Computing'.

17 Dino Buzzetti, E-mail message to the author (10 November 2012); Willard McCarty, *Humanities Computing* (Basingstoke: Palgrave Macmillan, 2005); John Unsworth, 'What Is Humanities Computing and What Is Not?', *Jahrbuch für Computerphilologie*, 4 (2002), http://computerphilologie.digital-humanities.de/jg02/unsworth.html

the domain of humanities and subjugates the computational/digital aspect as a partial property of that field. Or in the words of Willard McCarty: 'Note, please, the name "digital humanities" grammatically subordinates the digital [...] "Humanities computing" takes advantage of the ability in English to make a noun serve as an adjective while staying a noun, and it draws upon the participle/gerund ambiguity. But it seems I've lost this contest!'[18]

The trading zone and digital textual scholarship practice

Scholarly digital editions and the sites where they are conceived and created, virtual or concrete, are themselves methodological trading zones that materialise at two levels. There is a laboratory-like setting tied in a relatively small context to the practice of preparing and publishing a concrete digital scholarly edition—and possibly also the development of a specific technical infrastructure connected to it. At a more abstract level we find a theoretical discussion that connects to the methodological and epistemological histories of textual scholarship, knowledge representation and digital technology. The critical study of these trading zones along empirical ethnographic lines—another approach often applied in science and technology studies—would have much to tell about the methodological interaction between computer science and textual scholarship. Although such an elaborate study has yet to be undertaken, even fairly anecdotal observations nevertheless yield some intriguing insights.

The Huygens Institute for the History of the Netherlands is home to an example of a smaller-scale trading zone in a laboratory setting.[19] The institute encompasses a computer science and software development group that is relatively large by the standards of humanities research, numbering around fourteen professionally trained or educated IT developers. Various members of this group have distinct strengths, such as interface design, data modelling, architecture integration and text analytics. The group works closely with at least three researchers who are themselves closely involved in the national and international

---

18 Willard McCarty, 'Computationalists and Humanists', *Humanist Discussion Group*, 2013, http://lists.digitalhumanities.org/pipermail/humanist/2013-June/011052.html
19 https://www.huygens.knaw.nl/?lang=en

Digital Humanities community. Through numerous projects, group members are also in close productive contact with most of the other researchers in the institute and with external researchers active in relevant projects. The projects themselves cover a large part of the spectrum of Digital Humanities undertakings, from data modelling and repository building,[20] through digital scholarly editions such as the correspondence of Vincent van Gogh,[21] to analytical tool building, of which the text collation engine *CollateX*[22] is an example.[23]

The research staff of the institute originally had no particular focus on digital or computational activities. In 2005 the institute took the strategic decision to move into the domain of digital scholarly publications as well. The initiative began with the addition of a literary researcher and two developers to the institute. Staff at a related institute, later dissolved, had been developing a 'collaboratory' for the curation and analysis of humanities and social science data, which today would be called a Virtual Research Environment (VRE). At the Huygens Institute the part of this environment relevant to the humanities, consisting mainly of a transcription and publication environment for historical texts, was adopted and strongly pushed forward while the social science aspect was eventually abandoned. This eventually became the *eLaborate* online environment, 'in which scholars can upload scans, transcribe and annotate text and publish the results as an online text edition'.[24] *eLaborate* is a web-based environment where textual scholars find support for basic tasks in creating and editing a digital scholarly edition. A project in *eLaborate* is essentially a container for a series of scanned manuscript or print text pages that can be arranged arbitrarily in a tree structure. Fine-grained authorisation allows one to arrange access or restrictions down to page level and thus to arrange for private, collaborative or fully open edition workflows. A text editor is facilitated to aid in creating diplomatic and critical transcriptions which can be layered with annotations to serve the researcher's or reader's needs. All data is stored

---

20   https://github.com/HuygensING/timbuctoo
21   http://vangoghletters.org/vg
22   http://collatex.net
23   Ronald Haentjens Dekker et al., 'Computer-Supported Collation of Modern Manuscripts: CollateX and the Beckett Digital Manuscript Project', *Digital Scholarship in the Humanities*, 30 (2014), 452–70, http://dx.doi.org/10.1093/llc/fqu007
24   https://www.elaborate.huygens.knaw.nl

and retrievable as XML. *eLaborate* facilitates the automated publishing of web-based editions and provides a generalised graphical interface based on 'fluid' columns. Vertical areas of the screen can be arbitrarily arranged for visualising the reading text, connected annotations, browsing in the text structure, full text search and so forth. Given some basic training, *eLaborate* provides an out-of-the-box solution allowing textual scholars with only average computer skills to create basic digital scholarly editions without much need for technical support.

It is relevant to note that the IT team adopted an *Agile* software development methodology. This type of software development takes a manifest user-centred and evolutionary approach to software manufacturing. Short one- or two-week iterations deliver functioning parts of software that are evaluated by the client/user. This ensures the balancing of the software production with the evolving vision and knowledge of the client. Arguably this methodology feeds into the social shaping aspects of introducing new technologies and methodologies.[25]

A case study of the methodological dynamics surrounding the development of *eLaborate* serves to show that the trading zone metaphor is not unproblematic. Do the dynamics and interactions in the context—the work site—where *eLaborate* was developed point to the emergence of a methodological pidgin? Most certainly the developers and the researcher who headed the project started exchanging terminology. The developers began to refer to concepts such as 'page', 'annotation', 'transcription'. The researchers grew accustomed to using words such as 'user', 'interface', 'architecture', as well as the vocabulary that is rather typical for the agile methodology used by the developers: 'planning game', 'iteration'. Whether this constitutes a beginning of a methodological pidgin is debatable. The interactions that led to the exchange of vocabulary could equally be attributed to standard development practice in which there is a particular relationship between client and service provider and in which, certainly within agile methodology, the provider normally tries to understand the client's work process and concepts in order to model them into software. The objective of the developers in that case is simply to mimic as closely as possible the concepts the client is using. Arguably this could cause a medium shift in which the researcher ends up with

---

25 Robert C. Martin, *Agile Software Development, Principles, Patterns, and Practices* (Upper Saddle River: Prentice Hall, 2002).

a digital environment that is virtually identical to his or her known analogue work process and material. Once the work is done, the client and developer can go their separate ways, without having essentially influenced the methodologies on either side.

A clearer indicator of methodological change may be the actual *loss* of lexical items. During the *eLaborate* project it transpired that an index—in the sense of the keyword reference list in the back of a book—is not a very useful instrument to mimic in a digital environment if the texts at hand are automatically indexed and the interface includes a full-text search function that presents its result as a list of keywords in context. In various edition projects where *eLaborate* was deployed some friction and dissonance could be observed among users (either textual scholars or trained volunteers who transcribed manuscript material) about the lack of an index, but gradually the use of full text search as a replacement for the index became accepted, even appreciated, once the possibilities for wildcard and fuzzy search were understood. This is notwithstanding the fact that a full text search is not the epistemological equivalent of an index. Current full text indexing technology does not, for instance, facilitate named entity resolution in the same way as traditional indices may. Nevertheless, within projects based on *eLaborate* the concept of 'index' is no longer used except for references to the past; the concept of 'zoekfunctie' (search function) seems to have all but replaced it. For textual scholarship and scholarly editing I would argue that the loss of the 'analogue representation' of an index and even the lexical reference to it does indeed constitute a methodological change.

The same event shows the dynamics of social shaping and regression in a different way. With the indexing technology used in *eLaborate*—first *Lucene* and later *Solr*—it is possible to generate search result lists with text context ranked by 'relevance'.[26] Although the keyword-in-context search results list eventually found unanimous adoption, the concept of 'relevance' became a topic of recurring and fractious debate. *Lucene* applies a combination of Boolean and vector space models to determine the relevance of documents to a user's query. The Boolean measure selects the documents that correspond to the terms the user wishes to find or ignore. A vector space model is then applied to that selection to

---

26   http://lucene.apache.org; http://lucene.apache.org/solr

rank the relevance of each document to the query. Formally this model determines relevance by applying a cosine measure to the vectorised document vocabulary and query.[27] The vocabulary of any text can be expressed as a mathematical vector and the basic trigonometric function of the cosine can be applied to determine the size of the angle between two such vectors. This essentially means that the smaller the angle, the more the vocabularies of two texts are similar. In *Lucene* this measure is used to determine if requested search terms appear more often in a particular document than on average in the vocabulary of all documents retrieved with a specific query. The more such terms appear in a document, the higher the relevance ranking of that document. It transpired that the textual scholars and other users confronted with this technology were for the most part unimpressed with the relevance ranking, which appeared incomprehensible and alien to them. And although the feature was initially presented in the interface, most edition projects within *eLaborate* preferred canonical orderings such as sorting by folio number, name of author or text, shelf mark etc. As a result, word-weighted ranking is no longer offered in the editing and publication interfaces of *eLaborate*, and the researcher in charge of the development confirmed that in the several rounds of open testing that the software underwent, none of the trained users requested the function.[28]

The virtual disappearance of automatic ranking by relevance as a function in the current version of *eLaborate* is a case of social shaping of technology, and indeed of paradigmatic regression. Ranking by relevance could arguably be methodologically useful for textual scholars who must peruse a large corpus for occurrences of themes, words and motifs. Even if it is not the default, one would expect the option to be available. Technically there are no barriers to providing the function, as it is the default behaviour of the search engine used. In fact, it took additional development effort—though admittedly not much— to provide canonical ordering. Despite all this, the functionality that is standard from the technical point of view is no longer available—a strong signal that the IT developers and the textual scholars found a

---

27 Dominic Widdows, 'Word-Vectors and Search Engines', in *Geometry and Meaning* (Stanford: Center for the Study of Language and Information, 2004), pp. 131–265, http://www.puttypeg.net/book/chapters/chapter5.html

28 Karina van Dalen-Oskam, E-mail message to the author (10 January 2014).

barrier to knowledge exchange that they were unable to overcome. In other words, they could not create the required methodological pidgin to communicate or appreciate the possible utility of that function.

What is interesting here is not so much the disappearance of relevance-based ranking. There may be valid scholarly reasons to reject such an ordering principle—albeit that these have not been put forward by the users in this case. Rather, it serves as an example in which the pidgin, the 'reduced common language' used during the interaction between developers and researchers, was not sufficient to communicate the methodological potential of a relatively straightforward, seemingly useful and non-intrusive method, and so prevented its theoretical consideration. This example shows how difficult it actually is, both for researchers and for developers, to use the trading zone for methodological gain or innovation. The textual scholars involved first needed to know of the existence of such a thing as 'ranking by relevance' to be able to recognise its possible methodological potential. Next, to establish that potential would require them ultimately to drill down to the mathematics of cosine measure for vector comparison and understand how vectors can represent documents. As it has been argued elsewhere in a similar vein, without such a detailed level of knowledge, it is difficult to assess the methodological usefulness of new technologies.[29]

It should be noted additionally that this is a small example involving relatively standard digital technology. The syntactical and lexical distance that must be bridged in the case of a project such as *Circulation of Knowledge and Learned Practices in the 17th-century Dutch Republic* is significantly larger,[30] as in that project correspondences are visualised through network analysis.[31] A sensible understanding of what may be inferred from network visualisations and what this adds in terms of

---

29 D. Sculley and Bradley M. Pasanek, 'Meaning and Mining: The Impact of Implicit Assumptions in Data Mining for the Humanities', *Literary and Linguistic Computing*, 23 (2008), 409–24, http://dx.doi.org/10.1093/llc/fqn019

30 http://ckcc.huygens.knaw.nl

31 Charles van den Heuvel, 'Circulation of Knowledge in the Digital Republic of Letters: Making Correspondences of Manuscripts and Printed Editions Accessible for Research' (presented at the 5th *Liber Manuscript Conference: Promoting Access to Manuscript Content*, Paris Bibliothèque Nationale de France, 29–31 May 2012), http://ckcc.huygens.knaw.nl/wp-content/bestanden/2012/05/CHeuvel_LIBER_ParijsDEF.pdf

methodology requires a fairly deep grasp of the mathematical models underpinning not only network modelling and analysis in general, but also the topic modelling used to generate the network data.[32]

All in all, this raises the question of how much methodological interaction is actualised in a methodological trading zone in a smaller concrete context as some superficial vocabulary is certainly exchanged, of which some may be instrumental in future co-operation for both researchers and developers. But there is little in the way of deep methodological trading going on. Textual scholars are not providing knowledge about theoretical notions on scholarly editing and literary criticism to developers; and, vice versa, developers are not lecturing researchers about mathematical or computational principles. The common language does no more than create an interface that answers to the perceived needs of researchers in the humanities. The interface becomes an expression of these researchers' conceptions of how the digital technology might serve their purpose.

The methodological gain in this is rather superficial: access and discovery increase in scope, but concepts and processes hardly change. There is a digital translation, but little methodological innovation. The potential or realised methodological innovation furthermore happens rather covertly. In the case of the relevance ordering in *eLaborate* the potential is there, but hidden—again!—by a graphical interface, and by an apparently suboptimal methodological exchange between researchers and developers. In the case of the *Circulation of Knowledge* project, the mechanics, technology and methodology are almost completely covertly integrated into the resulting digital environment by the computer scientists. A further consequence was that the main technical developer struggled with negative feelings about lack of recognition for methodological merit. The covertness of this methodological innovation is far from trivial. If, as Peter Shillingsburg has pointed out, editions are scholarly and critical arguments about what a textual record means or about how it should be read, then a *digital*

---

32 Peter Wittek and Walter Ravenek, 'Supporting the Exploration of a Corpus of 17th-Century Scholarly Correspondences by Topic Modeling', in *Supporting Digital Humanities 2011: Answering the Unaskable*, ed. by Bente Maegaard (presented at the SDH 2011 Supporting Digital Humanities: Answering the Unaskable, Copenhagen, 2011), http://www.clarin.nl/sites/default/files/sdh2011-wittek-ravenek.pdf

edition is also such an argument.[33] Because both interface and model are constituents of the digital edition, they are both part of that intellectual argument. The model—i.e. the combination of the data model and the computer language logic that puts it into action—is entirely conceived by computer science experts. The interface and the view it offers on that model, including the functions of the model it exposes to or hides from the outside world, is to a very large degree conceived by developers and designers. The methodology used for this is effectively inaccessible to the textual scholars, who lack the skills to interpret and comprehend the technologies used. Given that the computer scientists create so much of the intellectual argument pertaining to a particular digital scholarly edition, it would seem that having a sufficiently broad common methodological language is pivotal to digital textual scholarship. But as we can see, our current dynamics of interaction are not helping to create it.

Trading theory in the larger textual scholarly context

Although the trading zone between computer science or digital technology and textual scholarship seems so problematic at the smaller more concrete level, there seems to be no shortage of methodological trading on the theoretical level. Exhaustively detailing and disentangling the intricately intertwined histories of textual scholarship, knowledge representation, literary criticism, computing and digital technologies, is hardly feasible in the span of this chapter. Moreover, creating history often suggests a falsely deterministic account of cause and effect. Nevertheless, it is important to identify a number of key developments. The beginnings of the Internet and the World Wide Web are usually identified with Vannevar Bush's vision of the Memex, an imaginary system to store, track, index and retrieve any information, and—crucially—to rewrite that information and keep versioning records so as to trace the development of our thoughts.[34] Visions of such knowledge systems reach far further back, however, at the very least to the work

---

33 Peter Shillingsburg, 'Is Reliable Social Scholarly Editing an Oxymoron?', *Social, Digital, Scholarly Editing* (Saskatoon: University of Saskatchewan, 2013), http://ecommons.luc.edu/ctsdh_pubs/1

34 Vannevar Bush, 'As We May Think', *The Atlantic* (July, 1945), pp. 112–24.

of Paul Otlet in the early twentieth century, as has been repeatedly shown.[35] It was Theodor Nelson who coined the term Hypertext and constructed a theory for it, inter alia referring back to Bush.[36] Nelson's attempts at implementing his visions failed to result in successful tools; instead it was Tim Berners-Lee whose team devised the Hypertext Transfer Protocol, which successfully kick-started the World Wide Web, with reference to the work of Nelson.[37] Although sympathetic to his endeavour, Nelson deeply hates Lee's technical solution:

> It is vital to point out that Tim's view of hypertext (only one-way links, invisible and not allowed to overlap) is entirely different from mine (visible, unbreaking n-way links by any parties, all content legally reweavable by anyone into new documents with paths back to the originals, and transclusions as well as links—as in Vannevar Bush's original vision).[38]

Imperfect or not, HTTP technology happens to align nicely with many ideas on the nature of knowledge and text that are emerging in literary criticism, textual theory and semiotics, which increasingly problematise a linear view of text and result in more post-structuralist approaches. George Landow summarises the convergence:

> Hypertext, an information technology consisting of individual blocks of text, or lexias, and the electronic links that join them, has much in common with recent literary and critical theory. For example, like much recent work by poststructuralists, such as Roland Barthes and Jacques Derrida, hypertext reconceives conventional, long-held assumptions

---

35   W. Boyd Rayward, 'Visions of Xanadu: Paul Otlet (1868–1944) and Hypertext', *JASIS*, 45 (1994), 235–50; Michael Buckland, 'What Is a "Document"?', *Journal of the American Society of Information Science*, 48 (1997), 804–09; Edward Vanhoutte, 'Paul Otlet (1868–1944) and Vannevar Bush (1890–1974)', *The Mind Tool: Edward Vanhoutte's Blog*, 2009 http://edwardvanhoutte.blogspot.nl/2009/03/paul-otlet-1868-1944-and-vannevar-bush.html; Charles van den Heuvel and W. Boyd Rayward, 'Facing Interfaces: Paul Otlet's Visualizations of Data Integration', *Journal of the American Society for Information Science and Technology*, 62 (2011), 2313–26.
36   Theodor Holm Nelson, *Literary Machines: The Report on, and of, Project Xanadu Concerning Word Processing, Electronic Publishing, Hypertext, Thinkertoys, Tomorrow's Intellectual Revolution, and Certain Other Topics Including Knowledge, Education and Freedom* (Sausolito: Mindful Press, 1993; first ed. 1981).
37   Tim Berners-Lee, 'Information Management: A Proposal' (CERN, 1989), http://info.cern.ch/Proposal.html
38   Theodor Holm Nelson, *POSSIPLEX: Movies, Intellect, Creative Control, My Computer Life and the Fight for Civilization* (Sausolito: Mindful Press, 2010).

about authors and readers and the texts they write and read. Electronic linking, which provides one of the defining features of hypertext, also embodies Julia Kristeva's notions of intertextuality, Mikhail Bakhtin's emphasis upon multivocality, Michel Foucault's conceptions of networks of power, and Gilles Deleuze and Felix Guattari's ideas of rhizomatic, 'nomad thought'. The very idea of hypertextuality seems to have taken form at approximately the same time that poststructuralism developed, but their points of convergence have a closer relation than that of mere contingency, for both grow out of dissatisfaction with the related phenomena of the printed book and hierarchical thought.[39]

Digital textual scholarship and more particularly the digital scholarly edition obviously rely on the technologies delivered by the development of the Internet and the hypertext protocol. In turn, these technologies are rooted in theory which sees the nature of knowledge, information and documents as highly interconnected and referential, or intertwingled and transclusional, as Nelson would in all likelihood phrase it. Peter Robinson expresses similar views when he discusses the idea of 'distributed editions', with attribution also to Peter Shillingsburg and Paul Eggert.[40] Robinson is interested in the volatile aspects of editions. He posits that readers may become writers too, and proposes that editions may exist in a distributed fashion in an interactive web-based space. Each reader may have a different representation: 'a manuscript transcription from one site, a layer of commentary from one scholar, textual notes and emendations from another, all on different servers around the globe. In a sentence: these will be fluid, co-operative and distributed editions, the work of many, the property of all'.[41] According to George P. Landow, this vision is strongly associated with the Docuverse, the ideas on nonlinear writing and hypertext systems described by Nelson:

> Perhaps the single most important development in the world of hypermedia has been the steady development of read-write systems—of the kind of systems, in other words, that the pioneering theorists Vannevar Bush and Theodor H. Nelson envisioned. Blogs, wikis [...] all represent

---

39 *Hyper/Text/Theory*, ed. by George P. Landow (Baltimore: Johns Hopkins University Press, 1994).
40 Peter Robinson, 'Where We Are with Electronic Scholarly Editions, and Where We Want to Be', *Jahrbuch für Computerphilologie*, 5 (2003), 125–46, http://computerphilologie.uni-muenchen.de/jg03/robinson.html
41 *Ibid.*

attempts to bring to the Web the features found in hypertext software of the 1980s that made readers into authors.[42]

But ideas on more interactive and volatile editions also refer to another complex of theory surrounding the fundamental instability of text. This complex encompasses a post-structuralist view of text where text is not a book but a hypertext, and where hypertext stresses the volatility of text, its heterogeneous, mutable, interactive and open-ended character — ideas rather opposed to that of text as an immutable form enclosed and bound by a front and back cover in a book. This theoretical complex also borrows from ideas on the fluidity of text as expressed for example by John Bryant who calls attention to the perpetual flux texts show trough preprint revisions, revised editions, and adaptations that shape literary works into forms specific to different audiences.[43] Similarly, the importance for scholarly editing of the volatile aspects of text is expressed through what has become known as *critique génétique*, an approach to editing that focuses on the *avant-texte*, the process of writing and revision that precedes the publication of a book.[44]

The instability and process aspects of text are also important to textual scholarship and the practice of scholarly editing from the point of view of the use of editions: of what happens after publication. The ideas behind hypertext, together with those about read-write systems, also inform ideas concerning the social aspects of text and scholarly editing. Read-write systems facilitate crowdsourcing and thus open up the process of scholarly editing to a potentially far larger source of labour by 'expert amateurs'[45] than the individual scholar could provide

---

42 George P. Landow, *Hypertext 3.0: Critical Theory and New Media in an Era of Globalization*, rev. ed. of Hypertext 2.0 1997 (Baltimore: Johns Hopkins University Press, 2006), p. xiv.

43 John Bryant, *The Fluid Text: A Theory of Revision and Editing for Book and Screen* (Ann Arbor: University of Michigan Press, 2002), http://books.google.nl/books?id=1w4wpOdPbu4C

44 Dirk Van Hulle, *Textual Awareness: A Genetic Study of Late Manuscripts by Joyce, Proust, and Mann* (Ann Arbor: University of Michigan Press, 2004); Domenico Fiormonte and Cinzia Pusceddu, 'The Text as a Product and as a Process: History, Genesis, Experiments', in *Manuscript, Variant, Genese—Genesis*, ed. by Edward Vanhoutte and M. de Smedt (Gent: KANTL, 2006), pp. 109–28, http://www.academia.edu/618689/The_Text_As_a_Product_and_As_a_Process._History_Genesis_Experiments

45 Katherine N. Hayles, *How We Think: Digital Media and Contemporary Technogenesis* (Chicago: University of Chicago Press, 2012).

for.[46] Crowdsourcing engages an audience of users in the scholarly process literally in the *avant-texte* phase of the creation of a scholarly edition. This potential need not be confined to, say, the transcription stage of a scholarly project. Meanwhile, ideas have been developed on the so-called social edition, which allows readers/users to add their knowledge to the edition and render its creation and use a community event under the guidance of scholarly experts.[47] Lastly, the process aspect of text is also highlighted through new computational engagements that readers/users may make with texts and scholarly editions. This aspect was already expressed as early as 1949 through what is now usually seen as the first application of Humanities Computing: the work of Roberto Busa,[48] which led to the computational means necessary to derive automatically a concordance to the works of St Thomas Aquinas.[49] This was the beginning of a long development that prefigured current computer-supported analytic engagement with literary texts such as distant reading, algorithmic reading and big data analysis.[50]

The shape of the digital edition according to reality

In short, the interaction between digital technology and textual scholarship places the focus of methodology on both the unstable and fluid aspects of text, and on the process aspects of texts. That is the fundamental tenet that computer science brings to textual scholarship.

---

46 Ben Brumfield, 'The Collaborative Future of Amateur Editions', *Collaborative Manuscript Transcription*, 2013, http://manuscripttranscription.blogspot.co.uk/2013/07/the-collaborative-future-of-amateur.html
47 Ray Siemens et al., 'Toward Modeling the Social Edition: An Approach to Understanding the Electronic Scholarly Edition in the Context of New and Emerging Social Media', *Literary and Linguistic Computing*, 27 (2012), 445–61, http://dx.doi.org/10.1093/llc/fqs013. See also the chapter by Siemens et al. in this book (p. 137).
48 Steven E. Jones, *Roberto Busa, S. J., and the Emergence of Humanities Computing* (New York and London: Routledge, 2016).
49 Hockey, 'The History of Humanities Computing'.
50 Dino Buzzetti, 'Digital Editions and Text Processing', in *Text Editing, Print and the Digital World*, ed. by Marilyn Deegan and Kathryn Sutherland (Farnham and Burlington: Ashgate, 2009), pp. 45–61, http://www.academia.edu/391823/Digital_Editions_and_Text_Processing; Franco Moretti, *Graphs, Maps, Trees*; Stephen Ramsay, *Reading Machines: Toward an Algorithmic Criticism* (Urbana-Champaign: University of Illinois Press, 2011); Matthew L. Jockers, *Macroanalysis: Digital Methods and Literary History* (Urbana-Champaign: University of Illinois Press, 2013).

Hypertext, unlike print, is fundamentally process- and context-oriented. Following a basic tenet of artificial intelligence theory, it views representing and acquiring knowledge as a problem of defining and searching information spaces, and it recognizes that these spaces and search methods will vary according to the purposes and abilities of particular users.[51]

Digital scholarly editions are indeed information spaces. But they are not often information spaces that line up with the theoretical pidgin discussed above. The theoretical notions of textual scholarship, and the scholarly digital edition that we find in the trading zones between textual scholarship and computer science, call for an expression of text and editions through which the information contained in the edition is expressed primarily according to the principles of hypertext. Current reality, however, is very different. In textual scholarship, Internet nodes are mostly placeholders that point via a URL to a digital document or to a digital edition as a whole, as a data silo. The edition of the Van Gogh letters, for instance, sits at the node identified by http://www.vangoghletters.org/vg/ as a fully integrated and monolithic pile of edited text from letters; the pile includes comments, annotations, translations and so on. The finest granularity presented to the network of the web is at the level of the individual letter (e.g. http://vangoghletters.org/vg/letters/let043/letter.html). Even that URL identifies a compound object, that is, a meaningful set of multiple scholarly objects: two facsimiles, a transcribed text, annotations, bound together by an interface that (again following Shillingsburg) represents an editorial argument about what constitutes the digital scholarly edition of this particular letter. According to this argument, there is no need to address the transcription, the facsimile, a particular annotation, in isolation. Most of the digital scholarly editions on the Web are expressed similarly. It is hardly better than a network of nodes in which each node represents a particular edition that is offered as a PDF. This situation renders it impossible to address texts (and thus editions) beyond their graphical interface in ways compatible with a hypertext model.

Digital editions often trumpet the ability to represent text exhaustively, celebrating the fact that there is no need to make decisions

---

51 Paul N. Edwards, 'Hyper Text and Hypertension: Post-Structuralist Critical Theory, Social Studies of Science, and Software', *Social Studies of Science*, 24 (1994), 229–78.

on what to leave out.⁵² Indeed, it is an asset that digital scholarly editions may be capacious almost without limit. In the case of an important and large tradition of a particular work, this potential may allow for the presentation of all witnesses as items in an inventory, or as a digital archive. Arguably this is not just an asset because of exhaustiveness of representation, but foremost because it allows for the expression of the relations between the witnesses, and thus *inter alia* the genesis and fluidity of texts—in fact the more process-like aspects of texts—for which the hypertext model as described offers technological expressive potential. In the reality of current digital scholarly digital editions, however, this potential seems seldom realised. A graphical interface will usually allow the user to select and view single witnesses, or perhaps to compare the texts of multiple witnesses, especially if the editor has integrated a collation or comparison tool such as *Juxta*.⁵³ The inventory will probably also allow a list of witnesses to be shown in chronological order. The order of that list will in all likelihood be based on a metadata property 'date' or similar in the relational database underlying the digital edition archive. The list itself is a generated GUI visualisation expressing that metadata. The point here is that a list so represented is not a hypertext representation of the chronological 'linkedness' of the witnesses, it is a mere list of individuated metadata. This is different from the idea of hypertext that all information is expressed as machine negotiable nodes and links, so that an expressive network of knowledge is created. This means that the chronological order of the witnesses in this case can only be inferred through human cognition from the metadata based list—it is not represented as knowledge in a computationally tractable form intrinsic to the hypertext medium. Much effort may thus be invested in gathering exhaustive representations of individual witnesses, but if the result of that effort only allows user-level navigation of relational metadata represented as a graphical interface, then the digital scholarly edition is not an effective hypertext knowledge space. Such an edition may still be valuable for the sheer wealth of information, but it remains

---

52 Cf. e.g. Kenneth M. Price, 'Electronic Scholarly Editions', in *A Companion to Digital Literary Studies*, ed. by Ray Siemens and Susan Schreibman (Oxford: Blackwell, 2008), http://www.digitalhumanities.org/companion/view?docId=blackwell/9781405148641/9781405148641.xml&chunk.id=ss1-6-5&toc.depth=1&toc.id=ss1-6-5&brand=9781405148641_brand

53 http://www.juxtasoftware.org

firmly at the level of document representation for human consumption without integrating the relations between witnesses in a computationally networked representation.

Regression and reaffirmation

There is nothing deterministic about technology, and indeed nothing much deterministic about hypertext. As a technology to express a text and to present it in the form of a digital scholarly edition, hypertext has been shaped by the scholarly community into little more than a filing cabinet for self-contained documents. Most digital scholarly editions on the Internet express the particular idea the scholar responsible for the edition has about what a digital edition is or should be; normally, that idea is a re-representation of the book. We find collections of page-based facsimiles and transcriptions presented as self-contained units, wrapped up in and bound by the front matter that is the interface. There is attention for fluid aspects, and for context. *The Hyperstack edition of Saint Patrick's 'Confessio'*,[54] for instance, explicitly offers its users the possibility to venture from the 'centrality of the text [...] through the dense net of textual layers and background information in answer to questions that are likely to arise in their minds'.[55] The dense net in question is effectively a star network radiating out from the main page into leaves containing pages of metadata, facsimiles of manuscript folia, or transcriptions of entire texts. Despite the impressive density of information, the information itself is not that densely networked. The relations between the texts and the contextualising information is *described*, but not expressed through the 'hyper fabric' of e.g. HTTP links. Even so, the *Confessio* is rather an exception to the rule—very few of today's digital editions seem to be particularly concerned with the core ideal of hypertext as an expression of linked information, of process and context.

Most digital scholarly editions, in fact, are all but literal translations of a book into a non-book-oriented medium. Peter Robinson, writing about the distinctions of text-as-work and text-as-document, argues

---

54 http://www.confessio.ie
55 Franz Fischer, 'About the HyperStack', *St. Patrick's Confessio*, 2011, http://www.confessio.ie/about/hyperstack#

that in the early days of digital editions—roughly until 2005—scholars would privilege the text-as-work perspective, focusing on the potential of digital technology to express and support the properties of text that construct its meaning.[56] In recent years, he continues, this trend has been exactly reversed. More recent digital scholarly editions harness the digital medium rather to represent the text-as-document—the faithful rerepresentation of a text according to its expression in the physical documents that carry it. As an example Robinson points to the online edition of Jane Austen's fiction manuscripts.[57] Elena Pierazzo, who was deeply involved with the methodological design of this edition, unsurprisingly offers a rationale for a text-as-document approach to the digital edition.[58] Robinson also notes that many collaborative transcription systems are designed to record text-as-document: not one of twenty-one tools listed in a survey by Ben Brumfield offers the possibility of recording text-as-work.[59] Indeed it is far easier to point to examples of digital scholarly editions that are in essence metaphors of the book, or in other words: translations of a print text to the digital medium, apparently for no other reason than to fulfil the same role as the print text.

Textual scholarly theory, as has been shown, embraces hypertext as a technology which enables the expression of post-structuralist ideas about information, with a focus on the fluid properties of text. It has often been suggested that the capabilities of digital technologies should become the focus and practice of digital scholarly editing. Despite all this, that ideal is not materialising in the form of concrete digital editions, and for similar reasons to those observed in the smaller context of the *eLaborate* project. Here, too, we find the dynamics of paradigmatic regression in the professional community surrounding the digital scholarly edition. The methodological potential of information technology is hidden by the incomplete metaphors of a paradigm that is itself reaffirmed by becoming the primary interface to the new technology. Robinson argues

---

56 Peter Robinson, 'Towards a Theory of Digital Editions', *Variants*, 10 (2013), 105–31.
57 http://www.janeausten.ac.uk
58 Elena Pierazzo, 'A Rationale of Digital Documentary Editions', *Literary and Linguistic Computing*, 26 (2011), 463–77, http://dx.doi.org/10.1093/llc/fqr033
59 Ben Brumfield, 'The Collaborative Future of Amateur Editions', *Collaborative Manuscript Transcription*, 2013, http://manuscripttranscription.blogspot.co.uk/2013/07/the-collaborative-future-of-amateur.html

that there is a strong continuity of previous contemplation of print editions present in the thinking of those scholars who first conceived of the digital scholarly edition, resulting in a kind of theoretical pidgin that embraces the new technology, but uses it to express digitally a familiar form for the scholarly edition: the printed book.[60] The print edition in that digital translation is a metaphor, but one that begins to hide hypertext's native potential for expressing referential and conceptual links between texts. The graphical interfaces of digital scholarly editions almost all refer strongly to this book metaphor, reaffirming thereby the paradigm from which that metaphor springs. In the end, the use of the technology has shaped it into a tool to recreate that which is already well known. It is also worth noting that the de facto *lingua franca* of current digital scholarly editions, TEI-XML, is instrumental in this reaffirmation.[61] As an encoding language it is geared fully towards describing text-as-document. Although not graphical in nature, TEI is thus an interface that, like graphical interfaces, hides many of the essential networking and process characteristics of hypertext. Instead, TEI-XML, with its text-inward orientation, print-text paradigm and hierarchical structure focus, constantly reaffirms the view of the digital edition as representing a text-as-document.

Beyond the book?

There is nothing deterministic about the Internet. The paradigmatic regression we currently see in the digital textual scholarship community is a clear demonstration of that. This community has devised a methodological pidgin that exploits a new technology to express a well-rehearsed paradigm of scholarly editing. Yet this must not be where the methodological shaping and disciplinary trading stops. The theoretical concepts pertaining to the fluidity of text are clearly important to the textual scholarly community, but they still need to be brought fully into the concrete methodological pidgin that is currently geared towards representing a text-as-document, rather than toward text-as-process. As long as scholarly editors keep producing digital metaphors of the book,

---

60 Robinson, 'Towards a Theory of Digital Editions'.
61 http://www.tei-c.org

this will hardly happen. Both textual theorists and computer science practitioners must intensify the methodological discourse to clarify what existing technology is needed to implement a form of hypertext that truly represents textual fluidity and text relations in a scholarly viable *and* computational tractable manner—a hypertext language inspired both by computer science and textual scholarship. Without that dialogue we relegate the *raison d'être* for the digital scholarly edition to that of a mere medium shift, we limit its expressiveness to that of print text, and we fail to explore the computational potential for digital text representation, analysis and interaction.

6. Exogenetic Digital Editing and Enactive Cognition

Dirk Van Hulle

The theoretical framework of this essay is a current paradigm in cognitive sciences, which may be relevant to the development of scholarly digital editing. In cognitive philosophy, the 'Extended Mind' hypothesis, first formulated by Clark and Chalmers, suggests that external features in the environment can become partly constitutive of the mind.[1] In other words, the mind is not limited to something inside the skull, but is regarded as being 'extended'.[2] Varieties of this post-Cartesian approach, which is being applied to cognitive narratology, are referred to as 'enactivism' and 'radical enactivism'.[3] The latter paradigm suggests that

---

1   Andy Clark and David J. Chalmers, 'The Extended Mind', *Analysis*, 58 (1998), 10–23 (p. 12).
2   Andy Clark, *Supersizing the Mind: Embodiment, Action, and Cognitive Extention* (Oxford: Oxford University Press, 2008); Andy Clark, 'Embodied, Embedded, and Extended Cognition', in *The Cambridge Handbook of Cognitive Science*, ed. by Keith Frankish and William M. Ramsey (Cambridge: Cambridge University Press, 2012), pp. 275–91; Richard Menary, 'Introduction', in *The Extended Mind*, ed. by Richard Menary (Cambridge, MA: MIT Press, 2010), pp. 1–25; *Enaction: Toward a New Paradigm for Cognitive Science*, ed. by John Steward, Olivier Gapenne and Ezequiel A. Di Paolo (Cambridge, MA: MIT Press, 2011).
3   David Herman, 'Re-minding Modernism', in *the Emergence of Mind: Representations of consciousness in Narrative Discourse in English*, ed. by David Herman (Lincoln: University of Nebraska Press, 2011), pp. 243–71; David Herman, 'Narrative and Mind: Directions for Inquiry', in *Stories and Minds: Cognitive Approaches to Literary Narrative*, ed. by Lars Bernaerts, Dirk De Geest, Luc Herman and Bart Vervaeck (Lincoln: University of Nebraska Press, 2013), pp. 199–209.

the mind is not just 'extended' but also 'extensive'.[4] David D. Hutto and Erik Myin suggest that the mind is constituted in an even-handed way by both the brain and the environment; the brain's contributions are not prioritised over those of the environment.[5] They abbreviate their hypothesis as REC for Radical Enactive (or Embodied) Cognition and suggest that 'If REC is right, basic cognition is not contentful; basic minds are fundamentally, constitutively already world-involving. They are, as we say, extensive'.[6] This view is presented in opposition to the 'Default Internal Mind assumption', which 'takes it for granted that, in their basic state, minds are unextended and brain-bound. If that is the case, then they become extended only when external resources are needed to complete certain cognitive tasks. On that model, what is fundamentally internal occasionally becomes extended'.[7] REC inverts this assumption: 'Basic minds are fundamentally extensive, whereas special kinds of scaffolded practices must be mastered before anything resembling internalised […] mentality appears on the scene'.[8] So, according to the REC hypothesis, knowledge and skills can evidently be internalised, but the proposed model of the mind is not 'internalist'.

In narratology, the 'internalist' model of the mind—usually referred to as the 'inward turn'—is currently regarded as a critical commonplace in the context of evocations of the mind in literary modernism.[9] As opposed to this 'inward turn', the extensive mind consists of the interplay between intelligent agents and their cultural as well as material circumstances which can be anything. In the case of a writer, for instance, this environment can simply be a piece of paper, a notebook or the margin of a book.[10]

---

4   Daniel D. Hutto and Erik Myin, *Radicalizing Enactivism: Basic Minds without Content* (Cambridge, MA: MIT Press, 2013), p. 135.
5   *Ibid.*, p. 137.
6   *Ibid.*, pp. xii, 137.
7   *Ibid.*, pp. 137–38.
8   *Ibid.*, p. 138.
9   Erich von Kahler, *The Inward Turn of Narrative*, trans. by Richard and Clara Winston (Princeton: Princeton University Press); Herman, 'Re-Minding Modernism'.
10 I have explored the relationship between manuscripts and the extended/extensive minds in *Modern Manuscripts: The Extended Mind and Creative Undoing from Darwin to Beckett and Beyond* (London: Bloomsbury, 2014).

This essay examines modernist authors' personal libraries, their reading notes and drafts as aspects of the 'extended mind', and investigates to what extent genetic digital editing can be deployed to study this form of enactive cognition. In 'Narrative and Mind: Directions for Inquiry', David Herman notes that interdisciplinary research in this area has so far been mainly *unidirectional* (literary studies 'borrowing from' cognitive sciences) and makes a plea for a *bidirectional* exchange of ideas.[11] Genetic digital editing may serve as a useful way of making this interdisciplinary research bidirectional, notably by indicating the markedly intertextual nature of many modernist texts and emphasising the interplay between 'exogenesis' and 'endogenesis' as a generative nexus in creative cognitive processes. The inclusion of the exogenesis (e.g. in the form of an author's personal library) in a genetic edition will be studied as a method (1) to visualise this nexus between exo- and endogenesis and (2) to analyse the enactive mind at work. In this way, genetic digital editing might be a way of contributing to the bidirectional exchange of ideas between literary studies and cognitive sciences. The case study to examine this research hypothesis is the *Beckett Digital Manuscript Project* (http://www.beckettarchive.org).

An intertextual ecosystem

A few years ago, Mark Nixon and I received permission from the Beckett Estate to work in Beckett's apartment for ten days to examine the marginalia in Beckett's books, and Anne Atik allowed us to do the same in the books Beckett gave to her husband, the visual artist Avigdor Arikha, who was a very good friend of Beckett's. We soon discovered that looking at the marginalia was not enough. Sometimes a book in his personal library was heavily marked, and yet Beckett eventually used an *un*marked passage for his own writing. To denote such passages that are *not* marked, Axel Gellhaus coined the term 'non-marginalia'.[12] This category applies to Beckett's copy of Petrarch's *Sonnets*, which Beckett

---

11 Herman, 'Narrative and the Mind'.
12 Axel Gellhaus, 'Marginalia: Paul Celan as a Reader', in *Variants: The Journal of the European Society for Textual Scholarship*, 2–3 (2004), pp. 207–19 (pp. 218–19).

first read in 1926.[13] The first volume bears no reading traces, whereas the second is heavily annotated. The first sonnets are marked with their rhyme schemes. Next to Sonnet XXI (2.36), opening with 'L'alma mia fiamma', Beckett has penciled 'Merde', and three pages further, next to Sonnet XXIV and especially the penultimate line 'Secca è la vena dell'usato ingegno', he has written: 'Macchè!' [not in the least, of course not].[14] But, strangely enough, Beckett's favourite line from Petrarch is *not* marked: 'chi può dir com'egli arde, è 'n picciol foco' — which Beckett translated as 'He who knows he is burning is burning in a small fire'. Beckett quoted it on several occasions, but it is unmarked in his copy of Petrarch's works.

My hypothesis is that he did not encounter it here, but in a quite different book, namely in Montaigne's essays. Beckett would not even have needed to read all of Montaigne's essays to encounter it, because it already features in the second essay of Book I: 'De la tristesse'. Corroborative evidence supporting this hypothesis can be found in the 'Sam Francis' Notebook (kept at the University of Reading, UoR MS2926, 19v) where the same line is quoted in isolation, followed by a reference to the name of the author *in French* ('Pétrarque'). In the 1777 translation by John Nott, the line ('chi può dir com'egli arde, è 'n picciol foco', in a literal translation: 'who can say how he burns is in little fire') reads as follows: 'Faint is the flame that language can express'.[15] Montaigne quotes this line as the expression of ardent lovers' unbearable passion,[16] but Beckett clearly interpreted the line in a more general sense, closer to

---

13 For more details about Beckett's reading and marginalia, see Dirk Van Hulle and Mark Nixon, *Samuel Beckett's Library* (Cambridge: Cambridge University Press, 2013). For the January 1926 Hilary Term Junior Sophister Examinations, Petrarch's poems and Dante's *Inferno* were among the set texts — see John Pilling, *A Samuel Beckett Chronology* (London: Palgrave Macmillan, 2006), p. 11 — and Beckett's library still contains several of the 'Prescribed Books'. The two-volume set of *Le Rime di Messer Francesco Petrarca* (from the Classica biblioteca italiana antica e moderna series, Milan: Nicolò Bettoni, 1824), which Beckett later gave to Avigdor Arikha and Anne Atik, was probably purchased in preparation for this examination. The library in Beckett's apartment contains a few other books by and on Petrarch, dating from after the war: *Le Rime* (with a preface by Luigi Baldacci, 1962) and Morris Bishop's *Petrarch and his World* (1964).

14 XXIV: 'Secca è la vena dell'usato ingegno' [dry is the vein of my old genius] (2.39; 2006).

15 *The Sonnets, Triumphs, and Other Poems of Petrarch*, with a Life of the Poet by Thomas Campbell (London: Henry G. Bohn, 1859), p. 160.

16 Michel de Montaigne, *Essais I* (Paris: Gallimard Folio Classique, 1965), p. 60.

his favourite line from *King Lear*: 'The worst is not, So long as one can say, "this is the worst"', jotted down in his 'Sottisier' Notebook (UoR MS2901, 14v).

All these allusions become a small intertextual ecosystem[17] in another notebook from the late period, the 'Super Conquérant' Notebook (UoR MS2934, 01r). Here, Beckett noted Seneca's line 'Curae leves loquuntur, ingentes stupent' [Light sorrows speak, deeper ones are silent] (from *Hyppolytus* Act 2, scene 3, line 607)—which is also quoted by Montaigne in the same essay 'De la tristesse' (61).[18] This intertextual network spans a period of more than fifty years, ranging from 1926 (when Beckett first read Petrarch) to 1983. Beckett's experience with the workings of his own extensive mind, not just in terms of space, but also combined with the factor 'time' is relevant to cognitive narratology, both on the level of the *writer's* mind (the production of the storyworld), and on the level of the evocation of his *characters'* minds.

The most obvious example is Krapp in *Krapp's Last Tape*. The intertextuality works (a) first of all in the most basic sense of allusions, but also (b) in a more complex way, involving intertextual cognition as a form of the extensive mind at work.

(a) In terms of cultural allusions, one recognises Petrarch's line 'He who knows he is burning is burning in a small fire' in the words 'burning' and 'fire' in Krapp's recorded speech on the tape, when he first talks about his dying mother, in the house on the canal, while he's sitting on a bench outside, '*wishing* she were gone' (emphasis added), and a few lines further on, while he is sitting on a bench in the park, '*wishing*' he himself were gone. Only in the fourth typescript did Beckett change '*wishing*' into '*burning*'. This '*burning*' to die is contrasted with the '*fire*' in the young Krapp, when he is talking about 'his vision', his aesthetic revelation, 'the *fire* that set it alight' (emphasis added) and especially 'the *fire* in me now' (emphasis added) at the very end of the play. In the fourth typescript, this last line reads: 'the fire burning in me now' (HRC MS SB 4/2/4, 7r). Beckett eventually deleted the burning, but in a letter to Patrick Magee, he explicitly asked the actor to emphasise the word 'burning' in the earlier passage ('burning to be gone') 'in order that "fire"

---

17 For a discussion of this intertextual ecosystem's relevance to Beckett's works, see Dirk Van Hulle, *The Making of Samuel Beckett's* Krapp's Last Tape/La Dernière Bande (London: Bloomsbury, 2015), pp. 177–80.

18 Michel de Montaigne, *Essais I*, p. 61.

at the end may carry all its ambiguity' (TCD MS 11313/1–2). So 'the fire that set it alight' in *Krapp's Last Tape*, the aesthetic vision or revelation, is at the same time the fire that consumes him, and the old Krapp is all too well aware of this ambiguity. While he knows this, he also realises that it must be a small fire since he can still say ('può dir') that he is burning.

(b) But what is perhaps more important is the way in which Beckett works not just with the allusion to Petrarch, but with the entire network of intertextuality in which it is entangled. My suggestion is that Beckett (and many modernists and late modernists) intuited and prefigured much of what cognitive philosophers and scientists are only now recognising to its full extent. Beckett found Petrarch in an essay by Montaigne. Montaigne published multiple versions of his *Essays*, and he kept adding marginalia to his own work, because he recognised that he (or 'his self') was constantly changing. What Beckett realised—to a large extent through the workings of intertextuality—was not just that the self consists of a succession of selves, but that these selves and the human mind are the result of constant storytelling, or what Daniel C. Dennett calls 'our narrative selfhood', for which the web of intertextuality is perhaps an adequate metaphor.[19] Dennett suggests that 'our fundamental tactic of self-protection, self-control, and self-definition is not spinning webs or building dams, but telling stories, and more particularly concocting and controlling the story we tell others—and ourselves—about who we are. [...] Our tales are spun, but for the most part we don't spin them; they spin us. Our human consciousness, and our narrative selfhood, is their product, not their source'.[20] But Dennett also adds that 'Unlike a spider, an individual human doesn't just *exude* its web; more like a beaver, it works hard to gather the materials out of which it builds its protective fortress'.[21] Or to refer to an older comparison, the fable of the spider and the bee in Swift's *Battle of the Books*: the bee is the one that draws the spider's attention to the fact that it is an illusion to think that you spin your web out of your own entrails. The spider may have wanted to build its own web 'with [its] own hands, and the materials extracted altogether out of [its] own person', as Swift puts it, but the Ancients point out that the spider also

---

19   Daniel C. Dennett, *Consciousness Explained* (London: Penguin, 1991), p. 418.
20   *Ibid.*
21   *Ibid.*, p. 416.

feeds on insects and the 'vermin of its age', otherwise it would not be able to make its web.[22] In this way, the methods of the bee and the spider are perhaps not as irreconcilable as Swift's fable suggests.

Without making reference to Swift, but building on Dennett, Andy Clark continues to develop the metaphor: 'The spider's web appears as a proper part of the spider's extended phenotype', which he compares to the extended mind. 'This perspective [...] is not compulsory, nor can it be simply proved (or disproved) by experiment. Its virtues lie rather in the ways of seeing familiar phenomena that it may breed, in that flip of perspective that invites us to view the larger organism-environment system in new and illuminating ways'.[23]

At first sight, intertextuality may seem anything but part of the Dennettian 'narrative selfhood' if one sees intertextuality as mere allusions to *other* people's writings, that is, not one's own writings. But if one sees consciousness in terms of the extensive mind, which is 'constitutively [...] world-involving' (cf. supra) then intertextuality is a natural component of this narrative selfhood.[24] Since modernists and late modernists are famous for their attempts to evoke the workings of the human mind, it is not a coincidence that intertextuality plays such an important role in their writings. Even though Beckett tried to work in a completely different way from Joyce's method, there is something fundamental about intertextuality that he did learn from Joyce. When they evoke the workings of the human mind, they do not *represent* it. Beckett's texts are not a representation of the experience of life; they are that experience itself. This aspect of his work accords with Joyce's 'Work in Progress', about which Beckett famously wrote: 'Here form *is* content, content *is* form. [...] His writing is not *about* something; *it is that something itself*'.[25] The same applies to Beckett's texts, to a large extent because of their subdued intertextuality: the intertext is not *about* a cognitive process, it 'is' that cognitive process itself.

---

22 Jonathan Swift, *A Tale of a Tub and Other Works* (Oxford: Oxford University Press, 1986), p. 112.
23 Andy Clark, 'Embodied', p. 287.
24 Hutto and Myin, *Radicalizing Enactivism*, p. 137.
25 Samuel Beckett, *Disjecta* (New York: Grove Press, 1984), p. 27 (emphasis in the original).

Exogenetic digital editing and the extensive mind

What digital scholarly editing can contribute to this combination of cognitive narratology and Genetic Criticism is the means to show how intertextuality functions as a model of the extensive mind. This requires an approach to scholarly digital editing that integrates the author's personal library. An integrated library—which could be seen as a step towards what Peter Shillingsburg called a 'knowledge site'—can contain both the author's extant library (the books that are still preserved, possibly featuring marginalia) and the reconstructed library (the books, newspapers, magazines, pamphlets that are no longer physically extant, but which we know the author read, thanks to notes he or she made in notebooks).

This integration of the library in an edition works best in an edition that is not limited to a single work, but encompasses the author's entire oeuvre. The advantage is that it allows researchers to map intertextual patterns and reconstruct the way one particular passage from one particular source recurs in several works; or, the other way round: how a particular passage in one of the author's works is the result of a complex combination of intertexts, including references to other texts within his or her own oeuvre.

Most genetic editions focus on what Raymonde Debray Genette called the 'endogenesis', 'la réécriture des documents' or the writing and revision process. A state-of-the-art example of the way in which this process can be visualised is Julie André and Elena Pierazzo's prototype for a genetic edition of Marcel Proust's manuscripts.[26] This prototype also illustrates the current focus on a *document-oriented* approach to genetic editing, linked to the materiality of the document (e.g. proceeding page by page in the case of a notebook or 'cahier'). This endogenetic aspect of digital genetic editing can be relevant to cognitive scientists as it maps the author's interaction with the direct environment, not just the writing surface, but also the text produced so far.

In addition to this focus on endogenesis, however, a genetic edition may also be expected to map the relationships between the endogenetic and the exogenetic dimensions of the writing process. The inclusion

---

26 Julie André and Elena Pierazzo, 'Le Codage en TEI des Brouillons de Proust: Vers L'Edition Numérique', *Genesis*, 36 (2013), 155–61.

of this exogenetic dimension opens up another aspect of the writer's environment, presenting intertextuality as a form of 'enactivism' at work. Next to the document-oriented approach, this integration of exogenesis also requires a textual orientation that is flexible enough to also include an *intertext*-oriented approach, enabling readers to compare textual versions of any passage, including the (often elliptic) early versions of marginalia or reading notes.

Inevitably, the integration of a writer's library in an edition raises several questions. A writer's library is part of what S. E. Gontarski dubbed the 'grey canon'.[27] If the published works are the 'black' canon (e.g. printed in books, black on white), the grey canon consists of related items (e.g. manuscripts, letters, biographical information, interviews, productions notes, marginalia, reading notes etc.). One of the characteristics of many writers' libraries is that some of the extant books have clearly been used for the writing of a particular work, whereas others may simply have been sitting on the author's shelves without ever having been read (Thomas Mann's library, for instance, features a copy of Joyce's *Finnegans Wake*, but only a few pages have been cut). The presence or absence of a book in the extant library is usually less meaningful for literary research than the traceable engagement with the source text and its functional incorporation in the endogenesis.

Writers' libraries and the canon's shades of grey

To some degree, it is possible to measure this intensity and develop a scale to indicate this measure. At the Centre for Manuscript Genetics at the University of Antwerp, we work with a 'grey scale' for writers' libraries, adding various shades to the notion of the 'grey canon'. This grey scale is adaptable to different projects, depending on the degree to which the digital scholarly edition is set up to incorporate the author's library. If the editor decides to include it only to a very limited extent, this library can for instance be reduced to the darkest shades in the grey scale, i.e. only those books that (1) are still extant in the author's personal library, (2) contain marginalia and/or have demonstrably been

---

27   S. E. Gontarski, 'Greying the Canon: Beckett in Performance', in *Beckett After Beckett*, ed. by S. E. Gontarski and Anthony Uhlman (Gainesville: University Press of Florida, 2006), pp. 141–57.

read by the author (e.g. because his or her reading notes are preserved in a notebook) and (3) have been used or are being alluded to in one of his or her works (this category can be further subdivided into smaller categories such as 'explicit' and 'implicit' references, resulting in a more refined grey scale with extra shades).

An example that would qualify for inclusion in such a limited version of Samuel Beckett's library is his copy of *Immanuel Kants Werke*, the complete works of Kant, edited with an essay (in the last volume) by Ernst Cassirer. In this essay, Cassirer explains that the motto of the *Critique of Pure Reason*, 'De nobis ipsis silemus' [We do not talk about ourselves], was taken from Francis Bacon: 'Das Wort "*De nobis ipsis silemus*", das er aus Bacon entnimmt, um es der "Kritik der reinen Vernunft" als Motto voranzuzetzen, tritt nun mehr und mehr in Kraft' [The phrase 'De nobis ipsis silemus', which he takes from Bacon as the epigraph to the 'Critique of Pure Reason', is becoming increasingly apt].[28]

Beckett was not only a 'marginalist', but also what Daniel Ferrer has termed an 'extractor':[29] in addition to marking this passage in the margin, he jotted it down in his 'Whoroscope' Notebook (UoR MS 300, 44r) towards the end of the 1930s. Then, after the war, he wrote it again on the inside of the back cover of the notebook containing the first draft of *L'Innommable*: 'De nobis ipsis silemus (Bacon, Intro. Novum Organon)' (HRC MS SB 3/10, inside back cover). This note can be seen as the pivot between exo- and endogenesis in this particular case, for Beckett subsequently incorporated it in the draft itself, on page 44v of the same notebook: '*De nobis ipsis silemus*, décidément cela aurait dû être ma devise' [*De nobis ipsis silemus*, decidedly that should have been my motto] (HRC MS SB 3/10, 44v) — which is of course very ironic, since the Unnamable (the narrator/narrated) is constantly talking about the self. In addition to incorporating digital facsimiles of *Kants Werke* — or at least the relevant pages — in a scholarly edition (a document-oriented approach), one could consider including *paralipomena* such as the note

---

28 Ernst Cassirer, 'Kants Leben und Lehre' in: *Immanuel Kants Werke*, I–XI, ed. by Ernst Cassirer (Berlin: Bruno Cassirer, 1921–1922), XI, pp. 1–385 (p. 5).
29 Daniel Ferrer, 'Towards a Marginalist Economy of Textual Genesis', *Variants: The Journal of the European Society for Textual Scholarship*, 2–3 (2004), pp. 7–8 (7–18).

'De nobis ipsis silemus (Bacon, Intro. Novum Organon)' in a synoptic survey of all the versions (a text-oriented approach). Although the word *paralipomenon* is derived from the Greek 'para-leipen', meaning 'what is left out', the *Samuel Beckett Digital Manuscript Project* does include it in the 'compare sentences' option (which enables readers to view all the versions of any sentence synoptically) to enrich the document- and text-oriented approaches with an intertextual dimension (Fig. 6.1).

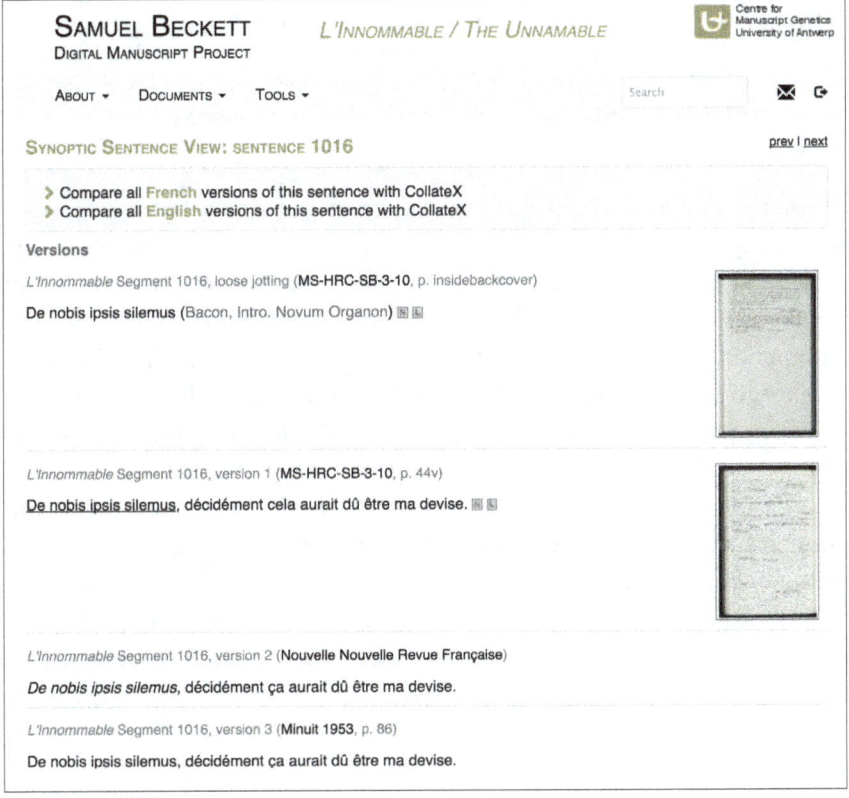

Fig. 6.1 Screenshot of the 'compare versions' option in the *Samuel Beckett Digital Manuscript Project*, module 2 (*BDMP2*), *Samuel Beckett's* L'Innommable/The Unnamable: *A Digital Genetic Edition*, ed. by Dirk Van Hulle, Shane Weller and Vincent Neyt (2013; http://www.beckettarchive.org).

From a cognitive perspective, the relevance of including these paralipomena in spite of the etymological suggestion to leave them out of a scholarly edition is that precisely these notes, marginalia and paralipomena (fragments of text that relate to, but are not strictly speaking part of, any version of the work) have the potential to visualise the 'extensive mind' at work. Excluding intertextual paralipomena from an edition is the equivalent of what Hutto and Myin call the 'Senior Partner Principle' (in the context of cognitive philosophy):

> To suppose that what is constitutive of mentality must reside in organisms or their brains alone is to endorse a Senior Partner Principle holding that, although a partnership with environmental factors may be causally necessary for cognition, the organism's or system's brain 'wears the trousers' in the relationship; only brains bring mentality to the party. In the place of this, we promote the more even-handed Equal Partner Principle as the right way to understand basic mental activity. Accordingly, contributions of the brain are not prioritized over those of the environment.[30]

Similarly, genetic editing has a tendency to focus on what is supposed (allegedly) to derive directly from the author's 'brain': the endogenesis. What a document-oriented, page-by-page mapping of the manuscript shows is that even this limited environment plays a role in the interaction that constitutes the extensive mind. Combining this with a text- and intertext-oriented approach can broaden the scope of this environmental interaction, and thus draw attention to the extensiveness of the creative mind at work. In conclusion, incorporating the exogenesis (e.g. by means of the writer's library) in a digital scholarly edition could be a way of including (at least some of) the 'environmental factors' that helped shape his or her work, thus promoting what Hutto and Myin call an 'Equal Partner Principle', in which endogenesis is not prioritised over exogenetic contributions from the author's cultural environment.[31]

---

30   Hutto and Myin, *Radicalizing Enactivism*, p. 137.
31   The research leading to these results has received funding from the Leverhulme Trust (Visiting Professorship at the University of Kent's School of European Culture and Languages) and from the European Research Council under the European Union's Seventh Framework Programme (FP7/2007–2013)/ERC grant agreement no. 313609.

7. Reading or Using a Digital Edition? Reader Roles in Scholarly Editions

Krista Stinne Greve Rasmussen

Hans Walter Gabler has said: 'We read texts in their native print medium, that is, in books; but we study texts and works in editions—in editions that live in the digital medium'.[1] This account of the difference between reading and studying texts is a fitting point of departure for the present chapter. On Gabler's account, texts should be read in their original media, but they are better studied in editions; and in today's publishing scene, scholarly editions live on in the digital medium, where the relationship between texts and works can better unfold and so be studied. This, at least, appears to be the general view in the publishing world, where many assumptions about the scholarly edition's digital potential derive from Peter Shillingsburg's descriptions of 'knowledge sites'.[2]

The quotation from Gabler indicates three key factors at work in modern scholarly editions: the shift from print to digital media, the relation between texts and editions, and, last but not least, the relationship between reading and studying. These factors can be defined as three basic assumptions that will always govern, to some degree, the work of textual studies. Although these basic assumptions affect the concept of

---

1   Hans Walter Gabler, 'Theorizing the Digital Scholarly Edition', *Literature Compass*, 7 (2010), 43–56 (p. 46), http://dx.doi.org/10.1111/j.1741-4113.2009.00675.x
2   Peter Shillingsburg, *From Gutenberg to Google: Electronic Representations of Literary Texts* (Cambridge: Cambridge University Press, 2006).

text, the shift in media and the reader, scholarly editors are not always conscious of how they approach these assumptions. Nor are they aware of how their work is affected by them.

The shift in media can be interpreted as a phase in the history of scholarly editing. During this phase, both the work of publishing scholarly editions and the editions themselves have been influenced by new media, affecting both working practices and the editions' actual forms of publication. Such changes have obviously been influenced by the possibilities for storage, manipulation and distribution that new media have introduced. Yet it is possible that these changes have been driven less by the concrete use of new media than by assumptions about their potential.

The relationship between text and work is a crucial distinction that often goes unexamined, despite the fact that it clearly affects the process of publishing scholarly editions. In what follows, a possible distinction between, and definition of, the concepts of *text* and *work* will be suggested, as these concepts are central to assumptions about both the reader and the user's possibilities in digital scholarly editions. The concepts of work and text are significant to readers because they, as readers, simultaneously operate on both an interpretive level and a manipulative level. This has led to the proposed definition of three *reader roles*—reader, user and co-worker—that can be adopted by readers of scholarly editions. Referring to these levels or modalities as *reader roles* emphasises, first of all, that taking up such a role presupposes certain conditions of possibility, and secondly, that even within such roles it is possible to be in and out of character. By working with these three categories of reader roles, a ground is prepared for a more precise discussion of whether (or, perhaps more accurately, of when) we are *reading* or *using* a scholarly edition, for the very act of studying such editions necessitates that we adopt both roles.

The concept of text

In many ways, the concept of text constitutes the core task of scholarly publishing. It governs both how we transfer texts to scholarly editions and how the editions themselves organise and display the texts they contain. Whereas uncertainty or disagreement about the definition of text can be said to prevail in literary studies,³ within the field of scholarly publishing we find a differently reflective notion of text. Here our concept of text not only governs our acts of transcription and markup,⁴ but is also decisive for our mode of perceiving the finished product.

If we return to the initial quotation from Hans Walter Gabler, in which he describes the digital scholarly edition as the best site for the study of works and texts, we find that his argument rests on a conception of text and work as two separate entities. A work is an immaterial entity that serves as a gathering point for all the texts that we classify under a certain title.⁵ Thus there exists no one-to-one correspondence between text and work. The latter fact is often exemplified by means of the distinction between stationary and sequential works: stationary works (such as paintings and sculptures) are conceived in space, while sequential works (such as literature and music) are conceived in time.⁶ Put another way, while stationary works generally have a single original, which can be described as both a work and its manifestation in one, sequential works as a rule comprise several instantiations, i.e. multiple texts that belong to the same work.

The text may be described as a recording or inscription that represents the work. It is important to emphasise that there does not necessarily exist any temporal relation between work and text. The work does not necessarily precede the text; it is not an *a priori* Platonic idea. The concept *work* does not presuppose the existence of an original idea that springs from to the author's intentions; it is, rather, an *a posteriori* category that

---

3   Johnny Kondrup, 'Tekst og værk — et begrebseftersyn', in *Betydning & forståelse: Festskrift til Hanne Ruus*, ed. by Dorthe Duncker, Anne Mette Hansen and Karen Skovgaard-Petersen (Copenhagen: Selskab for nordisk filologi, 2013), pp. 65–76.

4   Edward Vanhoutte, 'Prose Fiction and Modern Manuscripts: Limitations and Possibilities of Text Encoding for Electronic Editions', in *Electronic Textual Editing*, ed. by Lou Burnard, Katherine O'Brien O'Keeffe and John Unsworth (New York: Modern Language Association of America, 2006), pp. 161–80 (p. 171).

5   Johnny Kondrup, *Editionsfilologi* (Copenhagen: Museum Tusculanum Press, 2011), p. 34; Mats Dahlström, *Under utgivning: Den vetenskapliga utgivningens bibliografiska funktion* (Borås: Valfrid, 2006), p. 61.

6   The divide between stationary and sequential works originated in G. E. Lessing's 1766 essay *Laocoön*, but was further developed by G. Thomas Tanselle, from whom the Swedish bibliographer Rolf E. DuRietz derived it. DuRietz's book can serve as a basic reference book for bibliographical terminology. Rolf E. DuRietz, *Den tryckta skriften: Termer och begrepp: Grunderna till bibliografin, för biblioteken och antikvariaten, för bibliografer och textutgivare, för bokhistoriker och boksamlare* (Uppsala: Dahlia Books, 1999), p. 35.

we use to assemble various texts that all belong to the same work. That is to say, we have access to a work only through its texts, which serve as the basis for our readings and interpretations. Naturally, there may be works whose texts have gone missing, or which no longer exist. We can certainly talk about such works, but we cannot subject them to textual analysis or scholarly publication, which is our intention here. A revised second edition of a work, i.e. a new version, still belongs to the same work and in a sense expands it. But if new versions have variations that differ substantially enough from the previous ones, then we can speak of the emergence of a new work. Still, the boundaries are fluid here; only concrete individual assessments can determine whether it is appropriate to speak of a new work.

The text is not a homogenous entity. Rather, it exists on several partly independent levels. One can differentiate between three levels: ideal text, real text and material text.[7] The ideal text is an abstraction constructed on the basis of the real text, to which we have direct access through a material text, which is the materialisation of a text on a printed page or a screen. Thus the material text is not, strictly speaking, a text itself; it is a physical substrate attached to a material document. In printed texts, for example, the material text is the combination of ink and paper. In the case of digital texts, the relationship is more intricate; it can be debated whether the concept of material text may be used for the physical bits of a file, or for the appearance of the text on a screen. Finally, the designation *document* is also relevant when working with the concepts of work and text. When it comes to printed books, the document is simply 'the material bearer of one or more real texts'.[8] In print, a document serves both as a vehicle of representation (storage of the material text) and presentation (viewing of the real text); whereas these functions are separate for digital documents. When considering digital documents, one should also include the hardware and software that make presentation possible.[9]

---

[7] This schema of three levels and their definitions is indebted to the following authors: Kondrup, *Editionsfilologi*, pp. 36–38; Dahlström, *Under utgivning*, pp. 63–70; and DuRietz, *Den tryckta skriften*, pp. 41–53. Kondrup employs the same concepts that are introduced here.

[8] Kondrup, *Editionsfilologi*, p. 38 [my translation].

[9] Dahlström, *Under utgivning*, p. 72.

The interrelationship between work, text and document thus needs to be clarified, since it is crucial for the praxis of scholarly publishing. The goals that scholarly editors pursue reflect their approaches to each of these three entities. Gabler articulates this point as follows: 'For that product of criticism and humanities scholarship, the scholarly edition, the central question arises how it could, or should, relate to the reader's quest for the meaning of a work in and through a text'.[10] The reader, in other words, pursues an interpretation and understanding of the relevant work through a reading of particular texts. But it is never one single text that gives access to the work; rather, it is customary to regard the work as the sum of its texts.[11] It is indeed texts, rather than works, that are revised for publication in scholarly editions. The text of a scholarly edition is not necessarily the text that best represents the original work—although one might wish that were the case, as it is always only one among many textual representations of the work.[12]

It is the scholarly edition that relates most critically and reflectively to the relations between the work and its texts. But the text of the scholarly edition is always the scholarly editor's text, since the scrutiny of textual scholarship itself always represents another interpretation of the work. Scholarly publishing has long since abandoned the ideals of positivism; the editor's activity is no longer regarded as isolated from current research paradigms or theoretical constraints. Ultimately, the editor's explicit presence in the text helps to lend authority to the scholarly edition.[13] In digital scholarly editions, however, the editor's mark may at times seem blurred as a result of the encoding process. But the digital organisation and markup of such editions is just as much a product of the editor's interpretation and explicit intentions.

---

10 Hans Walter Gabler, 'Thoughts on Scholarly Editing', 2011, pp. 1–16 (p. 12), http://nbn-resolving.de/urn:nbn:de:0222-001542
11 Kondrup, *Editionsfilologi*, p. 34; Gabler, 'Thoughts on Scholarly Editing', p. 9; and Peter Shillingsburg, 'How Literary Works Exist: Implied, Represented, and Interpreted', in *Text and Genre in Reconstruction: Effects of Digitalization on Ideas, Behaviours, Products and Institutions*, ed. by Willard McCarty (Cambridge: Open Book Publishers, 2010), pp. 165–82 (p. 171), http://dx.doi.org/10.11647/OBP.0008
12 Gabler, 'Thoughts on Scholarly Editing', p. 9.
13 Mats Dahlström, 'The Compleat Edition', in *Text Editing, Print and the Digital World*, ed. by Marilyn Deegan and Kathryn Sutherland (Farnham: Ashgate, 2009), pp. 27–44 (p. 11).

The media shift

The 'media shift' addressed in this section is specifically defined in terms of the transition from print to digital online scholarly editions. Naturally, digital editions can also include editions published on external storage media, such as CD-ROM. The latter present an interesting intermediate stage, inasmuch as they are physically collected in a medium that is situated in the user's direct possession; but they will be left out of the present discussion, since they differ in status, ontologically speaking, from internet-based editions. Thus references to digital editions in what follows designate digital editions that are exclusively available online.

The media shift has also altered our notions of how a scholarly edition can represent the texts of a published work. A scholarly edition in print, one might say, is a complete and singular object in the world: the results of scholarly effort are locked in a printed edition that can be conceived of as completed and closed. The publisher or editors have completed a scholarly effort whose outcome can be accessed using the edition, which is frozen in time (the date of publication) and space (the physical edition). From this spatiotemporal point onward, such an edition's textual representation of the work can inscribe itself into the work's reception history, including the history of research about the work. Naturally, the original edition may be replaced by new and revised editions; but the original will always remain a unique statement about the work, constituting one among its many textual versions. Moreover, as mentioned above, it composes a statement that can be attributed to the edition's editor.

Digital scholarly editions, by contrast, have features that are practically the opposite of those of print editions. Digital scholarly editions are seemingly incomplete, ambiguous objects; certainly they can be frozen in the form of archived copies of the entire website, but in practice they are open to alteration in a much easier way than printed editions. To describe the difference between the two, Gabler distinguishes between information sites, which are composed of serially arranged collections in books, and knowledge sites, which are 'relational' and express 'creatively participatory intelligence'. Put another way, a knowledge site is 'a genuine research site'.[14] The concept of knowledge site is drawn

---

14 Gabler, 'Thoughts on Scholarly Editing', p. 15.

from Peter Shillingsburg's 2006 book *From Gutenberg to Google*, but is also found in earlier descriptions by Paul Eggert (the 'work site'),[15] and Peter Robinson, who label them 'fluid, collaborative, and distributed editions'[16] and 'interactive editions', respectively.[17] These designations for knowledge sites differ in their descriptions of what a knowledge site is, much as they use different names for them. But the starting point is still the same. Knowledge sites must take advantage of digital media's possibilities; they must give the reader the opportunity to interact with the edition. They are open, dynamic and interactive, as in the following description by Shillingsburg:

> Textual archives serve as a base for scholarly editions which serve in tandem with every other sort of literary scholarship to create knowledge sites of current and developing scholarship that can also serve as pedagogical tools in an environment where each user can choose an entry way, select a congenial set of enabling contextual materials, and emerge with a personalized interactive form of the work [...] always able to plug in for more information or different perspectives.[18]

Knowledge sites can thus better identify the relationship between the work's texts and other texts that relate to the work. In addition, they represent an unfinished research environment, facilitating readings that never end.

The ideal of the knowledge site is marked by a high degree of optimism about progress. In this view, the Internet can be a catalyst for scholarly studies, allowing scholars to engage more easily and personally in free knowledge exchange, with the user at the centre. Here we see traces of the ideology of freedom that commonly informs conceptions of digital media. Indeed, the ideologies of the Internet as a whole do not differ measurably from those bound up in the concept of the knowledge site. One can say that the knowledge site is a micro-Internet, and that both are based on the expectation that all relevant

---

15 Paul Eggert, 'Text-Encoding, Theories of the Text, and the 'Work-Site', *Literary & Linguistic Computing*, 20 (2005), 425–35, http://dx.doi.org/10.1093/llc/fqi050
16 Peter Robinson, 'Where We Are with Electronic Scholarly Editions, and Where We Want to Be', *Jahrbuch für Computerphilologie*, 5 (2003), http://computerphilologie.uni-muenchen.de/jg03/robinson.html
17 Peter Robinson, 'The Ends of Editing', *DHQ: Digital Humanities Quarterly*, 3 (2009) http://digitalhumanities.org/dhq/vol/3/3/000051/000051.html
18 Shillingsburg, *From Gutenberg to Google*, p. 88.

information can be gathered in a single place. With respect to scholarly editions, the expectation is to collect all knowledge of a work or an author in a single edition. The question, of course, is how much size really matters. There are good reasons not to let oneself get carried away completely with such optimism, and instead to ask certain basic critical questions about the object and purpose of these scholarly editions.

While scholarly editions may serve a variety of purposes, they share a common goal of facilitating study of the works that they reproduce. The aim is thus not simply to produce an edition, which amounts to conducting a research project; the aim is just as much to produce an edition for a specific intended audience. For this reason, scholarly editions tend to define their audiences in terms of various user groups—an initial manoeuvre that has not been altered by the media shift. Whereas one formerly spoke only of readers, the media shift has now introduced the reader as a user, but without drawing the requisite distinction between the two.

Reader roles

Our concept of text plays a significant role in how we theorise digital scholarly editions' possibilities for reading. The media shift, meanwhile, has had a decisive influence on how the theoretical conception of reading can be deployed in practice. I have chosen to work with a model that includes three reader roles: reader, user and co-worker. This model stems from reflections on the scholarly edition as a knowledge site, inasmuch as knowledge sites grant their readers the opportunity to participate in the publication of research. Meanwhile, in the wake of the media shift, readers have come to be called users just as often as readers—and that in itself is a change worth reflecting on. There can be no doubt that one who reads books is also a user, but he or she is a user whose handling of the medium has become transparent, since he or she has been trained in the medium over a lifetime. With the transition to digital editions it is therefore relevant to discuss the various interpretive levels of the scholarly edition and their relation to the reader. The aim here is not to devise a universal model for reading the text, but to try to theorise the distinctive mode of reading literary works that takes place within a scholarly edition.

The *reader* is mainly interested in scholarly editions as reliable academic versions of literary works. Such a reader will seek to interpret and understand the work in and through the texts of a scholarly edition. The degree of interpretation can vary, from the pleasure reading of an ordinary interested reader to a professional reader's deeper hermeneutical interpretation. The reader operates at a level where the focus is primarily on the relation between text and work. Nevertheless, the reader can also benefit from the edition's other texts, which could be called paratexts,[19] though that is open to debate. These may include introductions and notes, where they can contribute to a better understanding of the work.

The *user* also seeks an understanding of the work, but in a more intertextual context, where stress is placed either on the relation between the work's numerous texts and versions, or on the relation between the work's own texts and other texts that explain or relate to the work. The latter texts could be explanatory notes, general commentaries, or textual notes and lists of variants. The user may also be interested in the work's history of transmission, that is, in its various manifestations over time. All in all, what is in focus is the entire text-concept's three-part division into work, text(s) and original document(s). When the reader acts as a user of the edition, the emphasis is mainly on the edition's own structure and organisation: on how to use its individual parts, whether these are the texts themselves or the tools that can be used on them.

The *co-worker* seeks to go beyond the user and reader roles, and to contribute actively to the scholarly enterprise. This reader role could also have been called *contributor* or the like, but the term co-worker signals that, ideally speaking, the reader in this role is likely to take part in the editorial work at some level. This could consist of making annotations, reading proofs, adding encodings, or contributing in other ways to the site's total production of knowledge. The co-worker's contribution, in short, does not merely amount to additions or extensions, but forms a genuine part of the edition.[20]

These reader roles are neither definitive nor exclusive. They should rather be regarded as modalities — which the reader can inhabit

---

19 Gérard Genette, *Paratexts: Thresholds of Interpretation*, trans. by Jane E. Lewin (Cambridge: Cambridge University Press, 1997).
20 See the chapter by Ray Siemens et al. in the present volume.

simultaneously, even all three at once. Nevertheless, there is an order of progression to these roles, in the sense that one must be a reader in order to be able to be a user, and one must be both a reader and a user in order to be able to be a co-worker. Indeed, the role of co-worker presupposes considerable commitment to and knowledge of the work at issue: in order to contribute actively to the edition's production of knowledge, it is necessary to have prior knowledge of both the scholarly edition and the published work. To be sure, one can imagine situations in which one could contribute to an edition without knowing the work — as when transcriptions or encodings are crowdsourced. But in such a case we would be dealing with a contributor, rather than with a reader inhabiting a reader role. And it is entirely conceivable that a contributor might, for example, be participating in a project involving texts that he or she cannot read at all.

Reader roles are a function of how we manipulate and interpret an edition's texts, and so fulfilling each role involves action at two levels: the level of manipulation and the level of interpretation. In the wake of the media shift, the physical manipulation of an edition's documents has received increased attention. With printed books, physical manipulation goes more or less unarticulated, since it has become an integrated cultural habit. But when the medium takes centre stage, as occurred during the media shift, it can become unmanageable and problematic for the reader. At the same time, new media also make it possible to do things in new ways. They pave the way for discussions of what a digital scholarly edition actually is and can become — of which this anthology is an example.

In a 2008 article, Bertrand Gervais distinguishes among three levels of reading in relation to digital texts: the level of manipulation, focused on the handling of texts and on their actual acquisition; next the level of comprehension, directed at reading as an understanding of the linguistic text itself; and finally the level of interpretation, in which connections are drawn between the text and other texts that explain it.[21] In the article, Gervais discusses e-literature, which moves us (he claims) from a logic of discovery to a logic of revelation, in which knowledge

---

21 Bertrand Gervais, 'Is There a Text on This Screen? Reading in an Era of Hypertextuality', in *Companion to Digital Literary Studies*, ed. by Ray Siemens and Susan Schreibman (Oxford: Blackwell, 2008), http://www.digitalhumanities.org/companionDLS

and information are not arrived at by discovering meaningful similarities between texts on one's own, but are *given* to us by means of the hyperlink, as a revelation. This is because the connection between the two texts is already given to us by another, allowing us—thanks to the hyperlink—to move quickly and easily through the network of texts that the Internet as a whole represents. With the hyperlink's advent, meaning is revealed. And this turns the reader into a user, since responsibility for the discoveries rests with the one who has added the hyperlink, not the one who has activated it.

Gervais discusses e-literature, particularly hyperfictions, which are marked by their use of the hyperlink's logic of revelation as an explicit literary tool. Hypertext literature makes the hyperlink into an organising principle, so that the plot, action and progression of the literary work are determined by the reader's choice among various links. But Gervais' argumentation is also interesting in relation to scholarly editions, because even those in book form can readily be regarded as hyperlink-structured. After all, a printed note apparatus is comparable to hyperlinks; and indeed the hyperlink was first introduced, in the literature, as a generalised footnote.[22] The scholarly edition thus represents Gervais' logic of revelation par excellence. By virtue of the scholarly edition, the editor reveals relationships to the reader: not only relationships among the various texts that belong to the work, but also those between them and other texts related to the work.

My point is not that the universe of digital texts simply turns readers into users. Gervais' three levels (manipulation, comprehension and interpretation) do not function in quite the same way as do my three reader roles. Instead, one might say that each reader role contains all three of Gervais' levels, which serve as the foundation for every successful reading of literature. The reader must always act on all three of Gervais' levels, manipulation, comprehension and interpretation; but once the reader has taken up one of the three reader roles in relation to a scholarly edition, then it will mainly be the work, its texts and the edition (or website) that the reader, user or co-worker will respectively focus on. In all three reader roles, documents must be manipulated, and texts must be read and decoded. But for the reader *qua* reader it does not matter whether there are opportunities to contribute to the

---

22   Jakob Nielsen, *Hypertext and Hypermedia* (Boston: Academic Press, 1990), p. 2.

edition, or whether the page includes extra materials such as timelines, analyses etc. What mainly matters to the reader is that such features do not interfere with or impede the reading. This can be assured, for example, by allowing readers to download the edition. This is the case with *Henrik Ibsens Skrifter*, the online collected works of Henrik Ibsen.[23]

It should not be necessary to point out that the term 'physical documents' naturally also includes digital documents. Discussion of the concept of materiality would take us too far afield, so let a reference to Matthew Kirschenbaum's excellent analysis of the materiality of digital texts in *Mechanisms: New Media and the Forensic Imagination* suffice.[24] A distinction is often drawn between media in which representation and presentation are joined or separate. A printed book, for example, contains both representation and presentation, and so requires no external hardware or software in order to be read. Digital texts, on the other hand, just as was the case with LPs and CDs, are in a sense mere stored data, and require an external playback medium in order to be played. Indeed, this is the heart of the matter: digital texts cannot be read without playback. On the other hand, occasions where playback is a problem have become less and less frequent; as a result, the presentation of texts is not necessarily experienced as separate from their representation. With respect to digital editions, it may be said that as long as there is access to the Internet and to the site that houses the edition, there is also access to both storage and display of the documents. Even if there are technical problems with the display, it is still the case that once the reader has gained access to the edition, it reaches the reader as a package.

The difference between print and digital lies in our phenomenological understanding of a document. The physical book is present to us as a full-fledged object in the world even when we are not reading it. When we hold a printed book in our hands, even its unseen dimensions— e.g. the back cover—are present to us, and form a part of our overall phenomenological experience.[25] Digital texts, on the other hand,

---

23 *Henrik Ibsens Skrifter*, http://www.ibsen.uio.no/forside.xhtml
24 Matthew Kirschenbaum, *Mechanisms: New Media and the Forensic Imagination* (Cambridge, MA: MIT Press, 2008).
25 Anne Mangen, 'Hypertext Fiction Reading: Haptics and Immersion', *Journal of Research in Reading*, 31 (2008), 404–19 (p. 408), http://dx.doi.org/10.1111/j.1467-9817.2008.00380.x

are given to us only partially and piecemeal while we have them on our screens. At the same time, one may say that the hyperlink structure complicates our immersion in the texts, because we feel a psychological need to pursue the distractions offered by the links. Anne Mangen speaks of 'the urge to click', and explains: 'In order for phenomenological immersion to be obtained, our cognitive capacity needs to be more or less fully occupied in a cohering and consistent way so that we do not experience any perceptual or cognitive surplus of attention available to other tasks'.[26] The urge to click can easily become too tempting to resist, if we are cognitively or perceptually stimulated with possibilities that seem more exciting than what we are presently focused on. Knowledge sites have a wealth of potentials that can risk disrupting our phenomenological preoccupation with them, thereby limiting the possibility of hermeneutical reflection.[27]

Let us recall our initial quotation from Hans Walter Gabler. His point was precisely that works should be read not on knowledge sites, but on information sites, which he equates with printed books. His distinction seems correct, with the proviso that 'books' need not be printed. Books should be understood, instead, as phenomenologically limited devices that permit hermeneutical reflection. This means that there is no question of an ontological distinction between print and digital editions, but rather of a phenomenological distinction between finished and unfinished editions. The potential of knowledge sites is to develop relationships between the work, its text, and documents in a way that printed books cannot, because the individual parts cannot be put in direct contact with each other in the same way. Knowledge sites permit other types of studies of the scholarly edition than we have been accustomed to; and because they are dynamic, they can potentially be extended indefinitely, and so offer new paths into and out of the work. New versions of the work may be issued and offered to the reader, but these always will—or always should—stand side by side with previous versions as a series of standalone statements about the work. This means that when an editor issues a new or different edition, this new version does not overwrite the previous one—as might be the case with digital editions as a whole, for which updates to the site can delete and

---

26   *Ibid.*, p. 413.
27   *Ibid.*, p. 415.

replace previous versions. Of course, digital scholarly editions need not be knowledge sites, and can certainly be completed as research and scholarly publication projects; but they will always require some form of updating, or at least migration.

What seems to be needed is a more general discussion of the relation between scholarly editions *qua* research project and *qua* publication project. For example, when Shillingsburg states (in the citation provided earlier) that when it comes to knowledge sites, users can always go back online for more information, this is precisely because a knowledge site is a locus for continuous knowledge enhancement, much like a library or an archive. The same is true for digital editions that regularly publish new works. Research and reception are always in progress, a fact that may be relevant for the reader-as-user. However, for the reader-as-reader, it is not necessarily advantageous that the site on which the text is read changes continuously. Moreover, it is questionable to what extent the resources that are relevant to the user are at all of interest to the reader.

In his article 'Electronic Editions for Everyone', Peter Robinson points out that there are in fact very few readers who care to see all of a text's facsimiles, transcripts and collations.[28] Robinson argues that only very few readers have an interest in taking on the user role and making use of the resources made available to them; and this seems to be confirmed by Petra Söderlund's study of the actual use made of the information provided in variant apparatuses.[29] Söderlund found that information provided in the variant apparatuses included in Svenska Vitterhetssamfundet's editions is rarely deployed in arguments made in analyses of the works.

Sören A. Steding arrived at a similar result in his dissertation on *Computer-Based Scholarly Editions*. Steding conducted a survey of students and university staff on their use and knowledge of scholarly

---

28 Peter Robinson, 'Electronic Editions for Everyone', in *Text and Genre in Reconstruction: Effects of Digitalization on Ideas, Behaviours, Products and Institutions*, ed. by Willard McCarty (Cambridge: Open Book Publishers, 2010), pp. 145–63 (p. 150), http://dx.doi.org/10.11647/OBP.0008

29 Petra Söderlund, 'Tryckt eller elektronisk variantredovisning — Varför och för vem?', in *Digitala och tryckta utgåvor: Erfarenheter, planering och teknik i förändring*, ed. by Pia Forssell (Helsingfors: Svenska litteratursällskapet i Finland, 2011), pp. 93–109.

editions. Respondents were asked to describe, among other things, the motives that led them to select scholarly editions. The four reasons given most often were access to reliable texts, comments and annotations that facilitate comprehension, details of the published texts' bibliographic data and verification of quotations from published authors. Out of the ten possible answers, access to textual variants and use of manuscript facsimiles came in, respectively, sixth and tenth most frequently.[30] The question, then, is which of the reader's interests are being served with comprehensive, large-scale scholarly editions. For the readers, it is important to be able to use the texts to immerse themselves in the work. Authentic reading, therefore, requires a reliable edition that may not necessarily be the best textual representation of the work, but at least reflects the editor's own explicit statements and textual version. The reader needs a singular object in which the text can be read. For the user, on the other hand, it is interesting to explore the texts and relate them to one another and possibly to other texts. The user studies the work, rather than reading it; the co-worker takes part in the total knowledge production of the website that houses the edition.

So, do we read digital scholarly editions, or use them? The answer is obvious: we do both. While it can be useful to identify an explicit target audience as a starting-point for work on a scholarly edition, one should also take into account how readers can interact with the edition in these different roles, for how a work is made accessible to an audience is ultimately a question of how the texts are related to each other. Digital texts are material enough: they are neither ephemeral nor necessarily ever-changeable. But if digital editions are unfinished and open, then the relationship between the work's texts will be unfinished and open as well—a fact that will be of benefit to the user, but not necessarily to the reader.[31]

---

30 Sören A. Steding, *Computer-Based Scholarly Editions: Context, Concept, Creation, Clientele* (Berlin: Logos, 2002), p. 243.

31 This chapter has been translated from Danish by David Possen. The ideas and arguments presented here are further developed in my PhD thesis, 'Bytes, bøger og læsere: En editionshistorisk analyse af medieskiftet fra trykte til digitale videnskabelige udgaver med udgangspunkt i Søren Kierkegaards Skrifter' (Copenhagen: University of Copenhagen, 2015), http://forskning.ku.dk/find-en-forsker/?pure=files%2F131207090%2FPh.d._2015_Greve_Rasmussen.pdf

SECTION 2: PRACTICES

8. Building *A Social Edition of the Devonshire Manuscript*

Ray Siemens, Constance Crompton, Daniel Powell and Alyssa Arbuckle, with Maggie Shirley and the Devonshire Manuscript Editorial Group

The multivalent text of the Devonshire Manuscript

A Social Edition of the Devonshire Manuscript is an unconventional text: it blends traditional scholarly editing practices and standards with comparatively recent digital social media environments. In doing so, the edition aims to reflect both contemporary editorial theory, which recognises the inherently social form and formation of texts, as well as the writerly and readerly practices that shaped the original production of the Devonshire Manuscript (London, British Library, MS Add. 17492). Dating from the 1530s–1540s, the Devonshire Manuscript is a multi-authored verse miscellany compiled by a number of sixteenth-century contributors.[1] As an inherently collaborative document, the manuscript calls for a social investigation of its production. In this chapter, we detail

---

[1] Following Peter Beal's definition of a verse miscellany as 'a manuscript, a compilation of predominantly verse texts, or extracts from verse texts, by different authors and usually gleaned from different sources' in *A Dictionary of English Manuscript Terminology, 1450–2000* (Oxford: Oxford University Press, 2008), p. 429. Beal lists the Devonshire Manuscript as a pertinent example of a verse miscellany (Beal, *Dictionary*, p. 430).

the content, context, process and implications of *A Social Edition of the Devonshire Manuscript*.[2] We will begin with an exploration of the textual, paratextual and non-textual content of the Devonshire Manuscript. In section 2, we will focus on the process of building a social edition of the manuscript. To conclude, we will ruminate on the affordances of digital editing. Overall, we will consider how publishing in Wikibooks emphasises the collaborative, social ethos of the Devonshire Manuscript itself, and how in doing so we attempt to model the *social scholarly edition*.[3]

The Devonshire Manuscript, acquired in 1848 by the British Museum, contains approximately 200 items (the total sum of complete lyrics, verse fragments, excerpts from longer works, anagrams and other ephemeral jottings) bound in a handwritten volume and inscribed in over a dozen hands by a coterie of men and women gathered around the court of Queen Anne Boleyn.[4] Despite growing scholarly interest in the Devonshire Manuscript, no critical editions existed during the production of *A Social Edition of the Devonshire Manuscript*.[5] The manuscript has long been valued as a source of Sir Thomas Wyatt's poetry; 129 of the 200 items in the manuscript were composed (although not copied) by him. These verses, in turn, have been transcribed and published by Agnes K. Foxwell, Kenneth Muir and Patricia Thomson in their respective editions of Wyatt's poetry.[6] As scholar Arthur F.

---

2   http://en.wikibooks.org/wiki/The_Devonshire_Manuscript

3   Wikibooks is a Wikimedia project that continues the aim of Wikipedia; namely, to encourage, develop and disseminate knowledge in the public sphere. Wikibooks differs from other Wikimedia projects in that it is primarily designed for facilitating collaborative open-content textbook building.

4   On the origins, early history and enumeration of the Devonshire Manuscript, see especially Richard C. Harrier, *The Canon of Sir Thomas Wyatt's Poetry* (Cambridge, MA.: Harvard University Press, 1975), pp. 23–54; Raymond Southall, 'The Devonshire Manuscript Collection of Early Tudor Poetry, 1532–41', *Review of English Studies*, 15 (1964), 142–43; Paul Remley, 'Mary Shelton and Her Tudor Literary Milieu', in *Rethinking the Henrician Era: Essays on Early Tudor Texts and Contexts*, ed. by Peter C. Herman (Urbana: University of Illinois Press, 1994), pp. 40–77 (p. 41, pp. 47–48). See also Helen Baron, 'Mary (Howard) Fitzroy's Hand in the Devonshire Manuscript', *Review of English Studies*, 45 (1994), 318–35, and Elizabeth Heale, 'Women and the Courtly Love Lyric: The Devonshire MS (BL Additional 17492)', *Modern Language Review* 90.2 (1995), 297–301.

5   Elizabeth Heale's edition, *The Devonshire Manuscript: A Women's Book of Courtly Poetry* (Toronto: Centre for Reformation and Renaissance Studies, 2012), is based on a regularised version of the Devonshire Manuscript Editorial Group transcriptions of the manuscript and was published in October 2012.

6   *The Poems of Sir Thomas Wiat*, ed. by Agnes K. Foxwell (London: University of London Press, 1913); *Collected Poems of Sir Thomas Wyatt*, ed. by Kenneth Muir (London:

Marotti argues, however, the author-centred focus of these editions distorts the character of the Devonshire Manuscript in two ways: 'first, it unjustifiably draws the work of other writers into the Wyatt canon, and, second, it prevents an appreciation of the collection as a document illustrating some of the uses of lyric verse within an actual social environment'.[7] The Devonshire Manuscript is much more than an important witness in the Wyatt canon; it is also a snapshot into the scribal practices of male and female lyricists, scribes and compilers in the Henrician court.

A Social Edition of the Devonshire Manuscript seeks to publish the contents of the original manuscript in their entirety, move beyond the limitations of an author-centred focus on Wyatt's contributions and concentrate on the social, literary and historical contexts in which the volume is situated as a unified whole. In doing so, we remain mindful of the editorial theories championed by D. F. McKenzie and Jerome McGann (among others) that expand the notion of textual production beyond a simple consideration of authorial intention. For McGann, these 'nonauthorial textual determinants' should be considered alongside authorial presence to include in our critical gaze 'other persons or groups involved in the initial process of production', as well as the phases, stages, means, modes and materials of this initial production process.[8] D. F. McKenzie's call for a 'sociology of texts' further extends this concept of textual production by arguing for the significance of

---

Routledge and Kegan Paul, 1949); *Collected Poems of Sir Thomas Wyatt*, ed. by Kenneth Muir and Patricia Thomson (Liverpool: Liverpool University Press, 1969). Many of the remaining poems, unattributed to Wyatt, have been transcribed and published in Kenneth Muir, 'Unpublished Poems in the Devonshire Manuscript', *Proceedings of the Leeds Philosophical and Literary Society*, 6 (1947), 253–82. George Frederick Nott's important early two-volume edition, *The Works of Henry Howard, Earl of Surrey, and of Sir Thomas Wyatt, the Elder* (London: T. Bensley, 1815), does not include diplomatic transcriptions of verses.

7   Arthur F. Marotti, *Manuscript, Print, and the English Renaissance Lyric* (Ithaca: Cornell University Press, 1995), p. 40. Nott's misguided statement, that the manuscript 'contains Wyatt's pieces almost exclusively' (*Works*, p. vii), or Muir's comment, 'it is not always easy to decide whether a poem is written by a successful imitator or by Wyatt himself in an uninspired mood' (*Poems*, p. 253), are characteristic of the sort of dismissive author-centric views taken to task by Marotti.

8   Jerome McGann, 'The Monks and the Giants: Textual and Bibliographical Studies and the Interpretation of Literary Works', in *The Beauty of Inflections: Literary Investigations in Historical Method and Theory* (Oxford: Oxford University Press, 1988), pp. 79, 82. See also McGann's earlier study, *A Critique of Modern Textual Criticism* (Chicago: Chicago University Press, 1983).

the material form of a text and its ability to affect the text's meaning.[9] These theories have prompted critics to reevaluate the notion of authorship in order to account for nonauthorial (but nevertheless deeply significant) organisers, contributors and collaborators. Marotti's assertion, that 'literary production, reproduction and reception are all socially mediated, the resulting texts demanding attention in their own right and not just as legitimate or illegitimate variants from authorial archetypes', also reflects the changing landscape of editorial theory.[10] In keeping with McGann, McKenzie and Marotti, *A Social Edition of the Devonshire Manuscript* aims to preserve the socially mediated textual and extra-textual elements of the manuscript that have been elided or ignored in previous work. These ostensible 'paratexts' make significant contributions to the meaning and appreciation of the manuscript miscellany and its constituent parts: annotations, glosses, names, ciphers and various jottings. The telling proximity of one work to another, significant gatherings of materials, illustrations entered into the manuscript alongside the text and so forth all shape the way we understand the manuscript, but are often ignored when preparing scholarly editions.[11] To accomplish this goal, we have prepared a diplomatic transcription of the complete Devonshire Manuscript with extensive scholarly apparatus.

The manuscript collection consists of short courtly verses by Sir Thomas Wyatt (129 items, sixty-six unique to the manuscript) and Henry Howard, Earl of Surrey (one item); verses attributed to Lady Margaret Douglas (two items), Richard Hattfield (two items), Mary Fitzroy (née Howard) (one item), Lord Thomas Howard (three items), Sir Edmund Knyvett (two items), Sir Anthony Lee (one item; 'A. I'. has three items) and Henry Stewart, Lord Darnley (one item); transcribed portions of medieval verse by Geoffrey Chaucer (eleven items), Thomas Hoccleve (three items) and Richard Roos (two items); transcriptions of the work of others or original works by prominent court figures such as Mary Shelton, Lady Margaret Douglas, Mary (Howard) Fitzroy, Lord Thomas Howard and possibly Queen Anne Boleyn. Alongside these are some

---

9   D. F. McKenzie, *Bibliography and the Sociology of Texts* (London: British Library, 1986).
10 Marotti, *Manuscript, Print, and the English Renaissance Lyric*, p. 212.
11 We have interpreted 'paratext' broadly, as articulated in Gérard Genette, *Paratexts: Thresholds of Interpretation*, trans. by Jane E. Lewin (Cambridge: Cambridge University Press, 1997).

thirty unidentified or unattributed pieces.¹² These multiple contributors often comment on and evaluate each other's work through marginal notation and drawing, in-line interjection, exchanging epistolary verse and selectively altering transcribed texts.

A Social Edition of the Devonshire Manuscript follows Helen Baron's attribution of hands in the Devonshire Manuscript.¹³ Of the roughly twenty hands, some are even and regular while others are idiosyncratic and variable. Historically, the exceptional difficulty of transcribing the Devonshire Manuscript has impeded widespread research on the text. Approximately 140 entries are copies of extant or contemporary works and bear the signs of copying. The majority of the pieces may reflect the work of local amanuenses and secretaries with little professional regard for the expected standards of a presentation-copy manuscript. A full half of the manuscript's scribes (Hands 1, 3, 4, 5, 6, 8, 9, 10, 11 and Mary Howard Fitzroy) dedicate themselves to copying extant pieces; another five (Hands 1.1, 2, 7, Thomas Howard 2 and Margaret Douglas) enter a mix of extant material and material that appear unique to the manuscript. The remaining five (Hands 12, 13, Henry Stuart, Mary Shelton and Thomas Howard 1) enter solely original materials. The work of the ten hands entering potentially original material to the manuscript amounts to forty-five pieces (fifteen identified and/or attributed). The many layers and authors render the Devonshire Manuscript an ideal text for experimentation in social editing.

---

12 Scholars have only cautiously asserted an approximate number of items preserved in the Devonshire Manuscript: 'the number of poems in the manuscript can only be given as approximately 184' (Southall, 'The Devonshire Manuscript', p. 143); 'the manuscript preserves about 185 items of verse, but it is impossible to obtain an exact figure as many of these are fragments, medieval extracts or the like, and others are divided up differently by various editors' (Remley, 'Mary Shelton', p. 47). Ethel Seaton identified the medieval origin of the Richard Roos texts in 'The Devonshire Manuscript and its Medieval Fragments', *Review of English Studies*, 7 (1956), 55–56. Richard Harrier first noted the use of William Thynne's 1532 edition of Chaucer as the source for that poet's verse in the Devonshire Manuscript in 'A Printed Source for the "Devonshire Manuscript"', *Review of English Studies*, 11 (1960), 54.

13 See http://en.wikibooks.org/wiki/The_Devonshire_Manuscript/Detailed_Hand_List_Hand_1. The most recent examination of the hands in D is that of Helen Baron, especially Table 1 in 'Mary (Howard) Fitzroy's Hand'. See also the earlier findings in Edward A. Bond, 'Wyatt's Poems', *Athenaeum*, 27 (1871), 654–55. Where the transcribers differ from Baron's attribution, the project's identification is noted in the underlying TEI markup, http://hcmc.uvic.ca/~etcl/Devonshire_Manuscript_poems.zip

The manuscript itself bears traces of the original contributors' editorial processes. Besides writing epistolary verse, contributors to the manuscript interacted with one another through annotation. Occasionally, these marginal responses appear quite personal in nature. They include responses that evaluate the quality of certain lines or cross out one word and insert another. In doing so, the annotations reveal the compilers' social engagement and editorial collaboration. For example, the text of the poem 'Suffryng in sorow in hope to attayn' (fols 6v–7r; see Figure 8.1) is annotated in the left margin. A hand identified as Lady Margaret Douglas' writes 'fforget thys', to which a hand identified as Mary Shelton's responds, 'yt ys wor[t]hy' (fol. 6v). The poem is written in a male voice appealing for the love of a lady. 'Suffryng in sorow' and 'desyryng in fere', the poet pleads for his unnamed addressee to'ease me off my payn' (fol. 6v, ll. 1–2, 4).

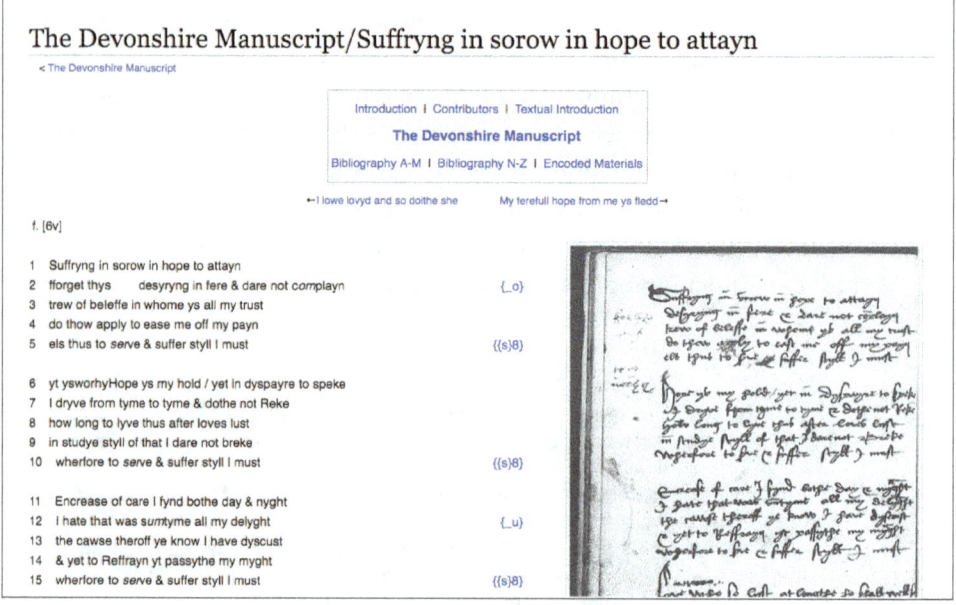

Fig. 8.1 'Suffryng in sorow in hope to attayn' (fol. 6v) in the Wikibook edition.

While its authorship remains debated, the acrostic of the verse suggests that Shelton is the intended recipient—the first letter of its seven stanzas spells out 'SHELTVN'.[14] The scribal annotations, which may only refer

---

14 The poem is entered in the Devonshire Manuscript by an unidentified hand (H2), and is also preserved in the Blage Manuscript (Trinity College, Dublin, MS 160,

to the quality of the verse, might therefore take on a more profound and personal meaning, as Douglas recommends rejecting the poem and its suit ('fforget thys'), but Shelton contradicts this advice with 'yt ys wor[t]hy'. At the end of the poem, Shelton adds a comment that has been variously transcribed as 'ondesyard sarwes/reqwer no hyar', 'ondesyrid favours/deserv no hyer', or perhaps 'ondesyard fansies/ requier no hyar'.[15] The transcription poses an interesting editorial crux: 'sarwes' might be read as 'service' or 'sorrows'.[16] Likewise, 'hyar' may be read as 'hire' or 'ear'.[17] Although the precise intentions behind Shelton's annotations and commentary remain obscure, their potential importance to the meaning and interpretation of the verse cannot be disputed.

---

fol. 159r). Modern editors of Wyatt's poems commonly attribute the poem to him (Foxwell, *The Poems of Sir Thomas Wiat*, pp. 257–58; Muir, *Poems*, pp. 96–97; Muir and Thomson, *Poems*, pp. 176–77; Nott, *Works*, p. 590). However, this attribution has not been universally accepted: Harrier argues that the poem 'must be excluded from the Wyatt canon' since it 'may be by Thomas Clere', Harrier, *The Canon*, pp. 41, 45, and Joost Daalder silently excludes the poem from his edition, *Collected Poems* (Oxford: Oxford University Press, 1975). Julia Boffey has argued the author is Shelton, mistaking Shelton's signed comment at the end of the poem as an attribution in 'Women Authors and Women's Literacy in Fourteenth- and Fifteenth-century England', in *Women and Literature in Britain 1150–1500*, ed. by Carol M. Meale (Cambridge: Cambridge University Press, 1996), pp. 159–82 (p. 173).

15 The first transcription as per Baron, 'Mary (Howard) Fitzroy's Hand', p. 331; Remley gives 'ondesyerd' in Remley, 'Mary Shelton', p. 50. The second as per Foxwell, *The Poems of Sir Thomas Wiat*, p. 258. The third as per Heale, *The Devonshire Manuscript*, p. 301. Heale also gives 'ondesiard fansies/requier no hiar' in *Wyatt, Surrey and Early Tudor Poetry* (London: Longman, 1998), p. 43, and 'ondesyred fansies/require no hyar' in '"Desiring Women Writing": Female Voices and Courtly "Balets" in Some Early Tudor Manuscript Albums', in *Early Modern Women's Manuscript Writing: Selected Papers from the Trinity/Trent Colloquium*, ed. by Victoria Elizabeth Burke and Jonathan Gibson (Farnham: Ashgate, 2004), pp. 9–31 (p. 21).

16 'Searwes' (device) is also possible, but unlikely. Alternatively rendering the word as 'fansies' or 'favours' is less problematic, but equally less probable.

17 S. P. Zitner argues, 'Whether Mary Shelton was saying that undesired service (attention) required no hire or that undesired sorrows required no ear, the response is pretty much the same in tone and substance', in 'Truth and Mourning in a Sonnet by Surrey', *English Literary History*, 50.3 (1983), 509–29 (p. 513). While this comment may be a 'remarkable example of an overtly critical rejoinder to a courtly lyric' written in the spirit described by Zitner, Remley argues that 'it seems equally probable that her words are meant ironically', that they offer a 'private recognition of the absurd spectacle of a man determined to get his way through protestations of extreme humility' Remley, 'Mary Shelton', p. 50. Similarly, Heale contends such 'unsympathetic replies may be part of the conventional exchange of courtly verse' and might be offered in jest, as 'such jesting offered some opportunities for female subject positions that seem to have appealed to the women using the manuscript', Heale, 'Desiring Women Writing', p. 21.

The Devonshire Manuscript embodies its compositional origins and circulation within the early Tudor court of Henry VIII, a body that was profoundly concerned with public and private performances of political loyalty and submission.[18] As Marotti notes, courtly manuscript miscellanies and poetic anthologies 'represent the meeting ground of literary production and social practices'.[19] The Devonshire Manuscript contains numerous examples of Marotti's assertion, especially in the form of epistolary verse and scribal annotation. Proximity and placement of poems often bear further significance. The poem 'My ferefull hope from me ys fledd' (fol. 7v), signed 'fynys quod n[o]b[od]y', is answered by the poem immediately following on the facing leaf, 'Yowre ferefull hope cannot prevayle' (fol. 8r), in turn signed 'fynys quod s[omebody]'. While this kind of playful imitation and formal echoing does not strictly rely on the relative proximity of the poems in the manuscript, the effect is more immediately apparent and more visually striking when the poems are placed, as they are, on facing leaves.[20] Poetry became yet another venue for the performance of public and private roles within the royal court, and the Devonshire Manuscript reflects this oscillation between public and private, personal and communal: within it, the private became public, the public was treated as private and all was deeply political. In addition to examining the volume as 'a medium of social intercourse',[21] other aspects of the Devonshire Manuscript— its multi-layered and multi-authored composition, its early history and transmission, the ways in which its contents engage with and

---

18 Alistair Fox writes, 'One striking phenomenon about early Tudor literature is that it was almost invariably concerned with politics, either directly or indirectly, and that this political bearing had a major impact on the nature of its literary forms' in *Politics and Literature in the Reigns of Henry VII and Henry VIII* (Oxford: Basil Blackwell, 1989), p. 3.

19 Marotti, *Manuscript, Print, and the English Renaissance Lyric*, p. 212.

20 The teasing blend of jest and earnestness in this pair of unattributed poems points to the role of much of the content in the manuscript as participating in the courtly 'game of love'. See John Stevens, *Music & Poetry in the Early Tudor Court* (Cambridge: Cambridge University Press, 1979), pp. 154–202; see also Roger Boase, *The Origin and Meaning of Courtly Love: A Critical Study of European Scholarship* (Manchester: Manchester University Press, 1977); David Burnley, *Courtliness and Literature in Medieval England* (New York: Longman, 1998) and Bernard O'Donoghue, *The Courtly Love Tradition* (Manchester: Manchester University Press, 1982).

21 Harold Love and Arthur F. Marotti, 'Manuscript Transmission and Circulation', in *The Cambridge History of Early Modern English Literature*, ed. by David Loewenstein and Janel Mueller (Cambridge: Cambridge University Press, 2002), pp. 55–80 (p. 63).

comment directly on contemporary political and social issues—invite further investigation and demand consideration when making critical assessments.

Like any of the other 'nonauthorial' textual determinants described above, compilation is an act of mediation. The selection of verses to be recorded, the manner in which they were entered and their position relative to one another all contribute to the meaning of the texts both individually and as a collection. Verses entered into the manuscript may have been selected on the basis of their popularity at court— perhaps accounting for the disproportionate number of Wyatt poems represented—or for more personal reasons; other verses were not simply selected and copied, but adapted and altered to suit specific purposes. The work of feminist literary critics and historians to rediscover texts by women and revise the canon of Western literature has further exposed the role of gender in the material and institutional conditions of textual production.[22]

To investigate the role of women in the production and circulation of literary works effectively, and building on the work of McGann and McKenzie, Margaret J. M. Ezell has persuasively proposed that the definition of 'authorship' needs to be re-examined and broadened.[23] Ezell's study of women's miscellanies demonstrates that these acts of

---

22 Representative studies include Elaine V. Beilin, *Redeeming Eve: Women Writers of the English Renaissance* (Princeton: Princeton University Press, 1987); Margaret J. M. Ezell, *Writing Women's Literary History* (Baltimore: The Johns Hopkins University Press, 1993); Margaret J. M. Ezell, *Social Authorship and the Advent of Print* (Baltimore: The Johns Hopkins University Press, 1999); Barbara K. Lewalski, *Writing Women in Jacobean England* (Cambridge, MA: Harvard University Press, 1993); Kim Walker, *Women Writers of the English Renaissance* (New York: Twayne, 1996) and Wendy Wall, *The Imprint of Gender: Authorship and Publication in the English Renaissance* (Ithaca, NY: Cornell University Press, 1993). See also the following representative essay collections: *The Renaissance Englishwoman in Print: Counterbalancing the Canon*, ed. by Anne M. Haselkorn and Betty S. Travitsky (Amherst: University of Massachusetts Press, 1990); *Silent but for the Word: Tudor Women as Patrons, Translators, and Writers of Religious Works*, ed. by Margaret P. Hannay (Kent: Kent State University Press, 1985); Susanne Woods and Margaret P. Hannay, *Teaching Tudor and Stuart Women Writers* (New York: Modern Languages Association, 2000); *Women and Literature in Britain, 1500–1700*, ed. by Helen Wilcox (Cambridge: Cambridge University Press, 1996); *Women, Writing, and the Reproduction of Culture in Tudor and Stuart Britain*, ed. by Mary E. Burke, Jane Donawerth, Linda L. Dove and Karen Nelson (Syracuse: Syracuse University Press, 2000).
23 Margaret J. M. Ezell, 'Women and Writing', in *A Companion to Early Modern Women's Writing*, ed. by Anita Pacheco (Oxford: Blackwell, 2002), pp. 77–94 (p. 79).

preservation and compilation often serve to reinforce religious and political loyalties and to 'cement social bonds during times of duress' within female literary circles.[24] In a similar vein, Elizabeth Clarke notes that 'compilation, rather than authorship of the writing in a document', was the 'dominant literary activity among women who could read and write' in the early modern period.[25] This is certainly true in the case of the Devonshire Manuscript, where women were, for the most part, directly responsible for the compilation and copying of the predominantly male-authored contents of the anthology. Some of the lyrics demonstrate close female friendship—Mary Shelton and Margaret Douglas kept close company, evidenced by the fact that Shelton's hand often immediately follows Douglas's—and these lyrics are now understood to have a definite subversive meaning for a select group of individuals.[26]

The Devonshire Manuscript is a rich, complex document. With its collection of courtly lyrics, pastiche of medieval and contemporary poetry, density of textual voices and often-uncertain authorship and attribution, the manuscript demonstrates how textual production and interpretation were foundational to those living within the Tudor court. By paying heed to the various texts in and around the document—the annotations, order of leaves and social context—one may obtain a fuller understanding of the source text and its various actors. We believe that the physical and social elements of the Devonshire Manuscript lend themselves to digital editing and publication processes that more readily represent these aspects than a print environment can. *A Social Edition of the Devonshire Manuscript* focuses on the editorial and scribal practices that inform the context and production of the Devonshire Manuscript. By shifting our own editorial process into an environment

---

24 Ezell, 'Women and Writing', p. 86.
25 Elizabeth Clarke, 'Women's Manuscript Miscellanies in Early Modern England', in *Teaching Tudor and Stuart Women Writers*, pp. 52–60 (p. 53).
26 Baron, 'Mary (Howard) Fitzroy's Hand', p. 328. Kathryn DeZur notes that early modern women's participation in circulating love lyrics might also indicate 'a possible site of resistance to the idealized cultural paradigm of women as chaste, silent, and obedient' in '"Vaine Books" and Early Modern Women Readers', in *Reading and Literacy in the Middle Ages and Renaissance*, ed. by Ian Frederick Moulton (Turnhout: Brepols, 2004), pp. 105–25 (p. 111). The continental trend of courtly love made it fashionable for noble ladies at Henry VIII's court to compile miscellanies. Regardless, DeZur emphasises that the tension between Christian values and courtly expectations meant that a woman's demeanour was always under scrutiny.

representative of the inherent sociality of texts, *A Social Edition of the Devonshire Manuscript* hearkens back to the multi-author roots of the text itself. In the following section, we focus on the specifics of *A Social Edition of the Devonshire Manuscript*, exploring the benefits (and drawbacks) of building a scholarly edition on the Wikibooks platform.

Building a social edition

A Social Edition of the Devonshire Manuscript manifests Ray Siemens's earlier argument that social media environments might enable new editing practices.[27] In order to build an edition of an early modern text on the principles of Open Access and editorial transparency (in both production and dissemination), we have integrated scholarly content with environments maintained by the social and social-editorial communities already existent on the web—most notably on Wikibooks, a cross-section of intellectual research activity and the social media practices that define Web 2.0. Early on, Web 2.0 was described as Internet technologies that allow users to be active authors rather than simply readers or consumers of web content.[28] Now, the term is most frequently associated with social media platforms (e.g. Facebook and Twitter) and blog applications (e.g. WordPress and wikis). In an experimental spirit, we have extended the editorial conversation into multiple pre-existing Web 2.0 and social media platforms, including Twitter, blogs, Wikibook discussion pages, dedicated Renaissance and early modern online community spaces and Skype-enabled interviews with our advisory group. As Tim Berners-Lee (the inventor of the World Wide Web as we know it) remarks, the internet was originally developed for workers to collaborate and access source documents; with wiki and Web 2.0 technology, it is now returning to its roots.[29] Wikibooks emphasises the

---

27 Ray Siemens, with Meagan Timney, Cara Leitch, Corina Koolen and Alex Garnett, and with the ETCL, INKE and PKP Research Groups, 'Toward Modeling the Social Edition: An Approach to Understanding the Electronic Scholarly Edition in the Context of New and Emerging Social Media', *Literary and Linguistic Computing*, 27.4 (2012), 445–61.
28 See Darcy DiNucci, 'Fragmented Future', *Print* (April 1999), 220–22.
29 Simon Mahony, 'Research Communities and Open Collaboration: The Example of the Digital Classicist Wiki', *Digital Medievalist*, 6 (2011), http://www.digitalmedievalist.org/journal/6/mahony

importance of multi-authored and multi-edited endeavours. In doing so, the platform exemplifies McGann, McKenzie and Marotti's earlier assertions that texts are created by a community of individuals. In what follows we offer a brief overview of the process and thinking that led to the Wikibook instantiation of the manuscript as *A Social Edition of the Devonshire Manuscript*.

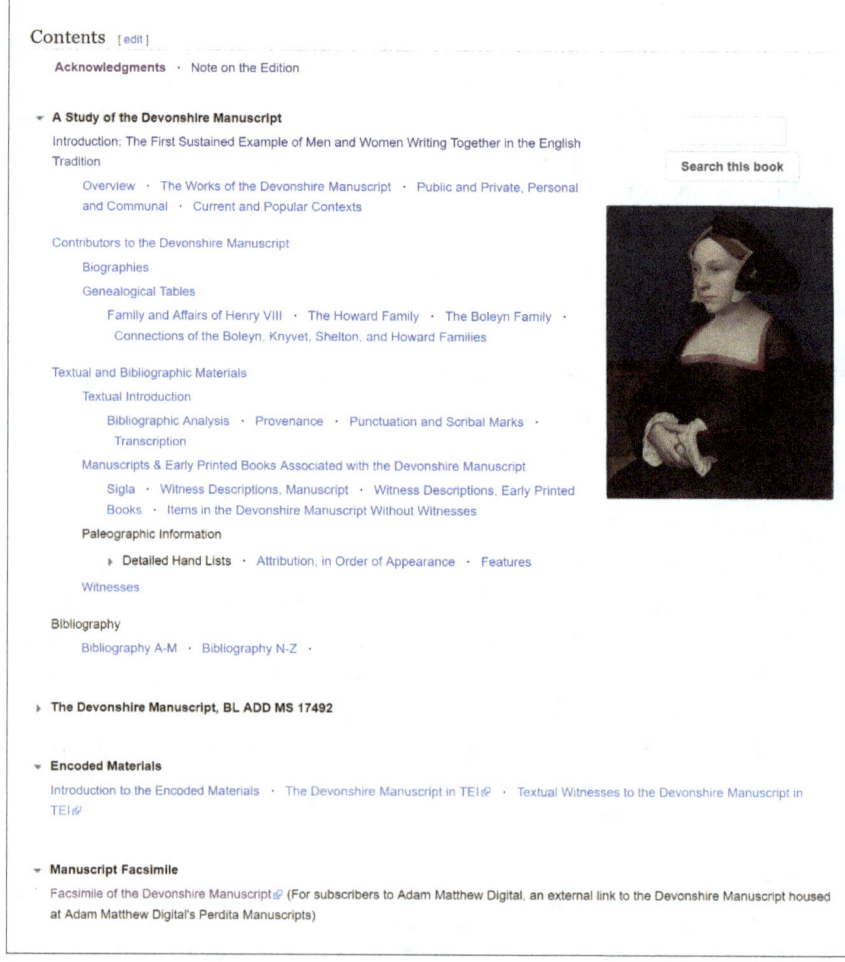

Fig. 8.2 The home page of *A Social Edition of the Devonshire Manuscript*.

Perhaps more than any other editorial choice, the iterative publication of *A Social Edition of the Devonshire Manuscript* departed most clearly from traditional scholarly editing practices. In effect we have published (or are in the perpetual process of publishing) versions of the edition in multiple media: a fixed PDF version, distributed to the project's advisory board, and a version housed on the publicly-editable Wikibooks. We are also currently working with multiple publishing partners to produce a second online edition, an e-reader edition and a print edition to meet the needs of a broad and varied readership. These versions were planned to inform and influence each other's development, with cross-pollination of editorial input across platforms. Although they did so, each medium also engendered difficulties in communication, coordination and expectations to be overcome or accommodated—with varying results.

The Wikibook edition's features stretch the limits of a print edition to the breaking point—especially in sheer size. Even if the manuscript facsimile pages and the XML files were excluded, *A Social Edition of the Devonshire Manuscript* would run to over 500 standard print pages. In addition to a general and textual introduction, the online edition includes: extensive hand sample tables that open our palaeographic attribution process to public scrutiny, witnesses that reflect the poem's textual legacy, biographies and genealogical diagrams that clarify the relationship between the manuscript's sixteenth century compiler-authors and an extensive bibliography of quoted and related sources. Courtesy of Adam Matthew Digital, we have also included the facsimile image of each page of the manuscript. The discussion sections on each page, a feature unique to Wikimedia projects, promote conversation on various aspects of the poem at hand. In this way, the Wikibook edition extends the social context of the Devonshire Manuscript by providing a space for ongoing discussion, collaboration and negotiation.

Editorial work on *A Social Edition of the Devonshire Manuscript* began long before we selected Wikibooks as a publication platform. In 2001, work on a digital edition of the manuscript began with a more recognisably traditional scholarly activity: primary source transcription. The transcription of the manuscript is based on examination of both the original document and a microfilm of the Devonshire Manuscript provided by the British Library. Members of the Devonshire Manuscript Editorial Group (or DMSEG, a team made up of up of scholars, postdoctoral fellows, graduate researchers and programmers,[30] working with two publishers,[31] an editorial board[32] and self-selected members of the public) prepared and transcribed (in a blind process) two independent paper copies from the microfilm. The transcribers collated the two paper copies manually as they were unable to perform a collation by electronic means using standard techniques; transcription of the *Devonshire Manuscript* is notoriously challenging, as the manuscript was inscribed by nineteen different hands, the majority of which used non-professional secretary script. The resultant rough transcription was resolved as far as possible using expanded paper prints and enlarged images. In general, their transcriptions were in accord with one another. Remaining areas of uncertainty were resolved with manual reference to the original document itself, housed at the British Library. This final, collated transcription forms the textual basis for *A Social Edition of the Devonshire Manuscript*.[33]

---

30   Ray Siemens, Karin Armstrong, Barbara Bond, Constance Crompton, Terra Dickson, Johanne Paquette, Jonathan Podracky, Ingrid Weber, Cara Leitch, Melanie Chernyk, Brett D. Hirsch, Daniel Powell, Alyssa Anne McLeod, Alyssa Arbuckle, Jonathan Gibson, Chris Gaudet, Eric Haswell, Arianna Ciula, Daniel Starza-Smith and James Cummings, with Martin Holmes, Greg Newton, Paul Remley, Erik Kwakkel, Aimie Shirkie and the INKE research group.
31   Iter, a not-for-profit consortium dedicated to the development and distribution of scholarly Middle Age and Renaissance online resources in partnership with Medieval and Renaissance Texts and Studies and Adam Matthew Digital, a digital academic publisher.
32   Robert E. Bjork (Director, Arizona Center for Medieval and Renaissance Studies, Arizona State University), William R. Bowen (Chair) (Director, Iter, University of Toronto Scarborough), Michael Ullyot (University of Calgary), Diane Jakacki (Georgia Institute of Technology), Jessica Murphy (University of Texas at Dallas), Jason Boyd (Ryerson University), Elizabeth Heale (University of Reading), Steven W. May (Georgetown College), Arthur F. Marotti (Wayne State University), Jennifer Summit (Stanford University), Jonathan Gibson (Queen Mary, University of London), John Lavagnino (King's College London) and Katherine Rowe (Bryn Mawr College).
33   For further information on the collation process, including collation tools used, see Ray Siemens with Caroline Leitch, 'Editing the Early Modern Miscellany: Modelling and Knowledge (Re)Presentation as a Context for the Contemporary Editor', in *New Ways of Looking at Old Texts IV*, ed. by Michael Denbog (Tempe: Renaissance English Text Society, 2009), pp. 115–30.

Guided by two principles, the team then encoded the text in XML according to the Text Encoding Initiative (TEI) Guidelines.[34] The first principle was consistency: even if the team discovered one of their previous choices to be less than optimal, they continued in that pattern until the text was complete. Rather than employ varying practices, consistently encoding the entire manuscript in XML allowed for global changes that could be, and indeed were, made after the conclusion of the initial encoding.[35] The second principle was accountability: as the team encoded, they maintained regular documentation to ensure that neither the original encoder nor any subsequent encoder would lack a basis from which to proceed. Another successful practice employed was to encode the manuscript by building layers of TEI in phases. The manuscript was completely encoded at a conservative level before commencing the second phase. The second layer of encoding, complete with annotations and regularisations, deepened, clarified and augmented the first. Although the project began in 2001, the particular implementation of the social edition method discussed here started with the formation of an advisory group in 2010. This provided a unique opportunity to invite potential critics to shape the process and the products associated with the social edition. As the final step before moving the edition into Wikibooks, the members of the DMSEG working in the Electronic Textual Cultures Lab (ETCL) at the University of Victoria prepared a static digital edition of the manuscript. This edition served as a base text against which our international advisory group of early modern and Renaissance scholars could compare the Wikibook edition as it evolved.[36]

Before deciding on Wikibooks as a platform, the team had considered hosting the edition on a stand-alone site. In response to public interest

---

34 TEI provides a standard for encoding electronic texts. By encoding a text in XML under TEI guidelines, one renders the text substantially more searchable, categorisable and preservable.
35 Please note that these global changes were not questions of transcription, but of encoding patterns and standards.
36 For a more in-detail description of transcription, collation and encoding practices, please see Ray Siemens, Barbara Bond and Karin Armstrong, 'The Devil is in the Details: An Electronic Edition of the Devonshire MS (British Library Additional MS 17,492), its Encoding and Prototyping', in *New Technologies and Renaissance Studies*, ed. by William R. Bowen and Ray Siemens (Tempe: Arizona Center for Medieval and Renaissance Studies, 2008), pp. 261–99.

in the project, coupled with the team's investment in emerging public knowledge communities, we devised an editorial experiment: as a control we produced a static PDF version of the edition, and as a variable we moved the same content onto a Wikimedia platform. Most famous for Wikipedia, Wikimedia is a small non-profit foundation, with less than one hundred and fifty employees responsible for management, fundraising and technological development. Volunteer editors contribute and moderate the content of the projects. We considered Wikisource, Wikibooks and Wikipedia as platforms, eventually deciding to mount our edition in Wikibooks. Acknowledging the dedicated community already engaged in Wikimedia, we sought to discover Wikibooks' affordances for the scholar. Even though Wikipedia has more editors, Wikibooks is purposefully structured to support the book-like form. And although Wikisource appears as a more appropriate environment for a scholarly edition, publishing *A Social Edition of the Devonshire Manuscript* on Wikisource would have prevented the inclusion of any and all scholarly material outside the transcription itself—including palaeographic expansions and bibliographies. With a book-like research environment as our end goal, we produced an edition in Wikibooks that is scholarly and peer reviewed in a traditional sense, but also enables citizen scholars to access, contribute and annotate material. Crucially, Wikibooks also archives each change in content, allowing us to track reversions and revisions to the text.

In order to keep the editorial and encoding process transparent, the Wikibook edition includes links to the baseline XML-encoded transcription.[37] Thus, in addition to being able to use the XML for their own projects, readers can see the encoder's TEI-based editorial choices. Others are able to download this XML and continue working with the document, potentially allowing the project to evolve in unanticipated ways. With the firm foundation of documented encoding, all those working with the document can refer to, build on or adapt the project's foundation. The markup did not simply help the team keep track of the process; it also facilitated an ongoing scholarly conversation about the text. Readers can compare our transcriptions to the facsimiles included

---

37 http://hcmc.uvic.ca/~etcl/Devonshire_Manuscript_poems.zip

on each page of the Wikibooks edition and are free to contest (and even alter) our regularisations or corrections.

In November 2011, ETCL-based members of the DMSEG began converting the TEI-encoded text into Wikimarkup, the Wikitext language. The team then moved the text, appendices, glosses, commentary and textual notes into Wikibooks, thereby providing a flexible collaboration environment for stakeholders inside and outside the lab. Wikibooks, like Wikimedia and institutional scholarship at large, has its own self-governing editorial culture, and *A Social Edition of the Devonshire Manuscript* received promising attention from Wikibooks' existing editorial community. Since then, the ETCL team has amplified the Wikibook with additional images of the manuscript, witness transcriptions, an extensive bibliography and the XML files containing the encoded transcription of the manuscript. Consequently, the Wikibook became an edition as well as a research environment for both early modern scholars and Tudor enthusiasts. Various authors have written on the value of employing wikis as collaborative research or authoring platforms. Best practice standards and protocols have developed as an increasing number of practitioners become versed in Wikipedia, and we have consciously developed *A Social Edition of the Devonshire Manuscript*, a scholarly Wikibook edition, with these priorities and standards in mind.[38]

The Wikibook form gives us the opportunity to recognise and assign credit for important editorial work that extends beyond the creation of original content. Activities like discussion and feedback are central to scholarly revision and authorship, but can be difficult to monitor and quantify within a large project. A print edition often only acknowledges these forms of labour with a line or two on the acknowledgments page. Originally, we considered the discussion pages ideal for this type of scholarly discussion and editorial record keeping. Like a private wiki

---

38 Bo Leuf and Ward Cunningham, authors of the first book on wikis, recognise that a wiki must fit the culture of the user community for it to be successful in *The Wiki Way* (Boston: Addison-Wesley Professional, 2001). Emma Tonkin advises that a collaborative authoring wiki should include the following: a page locking system to deter simultaneous editing, a versioning system to track changes and the ability to lock editing on a page in the case of an edit war, as well as an efficient search function, and navigation, categorisation and file management abilities, in 'Making the Case for a Wiki', *Ariadne* (30 January 2005), http://www.ariadne.ac.uk/issue42/tonkin

community, however, Wikibooks bears its own social conventions. Through conversation with an established Wikibooks editor we realised that the Wikibooks discussion pages are more often used for personal commentary and disputes than editorial suggestions. Reminiscent of Douglas' note in the margin of 'Suffryng in sorrow in hope to attyn' (fols 6v–7r) to 'fforget thys', and Shelton's contradiction 'yt ys wor[t] hy', the Wikibooks discussion pages are predominantly venues for editors to offer one another personal support (or criticism) rather than to discuss content analytically.

Thus, rather than relying on the discussion pages for editorial decisions, we made the most substantive changes in Wikibooks based on Skype and Iter interactions with our advisory group. Although our hope had been to have the advisors edit directly in Wikibooks, some found the technological threshold for contributing too high, and it became more practical to have the ETCL team make the proposed changes in the Wikibook. We responded to the advisors' recommendations in near-real time, adding (among other suggestions) navigation menus and images requested through our ongoing consultation. Many avenues for editorial conversation are necessary in order to foster the sense of a community that, as one of our advisors noted, is 'virtually there, as if everyone is crowded around a page, putting their two cents in on matters great and small'. Even when those giving editorial direction do not undertake the technical implementation, multiple social media platforms can facilitate social editing. Relying solely on one single communications platform could potentially impede the success of an evolving social edition.

Each social media platform attracts and enables specific types of interaction. Using social media allows us to integrate a new step into the editorial process—a step that fills the gap between an edition's initial planning stages and its concluding peer review. Producing an edition 'live' in consultation with various groups across multiple media allows for a publication that can quickly and productively meet the needs of its readers. Employing and participating in various platforms alerted us to different priorities across platforms, as well as forcing us to think through how we might create a multispatial experience for safe, productive and equitable interactions. In addition to producing an edition that allows for multiple editorial perspectives, the DMSEG gathered responses to the social edition-building methodology. In the interest of refining the process and expounding on its utility for collaborative editors in the Web 2.0 environment, the ETCL team used a combination of methods to gather data on the social edition building process. We conducted qualitative interviews with members of our advisory group to solicit their perspectives on the content of the evolving and fixed editions, as well as on issues of credit, peer review and collaborative editing. We also enumerated interaction in Wikibooks. Furthermore, we invited feedback via Twitter, guest blog posts and Iter's social media space. Rather than soliciting anonymous reader reports from our advisors, we brought them into conversation with one another over the fixed edition and the evolving Wikibooks edition. We facilitated this conversation in a social media space housed by Iter, which serves a broad community of early modern and Renaissance associations and scholars. In many cases, their suggestions have already been incorporated into the Wikibooks publication; those that have not will be integrated into a final, socially mediated edition of the Devonshire Manuscript for print and e-publication with Iter and Medieval and Renaissance Texts and Studies (MRTS).

Considered as a whole, *A Social Edition of the Devonshire Manuscript* suggests that social media technologies can be harnessed for productive interaction and discussion by those scholars invested in a content area or project, but that they do require comprehensive oversight by dedicated staff to develop and maintain participation in knowledge construction and dissemination. Regardless, social scholarly editions represent a step toward diversifying and democratising knowledge, and the Wikimedia suite of platforms is an established environment for this sort of work. Todd Presner reiterates this concept by considering Wikipedia as a model for the future of humanities research. Presner deems Wikipedia 'a truly innovative, global, multilingual, collaborative knowledge-generating community and platform for authoring, editing, distributing and versioning knowledge'.[39] Larger than a mere technological innovation, wikis represent a change in the philosophy and practice of knowledge creation. With this end in mind, we have published scholarly content in Wikibooks, an editable environment that

---

39   Todd Presner, 'Digital Humanities 2.0: A Report on Knowledge', *Connexions* (18 April 2010), http://cnx.org/contents/J0K7N3xH@6/Digital-Humanities-20-A-Report

allows for multithreaded conversation maintained by lay knowledge communities on the web. We hope that *A Social Edition of the Devonshire Manuscript* continues to serve all of the varying communities currently involved in the project: academic and non-academic alike.

Conclusion: Digital affordances for academic and non-academic editing

The Devonshire Manuscript's historically social structure and content informed our choice of Wikibooks as a publication venue. Recently emerged social media environments, including the Wikimedia suite, shape the way academic and citizen scholars work by providing new tools and platforms to perform scholarly activities. These technological innovations encourage academic researchers to open up scholarship and ask questions not previously possible. The intersection of social media and the scholarly edition has a destabilising effect, as it facilitates a model of textual interaction and intervention that represents the scholarly text as a process rather than a product. Moreover, these significant conceptual shifts in research, writing and editorial practices have provoked various reconsiderations of the ethos and methods inherent to academic scholarship in particular, and knowledge creation in general. For instance, the open source movement has morphed through its open scholarship instantiation to develop a new breed of academic: the open scholar.[40] According to Terry Anderson, open scholars

> create; use and contribute open educational resources; self archive; apply their research; do open research; filter and share with others; support emerging open learning alternatives; publish in open access journals; comment openly on the works of others; build networks.[41]

---

40 Don Tapscott and Anthony D. Williams outline five levels of open scholarship: (1) course content exchange; (2) course content collaboration; (3) course content co-innovation; (4) knowledge co-creation and (5) collaborative learning connection, in 'Innovating the 21st-Century University: It's Time!', *Educause* (January/February 2010), 22.

41 In Mahony, 'Research Communities and Open Collaboration'. Fred Garnett and Nigel Ecclesfield discuss the Open Scholar philosophy further in 'Towards a Framework for Co-Creating Open Scholarship', *Research in Learning Technology*, 19

True openness requires adopting values that the nature and scale of the electronic medium necessitates (i.e. collaboration and innovation across backgrounds, skill levels and disciplines).[42] These concepts vary considerably from the closed publication and professional cultures that have previously pervaded the university as an institution.

Technological advances potently shape how individuals and communities create new knowledge. As such, it behoves scholars to think through the affordances and implications of any collaborative publishing platform, space for social knowledge creation or multi-authored environment. Incorporating social media allowances and Web 2.0 practices into a scholarly edition recasts the primary editor as a facilitator, rather than progenitor, of textual knowledge creation. Conventionally, a single-authority editor determines and shapes what is important to the reader, focuses the editorial and analytical lens and ultimately exerts immense control over reader experience. A social media framework for the electronic scholarly edition pushes the boundaries of authority, shifting power from a single editor to a community of readers. As Kathleen Fitzpatrick writes, introducing different modes of reading and interpreting that take advantage of the capabilities of digital networks allows for new knowledge to develop:

> Scholars operate in a range of conversations, from classroom conversations with students to conference conversations with colleagues; scholars need to have available to them not simply the library model of texts circulating amongst individual readers but also the coffee house model of public reading and debate. This interconnection of individual

---

(2012), http://dx.doi.org/10.3402/rlt.v19i3.7795. Not to be confused with the Drupal software Open Scholar. Garnett and Ecclesfield reference *Academic Evolution*, a blog formerly run by Gideon Burton, who states: 'the Open Scholar is someone who makes their intellectual projects and processes digitally visible and who invites and encourages ongoing criticism of their work and secondary uses of any or all parts of it at any stage of its development', http://www.academicevolution.com/2009/08/the-open-scholar.html

42 Looking further than a mere series of activities, Charles M. Vest predicts the development of a meta-university: 'a transcendent, accessible, empowering, dynamic, communally constructed framework of open materials and platforms on which much of higher education worldwide can be constructed or enhanced', in 'Open Content and the Emerging Global Meta-University', *Educause* (May/June 2006), 18–30 (p. 18), http://www.hewlett.org/library/grantee-publication/open-content-and-emerging-global-meta-university

nodes into a collective fabric is, of course, the strength of the network, which not only physically binds individual machines but also has the ability to bring together the users of those machines, at their separate workstations, into one communal whole.[43]

The social edition models a new kind of scholarly discourse network that hopes to eschew traditional, institutionally reinforced, hierarchical structures and relies, instead, upon those that are community-generated.

A Social Edition of the Devonshire Manuscript brings communities together to engage in conversation around a text formed and reformed through an ongoing, iterative, public editorial process. A central aim of the project was to facilitate knowledge transfer and creation between multiple editorial communities with varying values and priorities. Ray Siemens has called for scholars 'to extend our understanding of the scholarly edition in light of new models of edition production that embrace social networking and its commensurate tools', and to develop 'the social edition as an extension of the traditions in which it is situated and which it has the potential to inform productively'.[44] Bringing practice to theory, we have modelled the social scholarly edition. We have worked as a team to extend scholarly best practice and Open Access methodology to collaborative editing in Web 2.0 environments. We have chosen to build an edition on Wikibooks, alongside (and with help from) the dedicated Wikibooks community. Our goal, manifested by community engagement via Wikibooks, Twitter, blogs and an Iter Drupal-based social media space, is to use existing social media tools to change the role of the scholarly editor from the *sole authority* on the text to a *facilitator* who brings traditional and citizen scholars into collaboration through ongoing editorial conversation. By privileging process of product, the DMSEG aims to render transparent the production of an online edition of the Devonshire Manuscript.

The edition-building process situated our text at the intersection of academic and wiki culture. As we traversed this admittedly new and multidisciplinary ground, we sought advice and feedback from a variety of sources. We developed the public editing process to encourage

---

43 Kathleen Fitzpatrick, 'CommentPress: New (Social) Structures for New (Networked) Texts', *Journal of Electronic Publishing*, 10.3 (2007), http://dx.doi.org/10.3998/3336451.0010.305

44 Siemens et al., 'Toward Modeling the Social Edition', p. 447.

communication between editorial communities while at the same time preserving the peer review process. Such open communication notwithstanding, conflicts in editorial norms exist, as standards and expectations concerning tone, feedback and content vary widely across our multiple communities. *A Social Edition of the Devonshire Manuscript* brings overlapping groups of partners and stakeholders together in a way that a traditional print edition cannot. The first group (the partners) consists of scholars and publishers invested in the shifting landscape of scholarly collaboration and dissemination: project advisors, publishing partners at Iter and Medieval and Renaissance Texts and Studies (MRTS), digital content partners at Adam Matthew Digital and members of the Digital Humanities community at the University of Alberta, who provided us with a tool to visualise Wikibooks contributions. The second group (the stakeholders) consists of individuals invested in early modern studies: project advisors, Wikimedia stakeholders, bloggers and traditional and citizen scholars on Twitter. Trusting the content contributed by partners and stakeholders means not only trusting both groups, but, perhaps more importantly, trusting our exploration of editable publication venues. In light of our experience with the iterative production of the social edition, we would argue for the importance of incorporating various social platforms and venues that enable conversation across previously divergent lines of knowledge production.

A Social Edition of the Devonshire Manuscript is designed to fill the void that Ezell notes has been left by the lack of effort made to 'Catalogue and reconstruct patterns in women's manuscript texts to provide an inclusive overview of literary activities rather than isolated, individual authors'.[45] Concurrently, the DMSEG planned the form of the social edition in response to Greg Crane and others' exhortation of the 'need to shift from lone editorials and monumental editions to editors [...] who coordinate contributions from many sources and oversee living editions'.[46] The editorial communities that have grown up around social media sites like Wikibooks indicate a public desire to expand knowledge

---

45   Ezell, *Social Authorship*, p. 23.
46   Greg Crane, 'Give Us Editors! Re-inventing the Edition and Re-thinking the Humanities', in *Online Humanities Scholarship: The Shape of Things to Come*, ed. by Jerome McGann (Houston: Rice University Press, 2010), pp. 81–97, http://cnx.org/contents/XfgqFrtg@2/Give-us-editors-Re-inventing-t

communities using accessible social technologies. Using the Devonshire Manuscript as a prototype, we have devised a method that addresses the questions that a social edition raises. Namely, how do we effectively integrate multiple communities with varying cultures and editorial standards while pushing the boundaries of editorial authority? How do we employ multiple social media platforms with varying degrees of openness to ensure a safe space for multiple individuals and opinions? And, how do we shift the power from a single editor, who shapes the reading of any given text, to a group of readers whose interactions and interpretations form a new method of making meaning out of the source material? It is our hope that this model of the social scholarly edition successfully straddles various communities of scholars and modes of creating and disseminating knowledge. *A Social Edition of the Devonshire Manuscript* represents the range of possibilities for social scholarly editing across contemporary editorial communities—communities who need not be limited by social, geographic or institutional boundaries.[47]

---

[47] This piece re-prints, with permission, an article in the journal *Renaissance and Reformation/Renaissance et Réforme*, 30.4 (2015), 131–56.

9. A Catalogue of Digital Editions

Greta Franzini, Melissa Terras and Simon Mahony

Introduction

Since the earliest days of hypertext, textual scholars have produced, discussed and theorised upon critical digital editions of manuscripts, in order to investigate how digital technologies can provide another means to present and enable the interpretative study of text. This work has generally been done by looking at particular case studies or examples of critical digital editions, and, as a result, there is no overarching understanding of how digital technologies have been employed across the full range of textual interpretations. This chapter will describe the creation of a catalogue of digital editions that could collect information about extant digital editions and, in so doing, contribute to research in related disciplines. The resulting catalogue will provide a means of answering, in the form of a quantitative survey, the following research questions: What makes a good digital edition? What features do digital editions share? What is the state of the art in the field of digital editions? Why are there so few electronic editions of ancient texts, and so many of texts from other periods? By collecting data regarding existing digital editions, and corresponding directly with the projects in question, we provide a unique record of extant digital critical editions of text across a range of subject areas, and show how this collaboratively edited catalogue can benefit the Digital Humanities community.[1]

---

1   For example, the *Digital Classicist* (http://www.digitalclassicist.org), *Digital Medievalist* (http://www.digitalmedievalist.org) and *Digital Byzantinist* (http://www.digitalbyzantinist.org) communities.

Digital editions and cataloguing

There is no universally accepted definition of *digital scholarly edition*.[2] Scholars continuously experiment with old and new tools in order to achieve the optimal digital experience of a manuscript and although there are online guidelines on how to produce scholarly editions,[3] the resulting projects often differ greatly. The term *edition* is generally used to describe the result of an interpretative study of a text. No matter how malleable, diverse and dynamic an edition is, it must be original or, in other words, must add new knowledge. Work that does not produce new knowledge is considered to be a mere reproduction of the primary source. Digital editions move beyond the mere translation into the digital. A digital facsimile is a good example of duplication inasmuch as it is a high-quality, faithful[4] photographic reproduction of the primary source, which can be used as an alternative consultation medium, thus avoiding repeated handling of the original. As a replica, this type of publication does not bear any new information and cannot, therefore, be considered an edition. Our area of interest is in the interpretative, digital publications of texts that allow new understanding of the original source material to be generated.

Unlike the past, where scholarly merit derived from expert and monumental pieces of work, (digital) editions today are constantly assuming different shapes; whether standalone projects or pieces of a larger whole,[5] digital editions are reassessing the notions of engagement and completeness. The latter often depends on the former, in that today's editions seek to embrace crowds—from both a reception and production standpoint—whose goal is to socialise, to exchange

---

2   Much literature exists on the topic; see e.g. Kenneth Price, 'Edition, Project, Database, Archive, Thematic Research Collection: What's in a Name?', *Digital Humanities Quarterly*, 3.3 (2009), http://www.digitalhumanities.org/dhq/vol/3/3/000053/000053. html; Hans Walter Gabler, 'Theorizing the Digital Scholarly Edition', *Literature Compass*, 7 (2010), 43–56, http://dx.doi.org/10.1111/j.1741-4113.2009.00675.x; Mats Dahlström, 'How Reproductive is a Scholarly Edition?', *Literary and Linguistic Computing*, 19 (2004), 17–33, http://dx.doi.org/10.1093/llc/19.1.17. See also Patrick Sahle's chapter in the present volume.

3   For example: *MLA Guidelines for Editors of Scholarly Editions* (2011), http://www.mla.org/cse_guidelines

4   As close as possible to the original.

5   Such as, digital libraries or archives showcasing various subprojects, items and collections.

views, to produce community knowledge and to help users read,[6] thus advancing research. This push for advancement is not only informed by our immersion in the rapid technological evolution but it is also dictated by people's need to assert their presence in an increasingly competitive and interdisciplinary field.

How might we understand the remit of digital editions, given this pace of technological change? Patrick Sahle's *Catalog of Digital Scholarly Editions*[7] presents a taxonomy which identifies when a digital edition is scholarly, providing various indicators to help understand the outputs of digital textual projects:[8]

> **S — Scholarly**: An edition must be critical, must have critical components. A pure facsimile is not an edition, a digital library is not an edition.[9]
>
> **D — Digital**: A digital edition cannot be converted to a printed edition without substantial loss of content or functionality. Vice versa: a retro-digitised printed edition is not a scholarly digital edition (but it may evolve into a scholarly digital edition through new content or functionalities).
>
> **E — Edition**: An edition must represent its material (usually as transcribed/edited text) — a catalogue, an index, a descriptive database is not an edition.
>
> **Complete/Prototype**: An SDE (Scholarly Digital Edition) is a publication of the material in question; an SDE project is not the same as an SDE, that means an SDE is more than a plan or a prototype.

In Sahle's model, a *scholarly* digital edition is a *critical* digital edition, understood as an analytical and accurate contextual study offering hypotheses and new insights into the source text under examination,

---

6 Peter Robinson, 'The One Text and the Many Texts', *Literary and Linguistic Computing*, 15 (2000), 5–14 (p. 13), http://dx.doi.org/10.1093/llc/15.1.5

7 As the name suggests, the *Catalog* lists only *scholarly editions*. Personal correspondence (14/06/2012) with Patrick Sahle revealed that the *Catalog* began in 2006 and saw only fifty new entries in the four years 2008 to 2012. The *Catalog* is available at http://www.uni-koeln.de/~ahz26/vlet/vlet-about.html

8 What follows is a summary of Patrick Sahle's analysis in the *About* page of his *A Catalog of Digital Scholarly Editions* website http://www.digitale-edition.de/vlet-about.html

9 Scholars in the field use the term *digital library* to describe a collection of electronic texts and/or visual materials, which typically does not add new knowledge to the primary source. It can be considered a digital exhibit. Digital libraries should not be confused with *variorum editions*, which are collections of variants of the same copy-text with appended commentary.

as elaborated by Peter Robinson.[10] Sahle's definitions help us define in more precise terms the intention and scope of the edition. To express it in Espen Ore's words:

> Any scholarly edition is better than none even if it is not a critical edition, and [...] editions that may not be critical digital editions do indeed have value and represent a kind of edition which are in fact the basis for critical text editions.[11]

These words bring to the fore the present and more social nature of digital editions, whereby multiple people can contribute—some more, some less—to a single edition.[12] Sahle's work also provides the starting point for analysing all digital editions, and offers an overarching catalogue that allows us to understand this field.

The need for a catalogue of digital critical editions is dictated by the absence of up-to-date, analogous resources. Caroline Macé called for a repository of digital editions at the *IV Incontro di Filologia Digitale*[13] in September 2012. Her rationale was that such a catalogue would provide a means of discovery, linking and advertisement of digital texts that may otherwise go unnoticed. We believe that an up-to-date, online catalogue of digital editions would provide an accessible, unique record of manuscripts that have had digital editions created based on them; allow an understanding of the digital editions created which are allied to a range of distinct historical periods; and providing a data bank of features, tools, licences, funding bodies and locations. This will give an insight into past, present and future digital edition projects, providing

---

10 Peter Robinson, 'What is a Critical Digital Edition?', *Variants: The Journal of the European Society for Textual Scholarship*, 1 (2002), 43–62. *Contextual* here is to be understood as a comprehensive study of the history, materiality and reception of the primary source under investigation.

11 Espen Ore, 'Monkey Business — or What is an Edition?', *Literary and Linguistic Computing*, 19 (2004), 35–44 (p. 35), http://dx.doi.org/10.1093/llc/19.1.35

12 Or, as Siemens et al. write: '[...] the 'social' edition is process-driven, privileging interpretative changes based on the input of many readers; text is fluid, agency is collective, and many readers/editors, rather than a single editor, shape what is important and, thus, broaden the editorial lens as well as the breadth, depth, and scope of any edition produced in this way'. Ray Siemens et al., 'Toward Modeling the Social Edition: An Approach to Understanding the Electronic Scholarly Edition in the Context of New and Emerging Social Media', *Literary and Linguistic Computing*, 27 (2012), 445–61 (p. 453), http://dx.doi.org/10.1093/llc/fqs013

13 The fourth meeting on Digital Philology was held in Verona, Italy (2012), http://www.filologiadigitale.it

the means to identify and view trends or patterns across the corpus (for example what time periods are covered most, which features are most prominent, or which institutions produce the largest number of digital editions), areas for improvement of errors, as well as projects which are no longer maintained or even available. This will inform future development of digital editions (from both technical and subject area perspectives), establish a hub around which collaborators can engage in community discussions, and become the source of updated information as it becomes available.

Fragmentary lists of digital editions projects already exist, but these do not record project features or provide an easy means of browsing, viewing and downloading the data, and often maintain links to projects which are no longer available.[14] Minor catalogues are curated by Paolo Monella, Cinzia Pusceddu, Aurélien Berra, the *Monastic Manuscript Project* and the wikis of Hunter College, the Digital Classicist and the *Associazione per l'Informatica Umanistica e la Cultura Digitale*.[15] With the exception of Sahle's *Catalog of Digital Scholarly Editions*, which currently records 386 projects, the catalogue emanating from our research is the most recent, and is certainly the most detailed in circulation, providing an overview of features and approaches, as well as details of the projects themselves. While Sahle's *Catalog* aims to record extant scholarly editions, our project brings together both scholarly and

---

14 See, for example, Ian Lancashire's *The Humanities Computing Yearbook 1989–1990* (Oxford: Oxford University Press, 1991). More recent resources include *arts-humanities.net* (http://www.arts-humanities.net), which also lists AHRC-funded projects (http://www.arts-humanities.net/ahrc_projects, last accessed February 2013), the *Zotero Digital Humanities Group* (http://www.zotero.org/groups/digital_humanities), *Romantic Circles Electronic Editions* (http://www.rc.umd.edu/editions) and *Rotunda Publications* (http://rotunda.upress.virginia.edu).

15 Monella's catalogue was formerly available at https://docs.google.com/document/d/1rmCkvtVJmLcJrJsUOXs90dSEcgs7MOOJdLDEb7, section 2.2 [last accessed February 2013]; Pusceddu's at http://www.digitalvariants.org/e-philology; Berra's at http://philologia.hypotheses.org/corpus; *Monastic Manuscript Project* list at http://earlymedievalmonasticism.org/listoflinks.html#Digital; Hunter College's at https://www.zotero.org/groups/hunter_college_engl_390.81/items/collectionKey/34ST6AVS; *Digital Classicist* lists, http://wiki.digitalclassicist.org/Greek_and_Latin_texts_in_digital_form and http://wiki.digitalclassicist.org/Digital_Critical_Editions_of_Texts_in_Greek_and_Latin; *Associazione per l'Informatica Umanistica e la Cultura Digitale* wiki, http://www.digitalclassicist.org/wip. Another notable catalogue is UCLA's *Catalogue of Digitized Medieval Manuscripts*, which, however, records some 3126 fully digitised manuscripts as opposed to digital editions http://manuscripts.cmrs.ucla.edu

non-scholarly resources, though it distinguishes between the two. Where Sahle gives useful summaries of each project, our catalogue also provides information on different categories and lists of technical and scholarly features. To date, we have examined and categorised 187 out of the total 325 editions harvested thus far.[16] The reason for not yet fully cataloguing all the digital editions collected is practical: listing editions is a relatively effortless process, but examining a project, on the other hand, is a slower and more labour-intensive activity, with much time spent looking for information (whether available via the project website or gathered directly from the creators). The number of projects suitable for further study will grow as our catalogue expands, and we aim fully to examine and categorise all projects listed as this research progresses.

Methodology

The editions present in the catalogue come from numerous sources, and their selection follows basic criteria: the electronic texts, whether available online or on CD-ROM, can be ongoing or complete projects,[17] born-digital editions[18] as well as electronic reproductions of print volumes. They were gathered from the previously mentioned catalogues, from lists such as *Projects using the TEI*,[19] RSS feeds,[20] publications (articles, reviews and books), Google Scholar alerts, Twitter, word of mouth, web browsing and chaining.[21]

---

16 The number is subject to change as the project progresses. The collection progress described in this chapter ran from August 2012 until December 2013.
Examined means that the authors have looked at the editions in great detail. In this sense, the catalogue will never be *complete*. New editions are systematically added to a queue waiting to be analysed in the same detail. The editions in Sahle's *Catalog* will also be included in our database, with the exception of those listed by him but appear no longer to exist, for example *Con2: An Edition of the Anglo-Saxon Chronicles, 924–983* (formerly available at http://www.slu.edu/departments/english/chron/index.html).
17 Still active on the web.
18 *Born-digital edition* refers to text born digital and edited for a digital publication.
19 Projects using TEI, http://www.tei-c.org/Activities/Projects/index.xml
20 Such as *The Ancient World Online* (http://ancientworldonline.blogspot.co.uk); arts-humanities.net (http://www.arts-humanities.net) and *Digital Classicist seminars* (http://www.digitalclassicist.org/wip).
21 For chaining, see David Ellis, 'Modeling the Information-seeking Patterns of Academic Researchers: A Grounded Theory Approach', *The Library Quarterly*, 63 (1993), 469–86 (p. 482), http://www.jstor.org/stable/4308867

In line with Klaus Krippendorf's content analysis method, the data was carefully collected and assessed both quantitatively and qualitatively, in order to make reliable inferences from which further research can stem and develop.[22] The content analysis was carried out along two parallel tracks: a data gathering approach, whereby each project team was contacted with a short questionnaire aimed at gaining a deeper understanding of both the production and user needs of the edition (see section 3.1.); and an observational examination of extant knowledge about the electronic edition through the analysis of the project website and its related publications. To date (March 2014), our catalogue showcases 187 digital editions, collected and examined over a period of sixteen months. As previously mentioned, the *Catalogue of Digital Editions* makes a distinction between scholarly and non-scholarly digital editions, and replicas of existing print volumes.[23] Of course, there are many more editions left to include and, indeed, many more to come.[24] Launched in May 2013,[25] the website showcases visualisations of the catalogue data, providing contextual information, as well as encouraging the community to contribute information, suggestions for improvement or feedback.

Data gathering

Creators of the digital editions collected were contacted directly between August 2012 and March 2013 and asked to provide information about their projects in structured categories. The questionnaire was disseminated and completed through email due to the scale of the

---

22 Klaus Krippendorf, *Content Analysis: An Introduction to Its Methodology*, 2nd ed. (Thousand Oaks: Sage, 2004). Statistically, the higher the number of editions, the more accurate and revealing the results (as they are less subject to sampling risk). Similarly, the more meticulous the qualitative analysis (the number of features under investigation), the clearer the implications.
23 Once again, it is important to stress that while making this distinction, this catalogue lists all electronic texts, regardless of their academic purpose.
24 To the authors' knowledge, there is no definitive or rough estimation of the total number of electronic editions active today on the web. However, based on the lists mentioned earlier, it seems fair to suggest a combined total of some 500 editions (excluding forthcoming and inactive projects archived in the *Wayback Machine* http://archive.org/web/web.php).
25 *A Catalogue of Digital Editions*, https://github.com/gfranzini/digEds_cat. The catalogue was initially set up as a *Google Sheet* (spreadsheet) viewable with any online reader but has now moved to GitHub.

research, and aimed to discover what the project goals and achievements were, what type of user enquiries or requests had been received, if the project had gathered any statistics regarding use of the resource, if the project understood who their main audience was, the project budget and team size needed to create the resource,[26] what lessons the team felt they had learnt from undertaking the project and sustainability issues in making the resource available over the longer term. Of the seventy-eight people contacted,[27] thirty-seven replied (some in full, some partly). Of the remaining forty-one, six emails bounced back due to expired email addresses and thirty-five have yet to, and may never, reply. Information gathered from this correspondence is stored in a separate file which is used as a log, an address book and as a reference tool to track changes and developments over time.

Content analysis of available information

Once a project has been identified for inclusion in the catalogue, the edition is subject to in-depth analysis, depending on the information that can be found in the available project data. The *Catalogue of Digital Editions* contains a variety of information: the *Catalogue*, or editions examined so far; *Institution coordinates* (a list of all institutions encountered thus far and their geographical coordinates, for reference and spatial/visual analysis); *Funding body coordinates*; *Repository coordinates* (the source document's current location or home); and *Place of origin coordinates* (the source document's presumed or known hometown or country and where it is now, if different). In the future, we will also note *Linked open data* when projects share source data. Additional features are grouped into *subject areas* encompassing ontological, technological and philological aspects.

The categories are the result of a comparative study of a number of editions whose aim was to identify commonalities between editions and

---

26   Given the potentially sensitive nature of the question, interviewees were given the option to not respond.

27   The number of emails sent out to project managers is smaller than that of editions as, more often than not, project managers are either co-investigators or work on multiple projects at the same time (in these instances, the questionnaire email addresses all relevant projects).

draw out the more useful and desirable features. None of the categories represent in any way compulsory features and while one might be more important than another to certain user groups, the catalogue does not make use of any weighting system. As is the nature of content analysis, categories are rather clear-cut and some projects may not entirely subscribe to their specificity. For example, ongoing projects will figure as incomplete or the digital text may be part replica and part born-digital. In such cases, the comments field allows details about classification choices. The edition illustrated in Figure 9.1, for example, is classified as scholarly but not digital for this version of the *Carmina* does not in any way enhance the printed text. It is also not complete, and so does not satisfy the aforementioned requirements to be considered critical.

	C	D	E	F	G	H	I
1	Edition_ID	URL	Scholarly	Digital	Edition	Prototype	Language
83	Claudii Claudiani Carmina Latina	http://www.curcu		1	1	1	0 LAT

Fig. 9.1 Example application of Sahle's rules to the *Claudii Claudiani Carmina Latina* project.

There is a full and detailed table available online that lists and describes all the fields in the *Catalogue of Digital Editions* and their respective numerical scoring, indicating the breadth of useful information that can be captured about digital editions to facilitate their analysis.[28] Whenever project websites are unclear or we cannot explicitly know the information, this is noted. Examples of the information recorded include: title and web address; the historical period the text belongs to (ancient, medieval or modern, with clarification of those terms); the project scope and perceived audience; does it qualify as a scholarly digital edition according to Sahle's classification?; does it include textual criticism and/or any *apparatus criticus*?; is the content encoded in TEI-compliant XML?; are there digital facsimiles of the primary sources?; what platform is used to host the project?; details of any analytic tools provided; ease of access; is there a CD-ROM edition?; details about the project itself; translations and

---

28 Table describing all fields and numerical scoring used in our catalogue, https://github.com/gfranzini/digEds_cat/wiki/Contribute

languages; any other useful and desirable information such as licences, open or proprietary, Open Source/Open Access.

Integration and visualisation

Once recorded, the information in the catalogue can be integrated and visualised. At present, the catalogue contains fifty-four columns and an ever-increasing number of rows, showcasing a large set of data, which can only be satisfactorily viewed and understood through visualisations and detailed queries; the data will only become more complex as more examples of editions are added.

Google Fusion Tables was used to extract data from the *Google Sheet* and visualise it as a map.[29] Maps can be used as data filters, displaying only certain sets of information, helping us contextualise data and better understand distribution and relationships. In our case, a map can help institutions survey their place in the world.[30]

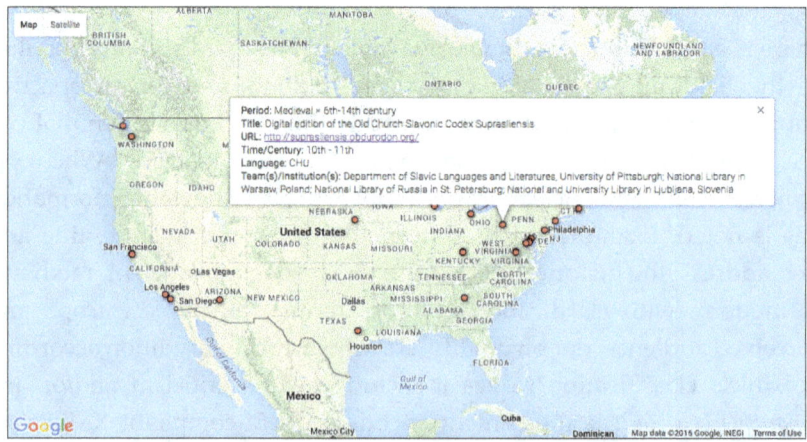

Fig. 9.2a Screenshot of a section of the map visualisation (March 2014). Location markers identify projects and pop-up windows provide information to the user.

---

29   See https://sites.google.com/site/digitaleds/mapping-editions
30   Martin Jessop, 'The Inhibition of Geographical Information in Digital Humanities Scholarship', *Literary and Linguistic Computing*, 23 (2008), 39–50 (p. 39), http://dx.doi.org/10.1093/llc/fqm041

9. A Catalogue of Digital Editions

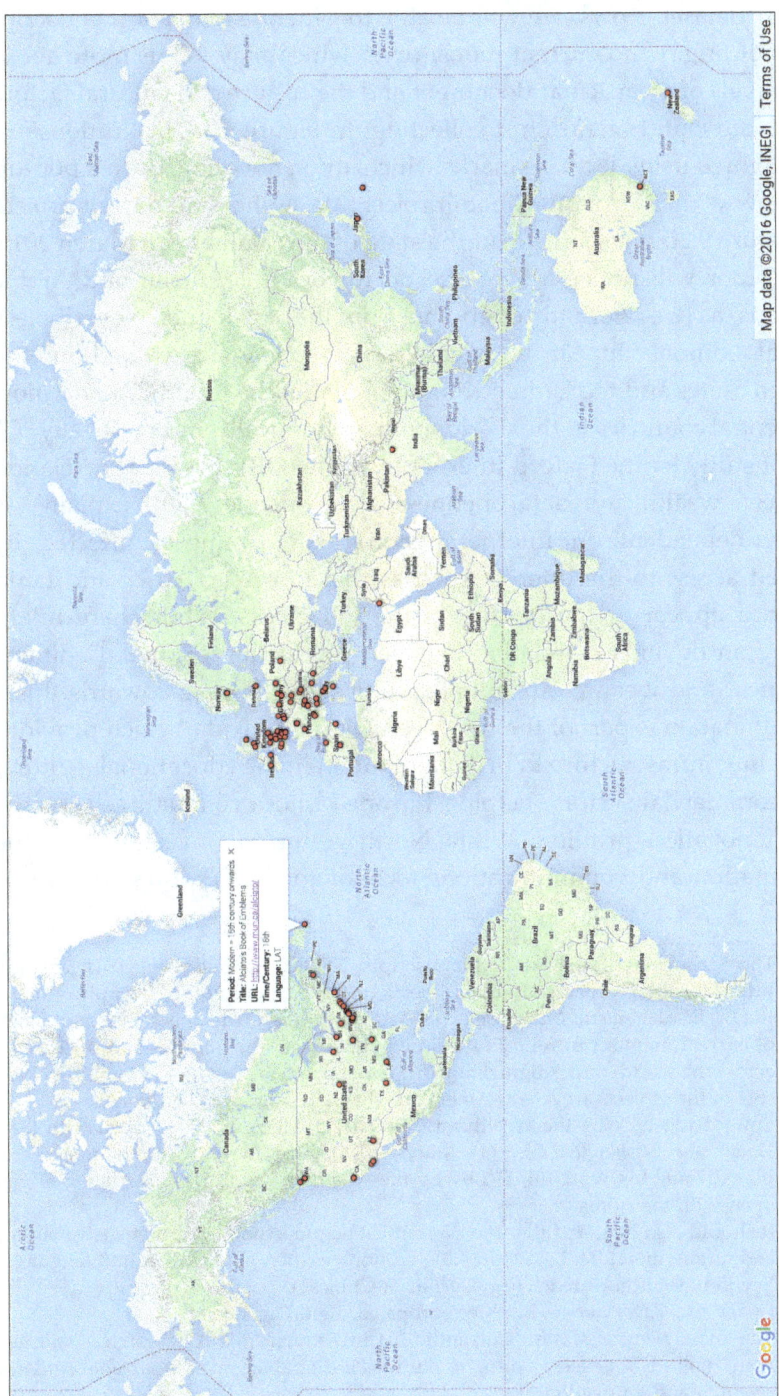

Fig. 9.2b Screenshot of the map visualisation of the editions present in the catalogue to this day (March 2014).

As our dataset grows, we will be able to generate maps of manuscript place of origin and current repository,[31] which may tell us more about the travels of a particular document and the culture and cultural factors which surround manuscript collecting. In Figure 9.2a, institutions are highlighted using location marks which, upon hovering, open a pop-up window with information about project title, author and date of project.

Figure 9.2b is a snapshot of the state of the catalogue in March 2014: the reader will notice a shortage of, for example, Asian and Arabic editions as we work through those in the catalogue. Nevertheless, digital editions appear to be a Western phenomenon, led by the United States and the United Kingdom, two of the wealthiest and most influential countries in the world, both economically and politically.[32] A recent study by the Oxford Internet Institute (OII) reveals a correlation between wealth and data openness; data openness, OII explains, is partly dependent on Internet penetration.[33] Countries affected by limited access to the Internet such as those in Asia, Africa and Latin America appear at the bottom of the OII charts. While there might not be an obvious correlation between production of digital editions, openness and wealth, our initial results seem to point towards this.[34] Dissemination is part of the European Digital Agenda, which provides a funding infrastructure to promote growth in the educational, cultural and commercial sectors, helping Europe build a competitive research and innovation profile.[35] While North American investment in the information and communications technology (ICT)[36] infrastructure is

---

31   The Schoenberg Database of Manuscripts (SDBM) is conducting such a study, http://dla.library.upenn.edu/dla/schoenberg/index.html; another example is that of the *Digitized Medieval Manuscripts* (*DMMMaps*) project, which is producing a map of current manuscript repositories in an attempt to link libraries and documents across the world, http://digitizedmedievalmanuscripts.org
32   65% of the projects are Anglo-American. That is 123 out of 187 editions.
33   Emily Badger, 'Why the Wealthiest Countries are also the Most Open with their Data', *The Washington Post* (14 March 2014), http://www.washingtonpost.com/blogs/wonkblog/wp/2014/03/14/why-the-wealthiest-countries-are-also-the-most-open-with-their-data
34   It should also be noted that the present catalogue is not a comprehensive survey and might, therefore, be overlooking editions written in alphabets and languages beyond the authors' reach (e.g. Cyrillic or Chinese).
35   *Digital Agenda for Europe*, http://ec.europa.eu/digital-agenda
36   The above website states: 'Currently, EU investment in ICT research is still less than half US levels', http://ec.europa.eu/digital-agenda/en/our-goals/pillar-v-research-and-innovation

much higher than that of Europe, both continents are at the forefront of the educational sector. Finally, we must remember that major associations and portals in the Digital Humanities are based in the US and UK.[37] We will be better able to define this relationship as the catalogue grows, and the data can be merged with other public tables to allow further analysis of trends emerging from the data collection.[38]

Results from the catalogue

Identifying and listing the features editions provide in a detailed and methodical fashion can help us refine our thoughts about digital editions. Projects are highly affected by the size of the corpus they select, the financial backing they can rely on and the timeframe within which they develop. We were able to gather much more information about the production than the usage of editions: many projects do not keep track of user statistics and, therefore, cannot provide information about how the resource is used.[39] Most editions address an intended scholarly audience but many projects do not provide basic editorial or technical information. There appears to be a tendency to leave out important information about the production process (imaging, for instance) and to place too much trust in the audience's knowledge of the field by way of assumption. Regardless of the intended audience, more could—and should—be done in terms of clarity and transparency, from both a content and contextual standpoint. However, as John Lavagnino writes:

> When we create editions, we are thinking about readers in two disciplines: readers who are editors, and readers who are not editors. [...] Making editions that work for both editors and for the popular audience will always be tricky, and moving into the digital world does not really make it much easier. [...] The most obvious problems that the popular audience has with editions stem from the apparatus, and such

---

37   Among many others, the Association for Computers and the Humanities (ACH); Alliance of Digital Humanities Organizations (ADHO); The European Association for Digital Humanities (formerly ALLC); arts-humanities.net; DHCommons; Digital Humanities Now; Humanities, Arts, Science, and Technology Advanced Collaboratory (HASTAC) and The Humanities and Technology Camp (THATCamp).

38   Some *Google Fusion Tables* users choose to make their data publicly available so that other users can merge multiple datasets to create custom and diverse visualisations.

39   One example is the digital edition of the Old Church Slavonic Codex Suprasliensis, http://suprasliensis.obdurodon.org

problems frequently have the undesirable effect of leading readers to ignore the apparatus or consider it too hard to use.[40]

It follows that editors should either strive for utmost clarity (with the end result that experts in the field might find some of the information redundant) or create layered content. The often-complex critical notes, for instance, could be organised in such a way that would allow users to filter by level of detail.

Projects urging the digital reunification of fragments or manuscript leaves housed in different locations are often internally fragmented themselves, having split the project management between different institutions. For instance, the computer and web development section of the British Library's Codex Sinaiticus project is managed by the University of Leipzig, which does not share user information with the British Library and the curators.[41]

The budget structures of projects are diverse: some small projects (e.g. *Phineas Fletcher's Sylva Poetica*) are the result of lengthy and free labour, whereby costs are either defrayed by the authors themselves or the work is carried out in their spare time; some editions hide behind pay walls or registrations forms (the fourteen *Rotunda* editions by the University of Virginia Press, for example), or can be fully accessed only by borrowing or purchasing the CD-ROM.

Technical trends emerge: the pie chart below (Figure 9.3) represents the 187 editions covered so far by the catalogue. The chart showcases the technologies used to encode the source texts and how many projects in the catalogue employ those technologies. Each slice is broken down even further to show, for example, how many ancient texts have been encoded using TEI as opposed to custom XML. Of the electronic editions collected and examined thus far only sixty-nine (37%) follow TEI encoding standards; fourteen (7%) use a bespoke set of XML tags to suit the features of the source text; thirty-seven (20%) employ other technologies, namely HTML, Cascading Style Sheets (CSS) and Plain Text; and the remaining sixty-seven projects (36% of the entire catalogue) do not clearly state if and how encoding was carried out, so we have

---

40 John Lavagnino, 'Access', *Literary and Linguistic Computing*, 24 (2009), 63–76 (pp. 65–66), http://dx.doi.org/10.1093/llc/fqn038

41 As orally reported to Greta Franzini by one of the British Library curators in charge of the project in May 2012.

labelled those 'unclear'.⁴² Two reasons were given why projects prefer to devise custom XML rather than adopt the recommended TEI tag-set. The first is purely practical: TEI has to be learnt and some projects feel they do not have the time to develop and apply this skill effectively. The second reason is editorial in that custom XML can be designed to better fit the nature and features of the source text. As for HTML, CSS and plain text editions, these technologies are typical of older projects, such as *D. Iunii Iuvenalis Saturae* or *Supliciae Conquestio*.⁴³

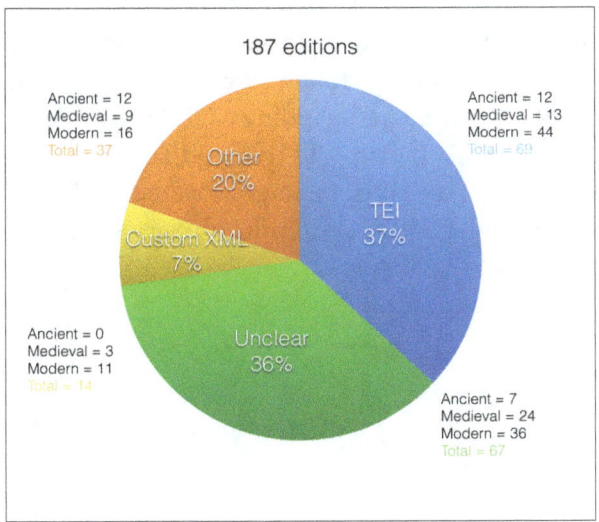

Fig. 9.3 Use of XML-TEI vs. other technologies in the digital editions featured in the catalogue.

These results are rather surprising considering TEI's promotional strategy.⁴⁴ The number of projects adopting TEI guidelines is gradually increasing, perhaps reflecting TEI's systematic growth and improvement.

---

42   These figures are based on the study of information explicitly available on the project website. It is likely that any implied or non-explicit information will fall under the 'unclear' slice of the pie chart (see Figure 9.3).

43   The former is available at http://www.curculio.org/Juvenal, the latter at http://www.curculio.org/Sulpiciae

44   The chief dissemination avenues being *The Journal of the Text Encoding Initiative* (http://journal.tei-c.org/journal), workshops, conference and seminar presentations given not only by members of the TEI community but also by project investigators who are adopting the standard, as well as publications and word of mouth. More recently (March 2014), the TEI advertised a Social Media Coordinator position as it seeks to improve outreach.

Nevertheless, the number of TEI editions is still low, suggesting some resistance to implementing this specific set of tags and structures. Today, at a time when scholars are gradually recognising the advantages of community-driven projects, standards need to be adopted if we are to push digital editions in a social direction or integrate their resources. Without guidelines such as the TEI, exchange and repurposing of data will not be possible and electronic editions will be used as standalone objects with their own set of characteristics, objectives and requirements.

The vast majority of texts encoded in TEI are written in English (and older variants thereof, i.e. Old and Middle English); the second most represented language is Latin, followed by French (including Old and Middle), Old Norse, German (including Middle High German), Welsh, Spanish, Ancient Greek, Italian, Old Irish and Hebrew.

Figure 9.4 below shows the languages covered by the catalogue and the predominance of English and Latin primary sources (which may change as we come to catalogue further Asian editions).

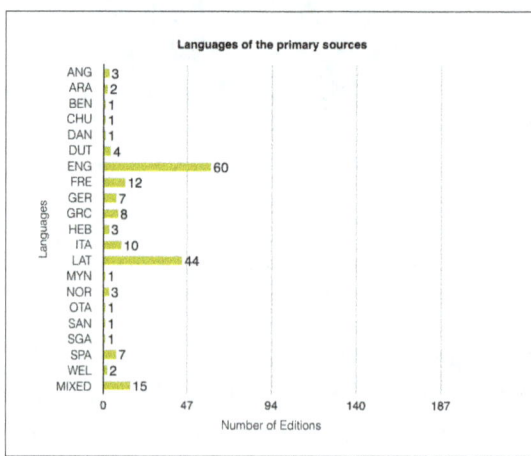

Fig. 9.4 Languages of the primary sources present in the catalogue. Some projects contain multiple texts in different languages. For the purpose of this calculation and illustration, these projects are categorised under *Mixed*. *Mixed* covers projects focussing on multiple texts and combinations of Ancient Greek, Aramaic, English, French, German, Hebrew, Latin, Middle English, Polish, Sanskrit and Vietnamese.

As the catalogue grows and more editions are added, it will be interesting to discover whether there is a relationship between a particular language and the use of XML. Are some languages easier to encode and therefore more likely to be digitally rendered using XML? As it stands, the predominance of English and Latin could be indicative of three things: apart from being the most widely known languages out of those featured in the catalogue, English and Latin texts are more likely to be encoded in XML because both are Latin-script languages;[45] XML is not yet easily implementable for non-Latin scripts (e.g. Cyrillic or Arabic); or the XML (and TEI) penetration is higher in academic environment where English and Latin are studied.

Most scholars working in the field of digital editions will be aware of Creative Commons licences[46] and how important it is to make work available under these conditions in order to promote research and further knowledge. Creative Commons licences appear to be becoming increasingly popular, and yet out of the 187 editions examined thus far, only thirty-two are available under a Creative Commons licence. The content of the remaining editions is either proprietary or available under different licences.

Other issues emerge from the survey, such as broken links, unavailable projects or expired email addresses, due to poor maintenance (for instance, the *purchase* button of the *Domesday Explorer* CD-ROM edition returns a 404 error[47]). Only a few people have provided information about project costs, or will allow this information to be shared.[48] Open projects are not always transparent, and funding appears to be a taboo topic.[49]

Digital editions of ancient vs. modern texts

Our catalogue of extant digital editions has led us to recognise a numerical disparity between the electronic reproduction of medieval and modern documents and manuscripts predating the fifth century AD.

---

45 Latin-script languages present fewer challenges when it comes to digitisation and encoding because computer software has been trained to recognise these characters.
46 For more information about these licences, see http://creativecommons.org
47 *Domesday Explorer*, http://www.domesdaybook.net
48 However, it does not seem unreasonable to expect publicly funded projects, such as those supported by JISC, to be open to such questions.
49 When asked about funding, one of the investigators of the *Orlando Furioso Hypertext Project*, http://stel.ub.edu/orlando, funded by the *Ministerio de Educación y Ciencia* and the *Istituto Italiano di Cultura di Barcelona*, replied: '*Su questa questione, capisce che non voglia dare forse i dati concreti*' [With regard to this matter, I am sure you can appreciate why I prefer not to disclose concrete numbers] (10 March 2013).

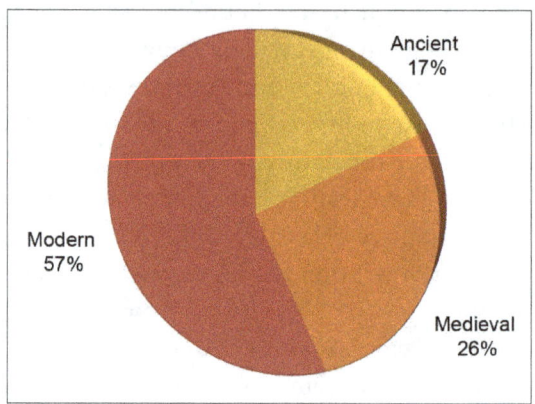

Fig. 9.5 Out of the 187 projects fully analysed, over half are electronic editions of modern texts.

Possible reasons for this could be that the number of modern manuscripts is larger than that of ancient manuscripts; that eighteenth- to twentieth-century manuscripts might be of more interest as they more closely relate to present times; that the absence of suitable, user-friendly tools supporting ancient scripts stops people from creating these resources. There are perhaps issues of funding: are modern topics better supported by funding councils? Or is the perceived degree of the usefulness of providing editions of texts less in cases where a relatively small proportion of society will have the skills to read them? Mats Dahlström, who also noticed a shortage of scholarly editions of classical works, offers further reasons:

> [...] shortages of time, resources, and competence. [...] Another reason for this conspicuous lack is the varying degrees of meritocratic prestige of print and digital media. Further reasons include: copyright restrictions; presumed illucrativity and consequential difficulty in finding financial support; authenticity, security, and long-time preservation uncertainties; as of yet severely primitive software for storing, presenting, encoding, and displaying the kind of complexity inherent in classical works. Finally, both the construction and the usage of existing digital SE:s [scholarly editions] need probably be thoroughly evaluated.[50]

---

50 Mats Dahlström, 'Digital Incunabules: Versionality and Versatility in Digital Scholarly Editions', in *ICCC/IFIP Third Conference on Electronic Publishing 2000, Kaliningrad State University, Kaliningrad/Svetlogorsk, Russia, 17th–19th August 2000* (Washington: ICCC Press, 2000).

Moreover, as John Lavagnino noted twenty years ago:

> In the last few decades, many textual scholars have come to believe that classical texts and modern texts have very different kinds of textual problems and constitute different kinds of literary works. Texts from classical antiquity have great textual problems: any manuscript that has survived to our day of such texts is the product of a long sequence of copyings and recopyings, so that it's likely to be full of errors in transmission that need to be corrected. These are errors on such a scale that the works are often simply unreadable without editorial correction. But for modern texts, the body of surviving evidence is very different. For texts circulated since the invention of movable type, and particularly for texts written since the seventeenth and eighteenth centuries, the problem of mistransmission is less and less imposing. The texts have been copied only a few times prior to the creation of our sources, rather than many times, and we often have many more of the sources, sometimes going back to the author's own drafts. Error will always be present, and is still sometimes a great problem, but it ceases to be the central problem.
>
> What we have for many modern works is not a shortage of reliable information, but an excess: often there is far too much textual information to include in any printed edition. We find, for example, cases in which a writer made extensive revisions over a span of many years, so that there may be a number of versions that were all produced by the same person and that all have good claims to our attention; but which one should be the text that a scholarly edition prints?[51]

The difference in numbers between classical and modern digital editions is a complex issue which deserves further attention.

A good digital edition? Some recommendations

The catalogue reveals just how different editions can be, despite them all sharing a core objective to disseminate and advance new knowledge about the text by means of the digital medium.[52] Structures and outputs are dictated by numerous variables, including readership, usage and resources. In this inevitably dynamic, ever-changing reality, there is perhaps no real necessity to set an axiom or formulate a strict definition

---

51 John Lavagnino, 'Reading, Scholarship and Hypertext Editions', *TEXT*, 8 (1995), 109–24 (p. 111), http://www.stg.brown.edu/resources/stg/monographs/rshe.html
52 *Digital medium* understood as an aid to, not a replacement of, the print publication, where available.

of digital scholarly edition. How does defining an edition affect that edition and its audience? Should we not be more concerned about generating usable and useful content?[53]

From creating the catalogue and analysing various digital editions in detail, we suggest that in order to be comprehensive and widely used, a digital edition should include descriptive information about the purpose of the edition, the manuscripts' history, production, significance and use, high definition images of the manuscript, optimised for the web, with the possibility of downloading or purchasing image files for personal or educational use,[54] documentation about the photographic process and technical metadata about the capture equipment and a transcription of the text and marginalia, including non-standard textual features (abbreviations, punctuation marks etc.) to make the manuscript more accessible to a non-expert audience. If the nature of the project is more scholarly, then

> The transcribed text must attain the usual levels of critical accuracy, meaning that the edition needs to follow diplomatic standards and be the product of expert work. The modern reader must have confidence in the edited text.[55]

Transcriptions should also conform to XML standards for searchability, worldwide integration, interchange and repurposing of data. 'A well-made electronic scholarly edition will be built on encoding of great complexity and richness'.[56] The digital edition should include searchable text and images[57] made possible with the use of appropriate and meaningful metadata, a critical apparatus, indices and word lists

---

53   Melissa Terras, 'Should We Just Send a Copy? Digitisation, Usefulness and Users', *Art Libraries Journal*, 35.1 (2010), 22–27, http://discovery.ucl.ac.uk/171096/1/Terras_Sendacopy.pdf

54   Greta Franzini purchased images of the primary source that her edition is based on for €100 (September 2011). The purchase came with an agreement whereby these images could only be published online if appropriately credited.

55   Jonas Carlquist, 'Medieval Manuscripts, Hypertext and Reading: Visions of Digital Editions', *Literary and Linguistic Computing*, 19 (2004), 105–18 (p.115), http://dx.doi.org/10.1093/llc/19.1.105

56   Peter Robinson, 'Where We Are with Electronic Scholarly Editions, and Where We Want to Be', *Jahrbuch für Computerphilologie*, 5 (2003), 125–46.

57   Susan Hockey, *Electronic Texts in the Humanities* (Oxford: Oxford University Press, 2010), pp. 141–42.

to facilitate filtering and more advanced searches, downloadable data (XML files), as well as print-friendly outputs or versions,[58] links to external resources, such as word or abbreviation dictionaries, clarifications of palaeographical terms and biographical information about the people mentioned within the text, different views of the text 'XML for analysis, XHTML for consultation on the screen and PDF for printing out as a reading edition',[59] a translation if necessary (whether internal to the website or a link to an existing, third party translation) for a wider appreciation of the text, space for users to comment, suggest improvements or corrections and discuss the material. The web platform or content management system (CMS) on which the edition runs should conform to W3C (World Wide Web Consortium) standards;[60] provide project documentation to allow the user to appreciate the edition's limitations or customisations and thus better utilise the resource; provide metadata (METS: Metadata Encoding and Transmission Standard) for all types of files (transcriptions, images etc.) in order to identify easily information and edition components as well as to understand better their mutual relationships,[61] text-image linking, as well as hyperlinking (desirable, not essential) and variant readings. If, however, the project is not a *variorum* edition, variant readings should at least be mentioned or referred to. If variants are used, these should be indicated as such by the authors.[62] Finally, the project should clearly state the type of licence the work is released under, not only as a means of stressing ownership but, more importantly, of telling users the extent to which they are allowed to repurpose content. Findings from this analysis will go onto inform the production Greta Franzini's diplomatic edition of St. Augustine's *De Civitate Dei*.

---

58 Carlquist, 'Medieval Manuscripts, Hypertext and Reading'.
59 Edward Vanhoutte, 'Every Reader his own Bibliographer—An Absurdity?', in *Text Editing, Print and the Digital World*, ed. Marilyn Deegan and Kathryn Sutherland (Farnham: Ashgate, 2009), pp. 99–110 (p. 109).
60 The *World Wide Web Consortium*, http://www.w3.org
61 The *Metadata Encoding and Transmission Standard*, http://www.loc.gov/standards/mets
62 Robinson, 'Where We Are with Electronic Scholarly Editions'.

Conclusion

The ultimate aim of our catalogue of digital editions is to record extant digital editions of texts and their features and functionality, helping us to establish an overview of past and current practice in the creation of digital editions and draw up a digital edition best practice profile. In building the catalogue this way, data is centralised and systematically organised into a unique bank which could be used in other studies and is useful to the community. While initially curated by Greta Franzini, a larger group of administrators are now carrying out regular updates, ensuring accurate data, providing support and broader outreach while integrating and populating the database on an ongoing basis. The catalogue itself raises issues about the nature of digital editions and the relationship of digital editions to source texts, institutions, and funding structures, while encouraging us to pause and establish the best way in which to support the user experience when engaging with such digital content. Trends emerge regarding the types of manuscripts which are supported and explored in digital editions, and we can begin to understand the larger issues that direct the work of the Digital Humanities community when they undertake a scholarly digital edition project. It is only by thoroughly cataloguing and analysing the hundreds of digital editions that now exist that we can understand and question the scope of the field, spot technical and procedural trends, and make recommendations as to how best to build digital editions that will provide the information required by users and expected by the Digital Humanities community.

10. Early Modern Correspondence: A New Challenge for Digital Editions

Camille Desenclos

The project of building a platform dedicated to early modern correspondence at the École Nationale des Chartes is the starting point for this contribution. Its reflections are based on the editing of two early modern corpora: the correspondence of Antoine Du Bourg, chancellor during the reign of Francis I (1536–1538),[1] and the correspondence of the extraordinary embassy led by the duke of Angoulême in the Holy Roman Empire (1620–1621).[2] The former encompasses approximately 1200 letters concerning every matter with which a chancellor had to deal (justice, royal finances, monitoring printed production, economic policies etc.), while the latter contains only 80 letters, which are longer and embrace the international network of French diplomacy in the early seventeenth century. Based on traditional editorial practices and the issues that we confronted while encoding, our aim was to build a documented schema that could support and highlight the specific characteristics of correspondence. Above all, this project has given us the opportunity to reconsider the issues and aims of digital scholarly editions of early modern correspondence. Through the process of highlighting

---

[1] *La correspondance du chancelier Antoine du Bourg*, a project at the École Nationale des Chartes, http://elec.enc.sorbonne.fr/dubourg. At this time, there are around 100 letters published, and the edition is still in progress.

[2] *L'ambassade extraordinaire des ducs d'Angoulême, comte de Béthune et abbé de Préaux*, a project at the École Nationale des Chartes, http://corpus.enc.sorbonne.fr/angouleme. This is only a beta version.

its formal and historical specificities, it has become quite clear that the present form of digital editions is not well suited to correspondence. This is especially the case for early modern correspondence.

Correspondence within the digital field

Editing correspondence: aims and general issues

Letters are one of the most important sources in the field of historical research.[3] They show, perhaps better than any other source, political, cultural and even commercial forces at work. They are not the result of a single act, but are, rather, part of a process, be it an exchange of information, a commercial transaction, a political negotiation, a cultural or spiritual discussion[4] etc. When editing them for scholarly purposes, we must first, therefore, reconstruct this process. An isolated letter can of course be understood and used by researchers, as it may contain historical information (the description of a battle or political audience etc.). But a single letter does not allow us to understand the context of the correspondence, the very reason for its existence: the origin and evolution of the relationship between the people involved. It is only through the analysis of several letters that we can gain a deeper understanding of the nature of that relationship. The main aim of a scholarly edition should therefore be to restore the general context, the continual dialogue between two individuals: one letter may refer to a previous one and call for a response, and this dialogue may be broken due to letters having been lost. An edition cannot of course overcome such losses, but it can attempt to build bridges between letters (through links, references to other correspondence or archives etc.) in order to restore the general meaning of the correspondence and consider it not as a collection of individual letters but as an intellectual entity. As far

---

3   *Les correspondances: Problématiques et économie d'un 'genre littéraire': Actes du colloque international 'Les correspondances'*, Nantes, 4–7 octobre 1982, ed. by Jean-Louis Bonnat, Mireille Bossis and Hélène Girard (Nantes: Université de Nantes, 1983).

4   Letters contributed for example greatly to the establishment and spread of late humanism, as the principal way in which the members shared and discussed their opinions. See Axel E. Walter, *Späthumanismus und Konfessionspolitik im konfessionellen Zeitalter: Die europäische Gelehrtenrepublik um 1600 im Spiegel der Korrespondenzen Georg Michael Lingelsheim* (Tübingen: Max Niemeyer Verlag, 2004).

as possible, therefore, a scholarly edition of correspondence must try to (re)present a coherent slice of life. But, if corpora are generally built around a typology of documents (e.g. royal acts), or more rarely on a theme (e.g. the legal status of religious minorities in medieval Christian and Islamic societies[5]), which give them a degree of consistency, epistolary documents are by their nature heterogeneous. They are produced by (at least) two people, writing in different locations, and contain a wealth of information of various kinds. The same letter might deal with information about political changes in France, military events in the Holy Roman Empire and the purchase of books. Editions of correspondence can thereby quickly appear jumbled. For editions based on the typology of documents, the aim seems quite clear: restoring the writing activity of a political or religious institution. The corpus itself is already established—the whole writing activity of one institution—and a chronological choice has to be made, but there is no need to justify the reason behind the edition. The choice is even simpler when the envisaged content of the edition comes from only one manuscript, such as for political discourses, memoirs or chronicles. For correspondence, however, the choice is more complex. The researcher must choose the sender, but must also decide upon one or more addressees. For example, he or she can only edit the active correspondence of ambassadors to their king or their active and passive correspondence with the king and/ or with other ambassadors and so on. Unlike charters and documents for which the context is obvious—an institution producing documents regardless of an envisaged public—there are as many choices as there are contexts for the production of letters.

At first sight, editions of correspondence seem to be the poor relation within the family of digital editions. The collection of digital editions at the École Nationale des Chartes, Élec,[6] corroborates this assertion: of the thirty editions available on the website, fourteen are scholarly editions, and only one is a scholarly edition of correspondence (that of Antoine

---

5 *Relmin: le statut légal des minorités religieuses dans l'espace euro-méditerranée (V^e–XVe siècle)*, project led by the University of Nantes and hosted at the L'Institut de recherche et d'histoire des textes (IRHT), http://www.cn-telma.fr/relmin/index
6 Élec (Éditions en ligne de l'École des chartes), http://elec.enc.sorbonne.fr. To this collection must be added another platform which contains beta versions of editions (http://corpus.enc.sorbonne.fr) with three other digital scholarly editions. Only one of them is an edition of correspondence.

Du Bourg). This observation is demonstrated more starkly by the *Telma* project, led by the Centre national de la recherche scientifique (CNRS),[7] which has six digital scholarly editions, none of them of correspondence. There are around twenty projects on correspondence in Europe and North America, barely ten per cent of the editions in the world.[8] Editions of manuscripts, or more generally of documentary units, seem to be preferred to those of correspondences: the text is already established and with an internal consistency.

How should we use metadata?

In addition to the editorial issues, the benefits of publishing digitally are not immediately apparent for series of correspondence. The characteristics of correspondence, such as the layout, which enables the reader to identify clearly the date, the signature and so on, can be expressed quite easily in a print edition. Yet the semantic step required by the encoding and the transfer to a digital framework turns these structural elements into editorial problems. Many issues need to be addressed: description of multiple metadata, concordance between layout and structure, semantic encoding for each part of the letter etc.

Metadata are crucial for digital scholarly editions of letters. They are the only way to identify and distinguish one letter from another. Above all, they give the letter a meaning, a formal proof of its place within the whole correspondence, by including details of the sender, addressee, date and place of writing, and sometimes even the date of receipt. As proof of the importance of metadata, almost every digital scholarly edition permits browsing of its corpus via these criteria.

If good structuring of the metadata offers a useful basis for the user, they must also be well displayed. Unfortunately, the display of the search

---

7   *Telma* (Traitement électronique des manuscrits et des archives), a project hosted by the Institut de recherche et d'histoire des textes, http://www.cn-telma.fr

8   There is no complete list of editions of correspondences. In order to find some quantitative information, we have compared various lists:
    - the Wiki-page of the TEI-SIG Correspondence, http://wiki.tei-c.org/index.php/SIG:Correspondence#Correspondence_Projects
    - the projects list of the Centre for Editing Lives and Letters, http://www.livesandletters.ac.uk
    - Greta Franzini, *A Catalogue of Digital Editions*, https://github.com/gfranzini/digEds_cat/wiki, for which see also the contribution by Franzini, Terras and Mahony in this volume.

results frequently fails to reflect the quality of the editions themselves, and does not reflect the global coherence of the correspondence. Most digital editions of correspondence, such as those of Carl-Maria von Weber[9] or Thomas Bodley,[10] allow access to a specific letter through these criteria, but only via their list of results. We cannot move on to another letter without going back to the list of results. By limiting the correspondence to a searchable object, the edition facilitates, in a sense, the research. Specific information can be found more easily without being lost within a number of letters. Thus a biographer can find useful information about a person under study simply by searching for his or her name within the edition.

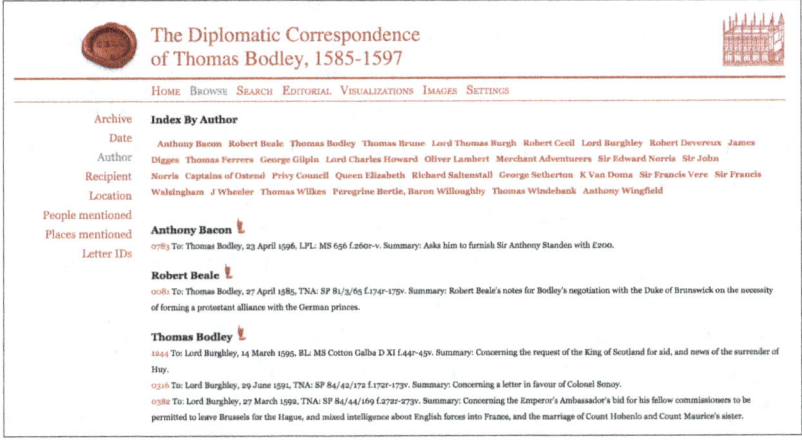

Fig. 10.1 Screenshot from the browsing page (and main access) to the correspondence of Thomas Bodley.

This breaks the dialogue created through the correspondence, however, and prevents the researcher from examining the wider context of the writing. No continuous reading, and consequently no global apprehension of the corpus, is allowed. This hides the true nature of a correspondence: that it is a flow of information. By offering a continuous reading, an edition places the letter in its proper context as

---

9   *Carl-Maria-von-Weber-Gesamtausgabe*, a project at the Akademie der Wissenschaften und der Literatur, Mainz, http://www.weber-gesamtausgabe.de/de/Index

10 *The Diplomatic Correspondence of Thomas Bodley*, a project at the Centre for Editing Lives and Letters at University College London, http://www.livesandletters.ac.uk/bodley/bodley.html

part of a dialogue, not just as a piece of information. Publishing digitally should not necessitate the loss of one of the advantages of paper: that of continuous reading. We do not deny the importance of providing several access points to facilitate navigation throughout sizeable corpora. But a scholarly edition of correspondence should, first and foremost, before providing search tools, transcribe a slice of life and make it understandable.

The main aim of producing a digital scholarly edition of a correspondence should not, then, be the creation of a database of letters—which can be a second step—but rather, editions should aim to offer a coherent object of study. The text must come first. At that point the edition can be used by researchers in various ways. An edition can, and should, be used by researchers for different purposes than those that were the initial aim of the edition. One edition can be produced, for instance, in order to recreate the intellectual network of Late Humanism, but another researcher may use it as a source of information about the Thirty Years War or about political habits. The aim therefore should be to build a solid and reusable structure with well identified metadata, for both straightforward study via the pages of the edition and more extensive use through the underlying XML files.

One of the major research aims of the study of early modern correspondence, and of correspondence in general, is the (re)construction of networks. Once perhaps considered less important, indexing, especially through traditional metadata such as sender, addressee and place of writing, has become the main value of such digital editions. We are preserving the advantages of the traditional edition (historical and prosopographical background) but with new possibilities for reconstitution of networks. By the links created first between the sender and the addressee and then between the different people mentioned within the letters, a social, commercial and even cultural network can be reconstructed. The analysis of correspondence is, for example, the first tool for studying the 'Republic of Letters', i.e. the long-distance intellectual community in the late seventeenth and eighteenth centuries. Different kinds of exploitation can be envisaged, from a simple prosopographical dictionary (linked to the letters) to a dynamic graph. For the time being, the first solution is the most common, through identification systems, sometimes supported by a database that provides access to the letters by date, place, sender, addressee or some other criteria. We can also find inspiration in other projects, such as the Pez correspondence.[11] Although not digital, this edition has been used to create a database of every book mentioned within the letters, to recreate the theoretical library of the brothers Pez and therefore to inform us about the general cultural environment of learned people in the eighteenth century.

Characteristics of early modern correspondence

TEI and early modern correspondence

A letter is identified first through its form: salutation, date, signature and address. These elements must be considered along with the edition and highlighted in order to facilitate a general understanding of the letter. Requirements differ, however, between early modern correspondence and that from nearer our own time. In the former, for example, there is no envelope,[12] as the address was normally written directly on the verso of the last folio. The editor does not need to describe an object such as the envelope, but rather a new block of text,[13] which has to be differentiated from the main text (the body of the letter), which was written on the same material. The form of the letter is also much more strictly structured in early modern correspondence. The form of early modern letters was not free and had to follow various rules, especially within the area of political correspondence, as part of a wider protocol: salutation, sometimes a formula of politeness, a courtesy formula, time and place, signatures.

---

11 *Monastic enlightenment and the Benedictine Republic of letters: The correspondence of the brothers Pez*, a project at the Institut für Österreichische Geschichte, http://www.univie.ac.at/monastische_aufklaerung/en/bernhard-and-hieronymus-pez

12 The envelope is a part of the letter as general object. Without the envelope, which contains the address, the letter cannot be identified. But the text written on the envelope cannot be considered as part of the content of the letter or even be considered purely as metadata. An appropriate form of encoding has to be found. A similar issue is represented by attachments that can be found within early modern correspondence. They complete the content of the letter but are written on a different piece of paper; they must be separated but linked at the same time. At present, no satisfactory solution has been found.

13 Most editors do not record addresses and similar text found on the last folio. This omission is unfortunate, as these often contain useful information, such as the date of reception or the exact rank of the addressee. At the very least, the possibility of encoding such text should be available to the editor.

This form should be re-transcribed clearly and accurately when preparing the digital part of the edition. These elements could be structured as simple sections of text, but this option would not capture their original meaning. Structures such as salutations, courtesy formulas or signatures could appear as equivalent to diplomatic structuring for charters. For correspondence, these elements are not optional, and furthermore a letter cannot be formally identified if they are not distinguished from the main body of its text. These structures are also objects of study for Diplomatics, which focuses on the critical analysis of the form of documents. However, the form is as important as the content, since it allows immediate identification of the nature of the text (a letter), its aims (who is writing to whom) and its context (through the choice of the politeness and courtesy formulas). Only the encoding of each specific element can accurately render the text, its coherence, legibility and initial form.

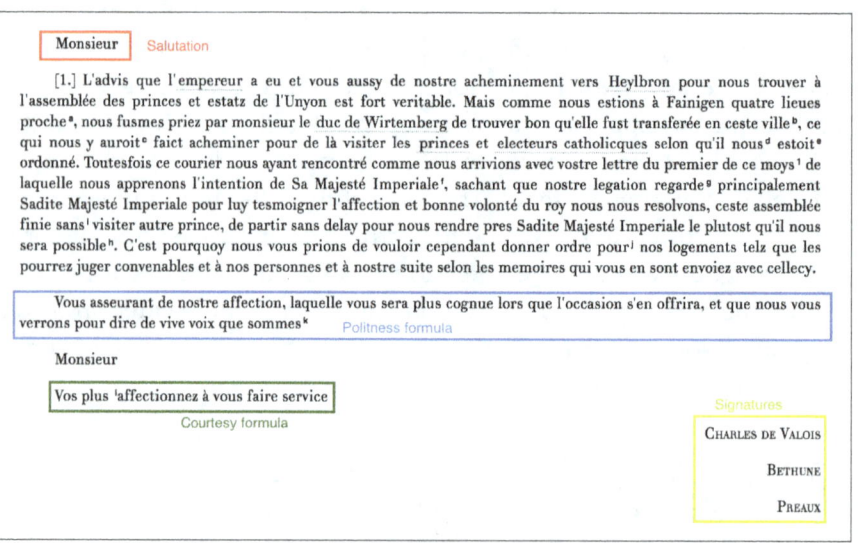

Fig. 10.2 Diplomatic formulas of early modern correspondence.

The encoding guidelines developed and maintained by the Text Encoding Initiative (TEI) are the most common standard used in the preparation of digital scholarly editions today.[14] Like many other projects, we have

---

14 *TEI P5: Guidelines for Electronic Text Encoding and Interchange*, 2016, http://www.tei-c.org/release/doc/tei-p5-doc/en/html

chosen these guidelines for the implementation of ours. The different structural features of the diplomatic letter are not sufficiently well distinguished by the TEI, however. These features can be encoded separately as various segments of text, but the TEI does not provide enough specific elements in order to identify clearly the meaning of each segment. Created to encompass a large variety of documents, the TEI is too general to cover the specifics of each particular kind of text. That is one of its major advantages. But correspondence is too specific to fit into this general standard. In fact, instead of making the encoding easier through the *Guidelines* and years of user experience, TEI complicates the encoding of early modern correspondence. It might indeed be possible to use some general TEI elements such as <seg> (segment), with a type attribute, to convey the features specific to this type of document. However, in order to achieve the required degree of granularity, it is necessary to use one or more attributes for each element: one can, for example, mark later additions with the help of a @type attribute, but it is then also necessary to add @subtype in order to state whether such the addition represents a date of reception, a summary etc., as one can see from the example below:

```
<p>
   <seg type="salutation">Monsieur,</seg>
</p>
<p xml:id="16-p1" n="1">L'avis que l'empereur a eu et vous aussy […]</p>
<p>
   <seg type="courtesy">Vous asseurant de nostre affection,
   laquelle vous sera plus cognue lors que l'occasion s'en
   offrira, et que nous vous verrons pour dire de vive
   voix que sommes, Monsieur, </seg>
   <seg type="courtesy">Vos plus affectionnez à vous faire
   service</seg>
   <seg type="signature"><name>Charles de Valois.</name>
   <name>Bethune</name><name>Preaux</name></seg>
   <seg type="mention" subtype="adresse">À monsieur,
   monsieur de Puisieux, conseiller du roi en ses conseils
   d'Estat et privé et premier secretaire des commandemens
   de Sa Majesté</seg>
</p>
```

A solution such as this, while TEI-conformant, results in verbose encoding which is open to mistakes. Some lighter semantic encoding is, however, possible with the TEI: in fact, the TEI offers a limited number of elements that can be used for this purpose, such as the element <opener> for opening formulas, <signed> for signatures and <closer> for closing formulas. But because of the general nature of the TEI, which offers support for every kind of text, these elements have a broader meaning than is required. As defined in the TEI *Guidelines*, the <opener> element 'groups together dateline, byline, salutation, and similar phrases appearing as a preliminary group at the start of a division, especially of a letter'.[15] Although clearly designed with modern letters in mind, these can be made to work with older material, but the *Guidelines* should offer better documentation and further examples to help researchers working with such material to make the appropriate choices.

Nor does the TEI offer elements designed for the semantic encoding of the final folio. The addressee often wrote on the back of the last folio the name of the sender, the date of the letter and sometimes the date of receipt, or even a brief summary of the letter. This practice is not yet documented or even envisaged by the TEI (or by the TEI Special Interest Group for correspondence, on which see below). At this point, two solutions can be envisaged: using a <seg> element—with the issues about the verbosity of encoding already mentioned—or creating a new element which could be added to the TEI schema. The use of <seg> or <div> (division) is therefore possible, but it is not really convincing as a solution, as these elements are too general in their scope. For scholarly purposes it would be much better to have a specific element that possesses the right semantics. This would permit, for instance, distinctions to be made between the different parts of the letter as hierarchical units. In this way the text on the back of the last folio would not be required to be part of the body of the letter, but could stand as a separate structure in its own right, which would enable the exploitation of the information it contains. Even if the last folio is not considered a priority for many scholars, the information contained in it should not be forgotten, as these folios form part of our understanding of the context of the correspondence.

---

15   http://www.tei-c.org/release/doc/tei-p5-doc/en/html/ref-opener.html

Semantic elements would bring the encoding closer to the original source and above all make it more understandable for the researcher, and perhaps even easier for him or her, as it forces the researcher to think of the structure of the letter no longer in terms of simple text divisions but rather as units of meaning. Thus the process of encoding becomes scholarly work in itself. This could encourage researchers to produce digital editions, or at least be part of the process and therefore link at last both the scholarly and technical parts of a digital edition. The definition of new elements at the local level should not be considered lightly, however, as adding new elements can present an obstacle for interoperability. It can be considered as a temporary solution, and indeed, the TEI itself is aware of the issues created by its generality and encourages the creation of new elements as the first step of a formal proposal to the TEI Council toward their integration into the general schema. Following this cautious and responsible approach, we have created at the École Nationale des Chartes a new element called <nota> based on a <seg>-like model in order to ensure a proper dialogue with the TEI.[16] The main purpose of this element is to make the encoding more precise by using a @type attribute to indicate the nature of the added text, such as address, date of receipt etc.

```
<enc:nota type="addresse" place="back">À monsieur le chancellier.</enc:nota>
```

We could even envisage, in future, the creation of even more specific elements for each kind of information, such as:

```
<enc:address place="back">À monsieur le chancellier.</enc:address>
<enc:reception place="back">L'empereur du XXII avril 1620. Receue le XIII may 1620</enc:reception>
```

---

16 This <nota> element could appear to overlap with the existing TEI element <note>. In our view, however, the content of the <nota> element is not, in a semantic way, an annotation, but rather a part of the letter which has been written either during the writing or the reading of the letter and should therefore not be considered as an addition but rather as a step in the writing process.

The former would be dedicated to each address, which appeared either on the last folio (for early modern correspondence) or on postcards or envelopes. The TEI *Guidelines* already offer an <address> element, which can be used within an <opener> element, for instance. But for the time being, the *Guidelines* restrain the use to postal addresses, so that plain text, or even a <p> (paragraph) element, cannot be inserted directly within this <address> element. Or if structured addresses exist for contemporary letters, for early modern ones they are mostly names without any precise address as 'To the chancellor, at the Court'. Ideally it would be good to find a solution that would fit with both contemporary correspondence (with envelopes) and that of the early modern period (with the address written directly on the last folio), by allowing both structured and unstructured encoding of the address. The latter would encode each addition made after the writing of the letter. Most of the time, these additions—the dates when the letter was sent and received, as well as sometimes a short abstract—were made after receiving the letter by the office of the secretary of state in order to manage more easily state papers and affairs. Other name elements or means of encoding could be envisaged. We have much to learn from the work currently being done on genetic editing for the encoding of different hands and other further additions.[17] The purpose of these examples is not to suggest new encoding elements, but more to highlight the need for further encoding specifications for correspondence. This work would require more than two corpora and would need to include various types of correspondence (commercial, personal etc.).

Documentation as a solution?

The main requirements for early modern correspondence are, however, not really new elements, but rather a more constrained encoding, to fit its specific structure. Writing, especially to a king or a secretary of state, is subject to various protocols or ceremonies, and the encoding should reflect this. This structure can also be considered as an advantage, since it forces the editor to think more carefully about the encoding requirements. For the two editions of correspondence at the École

---

17 See Elena Pierazzo, 'Un nouveau module de la TEI pour l'encodage des manuscrits modernes et les éditions génétiques', in *La génétique des textes et des formes: L'oeuvre comme processus*, ed. by Pierre-Marc De Biasi and Anne Pierrot Herschberg (forthcoming in 2016).

Nationale des Chartes, the first step has been to write a schema, based on TEI, but with a few additions, accompanied by a documentation that has been written specifically for early modern correspondence. The aim of this schema was to constrain the use of TEI and to document it in order better to adapt the elements to the particular nature of early modern correspondence, and therefore to make the use of TEI more straightforward for the researchers. The documentation is a result of a combination of both digital and traditional editorial practices. In fact, writing specific documentation provided an opportunity to link editorial norms to those of encoding. The École Nationale des Chartes has an established editorial practice through the publication of manuals such as *Conseils pour l'édition de textes médiévaux*[18] for medieval texts, *L'édition des textes anciens* for early modern ones[19] and very recently *L'édition critique des textes contemporains*.[20] Our documentation for early modern correspondence continues in this tradition, bringing it into the digital age.

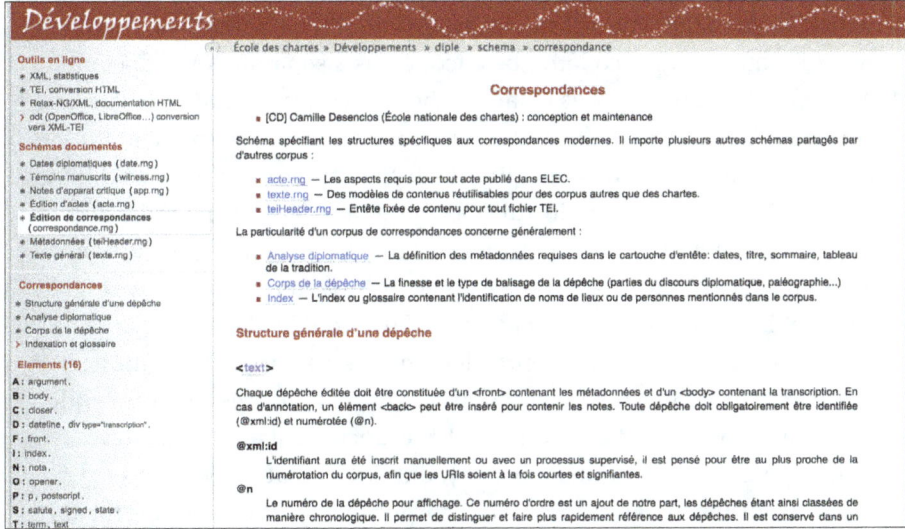

Fig. 10.3 Screenshot from the documentation for the general structure of a scholarly edition of early modern texts.

---

18 Groupe de recherches La civilisation de l'écrit au Moyen Âge, ed., *Conseils pour l'édition de textes médiévaux* (Paris: CTHS, 2001).

19 Bernard Barbiche and Monique Chatenet, *Conseils pour l'édition des textes de l'époque moderne (XVIe–XVIIIe siècle)* (Paris: Inventaire général, 1990).

20 Christine Nougaret and Élisabeth Parinet, *L'édition critique des textes contemporains (XIXe–XXIe siècle)* (Paris: École Nationale des Chartes, 2015).

The documentation is now composed both of editorial requirements and encoding recommendations, in order to provide an adapted and easily useable handbook for digital scholarly editions of early modern texts. This confers added scholarly value onto the schema, which is not only a computing tool but the result of an effective dialogue between researchers and developers, based on the meaning of the various segments. In fact, this makes its use easier for the researchers, since it not only talks about XML elements but also about editorial norms. Overall, correspondence projects, because of the large sizes of their corpora, are often collaborative projects. With such documentation, we can guarantee a common and consistent encoding which will permit interoperability between projects.

In order to make the encoding more meaningful for the researchers, we have made several choices which differ somewhat from the traditional recommendations of the TEI. The data required to identify the letter — title (i.e. sender and addressee), place and time of writing, witnesses, summary — are metadata and could be inserted into the <teiHeader>, which is probably the most common practice. This kind of encoding would require that each letter be encoded as a separate XML document. At the École Nationale des Chartes, the choice was made to create one single XML document for the entire corpus, in order to facilitate the creation of internal links and to match the structure of other editions, mostly those of charters. In this case, the <teiHeader> is dedicated to the general metadata of the corpus and the information specific to each letter is inserted within a <front> element. Moreover, the structure of that element is less constraining than that of the <teiHeader>. We were thus able to build, within the <front> element, a structure which duplicates the traditional structure of scholarly editions: addressee and sender, which are considered as the title of the documents in order to match to the structure of editions (<head>), date (<docDate>), witnesses (<div type="tradition">) and summary (<argument>). We would probably benefit from modifying this structure in further editions, especially for addressees and senders. Certainly we could simply encode sender, addressee and place name with <name> elements. But this is not as satisfactory a method for letters as it is for charters. In fact this practice requires the use of the same heavy encoding mentioned earlier in regard to the structure of the letter. Indeed, if we want to identify the sender and address with precision, we would need to use @role attributes as follows:

```
<head><name role="sender" ref="#FrançoisI">François Ier</name> à <name role="addressee" ref="#DuBourg">Antoine Du Bourg</name></head>
```

In this way, we should use the elements <sender> and <addressee>, as was suggested by the TEI — Special Interest Group on Correspondence within its proposal for a whole <correspDesc> element. We would only need to enlarge this use by allowing it both within the text and the <front> element.

The TEI-SIG on Correspondence was formed in 2008 and illustrates well the real encoding issues concerning these texts. To solve them, the work of the SIG relies mostly on the DALF schema and its documentation.[21] This is a specific schema for correspondence, particularly for features such as the main metadata (addressee, sender — who is considered as an author — etc.), envelopes and postscripts.[22] A task force for Correspondence Description was created in October 2013 during the TEI Members' Meeting in Rome and has led, very recently, to the addition to the TEI Guidelines of a new <correspDesc> element.[23] Contained by the <profileDesc> element, <correspDesc> allows the description of 'the actions related to one act of correspondence', including sender, addressee, place and time of writing, date of reception, type of correspondence etc. Only a few new specific elements have been introduced, however. For the sender and addressee for instance, the *Guidelines* still recommend general elements such as <name> or <persName> with a type attribute. If the introduction of new elements is an admirable first step towards recognising the specific characters of

---

21 *Digital Archives and Letters in Flanders*, a project at the Centre for Scholarly Editing and Document Studies in Gent, http://ctb.kantl.be/project/dalf
22 It is important however to note that the SIG Correspondence itself recognises the orientation of its current work and seeks to enlarge its perspectives. There are other projects of early modern correspondence, such as the projects developed by the CELL (Centre for Editing Lives and Letters, University College London), which do not offer any open documentation or access to their TEI files, therefore making it is also impossible to compare or to learn from their practices.
23 Release 2.8.0 (6 April 2015).

correspondence, things need to go further in order to provide a lighter, but still precise, encoding for correspondence, especially where the early modern period is concerned.

In our model, we have constrained the body of the letter in order to follow the strict structure of early modern correspondence: <opener> for the opening formulas (salutation), <p> for the text of the letter, <closer> for closing formulas (courtesy and politeness formulas, mention of the date and signatures), <postscript> for postscripts and <nota> for additional material (address, back notes etc.).

```
<body>
    <div type="transcription">
        <opener><salute>Mons<hi rend="sup">r</hi> le
        Chancellier,</salute></opener>
        <p xml:id="16-p1" n="1">Pour ce que je desire que le
        partaige de mon cousin le marquis de Rothelin […] Et
        vous me ferez service en ce faisant.</p>
        <closer>
            <salute>Priant Dieu, Mons<hi rend="sup">r</hi> le
            Chancellier, qu'il vous ayt en sa garde.</salute>
            <dateline>Escript à Valence le <hi rend="sc">ix</hi><hi rend="sup">e</hi> jour d'aoust mil <hi rend="sc">v<hi rend="sup">c</hi> xxxvi</hi>.</dateline>
            <signed>Françoys.</signed><signed>Bochetel.</signed>
        </closer>
        <enc:nota type="note" desc="note dorsale d'une
        écriture contemporaine">Le roy pour le faict du
        partaige de Mons<hi rend="sup">r</hi> le marquis de
        Rothelin.</enc:nota>
        <enc:nota type="adresse" desc="adresse au dos">À
        mons<hi rend="sup">r</hi> le chancellier.</enc:nota>
    </div>
</body>
```

Only the elements required for the structure of correspondence are permitted here. This is not a new standard but, rather, a proposal to stimulate discussion. Matters are not fixed and must be adapted according to each experience and practice of encoding. Our proposals solve some specific issues, but they do not cover the whole field of early modern correspondence.

Towards a general documentation

The TEI-SIG on Correspondence can be considered as a first important step towards much-needed collaboration. First of all, it tries to link different projects dealing with correspondence and encourages a general and free discussion through a mailing list and annual meetings.[24] Its work focuses on documenting and finding solutions for encoding the specific features of correspondence, which in turn enables researchers to identify and list the main issues they encounter when editing correspondence. The SIG does not offer immediate solutions, even if one of its eventual aims is to make some encoding proposals to the TEI Council. It is however a space in which to exchange and discuss proposals about topics such as

- the description of metadata (sender, addressee etc.);
- the content model of the postscript;[25] the issue of enclosures or attachments which are part of the letter but written on another leaf and need consequently to be distinguished from the letter but linked to it at the same time;
- the encoding of addresses.

In order to succeed, it is important that any proposal that will become part of the standard must take into consideration the largest dataset possible, covering material from many periods, countries and contexts. This is why we have to call for greater cooperation between DALF,

---

24   The aim of the TEI-SIGs is indeed to provide an opportunity for TEI users with similar interests to meet and exchange ideas. Eleven SIGs have been created: computer-mediated communication, correspondence, education, libraries, manuscripts, music, ontologies, scholarly publishing, TEI for linguists, text and graphics and tools. Each of these has a wiki space, a mailing-list and the opportunity to meet during the annual TEI Members' Meeting.

25   Until recently, the <postscript> element could not be inserted before the <closer> element, although in reality, it does not have a fixed place. It can be written after the signatures, on the same level within the letter or even before them. Since release 2.1.0 this element can be inserted anywhere within the body, which allows a better semantic encoding.

WeGa,[26] our own project and other projects in order to build a model that is as strong and efficient as possible.

The type of collaboration put in place by the EpiDoc community, which has built recommendations for the encoding of epigraphic documents, could inspire us. EpiDoc is indeed a specialisation of TEI for ancient documents, inscriptions and papyri, and all EpiDoc files are also TEI-conformant. However, its *Guidelines*[27] only contain those TEI elements which are required for this type of source material and have been constrained in order to fit to the epigraphic context. EpiDoc is therefore, as the *Guidelines* themselves assert, a supplement to, and not a replacement for the TEI *Guidelines*. We could envisage similar guidelines and an associated schema for correspondence.

Early modern correspondence requires, perhaps more than many other types of sources, a semantic and specialised encoding. Digital scholarly editions of such sources should not be a transposition of a text into a digital medium but a genuine restitution of the meaning of a text. Only by correctly labelling structures such as names or formulas can we retain the flow of the letter and consequently produce a virtual recreation of the relationship(s) inherent in a correspondence. In order to give to its specific structure sense and utility, a documented set of guidelines has to be created. The schema and documentation, created at the École Nationale des Chartes, should not be considered as anything other than a proposal for further development, especially by merging the documentation from our project with others such as DALF. We therefore call for the creation of a dynamic community around correspondence, so that we might build a general documentation that is suitable for correspondence of all kinds and from all periods.

---

26   Carl-Maria-von-Weber-Gesamtausgabe, mentioned above.
27   Tom Elliott et al., *EpiDoc Guidelines: Ancient Documents in TEI XML* (Version 8, 2007–2013), http://www.stoa.org/epidoc/gl/latest

11. Beyond Variants: Some Digital Desiderata for the Critical Apparatus of Ancient Greek and Latin Texts

Cynthia Damon

Introduction

Texts from the ancient world reach us via a long, complicated process of transmission from copy to copy. As printed today they are at best near approximations of what an ancient author wrote. A critical edition, which presents the text along with the surviving evidence of the transmission process and an editor's interpretation of it, allows the reader to go beyond a generalised expectation of error and to see whether any given bit of text is secure, or corrupt, or disputed, or weakly supported by the manuscripts that preserve it. No classical text can be read responsibly without one. Yet existing digital libraries of classical texts routinely strip out 'the surviving evidence of the transmission process and an editor's interpretation of it', presenting only the text.[1] They do so by the simple expedient of omitting the critical apparatus.

---

1   Some openly available digital libraries of Greek and Latin texts: http://pot-pourri.fltr.ucl.ac.be/files/AClassFTP/Textes (Greek and Latin); http://www.perseus.tufts.edu/hopper/collection?collection=Perseus:collection:Greco-Roman (Greek and Latin); https://www.hs-augsburg.de/~harsch/augustana.html#gr (Greek and Latin); http://latin.packhum.org (Latin). Some subscription-based libraries: http://stephanus.tlg.uci.edu (Thesaurus Linguae Graecae); http://www.brepolis.net (Library of Latin Texts, series A and B).

If we are going to reinstate the critical apparatus—as we must if digital editions of classical texts are to serve the needs of scholarship and if digital libraries are to become the go-to repositories of classical texts— we need to understand what the apparatus is. I am troubled by what I see as a trivialisation of the apparatus in the Text Encoding Initiative's *Guidelines for Electronic Text Encoding and Interchange*, which are meant to foster standardisation in digital editions. The TEI Guidelines define the apparatus as a repository of variants, and assert that 'individual readings are *the* crucial elements in any critical apparatus of variants'.[2] For classical texts, at least, a proper critical apparatus is far more than a repository of textual variants: it is a repository of *everything* that an editor judges necessary for a reader to understand why the text being read is what it is. More precisely, the apparatus is a set of notes designed to foster in the reader an awareness of the historical and editorial processes that resulted in the text he or she is reading and to give the reader what he or she needs to evaluate the editor's decisions.[3]

Some of the apparatus content is of course the variant readings in the manuscript tradition. But these variants only yield a text through the operation of an editor's theory about how the manuscripts that contain them are related to one another and to the authorial original. So the lists of variants have to be understood as embodiments of a theory. In other words, when the editor *reports* in the apparatus that manuscripts AB have the reading in the text, while CDE and FG have variants, what he or she *communicates* is likely to be something like this: 'Given my theory about how manuscripts ABCDEFG are related to one another, the reading of AB has manuscript authority and makes acceptable sense and is therefore printed, whereas the readings of CDE and FG are scribal innovations in the manuscript from which each group is separately descended and are therefore not used in the constitution of the text'. And beneath *that* message is a theory that defines what 'a reading with manuscript authority' is: basically, a reading that may have reached us through a continuous sequence of accurate copies of what the author wrote back

---

2 TEI Guidelines for the critical apparatus module are available at http://www.tei-c. org/release/doc/tei-p5-doc/en/html/TC.html, section 12.1.2, [my emphasis].

3 This point is also made in Marina Buzzoni's chapter in the present volume.

in antiquity and may therefore be authentic and (by definition) right.[4] This is much too much to write in small print at the bottom of the page for every lemma, but some variation on that reasoning is often implicit in notes that list manuscript variants. Furthermore, for most classical works the manuscript variants do not suffice for constituting the text. At best they allow one to reconstruct an archetype. But archetypes usually postdate the authorial original by centuries, often many centuries.[5] As copy succeeded copy corruptions must have entered the text, even if we can no longer trace the process in any detail. The situation is even worse when the process of transmission that produced the extant manuscripts cannot be represented genealogically, which means that one cannot reconstruct an archetype or make strong assertions about manuscript authority. In such traditions the manuscript variants will be even further removed, temporally and culturally, from the authorial text. They have to be evaluated on their merits, and all too often their merits are not enough to generate an acceptable text. In cases like these editors have recourse to emendation or declare the text irreparably corrupt. All of this is presented in the critical apparatus, which is therefore a repository not of variants but of arguments (in the best sense of the word) about variants.[6] We need to find a way to embody the arguments as well as the variants in the digital critical apparatus.

Arguments in the apparatus

I begin by illustrating something of the range of types of arguments found in the critical apparatus of a classical text with examples from

---

[4] Readings without manuscript authority can be right but they cannot be authentic. That is, they can be shown to have entered the tradition through innovation, and may be right if the innovation corrected an earlier error in such a way as to retrieve the original text.

[5] For a substantial portion of Petronius' wonderful *Satyrica*, for example, a work written in the first century CE, the archetype is a manuscript of the fifteenth century. See M. D. Reeve, 'Petronius', in *Texts and Transmission: A Survey of the Latin Classics*, ed. by L. D. Reynolds (Oxford: Oxford University Press, 1983), pp. 295–300.

[6] A point that is well made in general terms by Hans Walter Gabler in 'Theorizing the Digital Scholarly Edition', *Literature Compass* 7 (2010), 43–56, http://dx.doi.org/10.1111/j.1741-4113.2009.00675.x; esp. p. 45: 'The apparatus entries [...] thus function as argument for the establishment of the edition text' and on the apparatus as 'a discourse complementary to that of the edition text'. I have tried to offer some useful specifics.

recent major critical editions. Which types will appear in any given apparatus and their relative prevalence will depend on 'house style', editorial policy, transmission history and the nature of the work being edited, but in designing a digital apparatus we should be prepared to accommodate all of them and more.[7]

The simplest sort of note reports variants whose distribution enables the editor to reconstruct the archetype and arrive at a printable text. In a tradition with three branches, for example, such as that of Vegetius' *Epitoma rei militaris*, the agreement of two against the third will give you the reading of the archetype:

3.9.3 perscribam εβ : de- δ[8]

Here ε, β and δ represent the heads of the three principal families of the tradition. The editor, following the agreement of ε and β, prints *perscribam*. The variant *describam* in δ is an innovation. This note offers both an explanation of the reading in the text and evidence relevant to the assessment of the editor's stemma. (As will become clear as we proceed, the spatial compass of apparatus notes is usually reduced by the omission of things that can be assumed, such as the repetition of -*scribam* here; this increases the demand on the reader considerably.[9] Fonts, too, are part of the code: Roman font is used for words belonging to the text, italic font for words or symbols contributed by the editor.)

---

[7] Most of my examples in this first part of the paper are taken from a single series, the Oxford Classical Texts series, to minimise the variations due to house style. And I have chosen them from Latin texts but not Greek ones, to minimise the variations of language. (There is an irreducible minimum of Latin here, since the critical apparatus for classical texts is traditionally presented in Latin, but I have tried to make the point of each example independent of the language of the text and apparatus.) Variations in house style are illustrated in the discussion of the apparatuses for Ovid, *Amores* 1.13.1.

[8] *Vegetius, Epitoma rei militaris* (Oxford Classical Texts), ed. by M. D. Reeve (Oxford: Oxford University Press, 2004). This late-antique text is unusually well preserved in the manuscript tradition, such that the editor can say that 'at least one of the three reconstructed witnesses almost always has an acceptable reading' and 'it [...] seems unlikely that the tradition derives from an archetype more recent than a copy put into circulation by Vegetius himself' (p. xlviii).

[9] As does Reeve's assumption that the reader will identify '*per*' in *perscribam* as a prepositional prefix and infer that '*de*' has the same function. That is, he assumes that the reader will supply '*scribam*' after *de*, not the sequence of letters that follows the '*e*' in *perscribam*. The underlying policy is stated in general terms in the preface: 'I assume that the reader knows some Latin and expects the scribe [...] to have written a Latin word [...] not a monstrosity' (p. xlii).

If a reconstructable archetype has an unacceptable reading, the editor may want to explain why it has been discarded and/or what has taken its place. Thus, again from Vegetius:

1.4.1 imbibuntur δ : imbuu- εβ, *vix latine* (*cf. TLL 427.56–60*)

The archetype was the source of *imbuuntur* in ε and β, but that reading yields dubious Latin that is only paralleled by other doubtful passages listed in the reference work cited in the note, the *TLL*.[10] The reading in δ, *imbibuntur*, which the editor prints, is an innovation of some sort, but acceptable Latin. The editor of Vegetius does not justify his preferred reading here except by showing the argument against *imbuuntur*.

But you will also find notes with explicit justifications, such as this one in the newish OCT of Apuleius' *Metamorphoses*:

4.2.3 proprio F, corr. AU[11]

This tells the reader that the word in the text of 4.2.3 most closely resembling *proprio*, namely *proripio*, is misspelled in the manuscript F, which is the archetype of this tradition, but spelled correctly in two descendants of F. The correction was presumably made independently by A and U, since it does not appear in other descendants of their common parent from a generation between themselves and F. The editor's '*corr.*', meaning *correxerunt*, explains the genesis of the reading in the text. However, it may also provoke the reader to query the editor's explanation. If, for example, one feels that *proripio* is not a plausible correction for *proprio*, especially not one that would have been made twice, one may start looking for another explanation.

A very common type of note that requires considerable mental effort from the reader arises when each branch of a two-branch tradition preserves a construable reading from the archetype. The two branches in theory have equal authority, so how does the editor choose? Consider the following note from the OCT of Columella's *Res rustica*:

---

10   The *TLL* is the *Thesaurus linguae latinae*, an on-going major Latin dictionary project accessible in print and on-line by subscription at http://www.degruyter.com

11   *Apulei Metamorphoseon libri XI* (Oxford Classical Texts), ed. by M. Zimmerman (Oxford: Oxford University Press, 2012). The manuscript that is the source of all currently extant manuscripts, F, is itself extant but hard to read and damaged in spots, so that its descendants are sometimes called in as witnesses to the text.

1.pr. 7 relinquendique *SA* : retin- *R*[12]

Here SA and R represent the two branches. Both *relinquendique* and *retinendique* suit the context, which is about the honourable acquisition of wealth. The question is, once the wealth has been acquired, is the next step passing it on to your heirs, which would be the point of *relinquendique*, or holding onto it for yourself, via *retinendique*? Here the editor prints the reading that is less likely to have arisen from the other (or some common original) as an innovation, *relinquendique*. No explanation is given, or needed, so long as it can be taken for granted that the reader understands the principle of the *lectio difficilior*.[13] *Retinendique* simplifies the phrase since it does not require one to infer an indirect object, as *relinquendique* does.

Similarly challenging is the related scenario in which one branch of a two-branch tradition preserves a correct reading from the archetype, while the other goes astray but one or more of its constituents retrieves the correct reading. We can see this in a note pertaining to Macrobius' *Saturnalia*, where the two families are headed by α and β:

3.10.6 docte] te β *(recte V)*[14]

The word before the square bracket, *docte*, is what the editor prints. The note states explicitly that β reads *te*, and, armed with the knowledge—if we have read the edition's preface—that the tradition has two branches, we infer that *docte* is the reading transmitted by α. In β this has been corrupted to *te*, which makes no sense in the text. But '*recte V*', meaning 'V has it right', tells us that the scribe of V, a descendant of β, has recovered *docte*, either by conjecture or by contact with the family of α. These two explanations have very different implications for the transmission history of this text, so the note is a piece of the evidence necessary for evaluating the editor's account of that transmission.

---

12   *L. Iuni Moderati Columellae Res Rustica: Incerti auctoris Liber de arboribus* (Oxford Classical Texts), ed. by R. H. Rodgers (Oxford: Oxford University Press, 2010).

13   More fully, *lectio difficilior lectio potior*, a rule-of-thumb asserting that of two readings with equal manuscript authority the more difficult is to be preferred, on the grounds that it is more likely to be authentic, or rather less likely to have arisen from scribal innovation.

14   *Macrobii Ambrosii Theodosii Saturnalia* (Oxford Classical Texts), ed. by Robert A. Kaster (Oxford: Oxford University Press, 2011).

A different sort of challenge for the reader arises when a variant that needs reporting comes from an external source. Thus the editor of the *Saturnalia* informs us that Macrobius and Aulus Gellius quote Caesar's famous dictum about avoiding unusual words 'as one would a reef' using different terms for 'unusual':

> 1.5.2 infrequens] inauditum *Gell.*

This note tells us that the archetype of Macrobian tradition transmits *infrequens*, but also that the reading might not be right.

Some notes contain arguments about matters of interpretation. This is obviously a vastly extensible category and is for the most part excluded from the apparatus. But not always, and for this we should be grateful.

A note that efficiently explains the syntax of a difficult passage can save much head-scratching, as in this note from the OCT of Columella:

> 1.pr. 17 ut enim [...] uisos] *oratio obliqua ἀνακολούθως* (*cf. Varr. Rust.* 2.pr.1 maiores [...] praeponebant [...] ut ruri enim [...] desidiosiores putabant)

By identifying the construction as an incompletely expressed indirect statement ('*oratio obliqua ἀνακολούθως*') and by supplying a parallel passage in which one can see in *putabant* the sort of governing verb that seems implicit here, the editor allows us to read on unperturbed — unless we feel that it would be better after all to supply *putabant* or something like it in the text.

Another situation where interpretation may be felt to deserve mention in the apparatus is where ancient scholarship bears on the text. For example, on a description in Virgil's *Aeneid* that is presented in the text as part of a character's speech, the editor notes that the ancient grammarian Servius knew of a competing interpretation that took it as an utterance by the narrator:

> 6.573 "tunc [...] portae [...] *alii hoc a poeta dictum volunt [...] alii continuant narrationem*" *Serv.*[15]

A string of words running from *tunc* to *portae*, says Servius, is attributed by some authorities to the poet, by others to the character in the narrative;

---

15 *P. Vergili Maronis Opera*, ed. by M. Geymonat, 2nd ed. (Rome: Edizioni di storia e letteratura, 2008).

the editor follows the second group. This note does include a variant—Servius read *tunc* where the manuscripts used for constituting the text offer *tum*—but the variant is not the point.[16] The editor is prompting the reader to evaluate his editorial decision to treat the text as character-speech. This kind of challenge is present whenever the editor includes interpretative aids, be they ancient or modern.

The claim on the reader's attention is even more pressing when the editor indicates that the archetype's text is acceptable but nevertheless suspect for one reason or another. An editor has a variety of signals from which to choose. One can simply convey doubt. Thus in a passage from Ovid's *Metamorphoses* where the transmitted reading is unexceptionable in form and syntax but at odds with its context the editor draws attention to the passage with this brief note:

8.262 mitis habebatur *suspectum*[17]

The reader will find *mitis habebatur* in the text and infer that it is transmitted by the manuscripts, but he or she is invited by the editor to view it with suspicion.

Where possible and appropriate the suspicious editor may suggest an alternative, either one found in a manuscript or a modern scholar's proposal. This is the point of a note like the following from the *Metamorphoses*, which tells us that one or more manuscripts from the thirteenth century, here represented by the siglum χ, read *faciat* where the manuscripts used to constitute the text read *capiat*:

9.749 capiat] faciat *(cf. 1.469)* χ, *fort. recte*[18]

From this brief annotation one understands that the editor went looking for a way to improve upon the text's *capiat* and found it in a place that he would not normally cite. He cites it here on the strength of a parallel passage earlier in the poem (1.469) and indicates with his 'fort. recte',

---

16 To complicate matters further, the lemma for the note (*tum demum horrisono stridentes cardine sacrae/panduntur portae*) starts in line 573 (*tunc/tum*) but runs into line 574 (*portae*) and therefore overlaps with subsequent notes about *stridentes* and *sacrae*. The issues arising from multi-word lemmata will be need careful attention when the apparatus assumes digital form.

17 *P. Ovidi Nasonis Metamorphoses* (Oxford Classical Texts), ed. by Richard J. Tarrant (Oxford: Oxford University Press, 2004).

18 The meaning of the siglum χ is defined in the edition's introduction (p. xlvi).

meaning 'perhaps rightly', that the innovation in χ may retrieve what Ovid originally wrote.

A word can also be flagged as suspect by a list of attempts to emend it, even if the editor accepts none of them. Thus the puzzling word *reluctabant* in the description of a ragged and filthy robber in Apuleius' *Metamorphoses* gets the following note in the OCT edition:

> 7.5.3 reluctabant *F, def. Arminil (notione* relucendi), *aliter Helm ('i.q. specie discrepabant') aliter Hijmans3 ('were having a wrestling match')* : relucebant *uel* relucitabant *Gruterus*

The editor prints the reading of F, but the fact that three scholars explain it differently (*aliter*) while a fourth proposes two different emendations for it (*uel*) gives the reader plenty of reason to distrust the text here.

The editor may also want to float a suggestion of his or her own. Thus in Vegetius, where the archetype and the text read *duritia*, the reader is alerted to its metrical oddity by the editor's proposal to substitute a synonym:

> 1.6.4 *an* duritate *ob numeros?*

Duritate, the note explains, yields a more regular prose rhythm.

Or the editor may suggest that the text would be better off without the offending bit. That would be the case if, say, it made its way into the transmitted text from a source such as a marginal comment. Thus the note on *Met.* 9.749 that we looked at a moment ago in fact begins with the following warning:

> 9.749 del. *Heinsius*

In addition to the line's textual problems, of which *capiat* is just one, the line is a banal and self-contained aphorism, so it was excised (*del.*) by a great Renaissance editor of Ovid, Nicolaas Heinsius. Readers would do well, the editor indicates, to be cautious about embracing it as *echt* Ovid.

I could go on to illustrate notes that explain substantive repairs to the transmitted text, or notes that indicate by a lacuna or a crux that the editor has despaired of repairing the text, or notes about punctuation or orthography or illegible codices or the host of other issues that editors address in the critical apparatus, but the examples above suffice, I think, to show that the apparatus for a classical text is much more than a repository of variants. Its notes constitute a highly evolved form of philological argument.

Decoding the apparatus

The form may in fact be too highly evolved to move easily into a new medium. Apparatus notes cannot simply be read; they have to be decoded, not only by the expansion of abbreviations and the filling of omissions, but often also with the help of concepts and theories that are presented elsewhere in the edition or in the scholarly literature. In traditions where the relationships among manuscripts are essentially genealogical, for example, the stemma that charts those relationships is a key to the meaning of many apparatus notes.

The interpretative consequences that arise when a textual string in an apparatus has been properly decoded with the help of a stemma can be seen from the following example, taken from Loyen's 1970 Budé edition of the letters of Sidonius Apollinaris, a fifth-century bishop from Gaul.[19] The passage comes from Sidonius' travelogue description of Ravenna, and I give Loyen's translation:

> *Ep.* 1.5.5 insuper oppidum duplex pars interluit Padi, cetera pars alluit.
> "En outre la cité elle-même est coupée en deux par un bras du Pô, tandis que le reste de ses eaux la baigne".
> cetera *F* : certa *cett. codd.*

Ravenna is a two-part town, Sidonius tells us (*oppidum duplex*), because one branch of the Po runs through it (*interluit*), splitting it in two. He then adds something more about the river, which not only 'flows through' (*interluit*) but also 'flows alongside' (*alluit*). The apparatus reports the manuscript variants as follows: a manuscript called F reads *cetera*, the rest read *certa*. But what does it mean when Loyen prints F's *cetera* in his text? (Earlier editors either printed *certa* or marked the passage as irreparably corrupt.[20]) It is not a simple choice between manuscript

---

[19] *Sidoine Apollinaire, Poèmes et lettres*, ed. by André Loyen, 3 vols. (Paris: Belles Lettres, 1960–1970).

[20] *Certa* is printed in *C. Sollius Apollinaris Sidonius*, ed. by Paul Mohr (Leipzig: Teubner, 1895); †*certa* in *Gai Solii Apollinaris Sidonii Epistulae et carmina*, ed. by Christian Lütjohann (Berlin: Weidmann, 1887). Franz Dolveck is currently reassessing this stemma.

readings. A stemma for this text is given in Figure 11.1 below. (As is traditional in stemmata the capital letters represent actual manuscripts, the Greek letters represent lost manuscripts whose existence is inferred from the presence of shared errors in their descendants.)

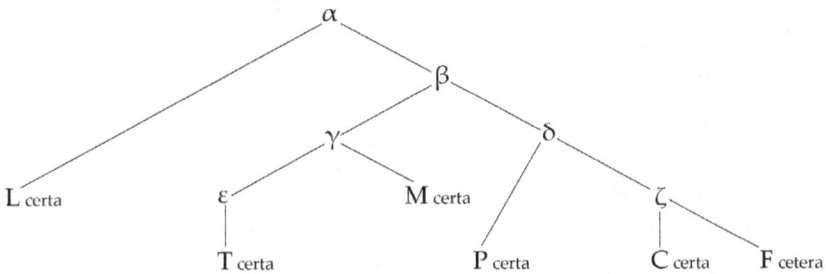

Fig. 11.1 Stemma for Sidonius, *Epistles* 1.5.5.

The earliest recoverable phase of the text is represented by α, the archetype, which passed down its readings to L and β, which passed its readings to γ and δ, and so on. The underlying principle is that the readings in, say, δ, are essentially those of α, together with the innovations introduced in the copying process. The innovations become visible when independent copies of a single model differ from one another. The editor's job is, in the first place, to identify the innovations at each stage of transmission and to work back to the reading of the archetype. What this stemma tells you is that the readings that reach F from α have been successfully transmitted through β, δ and ζ. For our passage it would have to work like this: α had *cetera*, β copied it correctly and L made an error, writing *certa*. Then δ copied *cetera* correctly and γ, the source of T and M, made an error, writing *certa*. Then ζ copied it correctly and P made an error, writing *certa*. And finally F copied it correctly, and C made an error, writing *certa*. The hypothesis that four scribes independently made the very same copying error is extremely improbable. Therefore the reading in F is probably the innovation. That is, although it is in the manuscripts, it has no manuscript authority. So when Loyen prints it he is saying that the archetype was corrupt and that this scribal innovation is the best available repair. The whole argument is implicit in the simple apparatus entry 'cetera *F* : certa *cett. codd.*'; but you have to decode it properly.

It is hard work to elicit arguments from the brief and cryptic notes that constitute a typical critical apparatus. But without the apparatus the text is a deceptively smooth and satisfying surface. We need both the variants and the arguments that make them interpretable. If a digital apparatus can provide something more user-friendly than the traditional print form, so much the better for the future of textual scholarship.

The need is in my view urgent. At present someone who wants a critical apparatus can go to the physical volume—provided that one exists with a competent *apparatus criticus* and provided that it is accessible. But a generation hence, when the use of online texts will have become the norm, readers will not expect or want to go to the physical volume. And a digital library that has equipped its texts with some kind of apparatus will be the only source that provides them with a fully adequate text. Back in 2000 Michael Reeve, a distinguished textual critic, observed that 'Until the apparatus can be restored, there is a danger that electronic texts will be trusted further than any text merits even if accurately reproduced'.[21] What readers need is a digital edition that not only gives them access to a given string of words but also enables them to understand why the string comprises just those words in just that order.[22] The balance of this paper offers some thoughts on how to achieve such a thing.

Where to start?

In a provocative opinion piece posted in 2012 Paolo Monella asked why classicists have been slow to embark on the project of creating digital critical editions for the works of Greco-Roman antiquity.[23] The answer that he proposed seems to me largely on-target, namely that the value that classicists place on the documentary basis of our texts is limited and

---

21 M. D. Reeve, '*Cuius in usum?* Recent and Future Editing', *Journal of Roman Studies*, 90 (2000), 196–206 (p. 200).
22 I am grateful to Bob Kaster for this neat formulation of the objective of a critical edition.
23 http://www.unipa.it/paolo.monella/lincei/why.html

pragmatic rather than ecumenical. That is, if I want to make a literary or historical argument about what Caesar wrote, any innovations in the text of Caesar by a medieval scribe are going to be a distraction if not a snare. So I rely on editors to give me the soundest possible text of Caesar's writings, as well as the evidence for it. And my interest in that evidence is pragmatic: does it support the reading that my argument is based on or not? If I try to imagine making a digital critical edition on the model widely considered to be fundamental[24]—where you start with page images of the witnesses, proceed to transcription and coding, then apply tools to produce collations and to link images and versions, and then you add annotations and so on—my first feeling is despair. I simply cannot imagine that any classicist—or funding agency—will invest the kind of time and money that would be needed to create digital critical editions of the whole corpus of Greek and Latin literature.

My next feeling, however, is exasperation. 'And why would we need so vast an investment?' After all, with classical texts, at least, we are far beyond the pioneering textual labours implied by this model. That work has been done and is recorded in the critical apparatuses of generations' worth of editions. Those apparatuses and editions are by no means perfect, but to redo the whole process that produced them would be a massive waste of effort. And yet—and yet. Classical texts risk being left behind at this juncture precisely because they started out ahead. What classicists need, I would argue, is a way to give digital form now to the mature state of textual scholarship represented by print editions, while leaving open the possibility of adding the underlying image and transcription data when and if opportunities arise. In other words, we need to start in the middle, not at the beginning. Can the TEI critical apparatus module help us do so? I have to say that it is sobering to report that one of the most tech-savvy classicists alive today, Donald Mastronarde, chose not to use TEI encoding for the apparatus of his Euripides Scholia project, which is otherwise TEI-based. As he explains in the discussion of the work's XML structure:

---

24 E.g. by Peter Robinson for the *Canterbury Tales*, http://www.tei-c.org/About/Archive_new/ETE/Preview/robinson.xml: 'A digital edition should be based on full-text transcription of the original texts into electronic form [...]'. Similarly, transcription is step 1 on the workflow proposed by Peter Shillingsburg for the HRIT project: https://sites.google.com/a/ctsdh.luc.edu/hrit-intranet/documentation/hrit-functions

The apparatus criticus is an area in which I have decided not to use the TEI mechanisms for apparatus criticus readings and variants, because in a project of this kind it seems to me that it would involve an unjustifiably large overhead of markup. I believe the information familiar to those who know how to read the apparatus criticus of a classical text can be provided in textual segments. This does mean that one will not be able to take my XML document and process it to produce a text that reflects the textual choices and errors of a particular witness, which probably would be possible with a more elaborate markup of readings and witnesses with pointers to specific words in the text. Such a project would require more personnel and a much larger budget, and I don't think the benefit would be worth the cost.[25]

Greg Crane's Open Philology project may give us a starting point.[26] He proposes to scan and make available versions of legacy editions that will be OCR-able with varying but ever-improving degrees of accuracy. In my view these images, and more particularly the images of the apparatuses, could serve as a foundational layer for transcription and encoding. That is, rather than start with the images of the manuscripts themselves, seductive as these are, we should start with the cryptic and crabbed text of the critical apparatus, which records the results of editorial collation of the manuscripts and the arguments that give those results meaning. The challenge will be to find new coding (TEI or other) that is flexible enough to enable meaningful collation of highly idiosyncratic expressions of comparable information.

A picture will help me convey what I mean by idiosyncratic. Below I give the apparatus entries from five modern editions on the first line of poem 13 in the first book of Ovid's *Amores* (Figure 11.2). In other words, a small subset of the data for one line of 750 or so in *Amores I*, which is one book of thirty-six by Ovid. A tiny fragment of the data needed for a digital critical edition of Ovid's work. And look how complicated it is. Almost everything here pertains to the preposition '*a*', which all five editors print in the text.[27]

---

25 http://euripidesscholia.org/EurSchStructure.html
26 http://sites.tufts.edu/perseusupdates/2013/04/04/the-open-philology-project-and-humboldt-chair-of-digital-humanities-at-leipzig
27 The editions are these: *P. Ovidi Nasonis Amores, Medicamina faciei femineae, Ars amatoria, Remedia amoris* (Oxford Classical Texts), ed. by Edward J. Kenney (Oxford: Oxford University Press, 1961) (I used this edition instead of its successor in order to highlight the effect of the re-evaluation of Y, which is used for the constitution

Ovid, *Amores* 1.13.1: Iam super Oceanum uenit a seniore marito

---

Kenney (1961)
a ω : *om. PSD*

McKeown (1987)
a yω : *om. PYSCD*

Munari (1955)
v. a seniore *recc.*, v. seniore *PS, defendunt Ehw., Burs. 167, 187, coll. Micone v. 261 (Poet. Carol. III 289) Ov. tr. 4, 5, 20 (v. l.) A. P. V 3, 1 ὄρθρος ἔβη 172, 1 ὄρθρε ἑτέστης et Eisenhut Gnomon 25, 1953, 447*

Ramirez de Verger (2003)
Oceanum *Marius, prob. McKeown 1989 coll. Bibac. frg. 7 Courtney; Verg. Aen. 4,129 (=11,1); 4,585 (= 9, 460); cf. TLL 2,1523,66sqq.* | a seniore marito *yT, recc. b, cf. u. 38, Heinsius, uide McKeown 1989* : seniore marito *PYS, recc. aliquot, Ehwald, cf. trist. 4,5,20, prob. Moore-Blunt coll. fast. 3,415* : seniore relicto *Heinsius in notis, cf. fast 1,461; 4,493; 6,473*

Lenz (1965)
a<Y(+a Y^c)PS, *vgl. Ehw., Burs. 167, 1914, 187; Eisenhut, Gnomon 25, 1953, 447*

Fig. 11.2 Apparatus notes on Ovid, *Amores* 1.13.1.

Basically what all of these apparatus notes say is that the preposition *a* is omitted by the principal manuscripts and is present in manuscripts of lesser authority (relevant text in green above). The fourth editor goes further, providing pointers to the arguments for printing the preposition (blue). He and two others also summarise or point to arguments against printing *a* (orange). And finally the very generous fourth editor reports a Renaissance conjecture (purple; the material in black justifies the capitalisation of *Oceanum*).

The editorial decision to print the preposition has significant interpretative consequences, since if the line includes the preposition, the verb *uenit* is present tense (short e), if it doesn't, the verb is *uenit* (long e), a perfect tense. The present tense verb 'she is coming' frames the poem as an address to Dawn as she arrives, a plea to the goddess to delay her arrival so that the lover and his beloved can enjoy a few more minutes of darkness before the day's round begins. A perfect tense verb

---

of the text after 1963); *Ovid, Amores: Text, prolegomena, and commentary*, ed. by J. C. McKeown, 4 vols. (Liverpool: Francis Cairns, 1987–2012); *P. Ovidi Nasonis Amores*, ed. by Franco Munari, 2nd ed. (Florence: Nuova Italia, 1955); *P. Ovidius Naso, Carmina amatoria: Amores, Medicamina faciei femineae, Ars amatoria, Remedia amoris*, ed. by Antonio Ramirez de Verger (Munich: Saur, 2003); *Die Liebeselegien*, ed. by Friedrich Walter Lenz (Darmstadt: Wissenschaftliche Buchgesellschaft, 1965).

in the first line frames the poem as a reproach: Dawn has come and I'm going to tell her just what her arrival means for us mortals. To make a long story short, the annotation *already available* for this line needs to accompany the line in its digital future. It is also worth noticing that the important information becomes visible when you compare the apparatus entries, not when you compare the texts of the editions, all of which print the same reading.

When I applied the 'starting from scratch' approach to this poem in the Juxtacommons program,[28] here is what emerged as the apparatus entry for the line:

a] **ed.**; *not in* **P, S, Y**

Because I had transcribed a published text, 'ed.', and the three principal manuscripts, P, S and Y, but not the more than 200 manuscripts of lesser authority, I ended up with a report that says that the edition prints *a*, which is absent from the principal manuscripts. This is significantly less than even the briefest of the existing apparatuses, that of Kenney, which at least tells us that the preposition is present in a class of manuscripts labelled ω. To put it differently, if we are going to spend time and money on digitising Ovid's *Amores* for the use of future scholarship, transcribing and encoding the apparatuses would allow us to start in the present rather than back in the humanist era when readers started comparing the medieval witnesses to the works of classical antiquity.

The problems, however, are considerable. The idiosyncratic and coded language of these notes would need to be translated into concepts before they could be properly re-encoded in a standardised TEI or other digital schema.

Consider the first part of the entry in Lenz's edition:

a<**Y**(+a **Yc**)**PS**

The concepts of omission, addition and correction expressed here are also present in McKeown's entry:

a *yω* : *om.* **PYSCD**

---

28 http://juxtacommons.org

But the form in which they are expressed is very different: Lenz uses the mathematical symbols < and + to convey omission and addition, and a suprascript c to convey correction, whereas McKeown uses the Latin abbreviation *om.*, meaning *omiserunt*, to convey omission and the layout of the note to convey addition, and he uses a lower-case letter (y) to convey correction: little y represents a later hand in big Y. Furthermore, the second entry has more information than the first: it reports the readings of ω and manuscripts labelled C and D as well as those of P, Y and S. But the first entry, when viewed in toto, has information not in the second, bibliographic information, also rather cryptic in form.

a<Y(+a Yc)**PS**, *vgl. Ehw., Burs. 167, 1914, 187; Eisenhut, Gnomon 25, 1953, 447*

Lenz sends you for starters to someone referred to as 'Ehw.', presumably in a publication referred to as 'Burs.', presumably to a volume or fascicle of that publication numbered 167 and published in 1914, and presumably to p. 187 of that volume. Any digital reader of that line would appreciate a translation, and not just because it is in German, unlike most apparatuses.

Doing the conceptual translations needed to correlate the five apparatus entries shown earlier will require a lot of work. However, even a minimal sort of coding that would simply allow you to stack up the entries as I did on the page here would be better than nothing.[29] So here is a more precise version of the question I asked before: Does (or could) the TEI critical apparatus module, despite its assertion that 'Individual readings are *the* crucial elements in any critical apparatus of variants', accommodate encoding that prioritises notes over witnesses? I would love to be able to extract readings from the subset of apparatus notes that concern variants, of course, but if I had to choose between recording the readings of five witnesses and recording the notes of five apparatuses I would choose the latter every time.

---

29 As my students and I found when producing just such 'stacks' for the *Annals* of Tacitus in the autumn of 2012, one immediate and unanticipated consequence was the ability to discover and render innocuous the errors and inconsistencies that have accumulated in the legacy of textual scholarship. Another was that the apparatus 'coding' became slightly more perspicuous with the juxtaposition of the same information in a variety of formats.

Conclusion

My aims in the three parts of this brief essay have been (1) to illustrate the inadequacy of the conceptualisation underpinning the current TEI module on the critical apparatus, (2) to demonstrate the power and complexity of the 'encoding' already present in the critical apparatus of classical texts, and (3) to encourage a pragmatic approach to the urgent need for digital libraries of critical editions of classical texts. Only with a comprehensive understanding of the content and assumptions of the traditional highly-evolved critical apparatus will we make the right strategic decisions for the future of textual scholarship on the literary legacy of Greece and Rome.[30]

---

30 I am grateful to my fellow speakers at the 2013 NeDiMAH Experts' seminar, and especially to the seminar's organisers, Matthew Driscoll and Elena Pierazzo, for a stimulating discussion of the wide world of digital critical editions, a topic that has been engaging my attention increasingly since 2008, when I organised a panel on 'Critical editions in the 21st century' for the American Philological Association. Further stimulus to thought was provided by the 'Digital Variorum Editions' project for an NEH 'Digging into Data' initiative, and I am grateful to Greg Crane both for the opportunity to be its respondent and for our many discussions on the digital future of classical texts. I have also learnt much from my fellow members of the Planning Committee for the Digital Latin Library, a project co-sponsored by the APA, the Medieval Academy of America and the Renaissance Society of America, especially its director, Sam Huskey, all of whom helped me to formulate desiderata and see opportunities for the ongoing development of critical editions. Especial thanks go to Bob Kaster and Richard Tarrant for many a conversation about the critical apparatus over the years.

12. The Battle We Forgot to Fight: Should We Make a Case for Digital Editions?

Roberto Rosselli Del Turco

Introduction

When Peter Robinson wrote 'Current Issues in Making Digital Editions of Medieval Texts—Or, Do Electronic Scholarly Editions Have a Future?',[1] he was looking back at what we may call the 'pioneer era' of digital editing and publishing: a time span of roughly ten years, from the early 90s to 2004.[2] It was during this time that important editorial projects such as the *Piers Plowman Electronic Archive*,[3] the *Electronic Beowulf*,[4] the *Canterbury Tales Project*,[5] the

---

1   Peter Robinson, 'Current Issues in Making Digital Editions of Medieval Texts—Or, Do Electronic Scholarly Editions Have a Future?', *Digital Medievalist*, 1.1 (2005), http://www.digitalmedievalist.org/journal/1.1/robinson
2   Robinson's article was received by the *Digital Medievalist* editors on January 6, 2005.
3   Hoyt N. Duggan, '1994 Prospectus: Archive Goals', *The Piers Plowman Electronic Archive (1994–2003)*, http://jefferson.village.virginia.edu/seenet/piers/archivegoals.htm
4   *The Electronic Beowulf*, ed. by Kevin S. Kiernan (London: British Library, 1999/2013) [CD-ROM]. See also Kevin S. Kiernan, 'Digital Preservation, Restoration, and Dissemination of Medieval Manuscripts', in *Gateways, Gatekeepers, and Roles in the Information Omniverse: Proceedings of the Third Symposium*, ed. by Ann Okerson and Dru Mogge (Washington: Office of Scientific and Academic Publishing, Association of Research Libraries, 1994), pp. 37–43.
5   *The Wife of Bath's Prologue on CD-ROM*, ed. by Peter Robinson (Cambridge: Cambridge University Press, 1996).

Parzival-Projekt[6] and many more[7] published the results of their efforts. The preferred publishing medium during this phase was that of an optical support, CD or DVD, but there were already in existence not only interesting experimental editions on the Web,[8] but also more complex, hypermedia-based ones.[9]

In spite of the great attention and interest that these editions enjoyed at the time of their publication, their acceptance and actual use by scholars was lower than expected:

> We thought then that we had a sound publication model for digital editions: major publishers would publish them, just as they have always done for print editions. But this has not happened. Further, we now know anecdotally that many scholars remain sceptical of electronic publication. Combined with the movement by leading academic publishers away from this field, this scepticism leads rather easily to the opinion that electronic publication is not real publication at all.[10]

This was all the more surprising since 'it is rather clear that well-made digital editions are better than print editions from the perspective of their users'.[11] The question remains 'if digital editions are so manifestly superior, then why indeed are we in the state of affairs described above? Why are so many scholars, and so many scholarly projects, still making print editions?'[12] According to Robinson, the answer lies in the

---

6   Michael Stolz, *Die St. Galler Epenhandschrift: Parzival, Nibelungenlied und Klage, Karl, Willehalm. Faksimile des Codex 857 der Stiftsbibliothek St. Gallen und zugehöriger Fragmente: CD-ROM mit einem Begleitheft*, Codices Electronici Sangallenses, 1 (Stiftsbibliothek St. Gallen/Basler Parzival-Projekt, 2003).

7   I will also cite Bernard James Muir's *The Exeter Anthology of Old English Poetry: An Edition of Exeter Dean and Chapter MS 3501* (Exeter: Exeter University Press, 2004) and a digital Facsimile of Oxford, Bodleian Library MS. Junius 11 (Oxford: Bodleian Library, 2004) as particularly significant for my area of research, that of medieval literary texts belonging to the Anglo-Saxon tradition.

8   *The Wanderer: Edition and Translation*, ed. by Tim Romano (1999), http://www.aimsdata.com/tim/anhaga/edition.htm

9   *The Complete Writings and Pictures of Dante Gabriel Rossetti: A Hypermedia Research Archive*, ed. by Jerome McGann (Charlottesville: Institute for Advanced Technology in the Humanities, 2000–), http://www.rossettiarchive.org

10   Robinson, 'Current Issues', § 11.

11   *Ibid.*, § 12.

12   *Ibid.*, § 13.

availability, or lack thereof, of suitable software tools that would allow editors to produce scholarly editions in digital form:

> Over the past two decades I have made two of the leading tools for making scholarly electronic editions. The first is the collation software *Collate*, which I first wrote as a set of VAX routines in the 1980s, and re-wrote into a Macintosh program in the 1990s. The second is the XML publication software *Anastasia*, which I initiated in the mid-1990s. Several of the electronic editions named above depend heavily on these two tools. One can assert that it is indeed possible to use them to make digital editions which offer all we could hope for. But as their creator I think I am uniquely qualified to note that they are not easy to use: if everyone who wanted to make digital editions was required to use these two tools, very few digital editions would ever be made.[13]

The rest of the article is devoted to a discussion of existing software tools and frameworks, and how to improve the workflow of scholars who wish to publish digital editions. Its conclusion is fairly optimistic:

> Throughout this article, I have expressed what I think should be our aim: that some time quite soon scholars wishing to make scholarly editions will naturally choose the electronic form. It follows then that all major series of scholarly editions, including those now published by the major academic presses, also will become digital. There will be exceptions: there always will be a place for a printed reader's edition or similar. But we should expect that for most of the purposes for which we now use editions, the editions we use will be electronic. We should do this not just to keep up with the rest of the world, but because indeed electronic editions make possible kinds of reading and research never before available and offer valuable insights into and approaches to the texts they cover.[14]

Roughly ten years after this article was written, we may now wonder about what has changed: has the balance between printed and digital editions tilted in favour of the latter? Surely there are many more digital editions available, but can we claim that they have 'succeeded'? Indeed, how do we measure success with regard to acceptance of scholarly editions in digital form?

---

13   *Ibid.*, § 11.
14   *Ibid.*, § 30.

Ten years later

Two recent surveys conducted by Ithaka S+R, part of the non-profit Ithaka group, on American[15] and British[16] academics' use of digital tools for research and teaching show that the acceptance and use of such tools is growing, albeit very slowly and that there is still considerable resistance. According to the surveys the use of Internet search engines and other web-based research tools is widespread, Open Access is increasingly considered as a dissemination method, although the majority of scholars still rely on printed monographs and A-level peer-reviewed journals to publish the results of their research. Moreover, the surveys shows that only a fraction of scholars actively use social media such as Facebook, Twitter and blogs for scholarly purposes. An interesting trend is that, in spite of the preference for traditional printed books both for research and dissemination of its results, there is a fast-growing acceptance of electronic-only versions of journal articles, to the extent that in 2012 about 40% of the respondents strongly agreed with the question 'Assuming that electronic collections of journals are proven to work well, I would be happy to see hard copy collections discarded and replaced entirely by electronic collections',[17] a percentage that has more than doubled since 2003. E-books are also increasingly valued as an alternative to printed books and textbooks for research and teaching purposes: 'After many years in which e-books were seen as the 'next big thing', they are firmly established in the mainstream marketplace and they are increasingly common among scholarly materials as well'.[18] Note, however, that

> Even while digital versions of scholarly monographs remain a relatively new feature on the mainstream scholarly communications landscape, some libraries have already begun to consider how library collections of print books will evolve, following the example of library journal collections. Very few respondents have historically agreed strongly with the statement: 'Within the next five years, the use of e-books will be so

---

15 US Faculty Survey 2012, http://www.sr.ithaka.org/research-publications/faculty-survey-2012-us
16 Ithaka S+R | Jisc | RLUK: UK Survey of Academics 2012, http://www.sr.ithaka.org/research-publications/ithaka-sr-jisc-rluk-uk-survey-academics-2012
17 *Ibid.*, pp. 28–29.
18 *Ibid.*, p. 31.

prevalent among faculty and students that it will not be necessary to maintain library collections of hard copy books'. This overall pattern did not change in this cycle of the survey.[19]

It is unfortunate that a study on such a large scale is not available for a specific type of monograph production, i.e. that of scholarly digital editions (SDEs), but we have a good approximation, even if limited to the field of medieval studies and (again) to English-speaking countries, thanks to Dot Porter's surveys conducted in 2002 and 2011.[20] This kind of survey is fundamental in order to assess the degree of acceptance and popularity of SDEs, but we can also rely on the following parameters:

- general discussion: either in public mailing lists, conferences or other forums of discussion; the risk is that information gathered by these means verges on the anecdotal while remaining incomplete;
- the number of digital editions published: on the assumption that, if more and more editions are published in digital form, there is a demand for and an appreciation of them;
- hard metrics: very few sites (or publishers) make publicly available data regarding number of hits per day/month/year (or actual number of CD/DVDs sold), but if it were available, such data would be a reliable indicator of actual use.

Let us put aside survey results and hard data for the moment and resort to the most unreliable form of evidence, i.e. the empirical and anecdotal evidence hinted at in the first bullet point above. First of all, I will quickly have to put aside my own country, Italy: use of digital resources, such as electronic facsimile and editions, is currently increasing, but it seems fairly safe to say that traditional formats are not on the verge of extinction, quite the contrary. If I look at the 'production side', i.e. scholars and researchers using IT methods and techniques to create scholarly digital editions, I can count those active in my field of study (myself included) on the fingers of a single hand; the same numerical proportion applies

---

19 *Ibid.*, p. 34.
20 Dorothy Carr Porter, 'Medievalists' Use of Electronic Resources: The Results of a National Survey of Faculty Members in Medieval Studies' (Phd thesis, UNC-Chapel Hill, 2002), http://ils.unc.edu/MSpapers/2807.pdf; Dot Porter, 'Medievalists and the Scholarly Digital Edition', *Scholarly Editing: The Annual of the Association for Documentary Editing*, 34 (2013), 1–26, http://www.scholarlyediting.org/2013/essays/essay.porter.html

when extending the research area to the whole of the medieval studies field, of course discounting specific and worthy exceptions. Therefore I will have to look to the world of the Digital Humanities in general, and in particular their application in the domain of Anglo-Saxon studies where they are stronger than in other areas of Medieval studies and on the upside of a growth curve.[21] There is a particular example that lends itself very well to show the problems that SDEs encounter when it comes not only to actual use, but also to receiving adequate recognition for the services they offer. In a thread about citation standards on the ANSAXNET mailing list,[22] several subscribers wrote that they routinely make use of digital resources, but they are quite wary of citing them in their works, with at least one person declaring that while he or she uses the online editions to do research, he or she then quotes from the printed equivalent. This statement caused understandable distress among those who are aware of the work and resources needed to create online resources: that people may not acknowledge the labour required to produce them, nor the high quality of many of them, struck many participants in the discussion as unfair. However, those who expressed 'uneasiness' at citing these resources were able to provide the reasoning behind it through a set of good points that I will take into account in the following section.

An increasing number of SDEs are published every year.[23] These editions seem to improve constantly in both their overall quality and the richness of features that they offer. Thus apparently all is well and good in regard to the second parameter.

With regard to the last criterion, I have personally visited about forty web-based digital editions, but could only find a single site which showed statistics about page hits—in the form of an apparent total number of visitors since the moment the site was created. While this is disappointing, it is also understandable: this feature hardly looks

---

21 See the reports quoted above; note, however, that there is a very strong push in favour of digital resources creation and fruition in many European countries.

22 A full-text database for the ANSAXNET mailing list has, until recently, been available at http://www.mun.ca/Ansaxdat, but this appears no longer to be active. The discussion thread I am referring to starts on 19 April 2013 with a message by C. E. Anderson with title 'Charter citation standards?'

23 See the chapter by Greta Franzini et al. in the present volume. Patrick Sahle's *A Catalog of Digital Scholarly Editions*, http://www.digitale-edition.de, is also a valuable resource.

essential when compared to all the other features required by a digital edition, and, in fact, it may be objected that the present writer is not himself open to criticism on this very point, since the *Digital Vercelli Book* web site is not able to count visitors (yet).[24] It is possible that these numbers are available for some web-based editions, but are simply not made accessible to the general public. In any case, it would be interesting to undertake more in-depth research on this topic, since we definitely need more evidence about the actual use of digital resources in general, and digital editions in particular.

The results of Dot Porter's surveys, which also allow us to assess the changes that occurred in a period of about ten years, confirm the situation described by the more general surveys mentioned above:

> The results of my survey bear out the continued usefulness, or at least continued use, of print editions: medievalists are using print editions more than they are using digital editions, and the use of digital editions has not grown over the past nine years, as it has, for example, for digital journals.[25]

The progress towards wider use of electronic editions is actually measurable, but unfortunately quite limited:

> Twenty-two percent of all respondents reported using only print editions (down from 48% in 2002), while 58% reported using mostly print (up from 44% in 2002). This is where the largest single shift occurred — not from a clear preference for print to a clear preference for electronic, but from a clear preference for print to a slightly less clear preference for print. Twelve percent of respondents (up from 7% in 2002) reported using electronic and print editions equally often, and 7% reported using mostly electronic editions.[26]

In spite of several excellent electronic editions having been published, therefore, not much seems to be different from the situation described by Robinson ten years ago:

> It is depressing to find cases where scholars do not use the digital editions one has gone to such trouble to make, even when they know of

---

24 http://vbd.humnet.unipi.it/beta2. Note that this is a beta version whose main purpose is that of soliciting feedback by its users.
25 Porter, 'Medievalists and the Scholarly Digital Edition', p. 8.
26 *Ibid.*, p. 9.

and have access to them. To give just one example: my edition of the *Wife of Bath's Prologue* and several later Canterbury Tales Project publications include Dan Mosser's descriptions of the *Canterbury Tales* manuscripts. These descriptions are the result of several decades of work by Professor Mosser, in the course of which he has inspected every manuscript and every complete incunable copy (and very many fragments too); consulted with every leading scholar; read every article of note; and built up a formidable expertise in palaeography, codicology, and watermarks. By all odds, these are not just the most recent, but also the most careful and comprehensive accounts ever made of the *Tales'* earliest texts. Despite this, I have come across several examples of work, even by senior scholars with access to Professor Mosser's research, where these essential resources have not been cited.[27]

In conclusion, if we combine general data about the steady but slow increase in use of general digital tools among academics with more specific information about digital editions use gathered through public surveys, in public discussions with colleagues or by other means, we have to acknowledge that the acceptance and use of such resources for research purposes is still far below the expectations that we had many years ago.[28] The apparent good health of scholarly editions in digital form, as witnessed by the growing number of projects, sharply contrasts a general perception of those editions and resources being underused and often undeservedly undercited.

Where the problem lies

Peter Robinson was surely right in citing the lack of user-friendly tools to create SDEs as a major reason for their (relative) scarcity at the time he was writing, but in my opinion this is just one of several factors that combine to produce the current state of affairs. First of all, however, it is necessary to distinguish the production aspect, i.e. why creating digital editions is perceived as being a complex, if not outright daunting task, and the enjoyment-and use-aspect, focusing on why digital editions are not used to the extent we would expect, and why, when used, they are often considered a useful resource, but one that does not enjoy the same degree of good standing as their printed counterparts.

---

27 Robinson, 'Current Issues', § 11.
28 The situation seems to be slightly better as regards the use of digital resources for teaching purposes.

Production

Robinson's remark about the lack of easy-to-use production tools is unfortunately still valid: there is no software tool nor suite of tools that allows a scholar to produce a full digital edition, be it image-based with a diplomatic text or a critical edition, in a way comparable to how printed editions are prepared.[29] Most of all, there is no 'standard way' to do it, so that right from the start the aspiring digital philologist will have to evaluate several alternatives, or rely on the opinion of technical support personnel or collaborators. Support from an IT centre is mandatory in the case of complex frameworks, such as those based on Drupal or Omeka, whose installation, configuration, data loading and maintenance is definitely beyond the reach of the average philologist, however enthusiastic he or she may otherwise be about the use of digital tools.

In fact, even in the best case scenario—that of a good, easy to use edition production software available for use—creating a SDE will always require more resources compared to a traditional one,unless you forgo such features as manuscript images, use of collation software, inclusion of a text search engine or of image-related tools. Not only that: the workflow of a traditional printed edition is dramatically simpler, since when you have finished working on the edition text you deliver it to a publisher, who will take care of printing and circulation. When embarking on a digital edition project, on the other hand, one has to start walking on an unfamiliar and possibly intimidating path, whose final destination may not be fully known in advance; this was especially the case for the 'pioneer era' projects described above, but even today, at least in my experience, there are often unexpected changes that the editor needs to be ready to perform so that the project can safely be concluded and an edition published. The progressive disappearance of the CD/DVD option, a surrogate of the book as a physical object that can be produced, distributed and sold, also means that traditional publishers are, at least for the moment, out of the equation:[30] as a

---

29 Scholars can rely on several software tools to prepare their editions, from word processors to more specifically philologically oriented programs such as CTE (http://cte.oeaw.ac.at), but usually the final typesetting stage is entrusted to the publisher.

30 A possible alternative would be that of web-based editions curated by publishers and made available for a subscription fee. As far as I know, this publishing model is not particularly popular in the Humanities, at least not for digital editions.

consequence, it is not usually possible to replicate the same workflow as the one used for printed editions, eventually entrusting the publisher with the task of taking care of the final processing and visualisation of the edition data. Although web-based editions are the better choice for too many reasons to be listed here, it remains to be seen who will take the role of the publisher. Since web space is now incredibly convenient and inexpensive, self-publishing is definitely a possibility, in some ways also a very desirable one, but it is characterised by significant limitations related to sustainability, maintenance and 'quotability' (see below). In conclusion, a single scholar wanting to explore the brave new world of digital philology is suddenly at a disadvantage compared to the colleague who opts to stick with the traditional methods inworking towards a printed edition.

Of the pariticipants in the aforementioned thread on the ANSAXNET mailing list, those who admitted to abstaining from citing digital resources reported two reasons for their uneasiness with these resources. The first is that since documents are displayed in a continuous HTML page, it is often difficult to refer to a specific text passage; secondly, and most importantly, web-based resources have an unpleasant tendency to be less reliable than print editions. Citing a web page only to lead to a '404—Page not found' error because the site, for whatever reason, is not available any more, is not an acceptable feature for a scholarly-level publication. While the first objection may be easily fixed by numbering and indexing text paragraphs, the second one highlights a crucial problem of digital publications, either based on optical media or on the Web framework: the sometimes rapid obsolescence of standalone software in the case of CD/DVD-based editions, and the sudden disappearance of web-based ones or, in some cases, the creeping of similar incompatibilities in the visualisation software when used with more modern operating systems and browsers. While manuscripts may have lasted hundreds of years, it is discomforting to note how the life span of a digital facsimile/edition is sometimes less than 4–5 years. For web-based editions the problem is twofold:

- software compatibility: web browser extensions, such as Java applets, ActiveX controls and Flash applications, may look like a good idea at the time of implementation, but nothing guarantees that they will continue to function, especially in the case of closed, proprietary extensions;

- long-term sustainability: if you look towards persistence and actual usability of your edition for the next 10–20 years at least, it is essential to make sure that the web server on which the edition is published is sufficiently reliable, both on the technical side and on the financial one; complex software running on the server will require more financial resources to ensure its maintenance, and may be more prone to incur the compatibility problems described in the previous point.

Last, but definitely not least, there are also some issues of a strictly theoretical nature that have to be addressed in order to make SDEs appealing to scholars from a range of philological schools. A web-based publishing framework, a general term which I use to refer to all necessary software and server resources needed to publish a digital edition on the web, should be a complete and neutral tool, but at the present moment it seems to be neither: currently the most popular type of web-based digital edition,[31] the image-based digital facsimile accompanied by a diplomatic transcription, although clearly suitable for a 'best text' or 'new philology' edition, is less useful to editors aiming at establishing a critical text. Is the fact that the production method apparently lacks neutrality a reason why Neo-/Post-Lachmannian scholars do not use it more often? Or is their non-use simply related to the shortcomings of the current set of software tools?

Consumption

Compared to the problems involved in production, problems in fruition of SDEs are, while still significant, much fewer in number and less troubling.

Any resource that requires a computer screen to be used is already at a disadvantage when compared to the traditional medium, the printed book. The simple fact that you need an LCD monitor to browse any kind of digital resource implies several drawbacks related to ergonomics, mobility, availability and quality of the Internet connection, among

---

[31] On this topic see Odd Einar Haugen, 'The Spirit of Lachmann, the Spirit of Bédier: Old Norse Textual Editing in the Electronic Age', in *Annual Meeting of The Viking Society, University College London*, 8 (2002), pp. 1–21, http://www.ub.uib.no/elpub/2003/a/522001/haugen.pdf, especially the section 'The Drift towards Monotypic Editions'.

others. This is a well-known limitation, but also one which does not prevent successful use of digital editions as study and research tools, which should be their primary purpose.

Another obstacle to overcome is the high fragmentation of user interfaces and the resulting difficulty in the use of each SDE, considering that some effort to learn layout and function of all GUI elements, as well as general navigation of the edition, will be required in any case. While there is a slow trend towards a sort of 'canon' or standard set of tools expected to be available (such as image-related tools, a text search engine and so on), no standardised user interface exists, especially when it comes to the general layout of the web site. This problem would not be so bad if it were not for the fact that many web designers, and programmers of stand-alone SDEs on CD/DVD, often seem to make their creations more difficult to use than necessary.[32]

Furthermore, while we are well aware of the advantages of SDEs as research tools when compared to their printed counterparts,[33] a precise awareness of their benefits, together with the perception of what exactly a SDE is, may not be sufficiently clear to users, who are often scholars that may be interested in venturing out onto the digital path at some point in the future. The question that I have been trying to answer during the last few years, both at conferences and by other means of public discussion, is as follows: 'In terms of scientific efficiency, in which ways is a digital edition superior to a traditional printed edition?'[34] This is a very legitimate question showing how much the wondrous 'dynamic device', or at least its potential, is still largely unknown to a large part of the prospective users of such editions. At surface level, hypertext navigation or a diplomatic transcription accompanied by manuscript images may not appear more than a convenient set of functionalities granted by a brand-new medium (see above), but, again, this is just an adherence to an old, outdated perception of SDEs. As a consequence, since the 'manifest superiority' of SDEs is not 'rather clear', at least not for all users, the risk of underuse and underappreciation is high.

---

32 On this topic see Roberto Rosselli Del Turco, 'After the Editing Is Done: Designing a Graphic User Interface for Digital Editions', *Digital Medievalist*, 7 (2011), http://www.digitalmedievalist.org/journal/7/rosselliDelTurco

33 See for instance Marina Buzzoni's chapter in the present volume.

34 Question asked by colleague and friend Marcello Meli at the *'Incontri di Filologia Digitale'* conference (Verona, 15–16 January 2009).

Perception

Another small piece of evidence concerning the problems afflicting SDEs is the way that we sometimes address less 'digital-savvy' colleagues: I find it telling when a speaker at a conference or workshop takes great pains to distinguish between a 'digitised edition' and a proper digital edition; indeed, the present writer had to make this very clarification on more than one occasion. That it is necessary to explain this to anyone who is not an undergraduate student, today, is symptomatic of a problem that goes beyond the mode of production or the appropriateness of citing from a digital edition.[35] To quote Dot Porter again:

> The serious issue in the scholarly community is credit toward tenure and promotion for scholars who focus their efforts on creating digital editions and other projects. If we say 'digital edition' and our colleagues and administrators think 'Google Books' when what we really mean is 'Electronic Beowulf', that is a huge gulf.[36]

Actually the problem may be more severe and difficult to resolve because sometimes even those who produce such editions do not seem to understand fully the underlying concepts. In an article dating back to 2004, approximately contemporary with Robinson's, Lina Karlsson and Linda Malm perform a survey of thirty-one web-based scholarly editions and conclude that 'web editions seem to reproduce features of the printed media and do not fulfil the potential of the Web to any larger extent'.[37] Today, web editions have become much more sophisticated and can now conceivably fulfil the 'potential of the Web': the powerful, dynamic device to visualise SDEs theorised by Robinson is slowly becoming a reality, at least in a few select cases, but the true potential of this concept and its full implications must be very clear to those who start a digital edition, or what we will see will be more imitations of the traditional layout and features of printed editions. In other words, if an editor thinks that a digital edition is simply a traditional edition on a

---

35 On this subject, see Patrick Sahle's chapter in the present volume.
36 Porter, 'Medievalists and the Scholarly Digital Edition', p. 14.
37 Lina Karlsson and Linda Malm, 'Revolution or Remediation? A Study of Electronic Scholarly Editions on the Web', *Human IT*, 7.1 (2004), p. 1, http://etjanst.hb.se/bhs/ith/1-7/lklm.pdf

digital medium, he or she is actually missing the real point of it and will produce no more than a digital replica of a printed edition.[38]

How to fix things

While I will discuss each point in roughly the same order as they were presented above, let me state beforehand that availability of easy-to-use tools, amount of resources, time required, and streamlining of the workflow are all different facets of the same problem: how to make production of a scholarly digital edition as simple as possible for a scholar or researcher who is used to working mostly alone and on a limited budget.

Production and visualisation tools

The 'perfect' software tool for any purpose is one requiring little to no training on the part of the user, ideally being ready to be used out of the box, no hefty manual study required. Judging from the current state of affairs as regards both production and visualisation tools, we are still quite far from that goal, but progress in that direction is undisputedly being made. A recent development is that of authoring tools for the encoding of edition texts.[39] While this can surely lower the bar for SDE production, I would be wary of relying on this kind of software exclusively, especially after web developers enjoyed a less than satisfying experience with similar tools (code produced by HTML authoring tools was often bloated and unreliable). What is recommended, if not required, from the scholar? Surely a good knowledge of the markup language is needed to create the edition, but anything beyond XSLT stylesheets application to XML documents, for instance XSLT programming or installation/configuration of server software, would require too much

---

38 For a different point of view see Daniel Paul O'Donnell, 'Resisting the Tyranny of the Screen, or, Must a Digital Edition be Electronic?', *Heroic Age*, 8 (2008), http://www.heroicage.org/issues/11/em.php

39 See, for instance, the TextLab transcription tool developed by John Bryant at Hofstra University (available on the project's website: http://mel.hofstra.edu/textlab.html) and the DTA-oXygen-Framework (DTAoX: http://www.deutschestextarchiv.de/doku/software#dtaox), which uses the oXygen XML editor to build an authoring tool for text annotation.

time and resources from the 'traditional' scholar (i.e. one working alone on his or her edition, not in a research group, and often on a limited budget), especially if he or she is approaching the digital scholarly editing path for the first time. Assuming that the scholar is equipped with this fundamental knowledge, whatever the markup language used, the tools available for creating an SDE fall in one of two general categories:

- production tools: any good XML editor is an effective production tool, but new authoring environments are currently developed to assist the scholar in this phase;[40] provided that the encoded text is always available to inspection and human readable, this is probably the best solution since these environments usually offer image-related functionality (such as text-image linking tools) which should otherwise be looked for elsewhere;

- visualisation tools: one could maintain that, if you correctly encode your text, the edition is already there and only needs to be 'extracted' from the XML document base, but of course this phase is at least as delicate and complex as the previous one (especially considering the usability issues hinted above). This is also an area where tool development is particularly intense.

A survey of the existing visualisation tools undertaken by the *Digital Vercelli Book* project team in 2012, and the conclusion that none of the evaluated software was suitable for our purposes, led to the birth of EVT (Edition Visualisation Technology) software:[41] a framework to build a web-based diplomatic edition applying a chain of XSLT transformations to the TEI XML document holding the encoded text. Creating the edition

---

40 Another example is Ediarum — an easy tool for editing manuscripts with TEI XML: http://www.bbaw.de/en/telota/software/ediarum; see also eCodicology — Algorithms for the Automatic Tagging of Medieval Manuscripts, http://ipelsdf1.lsdf.kit.edu/index.php/nav-pro-projects/nav-pro-act-ecodicology

41 Roberto Rosselli Del Turco and Raffaele Masotti, *Edition Visualization Technology: Digital Edition Visualization Software*, 2013–, http://sourceforge.net/projects/evt-project. For more information about this tool see Roberto Rosselli Del Turco, Giancarlo Buomprisco, Chiara Di Pietro, Julia Kenny, Raffaele Masotti and Jacopo Pugliese, 'Edition Visualization Technology: A Simple Tool to Visualize TEI-based Digital Editions', *Journal of the Text Encoding Initiative*, 8 (2014–2015), http://jtei.revues.org/1077; see also Roberto Rosselli Del Turco, 'EVT Development: An Update (and Quite a Bit of History)', in Edition Visualization Technology blog, 2014, http://visualizationtechnology.wordpress.com/2014/01/26/evt-development-an-update-and-quite-a-bit-of-history

is as simple as applying a stylesheet to the marked-up text. This is the software used to create the Digital Vercelli Book edition mentioned above, while for production we resorted to several different XML editors for text encoding and the Image Markup Tool[42] for annotating the manuscript areas corresponding to text lines and other points of interest.

Long-term sustainability

One way to look at the preservation problem is to consider it as a consequence of the continuous, uninterrupted evolution of software, even 'slow motion' development of critical components of the modern web infrastructure such as the standards promoted by the W3C.[43] This is why the only viable solution to ensure that an edition is usable for the foreseeable future is to completely decouple the edition data from the visualisation mechanism: if the editor makes use of standard-based data formats (such as TIFF, JPEG for digitised images, (X)HTML or XML for texts etc.), he or she can be reasonably confident that the core of the edition will still be readable and usable for a very long time. The visualisation framework, on the other hand, may require periodic maintenance, up to the point when a total replacement will be a better option as a result of the availability of new technology, but that is probably unavoidable in the long term.

How can we make web publishing as simple and painless as possible for the 'traditional' scholar, who usually works independently and cannot count on the support of technical staff to handle electronic publishing? As noted above, hosting services are cheap and there are plenty to choose from, but this is not a solution except for beta-testing and short-term experimental editions. Entrusting a significant SDE to such a fickle support would only make it all the more frustrating when a good resource is lost, temporarily or forever, because the person responsible for its accessibility has forgotten to renew the yearly domain license, or has just abandoned the project. We need a reliable third party, such

---

42   The Image Markup Tool project, http://tapor.uvic.ca/~mholmes/image_markup/index.php
43   The World Wide Web Consortium (W3C), http://www.w3.org

as universities and other research institutions,[44] offering support and preparing an adequate infrastructure for long-term publishing of select digital editions. This is, in fact, also an opportunity to ensure visibility and support for those SDEs that exceed certain quality criteria and are therefore eligible to be hosted on institutional web sites. Last but not least, a stable, institution-guaranteed 'home' for SDEs would also solve the quotability problem, since this would undoubtedly ensure that a specific digital resource would stay online for the foreseeable future.

Usability

Two concepts as different as hypertext theory and the e-book were have been theorised years (many years, in the case of hypertext theory) before a suitable medium would allow them to succeed. The situation is less clear-cut when it comes to SDEs: on a purely technical ground we have all that is needed already, and in fact many excellent editions are already available to be used for research purposes which are superior to traditional printed ones, even though possibly not 'manifestly superior'; but, as remarked above, some rough edges still exist and have to be addressed. Progress on the usability front will be slow but hopefully steady if visualisation tool designers take into account usability and accessibility standards, conforming to best practice guidelines. A particularly delicate point will be the implementation of the most advanced features that are being discussed and deployed in experimental form right now (shared annotation, social editions, linked open data etc.).

It is also important to consider the inherent limitations of the physical media conveying the digital editions: for the great majority of users it is not a problem to use a SDE as a research tool,[45] even for extended periods of time; anyone intending to use such a resource as a reading edition on a computer, on the other hand, will have to face both the

---

44 Also cultural heritage bodies such as Europeana, http://europeana.eu
45 Although it is surely essential to follow usability and accessibility best practices to avoid making use of such digital resources difficult for certain classes of users (for example users suffering from colour blindness).

physical constraint of the typical PC workstation and the well-known Visual Fatigue phenomenon induced by LCD monitors.[46]

The e-book story may teach something useful here. In fact e-books only started being popular when e-reader devices with suitable characteristics (e-ink display) and reasonable prices were introduced to the market. In a similar way, we already have cheap mobile devices, namely tablets, with all the features needed to visualise an SDE (processing power, medium size but often high resolution screens); the e-codices iOS app[47] shows how even on smaller, smartphone screens you can have a usable and useful opportunity to search and browse digital facsimiles of medieval manuscripts. Moreover, new and more sophisticated displays combined with the inherent mobility of such devices would allow us to overcome the limitations of PC monitors hinted at above. The considerable difference and peculiarities of a Touch User Interface will require special attention and a determined search for effective solutions to implement in such an app, but the challenge is well worth the effort.

---

46 Note that, while the subject is still very much open to research and debate, at the present moment the e-ink displays of e-book readers such as the Kindle or the Nook seem to have an edge over smartphones and tablets based on LCD screens. In part this was caused by the relatively low resolution of the first tablets: a comparison of the original iPad with the contemporary Kindle model by means of a high resolution microscope done in 2010 (see Keith Peters, 'Kindle and iPad Displays: Up Close and Personal', *BIT-101* (2010), http://www.bit-101.com/blog/?p=2722) showed how the e-ink display is much more similar to printed paper with regard to resolution and appearance, which explained why it was felt to be a lot less tiring on the eyes by its users. Subsequent iPad models, as well as the great majority of tablets now sold by other brands, greatly improved screen resolution, so that according to some researchers (for example Eva Siegenthaler, Yves Bochud, Per Bergamin and Pascal Wurtz, 'Reading on LCD vs. e-Ink Displays: Effects on Fatigue and Visual Strain', *Ophthalmic and Physiological Optics*, 32 (2012), 367–74) the gulf has been bridged and e-ink displays are no longer to be considered better than tablets for reading purposes. A recent article, however, brought up the backlit nature of LCD as a significant factor increasing Visual Fatigue; see Simone Benedetto, Véronique Drai-Zerbib, Marco Pedrotti, Geoffrey Tissier and Thierry Baccino, 'E-Readers and Visual Fatigue', *PLoS ONE*, 8.12 (2013), http://www.ncbi.nlm.nih.gov/pmc/articles/PMC3873942, http://dx.doi.org/10.1371/journal.pone.0083676. Tablet displays are constantly improved and new technologies are introduced at an impressive rhythm, however, so the problem of 'visual fatigue' will hopefully be eliminated or greatly reduced in the near future.

47 E-codices — Virtual Manuscript Library of Switzerland iPhone and iPad app developed by text & bytes LLC and e-codices, http://e-codices.textandbytes.com

Theoretical issues

The discussion about topics that relate to the digital philology field is very lively,[48] but I think that we still need to formulate a convincing definition of SDE, including a description of what makes it different from a 'digitised edition' and a description of types and sub-types, that can be offered to our colleagues who want to know more about philology and 'computer stuff'.[49] Dot Porter concludes her essay with the following recommendation:

> My findings strongly suggest that there is a disconnect between scholarly interest in electronic resources in general and in reported use of digital scholarly editions, and that this disconnect may be related not only to a relative lack of digital editions but also to a lack of understanding by non-digital-editing medievalists about what exactly a digital scholarly edition is. Before we can encourage the scholarly community to take up tools and develop digital editions instead of print, we need to ensure that there are clear definitions regarding 'digital' vs. 'digitised' editions so that scholars are aware of what they are getting into.[50]

We should also explain in detail the advantages and (current) drawbacks of the SDE concept, highlighting its potential without hiding the pitfalls and the differences from the traditional way of preparing a scholarly edition. This 'general survey' of digital philology studies should also take into account how the SDE concept relates to different ecdotic theories, again pinpointing benefits but also shortcomings in some cases.

Success and acceptance

It cannot be considered a predetermined outcome, but I am confident that the act of attending to all the issues discussed above, together with digital editing work ending in excellent SDEs being published, will result in the greater acceptance and popularity of digital scholarly editing.

---

48 See for instance the special issue 'Computing the Edition', *Literary & Linguistic Computing*, 24.1 (2009), and the special issue 'Scholarly Editing in the Twenty-First Century', *Literature Compass*, 7.2 (2010). On the specific subject of defining SDEs see Peter Robinson, 'Towards a Theory of Digital Editions', *Variants: The Journal of the European Society for Textual Scholarship*, 10 (2013), 105–31.

49 Patrick Sahle's chapter in the present volume, mentioned above, goes a long way toward formulating that definition.

50 Porter, 'Medievalists and the Scholarly Digital Edition', p. 14.

A critical point will be that of evaluation: there are already initiatives, such as NINES[51] and MESA,[52] that aim at aggregating scholarly digital resources and that can also work as peer-reviewing bodies to improve the perception of SDEs by the academic community.[53] Adding a rigorous selection at an institutional level to grant hosting and maintenance of web-based digital editions would reinforce the process of perception change and increased acceptance for digital scholarly editing.

Conclusion

We are at a crucial moment in the evolution of digital scholarly editing: if we want it to succeed, to be accepted by our own colleagues, we should continue to discuss and improve its fundamental methodologies not only among us 'pioneers', but also with the numerous scholars who may be interested in adopting such methods, and have thus far refrained from doing so because of the many hurdles they assume they have to overcome. It is not by accident that so many papers given at the Experts' Seminar on Digital Editions, and now so many chapters in the present book, revolve around the core themes that I have briefly hinted at as fundamental to ensure success and acceptance for SDEs: what a digital edition really is (Patrick Sahle), advantages of SDEs and problems in apparatus visualisation (Marina Buzzoni), a catalogue and taxonomy of SDEs (Greta Franzini), readers' role in scholarly editions (Krista Stinne Greve Rasmussen) and more. The fact that the researchers contributing to the present volume worked independently and touched deeply interconnected topics to reach similar conclusions means that there exists a general consensus about the direction to take, which is an encouraging sign and an invitation to persevere in expanding the field of Digital Philology.

---

51 NINES (Networked Infrastructure for Nineteenth-Century Electronic Scholarship), http://www.nines.org

52 MESA (The Medieval Electronic Scholarly Alliance), http://www.mesa-medieval.org

53 This is one of the primary goals of NINES: 'Digital humanities projects have long lacked a framework for peer review and thus have often had difficulty establishing their credibility as true scholarship. NINES exists in part to address this situation by instituting a robust system of review by some of the most respected scholars in the field of nineteenth-century studies, British and American' (http://www.nines.org/about/scholarship/peer-review).

Bibliography

André, Julie and Elena Pierazzo, 'Le Codage en TEI des Brouillons de Proust: Vers l'Edition Numérique', *Genesis*, 36 (2013), 155–61.

Apollon, Daniel, Claire Bélisle and Philippe Régnier, eds., *Digital Critical Editions* (Urbana-Champaign: University of Illinois Press, 2014).

Badger, Emily, 'Why the Wealthiest Countries are also the Most Open with Their Data', *The Washington Post* (14 March 2014), http://www.washingtonpost.com/blogs/wonkblog/wp/2014/03/14/why-the-wealthiest-countries-are-also-the-most-open-with-their-data

Baecker, Ronald M., Jonathan Grudin, William A. S. Buxton and Saul Greenberg, eds., *Readings in Human-Computer Interaction: Toward the Year 2000*, 2nd ed. (San Mateo, CA: Morgan Kaufmann, 1995).

Barbi, Michele, *La nuova filologia e l'edizioni dei nostri scrittori da Dante a Manzoni* (Florence: Le Monnier, 1938).

Barbiche, Bernard and Monique Chatenet, eds., *Conseils pour l'édition des textes de l'époque moderne (XVIe–XVIIIe siècle)* (Paris: Inventaire général, 1990).

Baron, Helen, 'Mary (Howard) Fitzroy's Hand in the Devonshire Manuscript', *Review of English Studies*, 45 (1994), 324–29.

Beal, Peter, *A Dictionary of English Manuscript Terminology, 1450–2000* (Oxford: Oxford University Press, 2008).

Beckett, Samuel, *Disjecta* (New York: Grove Press, 1984).

Bédier, Joseph, ed., *La Chanson de Roland* (Paris: L'édition d'art, 1921).

Beilin, Elaine V., *Redeeming Eve: Women Writers of the English Renaissance* (Princeton: Princeton University Press, 1987).

Benedetto, Simone, Véronique Drai-Zerbib, Marco Pedrotti, Geoffrey Tissier and Thierry Baccino, 'E-Readers and Visual Fatigue', *PLoS ONE*, 8.12 (2013), http://www.ncbi.nlm.nih.gov/pmc/articles/PMC3873942, http://dx.doi.org/10.1371/journal.pone.0083676

Bergmann Loizeaux, Elizabeth and Neil Fraistat, eds., *Reimagining Textuality: Textual Studies in the Late Age of Print* (Madison: University of Wisconsin Press, 2002).

Berners-Lee, Tim, 'Information Management: A Proposal' (Geneva: CERN, 1989), http://info.cern.ch/Proposal.html

Bishop, Morris, *Petrarch and his World* (Bloomington: Indiana University Press, 1963).

Boase, Roger, *The Origin and Meaning of Courtly Love: A Critical Study of European Scholarship* (Manchester: Manchester University Press, 1977).

Boffey, Julia, 'Women Authors and Women's Literacy in Fourteenth- and Fifteenth-Century England', in *Women and Literature in Britain 1150–1500*, ed. by Carol M. Meale (Cambridge: Cambridge University Press, 1996), pp. 159–82.

Bond, Edward A., 'Wyatt's Poems', *Athenaeum*, 27 (1871), 654–55.

Bonnat, Jean-Louis, Mireille Bossis and Hélène Girard, eds., *Les correspondances: Problématiques et économie d'un 'genre littéraire': Écrire, publier, lire: Actes du Colloque international Les Correspondances* (Nantes: Université de Nantes, 1983).

Boot, Peter and Joris van Zundert, 'The Digital Edition 2.0 and The Digital Library: Services, not Resources', *Digitale Edition und Forschungsbibliothek, Bibliothek und Wissenschaft*, 44 (2011), 141–52, http://peterboot.nl/pub/vanzundert-boot-services-not-resources-2011.pdf

Borgman, Christine L, *Scholarship in the Digital Age: Information, Infrastructure, and the Internet* (Cambridge, MA: MIT Press, 2007).

—, 'The Digital Future Is Now: A Call to Action for the Humanities', *Digital Humanities Quarterly*, 3 (2009), http://www.digitalhumanities.org/dhq/vol/3/4/000077/000077.html

Bowers, Fredson, *Principles of Bibliographical Description* (Princeton: Princeton University Press, 1949).

—, 'Principle and Practice in the Editing of Early Dramatic Texts', in *Textual and Literary Criticism: The Sandars Lectures in Bibliography 1957–1958* (Cambridge: Cambridge University Press, 1966), pp. 117–50.

Brumfield, Ben, 'The Collaborative Future of Amateur Editions', *Collaborative Manuscript Transcription*, 2013, http://manuscripttranscription.blogspot.co.uk/2013/07/the-collaborative-future-of-amateur.html

Bryant, John, *The Fluid Text: A Theory of Revision and Editing for Book and Screen* (Ann Arbor: University of Michigan Press, 2002).

Buckland, Michael, 'What Is a "Document"?', *Journal of the American Society of Information Science*, 48 (1997), 804–09.

Burgio, Eugenio et al., eds., *Giovanni Battista Ramusio 'editor' del 'Milione': Trattamento del testo e manipolazione dei modelli: Atti del seminario di ricerca, Venezia, 9–10 settembre 2010* (Rome/Padua: Antenore, 2011).

Burke, Mary E., Jane Donawerth, Linda L. Dove and Karen Nelson, eds., *Women, Writing, and the Reproduction of Culture in Tudor and Stuart Britain* (Syracuse, NY: Syracuse University Press, 2000).

Burnley, David, *Courtliness and Literature in Medieval England* (London: Longman, 1998).

Bush, Vannevar, 'As We May Think', *The Atlantic* (July 1945), 112–24.

Buzzetti, Dino, 'Digital Edition and Text Processing', in *Text Editing, Print, and the Digital World*, ed. by Marilyn Deegan and Kathryn Sutherland (Farnham: Ashgate, 2009), pp. 45–61.

Buzzoni, Marina, '*Uuarth thuo the hêlago gêst that barn an ira bôsma*: Towards a Scholarly Electronic Edition of the *Hêliand*', in *Medieval Texts — Contemporary Media: The Art and Science of Editing in the Digital Age*, ed. by Maria Grazia Saibene and Marina Buzzoni (Pavia: Ibis, 2009), pp. 35–55.

—, 'The "Electronic *Heliand* Project": Theoretical and Practical Updates', in *Linguistica e filologia digitale: Aspetti e progetti*, ed. by Paola Cotticelli Kurras (Alessandria: Edizioni dell'Orso, 2011), pp. 55–68.

Buzzoni, Marina and Eugenio Burgio, 'The Italian "Third Way" of Editing Between Globalization and Localization', in *Internationalität und Interdisziplinarität der Editionswissenschaft*, Beihefte zu *Editio* 38, ed. by Michael Stolz and Yen-Chun Chen (Berlin: Walter de Gruyter, 2014), pp. 171–80.

Cammarota, Maria Grazia, ed., *Freidank: L'indignazione di un poeta-crociato: I versi gnomici su Acri* (Rome: Carocci Editore, 2011).

Carlquist, Jonas, 'Medieval Manuscripts, Hypertext and Reading: Visions of Digital Editions', *Literary and Linguistic Computing*, 19 (2004), 105–18, http://dx.doi.org/10.1093/llc/19.1.105

Carpenter, David, Louise Wilkinson, David Crook and Harold Short, eds., *Henry III Fine Rolls Project* (London: King's College London, 2009–2013), http://www.finerollshenry3.org.uk/home.html

Cerquiglini, Bernard, *Éloge de la variante: Histoire critique de la philologie* (Paris: Seuil, 1989).

—, *In Praise of the Variant: A Critical History of Philology*, trans. by Betsy Wing (Baltimore, MD: The Johns Hopkins University Press, 1999).

Chernaik, Warren L., Marilyn Deegan and Andrew Gibson, eds., *Beyond the Book: Theory, Culture, and the Politics of Cyberspace*, (Oxford: Office for Humanities Communication, 1996).

Ciula, Arianna and Francesco Stella, eds., *Digital Philology and Medieval Texts* (Pisa: Pacini editore, 2006).

Clark, Andy, *Supersizing the Mind: Embodiment, Action, and Cognitive Extension* (Oxford: Oxford University Press, 2008).

—, 'Embodied, Embedded, and Extended Cognition', in *The Cambridge Handbook of Cognitive Science*, ed. by Keith Frankish and William M. Ramsey (Cambridge: Cambridge University Press, 2012), pp. 275–91.

Clark, Andy and David J. Chalmers, 'The Extended Mind', *Analysis*, 58 (1998), 10–23.

Clarke, Elizabeth, 'Women's Manuscript Miscellanies in Early Modern England', in *Teaching Tudor and Stuart Women Writers*, ed. by Susanne Woods and Margaret P. Hannay (New York: Modern Languages Association, 2000), pp. 52–60.

Contini, Gianfranco, 'La critica testuale come studio di strutture', in *La critica del testo: Atti del II Congresso Internazionale della Società Italiana di Storia del Diritto*, 2 vols. (Florence: Olschki, 1971), I, 11–23.

—, 'Filologia', in *Enciclopedia del Novecento*, 7 vols. (Rome: Istituto della Enciclopedia Italiana, 1975–1984), II, 954–72.

—, *Breviario di ecdotica* (Turin: Einaudi, 1990; 1st ed. 1986).

Crane, Greg, 'Give Us Editors! Re-inventing the Edition and Re-thinking the Humanities', in *The Shape of Things to Come*, ed. by Jerome J. McGann (Houston: Rice University Press, 2010), pp. 81–97, http://cnx.org/contents/XfgqFrtg@2/Give-us-editors-Re-inventing-t

Culkin, John M., SJ, 'A Schoolman's Guide to Marshall McLuhan', *Saturday Review* (18 March 1967), pp. 51–53, 71–72.

Daalder, Joost, ed., *Sir Thomas Wyatt: Collected Poems* (Oxford: Oxford University Press, 1975).

Dahlström, Mats, 'Digital Incunabules: Versionality and Versatility in Digital Scholarly Editions', in *ICCC/IFIP Third Conference on Electronic Publishing 2000, Kaliningrad State University, Kaliningrad/Svetlogorsk, Russia, 17th–19th August 2000* (Washington: ICCC Press, 2000), https://www.researchgate.net/researcher/70619446_Mats_Dahlstroem

—, 'How Reproductive is a Scholarly Edition?', *Literary and Linguistic Computing*, 19 (2004), 17–33, http://dx.doi.org/10.1093/llc/19.1.17

—, *Under utgivning: Den vetenskapliga utgivningens bibliografiska funktion* (Borås: Valfrid, 2006).

—, 'The Compleat Edition', in *Text Editing, Print and the Digital World*, ed. by Marilyn Deegan and Kathryn Sutherland (Farnham: Ashgate, 2009), pp. 27–44.

—, 'Critical Editing and Critical Digitization', in *Text Comparison and Digital Creativity: The Production of Presence and Meaning in Digital Text Scholarship*, ed. by Ernst Thoutenhoofd, Adrian van der Weel and Willem Th. van Peursen (Amsterdam: Brill, 2010), pp. 79–97.

Daisne, Johan, *De Trein der Traagheid*, ed. by Xavier Roelens, Edward Vanhoutte and Ron Van der Branden (Gent: Centrum voor Teksteditie en Bronnenstudie, 2012), http://edities.ctb.kantl.be/daisne/index.htm

Debray Genette, Raymonde, 'Génétique et poétique: Le cas Flaubert', *Essais de critique génétique*, ed. by Louis Hay (Paris: Flammarion, 1979), pp. 21–67, http://www.item.ens.fr/index.php?id=187284

Deegan, Marilyn and Kathryn Sutherland, *Transferred Illusions: Digital Technology and the Forms of Print* (Farnham: Ashgate, 2009).

Dennett, Daniel C., *Consciousness Explained* (London: Penguin, 1991).

De Robertis, Domenico, 'Problemi di filologia delle strutture', in *La critica del testo: Problemi di metodo ed esperienze di lavoro*: *Atti del Convegno di Lecce 1984* (Rome: Salerno editrice, 1985), pp. 383–404.

DeZur, Kathryn, '"Vaine Books" and Early Modern Women Readers', in *Reading and Literacy in the Middle Ages and Renaissance*, ed. by Ian Frederick Moulton (Turnhout: Brepols, 2004), pp. 105–25.

Driscoll, Matthew James, 'The Words on the Page: Thoughts on Philology, Old and New', in *Creating the Medieval Saga: Versions, Variability, and Editorial Interpretations of Old Norse Saga Literature*, ed. by Judy Quinn and Emily Lethbridge (Odense: University Press of Southern Denmark, 2010), pp. 85–102.

Duggan, Hoyt N., '1994 Prospectus: Archive Goals', *The Piers Plowman Electronic Archive* (1994–2003), http://jefferson.village.virginia.edu/seenet/piers/archivegoals.htm

DuRietz, Rolf E., *Den tryckta skriften: Termer och begrepp: grunderna till bibliografin: för biblioteken och antikvariaten, för bibliografer och textutgivare, för bokhistoriker och boksamlare* (Uppsala: Dahlia Books, 1999).

Ebbinghaus, Ernst A., ed., *Althochdeutsches Lesebuch*, ed. by Wilhelm Braune and Karl Helm, 17th ed. by Ernst A. Ebbinghaus (Tübingen: Max Niemeyer Verlag, 1994).

Edwards, Paul N., 'Hyper Text and Hypertension: Post-Structuralist Critical Theory: Social Studies of Science, and Software', *Social Studies of Science*, 24 (1994), 229–78.

Eggert, Paul, 'Text-Encoding, Theories of the Text, and the "Work-Site"', *Literary and Linguistic Computing*, 20 (2005), 425–35, http://dx.doi.org/10.1093/llc/fqi050

Eisenstein, Elizabeth L., *The Printing Press as an Agent of Change* (Cambridge: Cambridge University Press, 1982).

Elliott, Tom et al., *EpiDoc Guidelines: Ancient documents in TEI XML* (Version 8) (2007–2013), http://www.stoa.org/epidoc/gl/latest

Ellis, David, 'Modeling the Information-Seeking Patterns of Academic Researchers: A Grounded Theory Approach', *The Library Quarterly*, 63 (1993), 469–86, http://www.jstor.org/stable/4308867

Ezell, Margaret J. M., *Writing Women's Literary History* (Baltimore: The Johns Hopkins University Press, 1993).

—, *Social Authorship and the Advent of Print* (Baltimore: The Johns Hopkins University Press, 1999).

—, 'Women and Writing', in *A Companion to Early Modern Women's Writing*, ed. by Anita Pacheco (Oxford: Blackwell, 2002), pp. 77–94.

Ferrari, Fulvio and Massimiliano Bampi, eds., *Storicità del testo, Storicità dell'edizione* (Trento: Dipartimento di Studi Letterari, Linguistici e Filologici, 2009).

Ferrer, Daniel, 'Towards a Marginalist Economy of Textual Genesis', *Variants: The Journal of the European Society for Textual Scholarship*, 2–3 (2004), 7–18.

Finneran, Richard J., ed., *The Literary Text in the Digital Age* (Ann Arbor: University of Michigan Press, 1996).

Fiormonte, Domenico and Cinzia Pusceddu, 'The Text as a Product and as a Process: History, Genesis, Experiments', in *Manuscript, Variant, Genese— Genesis*, ed. by Edward Vanhoutte and Marcel de Smedt (Gent: KANTL, 2006), pp. 109–28, http://www.academia.edu/618689/The_Text_As_a_Product_and_As_a_Process._History_Genesis_Experiments

Fischer, Franz, 'About the HyperStack', *St. Patrick's Confessio*, 2011, http://www.confessio.ie/about/hyperstack#

Fitzpatrick, Kathleen, 'CommentPress: New (Social) Structures for New (Networked) Texts', *Journal of Electronic Publishing*, 10.3 (2007), http://dx.doi.org/10.3998/3336451.0010.305

Folsom, Ed and Kenneth M. Price, eds., *The Walt Whitman Archive* (University of Nebraska-Lincoln: Center for Digital Research in the Humanities, 1995–), http://www.whitmanarchive.org

Fox, Alistair, *Politics and Literature in the Reigns of Henry VII and Henry VIII* (Oxford: Basil Blackwell, 1989).

Foxwell, Agnes K., ed., *The Poems of Sir Thomas Wiat* (London: University of London Press, 1913).

Foys, Martin K., ed., *Bayeux Tapestry* [CD-ROM] (Woodbridge: Scholarly Digital Editions, 2002).

Gabler, Hans Walter, 'Das wissenschaftliche Edieren als Funktion der Dokumente', *Jahrbuch für Computerphilologie*, 8 (2006), 55–62, http://computerphilologie.tu-darmstadt.de/jg06/gabler.html

—, 'The Primacy of the Document in Editing', *Ecdotica*, 4 (2007), 197–207.

—, 'Theorizing the Digital Scholarly Edition', *Literature Compass*, 7 (2010), 43–56, http://dx.doi.org/10.1111/j.1741-4113.2009.00675.x

—, 'Thoughts on Scholarly Editing', *Journal of Literary Theory* (2011), http://www.jltonline.de/index.php/reviews/article/view/307/893; http://nbn-resolving.de/urn:nbn:de:0222-001542

Galison, Peter, 'Trading with the Enemy', in *Trading Zones and Interactional Expertise: Creating New Kinds of Collaboration*, ed. by Michael E. Gorman (Cambridge, MA: MIT Press, 2010), pp. 25–52.

Garnett, Fred and Nigel Ecclesfield, 'Towards a Framework for Co-Creating Open Scholarship', *Research in Learning Technology*, 19 (2012), http://dx.doi.org/10.3402/rlt.v19i3.7795

Gellhaus, Axel, 'Marginalia: Paul Celan as Reader', in *Reading Notes*, Special Issue of *Variants: The Journal of the European Society for Textual Scholarship*, ed. Dirk Van Hulle and Wim van Mierlo, 2–3 (2004), 207–19.

Genette, Gérard, *Palimpsests: Literature in the Second Degree*, trans. by Channa Newman and Claude Doubinsky (Lincoln: University of Nebraska Press, 1997).

—, *Paratexts: Thresholds of Interpretation*, trans. by Jane E. Lewin (Cambridge: Cambridge University Press, 1997).

Gervais, Bertrand, 'Is There a Text on This Screen? Reading in an Era of Hypertextuality', in *Companion to Digital Literary Studies*, ed. by Ray Siemens and Susan Schreibman (Oxford: Blackwell, 2008), pp. 183–201, http://www.digitalhumanities.org/companion/view?docId=blackwell/9781405148641/9781405148641.xml&chunk.id=ss1-5-3&toc.depth=1&toc.id=ss1-5-3&brand=9781405148641_brand

Geymonat, M., ed., *P. Vergili Maronis opera*, 2nd ed. (Rome: Edizioni di storia e letteratura, 2008).

Gontarski, S. E., 'Greying the Canon: Beckett in Performance', in *Beckett After Beckett*, ed. by S. E. Gontarski and Anthony Uhlman (Gainesville: University Press of Florida, 2006), pp. 141–57.

Gorman, Michael E., Lekelia D. Jenkins and Raina K. Plowright, 'Human Interactions and Sustainability', in *Sustainability: Multi-Disciplinary Perspectives*, ed. by Heriberto Cabezas and Urmila Diwekar (Sharjah: Bentham Science Publishers, 2012), pp. 88–111.

Grafton, Anthony, *The Culture of Correction in Renaissance Europe (Panizzi Lectures)* (London: British Library, 2011).

Greetham, David, 'Editorial and Critical Theory: From Modernism to Postmodernism', in *Palimpsest: Editorial Theory in the Humanities*, ed. by George Bornstein and Ralph G. Williams (Ann Arbor, University of Michigan Press, 1993), pp. 9–28.

—, *Textual Scholarship: An Introduction* (New York: Garland, 1994).

—, 'A History of Textual Scholarship', in *The Cambridge Companion to Textual Scholarship*, ed. by Neil Fraistat and Julia Flanders (Cambridge: Cambridge University Press, 2013), pp. 16–41.

Greg, W. W., 'The Rationale of Copy-Text', *Studies in Bibliography*, 3 (1950–1951), 19–36.

Grésillon, Almuth, *Eléments de critique génétique: Lire les manuscrits modernes* (Paris: Presses universitaires de France, 1994).

Guyotjeannin, Olivier, ed., *Conseils pour l'édition de textes médiévaux*, 3 vols. (Paris: CTHS, 2003–2014).

Haentjens Dekker, Ronald, Dirk Van Hulle, Gregor Middell, Vincent Neyt and Joris van Zundert, 'Computer Supported Collation of Modern Manuscripts: CollateX and the Beckett Digital Manuscript Project', *Digital Scholarship in the Humanities*, 25 (2014), 1–19, http://dx.doi.org/10.1093/llc/fqu007

Hannay, Margaret P., ed., *Silent but for the Word: Tudor Women as Patrons, Translators, and Writers of Religious Works* (Kent, OH: Kent State University Press, 1985).

Harrier, Richard C., 'A Printed Source for the "Devonshire Manuscript"', *Review of English Studies*, 11 (1960), 54.

—, *The Canon of Sir Thomas Wyatt's Poetry* (Cambridge, MA: Harvard University Press, 1975).

Haselkorn, Anne M. and Betty S. Travitsky, eds., *The Renaissance Englishwoman in Print: Counterbalancing the Canon* (Amherst: University of Massachusetts Press, 1990).

Hassner, Tal, Malte Rehbein, Peter A. Stokes and Lior Wolf, 'Computation and Palaeography: Potentials and Limits: Manifesto from Dagstuhl Perspectives Workshop 12382', *Dagstuhl Manifestos*, 2 (2013), 14–35, http://drops.dagstuhl.de/opus/volltexte/2013/4167/pdf/dagman-v002-i001-p014-12382.pdf

Haugen, Odd Einar, 'The Spirit of Lachmann, the Spirit of Bédier: Old Norse Textual Editing in the Electronic Age', in Annual Meeting of The Viking Society, University College London, 8 (2002), pp. 1–21, http://www.ub.uib.no/elpub/2003/a/522001/haugen.pdf

Hayles, Katherine N., *How We Think: Digital Media and Contemporary Technogenesis* (Chicago: University of Chicago Press, 2012).

Heale, Elizabeth, 'Women and the Courtly Love Lyric: The Devonshire MS (BL Additional 17492)', *Modern Language Review,* 90.2 (1995), 297–301.

—, *Wyatt, Surrey and Early Tudor Poetry* (London: Longman, 1998).

—, '"Desiring Women Writing": Female Voices and Courtly "Balets" in Some Early Tudor Manuscript Albums', in *Early Modern Women's Manuscript Writing: Selected Papers from the Trinity/Trent Colloquium,* ed. by Victoria Elizabeth Burke and Jonathan Gibson (Farnham: Ashgate, 2004), pp. 9–31.

—, ed., *The Devonshire Manuscript: A Women's Book of Courtly Poetry* (Toronto: Centre for Reformation and Renaissance Studies, 2012).

Henrik Ibsens Skrifter, http://www.ibsen.uio.no/forside.xhtml

Herman, David, 'Re-Minding Modernism', in *The Emergence of Mind: Representations of Consciousness in Narrative Discourse in English,* ed. by David Herman (Lincoln: University of Nebraska Press, 2011), pp. 243–71.

—, 'Narrative and Mind: Directions for Inquiry', in, *Stories and Minds: Cognitive Approaches to Literary Narrative,* ed. by Lars Bernaerts, Dirk De Geest, Luc Herman and Bart Vervaeck (Lincoln: University of Nebraska Press, 2013), pp. 199–209.

Heuvel, Charles van den, 'Circulation of Knowledge in the Digital Republic of Letters: Making Correspondences of Manuscripts and Printed Editions Accessible for Research', http://ckcc.huygens.knaw.nl/wp-content/bestanden/2012/05/CHeuvel_LIBER_ParijsDEF.pdf

Heuvel, Charles van den and W. Boyd Rayward, 'Facing Interfaces: Paul Otlet's Visualizations of Data Integration', *Journal of the American Society for Information Science and Technology,* 62 (2011), 2313–26.

Hockey, Susan, 'The History of Humanities Computing', in *A Companion to Digital Humanities,* ed. by Susan Schreibman, Ray Siemens and John Unsworth (Oxford: Blackwell, 2004), pp. 3–19, http://www.digitalhumanities.org/companion/view?docId=blackwell/9781405103213/9781405103213.xml&chunk.id=ss1-2-1&toc.depth=1&toc.id=ss1-2-1&brand=default

—, *Electronic Texts in the Humanities* (Oxford: Oxford University Press, 2010).

Hutto, Daniel D. and Erik Myin, *Radicalizing Enactivism: Basic Minds without Content* (Cambridge, MA: MIT Press, 2013).

Huygens, R. B. C., *Ars edendi: A Practical Introduction to Editing Medieval Latin Texts* (Turnhout: Brepols, 2000).

Jannidis, Fotis, 'Digital Editions in the Net: Perspectives for Scholarly Editing in a Digital World', in *Beyond the Screen: Transformations of Literary Structures, Interfaces and Genre,* ed. by Jörgen Schäfer and Peter Gendolla (Bielefeld: Transcript Verlag, 2010), pp. 543–60.

Jessop, Martin, 'The Inhibition of Geographical Information in Digital Humanities Scholarship', *Literary and Linguistic Computing*, 23 (2008), 39–50, http://dx.doi.org/10.1093/llc/fqm041

Jockers, Matthew L., *Macroanalysis: Digital Methods and Literary History* (Urbana-Champaign: University of Illinois Press, 2013).

Kahler, Erich von, *The Inward Turn of Narrative*, trans. by Richard and Clara Winston (Princeton: Princeton University Press, 1973).

Kant, Immanuel, *Immanuel Kants Werke*, ed. by Ernst Cassirer, 11 vols. (Berlin: Bruno Cassirer, 1921–1922).

Karlsson, Lina and Linda Malm, 'Revolution or Remediation? A Study of Electronic Scholarly Editions on the Web', *Human IT*, 7.1 (2004), 1–46, http://etjanst.hb.se/bhs/ith/1-7/lklm.pdf

Kaster, R. A., ed., *Macrobii Ambrosii Theodosii Saturnalia* (Oxford: Oxford University Press, 2011).

Kenney, E. J., ed., *P. Ovidi Nasonis Amores, Medicamina faciei femineae, Ars amatoria, Remedia amoris* (Oxford: Oxford University Press, 1961).

Kiernan, Kevin S., 'Digital Preservation, Restoration, and Dissemination of Medieval Manuscripts', in *Gateways, Gatekeepers, and Roles in the Information Omniverse: Proceedings of the Third Symposium*, ed. by Ann Okerson and Dru Mogge (Washington, DC: Office of Scientific and Academic Publishing, Association of Research Libraries, 1994), pp. 37–43.

—, ed., *The Electronic Beowulf* (London: British Library, 1999/2013) [CD-ROM].

Kirschenbaum, Matthew, *Mechanisms: New Media and the Forensic Imagination* (Cambridge, MA: MIT Press, 2008).

—, 'What Is Digital Humanities and What's It Doing in English Departments?', in *Debates in the Digital Humanities*, ed. by Matthew K. Gold (Minneapolis: University of Minnesota Press, 2012), pp. 3–11, http://dhdebates.gc.cuny.edu/debates/text/38

Kondrup, Johnny, *Editionsfilologi* (Copenhagen: Museum Tusculanum Press, 2011).

—, 'Tekst og værk—et begrebseftersyn', in *Betydning & forståelse: Festskrift til Hanne Ruus*, ed. by Dorte Duncker, Anne Mette Hansen and Karen Skovgaard-Petersen (Copenhagen: Selskab for nordisk filologi, 2013), pp. 65–76.

Krippendorf, Klaus, *Content Analysis: An Introduction to Its Methodology*, 2nd ed. (Thousand Oaks, CA: Sage, 2004).

Lancashire, Ian, ed., *The Humanities Computing Yearbook 1989–1990: A Comprehensive Guide to Software and other Resources* (Oxford: Oxford University Press, 1991).

Landow, George P., ed., *Hyper/Text/Theory* (Baltimore: The Johns Hopkins University Press, 1994).

—, *Hypertext 3.0: Critical Theory and New Media in an Era of Globalization* (Baltimore: The Johns Hopkins University Press, 2006).

Latour, Bruno, *Science in Action: How to Follow Scientists and Engineers through Society* (Cambridge, MA: Harvard University Press, 1988).

Lavagnino, John, 'Reading, Scholarship and Hypertext Editions', *Text: Transactions of the Society for Textual Scholarship*, 8 (1995), 109–24, http://www.stg.brown.edu/resources/stg/monographs/rshe.html

—, 'Access', *Literary and Linguistic Computing*, 24 (2009), 63–76, http://dx.doi.org/10.1093/llc/fqn038

Lee, Gwanhoo and Weidong Xia, 'Toward Agile: An Integrated Analysis of Quantitative and Qualitative Field Data on Software Development Agility', *MIS Quarterly*, 34 (2010), 87–114.

Lenz, Friedrich Walter, ed., *Die Liebeselegien* (Darmstadt: Wissenschaftliche Buchgesellschaft, 1965).

Leuf, Bo and Ward Cunningham, *The Wiki Way* (Boston: Addison-Wesley Professional, 2001).

Levallois, Clement, Stephanie Steinmetz and Paul Wouters, 'Sloppy Data Floods or Precise Methodologies? Dilemmas in the Transition to Data-Intensive Research in Sociology and Economics', in *Virtual Knowledge: Experimenting in the Humanities and the Social Sciences*, ed. by Paul Wouters, Anne Beaulieu, Andrea Scharnhorst and Sally Wyatt (Cambridge, MA: MIT Press, 2013), pp. 151–82.

Lewalski, Barbara K., *Writing Women in Jacobean England* (Cambridge, MA: Harvard University Press, 1993).

Love, Harold and Arthur F. Marotti, 'Manuscript Transmission and Circulation', in *The Cambridge History of Early Modern English Literature*, ed. by David Loewenstein and Janel Mueller (Cambridge: Cambridge University Press, 2002), pp. 55–80.

Loyen, André, ed., *Sidoine Apollinaire, Poèmes et lettres*, 3 vols. (Paris: Belles Lettres, 1960–1970).

Luiselli Fadda, Anna Maria, *Tradizioni manoscritte e critica del testo nel Medioevo germanico* (Rome and Bari: Laterza, 1994).

—, 'Quale edizione-nel-tempo (Contini) per i documenti e i testi germanici nel ventunesimo secolo?', in *Storicità del testo, Storicità dell'edizione*, ed. by Fulvio Ferrari and Massimiliano Bampi (Trento: Dipartimento di Studi Letterari, Linguistici e Filologici, 2009), pp. 11–22.

Lütjohann, Christian, ed., *Gai Solii Apollinaris Sidonii Epistulae et carmina* (Berlin: Weidmann, 1887).

Macé, Caroline and Philippe V. Baret, 'Why Phylogenetic Methods Work: The Theory of Evolution and Textual Criticism', in *The Evolution of Texts: Confronting Stemmatological and Genetical Methods*, ed. by Caroline Macé et al. (Pisa/Rome: Istituti Editoriali e Poligrafici Internazionali, 2006).

Mahony, Simon, 'Research Communities and Open Collaboration: The Example of the Digital Classicist Wiki', *Digital Medievalist*, 6 (2011), http://www.digitalmedievalist.org/journal/6/mahony

Mahony, Simon and Elena Pierazzo, 'Teaching Skills or Teaching Methodology', in *Digital Humanities Pedagogy: Practices, Principles and Politics*, ed. by Brett D. Hirsch (Cambridge: Open Book Publishers, 2013), pp. 215–25, http://dx.doi.org/10.11647/OBP.0024

Mangen, Anne, 'Hypertext Fiction Reading: Haptics and Immersion', *Journal of Research in Reading*, 31 (2008), 404–19, http://dx.doi.org/10.1111/j.1467-9817.2008.00380.x

Marotti, Arthur F., *Manuscript, Print, and the English Renaissance Lyric* (Ithaca, NY: Cornell University Press, 1995).

Martin, Robert C., *Agile Software Development, Principles, Patterns, and Practices* (Upper Saddle River: Prentice Hall, 2002).

McCarty, Willard, *Humanities Computing* (Basingstoke: Palgrave Macmillan, 2005).

—, ed., *Text and Genre in Reconstruction: Effects of Digitalization on Ideas, Behaviours, Products and Institutions* (Cambridge: Open Book Publishers, 2010), http://dx.doi.org/10.11647/OBP.0008

—, 'Computationalists and Humanists', *Humanist Discussion Group* (2013), http://lists.digitalhumanities.org/pipermail/humanist/2013-June/011052.html

McGann, Jerome J., *A Critique of Modern Textual Criticism* (Chicago: University of Chicago Press, 1983).

—, 'The Monks and the Giants: Textual and Bibliographical Studies and the Interpretation of Literary Works', in *The Beauty of Inflections: Literary Investigations in Historical Method and Theory* (Oxford: Oxford University Press, 1988), pp. 68–89.

—, ed., *The Complete Writings and Pictures of Dante Gabriel Rossetti: A Hypermedia Research Archive* (Charlottesville, VA: Institute for Advanced Technology in the Humanities, 2000–), http://www.rossettiarchive.org

—, 'Electronic Archives and Critical Editing', *Literature Compass*, 7.2 (2010), 37–42.

McKenzie, D. F., *Bibliography and the Sociology of Texts (The Panizzi Lectures, 1985)* (London: British Library, 1986).

McKeown, J. C., ed., *Ovid, Amores: Text, Prolegomena, and Commentary*, 4 vols. (Liverpool: Francis Cairns, 1987–2012).

McKerrow, Ronald B., *An Introduction to Bibliography for Literary Students* (Winchester: St Paul's Bibliographies, 1994).

McLuhan, Marshall, *Understanding Media: The Extensions of Man* (New York: McGraw-Hill, 1964).

Meister, Jan Christoph, 'Computationalists and Humanists', *Humanist Discussion Group* (2013), http://lists.digitalhumanities.org/pipermail/humanist/2013-June/011053.html

Menary, Richard, 'Introduction', in *The Extended Mind*, edited by Richard Menary (Cambridge, MA: MIT Press, 2010), pp. 1–25.

MLA Guidelines for Editors of Scholarly Editions (2011), https://www.mla.org/Resources/Research/Surveys-Reports-and-Other-Documents/Publishing-and-Scholarship/Reports-from-the-MLA-Committee-on-Scholarly-Editions/Guidelines-for-Editors-of-Scholarly-Editions

Mohr, Paul, ed., *C. Sollius Apollinaris Sidonius* (Leipzig: Teubner, 1895).

Montaigne, Michel de, *Essais*, ed. by Pierre Michel, 3 vols. (Paris: Gallimard, 1965).

Moretti, Franco, *Graphs, Maps, Trees: Abstract Models for Literary History* (London: Verso, 2007).

Muir, Bernard James, ed., *A Digital Facsimile of Oxford, Bodleian Library MS. Junius 11* (Oxford: Bodleian Library, 2004).

—, ed., *The Exeter Anthology of Old English Poetry: An Edition of Exeter Dean and Chapter MS 3501*, 2nd ed. (Exeter: Exeter University Press, 2004) [CD-ROM].

Muir, Kenneth, 'Unpublished Poems in the Devonshire Manuscript', *Proceedings of the Leeds Philosophical and Literary Society*, 6 (1947), 253–82.

—, ed., *Collected Poems of Sir Thomas Wyatt* (London: Routledge and Kegan Paul, 1949).

Muir, Kenneth and Patricia Thomson, eds., *Collected Poems of Sir Thomas Wyatt* (Liverpool: Liverpool University Press, 1969).

Munari, Franco, ed., *P. Ovidi Nasonis Amores*, 2nd ed. (Florence: Nuova Italia, 1955).

Nelson, Theodor Holm, *Literary Machines: The Report On, and Of, Project Xanadu Concerning Word Processing, Electronic Publishing, Hypertext, Thinkertoys, Tomorrow's Intellectual Revolution, and Certain Other Topics Including Knowledge, Education and Freedom* (Sausolito, CA: Mindful Press, 1993; first published 1981).

—, *POSSIPLEX: Movies, Intellect, Creative Control, My Computer Life and the Fight for Civilization* (Sausolito, CA: Mindful Press, 2010).

Nichols, Stephen G., 'Introduction: Philology in a Manuscript Culture', *Speculum*, 65.1 (1990), 1–10.

Nielsen, Jakob, *Hypertext and Hypermedia* (Boston, MA: Academic Press, 1990).

Nott, George Frederick, *The Works of Henry Howard, Earl of Surrey, and of Sir Thomas Wyatt, the Elder* (London: T. Bensley, 1815).

Nougaret, Christine and Élisabeth Parinet, *L'édition critique des textes contemporains (XIXe–XXIe siècle)* (Paris: École Nationale des Chartes, 2015).

O'Donnell, Daniel Paul, 'Resisting the Tyranny of the Screen, or, Must a Digital Edition be Electronic?', *Heroic Age*, 8 (2008), http://www.heroicage.org/issues/11/em.php

O'Donnell, James J., *Avatars of the Word: From Papyrus to Cyberspace* (Cambridge, MA: Harvard University Press, 1998).

O'Donoghue, Bernard, *The Courtly Love Tradition* (Manchester: Manchester University Press, 1982).

Ore, Espen, 'Monkey Business — or What is an Edition?', *Literary and Linguistic Computing*, 19 (2004), 35–44, http://dx.doi.org/10.1093/llc/19.1.35

Pakis, Valentine A., ed., *Perspectives on the Old Saxon Heliand: Introductory and Critical Essays, with an Edition of the Leipzig Fragment* (Morgantown: West Virginia University Press, 2010).

Pasquali, Giorgio, *Storia della tradizione e critica del testo* (Florence: Le Monnier, 1934).

Peters, Keith, 'Kindle and iPad Displays: Up Close and Personal', *BIT-101* (2010), http://www.bit-101.com/blog/?p=2722

Petrarca, Francesco, *The Sonnets, Triumphs, and Other Poems of Petrarch*, ed. by Thomas Campbell (London: Henry G. Bohn, 1859).

—, *Le rime*, ed. by Luigi Baldacci (Bologna: Zanichelli, 1962).

Pierazzo, Elena, 'A Rationale of Digital Documentary Editions', *Literary and Linguistic Computing*, 26 (2011), 463–77, http://dx.doi.org/10.1093/llc/fqr033

—, 'Digital Documentary Editions and the Others', *Scholarly Editing*, 35 (2014), http://www.scholarlyediting.org/2014/essays/essay.pierazzo.html

—, *Digital Scholarly Editing: Theories, Models and Methods* (Farnham: Ashgate, 2015).

—, 'Disciplinary Impact: The Effect of Digital Editing', *Digital Humanities 2015 (Sydney, 2015)*, http://dh2015.org/abstracts/xml/PIERAZZO_Elena_Disciplinary_Impact__The_Effect_of/PIERAZZO_Elena_Disciplinary_Impact__The_Effect_of_Digit.html

—, 'Un nouveau module de la TEI pour l'encodage des manuscrits modernes et les éditions génétiques', in *La génétique des textes et des formes: L'œuvre comme processus*, ed. by Pierre-Marc De Biasi and Anne Pierrot Herschberg (2016 [forthcoming]).

Pilling, John, *A Samuel Beckett Chronology* (Basingstoke: Palgrave Macmillan, 2006).

Porter, Dorothy C., *Medievalists' Use of Electronic Resources: The Results of a National Survey of Faculty Members in Medieval Studies* (Thesis, University of North Carolina—Chapel Hill, 2002), http://ils.unc.edu/MSpapers/2807.pdf and in IUScholarWorks, http://hdl.handle.net/2022/14060

—, 'Medievalists and the Scholarly Digital Edition', *Scholarly Editing: The Annual of the Association for Documentary Editing*, 34 (2013), 1–26, http://www.scholarlyediting.org/2013/essays/essay.porter.html

Presner, Todd, 'Digital Humanities 2.0: A Report on Knowledge', *Connexions* (18 April, 2010), http://cnx.org/contents/J0K7N3xH@6/Digital-Humanities-20-A-Report

Price, Kenneth M., 'Electronic Scholarly Editions', in *A Companion to Digital Humanities*, ed. by Susan Schreibman, Ray Siemens and John Unsworth (Oxford: Blackwell, 2004), http://www.digitalhumanities.org/companion/view?docId=blackwell/9781405148641/9781405148641.xml&chunk.id=ss1-6-5&toc.depth=1&toc.id=ss1-6-5&brand=9781405148641_brand

—, 'Edition, Project, Database, Archive, Thematic Research Collection: What's in a Name?', *Digital Humanities Quarterly*, 3.3 (2009), http://www.digitalhumanities.org/dhq/vol/3/3/000053/000053.html

Pugliatti, Paola, 'Textual Perspectives in Italy: From Pasquali's Historicism to the Challenge of "Variantistica" (and Beyond)', *Text: An Interdisciplinary Annual of Textual Studies*, 11 (1998), 155–88.

Quentin, Henri, *Essais de critique textuelle* (Paris: Picard, 1926).

Ramirez de Verger, Antonio, ed., *P. Ovidius Naso, Carmina amatoria: Amores, Medicamina faciei femineae, Ars amatoria, Remedia amoris* (Munich: Saur, 2003).

Ramsay, Stephen, *Reading Machines: Toward an Algorithmic Criticism* (Urbana-Champaign: University of Illinois Press, 2011).

Rasmussen, Krista Stinne Greve, 'Bytes, bøger og læsere: En editionshistorisk analyse af medieskiftet fra trykte til digitale videnskabelige udgaver med udgangspunkt i Søren Kierkegaards Skrifter' (PhD thesis, University of Copenhagen, 2015), http://forskning.ku.dk/find-enforsker/?pure=files%2F131207090%2FPh.d._2015_Greve_Rasmussen.pdf

Ravasio, Pamela and Vincent Tscherter, 'Users' Theories on the Desktop Metaphor—or Why We Should Seek Metaphor-Free Interfaces', in *Beyond the Desktop Metaphor: Designing Integrated Digital Work Environments*, ed. by Victor Kaptelinin and Mary Czerwinski (Cambridge, MA: MIT Press, 2004), pp. 265–94.

Rayward, W. Boyd, 'Visions of Xanadu: Paul Otlet (1868–1944) and Hypertext', *JASIS*, 45 (1994), 235–50.

Reeve, M. D., 'Petronius', in *Texts and Transmission: A Survey of the Latin Classics*, ed. by L. D. Reynolds (Oxford: Oxford University Press, 1983), pp. 295–300.

—, '*Cuius in usum*? Recent and Future Editing', *Journal of Roman Studies*, 90 (2000), 196–206.

—, ed., *Vegetius, Epitoma rei militaris* (Oxford: Oxford University Press, 2004).

Remley, Paul, 'Mary Shelton and Her Tudor Literary Milieu', in *Rethinking the Henrician Era: Essays on Early Tudor Texts and Contexts*, ed. by Peter C. Herman (Urbana-Champaign: University of Illinois Press, 1994), pp. 40–77.

Robinson, Peter, ed., *The Wife of Bath's Prologue on CD-ROM* (Cambridge: Cambridge University Press, 1996).

—, 'The One Text and the Many Texts', *Literary and Linguistic Computing*, 15 (2000), 5–14, http://dx.doi.org/10.1093/llc/15.1.5

—, 'What is a Critical Digital Edition?', *Variants: The Journal of the European Society for Textual Scholarship*, 1 (2002), 43–62.

—, 'Where We Are with Electronic Scholarly Editions, and Where We Want to Be', *Jahrbuch für Computerphilologie*, 5 (2003), 125–46, http://computerphilologie.uni-muenchen.de/jg03/robinson.html

—, 'Current Issues in Making Digital Editions of Medieval Texts—Or, Do Electronic Scholarly Editions Have a Future?', *Digital Medievalist*, 1.1 (2005), http://www.digitalmedievalist.org/journal/1.1/robinson

—, 'The Ends of Editing', *DHQ: Digital Humanities Quarterly* (2009), http://digitalhumanities.org/dhq/vol/3/3/000051/000051.html

—, 'Electronic Editions for Everyone', in *Text and Genre in Reconstruction: Effects of Digitalization on Ideas, Behaviours, Products and Institutions*, ed. by Willard McCarty (Cambridge: Open Book Publishers, 2010), pp. 145–63, http://dx.doi.org/10.11647/OBP.0008

—, 'Towards a Theory of Digital Editions', *Variants: The Journal of the European Society for Textual Scholarship*, 10 (2013), 105–32.

Rodgers, R. H., ed., *Columellae Res rustica* (Oxford: Oxford University Press, 2010).

Romano, Tim, ed., *The Wanderer: Edition and Translation* (1999), http://www.aimsdata.com/tim/anhaga/edition.htm

Rosselli Del Turco, Roberto, 'After the Editing Is Done: Designing a Graphic User Interface for Digital Editions', *Digital Medievalist*, 7 (2011), http://www.digitalmedievalist.org/journal/7/rosselliDelTurco

—, 'EVT Development: An Update (and Quite a Bit of History)', in Edition Visualization Technology blog, 2014, http://visualizationtechnology.wordpress.com/2014/01/26/evt-development-an-update-and-quite-a-bit-of-history

Rosselli Del Turco, Roberto, Chiara Di Pietro, Julia Kenny and Raffaele Masotti, *Edition Visualization Technology: Digital Edition Visualization Software*, 2013–, http://sourceforge.net/projects/evt-project

Rosselli Del Turco, Roberto, Giancarlo Buomprisco, Chiara Di Pietro, Julia Kenny, Raffaele Masotti and Jacopo Pugliese, 'Edition Visualization Technology: A Simple Tool to Visualize TEI-based Digital Editions', *Journal of the Text Encoding Initiative*, 8 (2014–2015), http://jtei.revues.org/1077

Sahle, Patrick, *A Catalog of Digital Scholarly Editions*, http://www.digitale-edition.de

—, 'Digitales Archiv—Digital Edition: Anmerkungen zur Begriffsklärung', in *Literatur und Literaturwissenschaft auf dem Weg zu den neuen Medien: Eine Standortbestimmung*, ed. by Michael Stolz et al. (Zürich: germanistik.ch, 2007), pp. 64–84.

—, 'Die disziplinierte Edition—eine kleine Wissenschaftsgeschichte', *Editionswissenschaftliche Kolloquien 2005/2007: Methodik—Amtsbücher—Digitale Edition—Projekte*, ed. by Matthias Thumser and Janusz Tandecki (Toruń: Deutsch-Polnischer Gesprächskreis für Quellenedition, 2008), pp. 35–52.

—, 'Zwischen Mediengebundenheit und Transmedialisierung: Anmerkungen zum Verhältnis von Edition und Medien', *editio—International Yearbook of Scholarly Editing*, 24 (2010), 23–36.

—, *Digitale Editionsformen: Zum Umgang mit der Überlieferung unter den Bedingungen des Medienwandels*, 3 vols., Schriften des Instituts für Dokumentologie und Editorik 7–9 (Norderstedt: BOD, 2013).

Schomaker, Lambert, 'Writer Identification and Verification', in *Advances in Biometrics: Sensors, Algorithms and Systems*, ed. by N. K. Ratha and Venu Govindaraju (London: Springer, 2008), pp. 247–64.

Schreibman, Susan, Ray Siemens and John Unsworth, eds., *A Companion to Digital Humanities* (Oxford: Blackwell, 2004), http://www.digitalhumanities.org/companion

Sculley, D. and Bradley M. Pasanek, 'Meaning and Mining: The Impact of Implicit Assumptions in Data Mining for the Humanities', *Literary and Linguistic Computing*, 23 (2008), 409–24, http://dx.doi.org/10.1093/llc/fqn019

Seaton, Ethel, 'The Devonshire Manuscript and its Medieval Fragments', *Review of English Studies*, 7 (1956), 55–56.

Segre, Cesare, ed., *La Chanson de Roland* (Milan and Naples: Ricciardi, 1971).

—, 'Critique textuelle, théorie des ensembles et diasystèmes', *Académie royale de Belgique: Bulletin de la classe des lettres et des sciences morales et politiques*, 62 (1976), 279–92.

—, 'La critica testuale', in *XIV Congresso internazionale di linguistica e filologia romanza (Napoli, 15–20 Aprile 1974)*, ed. by Alberto Varvaro, 5 vols. (Amsterdam: John Benjamins, 1978), I, pp. 493–99.

—, *Semiotica filologica: Testo e modelli culturali* (Turin: Einaudi, 1978).

Seifert, Sabine, Marcel Illetschko and Peter Stadler, 'Towards a Model for Encoding Correspondence in the TEI', *Journal of the Text Encoding Initiative*, 9 (forthcoming).

Shillingsburg, Peter L., 'Text as Matter, Concept, and Action', *Studies in Bibliography*, 44 (1991), 31–82.

—, *Scholarly Editing in the Computer Age: Theory and Practice*, 3rd ed. (Ann Arbor: University of Michigan Press, 1996).

—, *From Gutenberg to Google: Electronic Representations of Literary Texts* (Cambridge: Cambridge University Press, 2006).

—, 'How Literary Works Exist: Implied, Represented, and Interpreted', in *Text and Genre in Reconstruction: Effects of Digitalization on Ideas, Behaviours, Products and Institutions*, ed. by Willard McCarty (Cambridge: Open Book Publishers, 2010), pp. 165–82, http://dx.doi.org/10.11647/OBP.0008

—, 'Is Reliable Social Scholarly Editing an Oxymoron?', *Social, Digital, Scholarly Editing* (Saskatoon: University of Saskatchewan, 2013), http://ecommons.luc.edu/ctsdh_pubs/1

Siegenthaler, Eva, Yves Bochud, Per Bergamin and Pascal Wurtz, 'Reading on LCD vs. e-Ink Displays: Effects on Fatigue and Visual Strain', *Ophthalmic and Physiological Optics*, 32 (2012), 367–74.

Siemens, Ray and Susan Schreibman, *A Companion to Digital Literary Studies* (Oxford: Blackwell, 2008), http://www.digitalhumanities.org/companionDLS

Siemens, Ray, with Barbara Bond and Karin Armstrong, 'The Devil is in the Details: An Electronic Edition of the Devonshire MS (British Library Additional MS 17,492), its Encoding and Prototyping', in *New Technologies and Renaissance Studies*, ed. by William R. Bowen and Ray Siemens (Tempe: Arizona Center for Medieval and Renaissance Studies, 2008), pp. 261–99.

Siemens, Ray, with Caroline Leitch, 'Editing the Early Modern Miscellany: Modelling and Knowledge (Re)Presentation as a Context for the Contemporary Editor', in *New Ways of Looking at Old Texts IV*, ed. by Michael Denbo (Tempe, AZ: Renaissance English Text Society, 2009), pp. 115–30.

Siemens, Ray, with Meagan Timney, Cara Leitch, Corina Koolen and Alex Garnett, and with the ETCL, inKE and PKP Research Groups, 'Toward Modeling the Social Edition: An Approach to Understanding the Electronic Scholarly Edition in the Context of New and Emerging Social Media', *Literary and Linguistic Computing*, 27 (2012), 445–61, http://dx.doi.org/10.1093/llc/fqs013

Simon, Herbert A., 'Technology Is Not the Problem', in *Speaking Minds: Interviews with Twenty Eminent Cognitive Scientists*, ed. by Peter Baumgarter and Sabine Payr (Princeton: Princeton University Press, 1995), pp. 232–48.

Söderlund, Petra, 'Tryckt eller elektronisk variantredovisning — Varför och för vem?', in *Digitala och tryckta utgåvor: Erfarenheter, planering och teknik i förändring* (Helsingfors: Svenska litteratursällskapet i Finland, 2011), pp. 93–109.

Southall, Raymond, 'The Devonshire Manuscript Collection of Early Tudor Poetry, 1532–41', *Review of English Studies*, 15 (1964), 142–50.

Spencer, Matthew, Elizabeth A. Davidson, Adrian C. Barbrook and Christopher J. Howe, 'Phylogenetics of Artificial Manuscripts', *Journal of Theoretical Biology*, 227 (2004), 503–11.

Sperberg-McQueen, C. Michael, 'How to Teach Your Edition How to Swim', *Literary and Linguistic Computing*, 24 (2009), 27–52, http://dx.doi.org/10.1093/llc/fqn034

Stadler, Peter, 'Interoperabilität von digitalen Briefeditionen', in *Fontanes Briefe ediert*, ed. by Hanna Delf von Wolzogen and Rainer Falk (Würzburg: Königshausen & Neumann, 2014), pp. 278–87.

Stahl, Peter, 'Kollation und Satztechnik als Vorbereitung für eine kritische Edition', in *Maschinelle Verarbeitung altdeutscher Texte* IV, ed. by Kurt Gärtner et al. (Tübingen: Max Niemeyer Verlag, 1991), pp. 142–47.

Steding, Sören A., *Computer-Based Scholarly Editions: Context, Concept, Creation, Clientele* (Berlin: Logos, 2002).

Stella, Francesco, 'Tipologie di edizione digitale per i testi medievali', in *Poesía medieval: Historia literaria y transmisión de textos*, ed. by Vitalino Valcárcel Martinez and Carlos Pérez González (Burgos: Fundación Instituto Castellano y Leonés de la Lengua, 2005), pp. 327–62.

—, 'Digital Philology, Medieval Texts, and the *Corpus* of Latin Rhythms: A Digital Edition of Music and Poems', in *Digital Philology and Medieval Texts*, ed. by Arianna Ciula and Francesco Stella (Pisa: Pacini editore, 2006), pp. 223–49.

—, ed., *Corpus rhythmorum musicum saec. IV–IX* (Florence: SISMEL-Edizioni del Galluzzo, 2007).

Stevens, John, *Music and Poetry in the Early Tudor Court* (Cambridge: Cambridge University Press, 1979).

Stewart, John, Olivier Gapenne and Ezequiel A. Di Paolo, eds., *Enaction: Toward a New Paradigm for Cognitive Science* (Cambridge, MA: MIT Press, 2011).

Stokes, Peter A., 'Computer-Aided Palaeography, Present and Future', in *Kodikologie und Paläographie im Digitalen Zeitalter — Codicology and Palaeography in the Digital Age*, ed. by Malte Rehbein, Patrick Sahle and Torsten Schassan, in collaboration with Bernhard Assman, Franz Fischer and Christiane Fritze (Norderstedt: BOD, 2009), pp. 313–42.

—, 'Teaching Manuscripts in the "Digital Age"', in *Kodikologie und Paläographie im Digitalen Zeitalter 2 — Codicology and Palaeography in the Digital Age 2*, ed. by Franz Fischer, Christiane Fritze and Georg Vogeler, in collaboration with Bernhard Assmann, Malte Rehbein and Patrick Sahle, Schriften des Instituts für Dokumentologie und Editorik 3 (Norderstedt: BOD, 2010), pp. 229–45.

—, 'The Problem of Digital Dating: A Model for Uncertainty in Medieval Documents', in *Digital Humanities 2015 Book of Abstracts* (Sydney, 2015), http://dh2015.org/abstracts/xml/STOKES_Peter_Anthony_The_Problem_of_Digital_Datin/STOKES_Peter_Anthony_The_Problem_of_Digital_Dating__A_M.html

Stolz, Michael, ed., *Die St. Galler Epenhandschrift: Parzival, Nibelungenlied und Klage, Karl, Willehalm: Faksimile des Codex 857 der Stiftsbibliothek St. Gallen und zugehöriger Fragmente: CD-ROM mit einem Begleitheft*, Codices Electronici Sangallenses, 1 (Stiftsbibliothek St. Gallen/Basler Parzival-Projekt, 2003).

Stussi, Alfredo, ed., *Fondamenti di critica testuale*, 2nd ed. (Bologna: il Mulino, 2006).

—, *Introduzione agli studi di filologia italiana*, 4th ed. (Bologna: il Mulino, 2011).

Sutherland, Kathryn, ed., *Electronic Text: Investigations in Method and Theory* (Oxford: Oxford University Press, 1997).

—, *Jane Austen's Textual Lives: From Aeschylus to Bollywood* (Oxford: Oxford University Press, 2005).

Swift, Jonathan, *A Tale of a Tub and Other Works*, ed. by ed. Angus Ross and David Woolley (Oxford: Oxford University Press, 1986).

Taeger, Burkhard, ed., *Heliand und Genesis*, ed. by Otto Behaghel, 10th ed. by Burkhard Taeger (Tübingen: Max Niemeyer Verlag, 1996).

Tapscott, Don and Anthony D. Williams, 'Innovating the 21st-Century University: It's Time!', *Educause* (January/February 2010), 17–29.

Tarrant, R. J., ed., *P. Ovidi Nasonis Metamorphoses* (Oxford: Oxford University Press, 2004).

Terras, Melissa, 'Should We Just Send a Copy? Digitisation, Usefulness and Users', *Art Libraries Journal*, 35.1 (2010), 22–27, http://discovery.ucl.ac.uk/171096/1/Terras_Sendacopy.pdf

Thorburn, David and Henry Jenkins, eds., *Rethinking Media Change: The Aesthetics of Transition* (Cambridge, MA: MIT Press, 2003).

Timpanaro, Sebastiano, *La genesi del metodo del Lachmann* (Florence: Le Monnier, 1963).

—, *The Genesis of Lachmann's Method*, ed. and trans. by Glenn W. Most (Chicago: University of Chicago Press, 2005).

Tonkin, Emma, 'Making the Case for a Wiki', *Ariadne* (30 January 2005), http://www.ariadne.ac.uk/issue42/tonkin

Trovato, Paolo, *Everything You Always Wanted to Know about Lachmann's Method: A Non-Standard Handbook of Genealogical Textual Criticism in the Age of Post-Structuralism, Cladistics, and Copy-Text* (Padua: libreriauniversitaria.it edizioni, 2014).

Twycross, Meg, 'Virtual Restoration and Manuscript Archeology', in *The Virtual Representation of the Past*, ed. by Mark Greengrass and Lorna Hughes (Farnham: Ashgate, 2008), pp. 23–47.

Unsworth, John, 'What Is Humanities Computing and What Is Not?', *Jahrbuch für Computerphilologie*, 4 (2002), http://computerphilologie.digital-humanities.de/jg02/unsworth.html

Van Hulle, Dirk, *Textual Awareness: A Genetic Study of Late Manuscripts by Joyce, Proust, and Mann* (Ann Arbor: University of Michigan Press, 2004).

—, *The Making of Samuel Beckett's* Krapp's Last Tape/La Dernière Bande (London: Bloomsbury, 2015).

—, *Modern Manuscripts: The Extended Mind and Creative Undoing from Darwin to Beckett and Beyond* (London: Bloomsbury, 2014).

Van Hulle, Dirk and Vincent Neyt, eds., *The Beckett Digital Manuscript Project (BDMP1), Module 1:* Stirrings Still / Soubresauts *and 'Comment dire' / 'what is the word': A Digital Genetic Edition* (Brussels: ASP/University Press Antwerp, 2011), http://www.beckettarchive.org

Van Hulle, Dirk, Mark Nixon and Vincent Neyt, eds., *Samuel Beckett Digital Manuscript Project* (Antwerp: University Press Antwerp, 2013), http://www.beckettarchive.org

Van Hulle, Dirk and Mark Nixon, *Samuel Beckett's Library* (Cambridge: Cambridge University Press, 2013).

Van Hulle, Dirk, Shane Weller and Vincent Neyt, eds., *The Beckett Digital Manuscript Project (BDMP2), Module 2:* L'Innommable / The Unnamable: *A Digital Genetic Edition* (Brussels: ASP/University Press Antwerp, 2013), http://www.beckettarchive.org

Vandendorpe, Christian, *From Papyrus to Hypertext: Toward the Universal Digital Library* (Urbana-Champaign: University of Illinois Press, 2009).

Vanhoutte, Edward, 'Prose Fiction and Modern Manuscripts: Limitations and Possibilities of Text Encoding for Electronic Editions', in *Electronic Textual Editing*, ed. by Lou Burnard, Katherine O'Brien O'Keeffe and John Unsworth (New York: Modern Languages Association, 2006), pp. 161–80.

—, 'Every Reader his own Bibliographer—An Absurdity?', in *Text Editing, Print and the Digital World*, ed. by Marilyn Deegan and Kathryn Sutherland (Farnham: Ashgate, 2009), pp. 99–110.

—, 'Paul Otlet (1868–1944) and Vannevar Bush (1890–1974)', *The Mind Tool: Edward Vanhoutte's Blog*, 2009, http://edwardvanhoutte.blogspot.nl/2009/03/paul-otlet-1868-1944-and-vannevar-bush.html

Vázquez, Nila, ed., *The Tale of Gamelyn of the Canterbury Tales: An Annotated Edition* (Lewiston, NY: The Edwin Mellen Press, 2009).

Vest, Charles M., 'Open Content and the Emerging Global Meta-University', *Educause* (May/June 2006), http://www.hewlett.org/library/grantee-publication/open-content-and-emerging-global-meta-university

Walker, Kim, *Women Writers of the English Renaissance* (New York: Twayne, 1996).

Wall, Wendy, *The Imprint of Gender: Authorship and Publication in the English Renaissance* (Ithaca, NY: Cornell University Press, 1993).

Walter, Axel E., *Späthumanismus und Konfessionspolitik im konfessionellen Zeitalter: Die europäische Gelehrtenrepublik um 1600 im Spiegel der Korrespondenzen Georg Michael Lingelsheim* (Tübingen: Max Niemeyer Verlag, 2004).

Weaver, Warren and Claude E. Shannon, *The Mathematical Theory of Communication* (Urbana-Champaign: University of Illinois Press, 1963).

Weinreich, Uriel, 'Is a Structural Dialectology Possible?', *Word*, 10 (1954), 388–400.

Widdows, Dominic, 'Word-Vectors and Search Engines', in *Geometry and Meaning* (Stanford, CA: Center for the Study of Language and Information, 2004), pp. 131–265, http://www.puttypeg.net/book/chapters/chapter5.html

Wilcox, Helen, ed., *Women and Literature in Britain, 1500–1700* (Cambridge: Cambridge University Press, 1996).

Wilson, Christo, Bryce Boe, Alessandra Sala, Krishna P. N. Puttaswamy and Ben Y. Zhao, 'User Interactions in Social Networks and their Implications', in *EuroSys '09: Proceedings of the 4th ACM European Conference on Computer Systems* (New York: ACM, 2009), pp. 205–18, http://dx.doi.org/10.1145/1519065.1519089

Wittek, Peter and Walter Ravenek, 'Supporting the Exploration of a Corpus of 17th-Century Scholarly Correspondences by Topic Modeling', in *Supporting Digital Humanities 2011: Answering the Unaskable*, ed. by Bente Maegaard (Copenhagen, 2011), http://www.clarin.nl/sites/default/files/sdh2011-wittek-ravenek.pdf

Wolf, Lior et al., 'Identifying Join Candidates in the Cairo Genizah', *International Journal of Computer Vision*, 94 (2011), 118–35.

Woods, Susanne and Margaret P. Hannay, *Teaching Tudor and Stuart Women Writers* (New York: Modern Languages Association, 2000).

Zimmerman, M., ed., *Apulei Metamorphoseon libri XI* (Oxford: Oxford University Press, 2012).

Zitner, S. P., 'Truth and Mourning in a Sonnet by Surrey', *English Literary History*, 50 (1983), 509–29.

Zumthor, Paul, *Essai de poétique médiévale* (Paris: Éditions du Seuil 1972).

—, *La lettre et la voix* (Paris: Éditions du Seuil, 1987).

—, *Toward a Medieval Poetics*, trans. by Philip Bennet (Minneapolis: University of Minnesota Press, 1992).

Zundert, Joris van, 'The Case of the Bold Button: Social Shaping of Technology and the Digital Scholarly Edition', *Digital Scholarship in the Humanities*, advanced access (8 March 2016), http://dx.doi.org/10.1093/llc/fqw012

Index

accountability 10, 60, 151
Alliance of Digital Humanities
  Organizations (ADHO) 173
Anastasia 221
Anderson, Terry 156
André, Julie 114
annotation 11, 24, 90, 91, 101, 127,
  142, 146, 235
Apollon, Daniel 59
Apuleius, Lucius 205, 209
Arbuckle, Alyssa 150
archetype 203, 204, 205, 206, 207–213
Arikha, Avigdor 109, 110
Armstrong, Karin 150, 151
arts-humanities.net 165, 166, 173
Assmann, Bernhard 2
Association for Computers and the
  Humanities (ACH) 173
Associazione per l'Informatica
  Umanistica e la Cultura Digitale
  165
Atik, Anne 109, 110
Aulus Gellius 207
Austen, Jane 42, 104
authorship attribution 56
Baccino, Thierry 236
Bacon, Francis 116
Badger, Emily 172
Baecker, Ronald M. 86
Bakhtin, Mikhail 98
Baldacci, Luigi 110
Bampi, Massimiliano 64

Barbi, Michele 72
Barbrook, Adrian C. 7
Baret, Philippe V. 7
Baron, Helen 138, 141, 143, 146
Barthes, Roland 97
Baumgarter, Peter 83
Bayeux Tapestry 22
Beckett Digital Manuscript Project
  49, 109, 117
Beckett, Samuel 11, 49, 108, 109, 110,
  111, 112, 113, 115, 116, 117
Bédier, Joseph 44, 62, 63, 229
Behaghel, Otto 66
Beilin, Elaine V. 145
Belisle, Claire 59
Bembo, Pietro 43
Benedetto, Simone 236
Bergamin, Per 236
Bergmann Loizeaux, Elizabeth 28
Bernaerts, Lars 107
Berners-Lee, Tim 97, 147
Berra, Aurélien 165
Bishop, Morris 110
Bjork, Robert E. 150
Boase, Roger 144
Bochud, Yves 236
Bodley, Thomas 187
Boe, Bryce 80
Boffey, Julia 143
Boleyn, Anne, Queen of England 138,
  140
Bond, Barbara 150, 151

Bond, Edward A. 141
Bonnat, Jean-Louis 184
Boot, Peter 37
Borgman, Christine L. 57, 84
Bossis, Mireille 184
Bowen, William R. 150, 151
Bowers, Fredson 42, 48
Boyd, Jason 150
Braune, Wilhelm 67
Brumfield, Ben 100, 104
Bryant, John 41, 49, 99, 232
Buckland, Michael 97
Buomprisco, Giancarlo 233
Buonarroti, Michelangelo 47
Burghart, Marjorie 76
Burgio, Eugenio 78
Burke, Mary E. 145
Burke, Victoria Elizabeth 143
Burnard, Lou 121
Burnley, David 144
Burton, Gideon 157
Busa, Roberto 100
Bush, Vannevar 96, 98
Buzzetti, Dino 61, 71, 88, 100
Buzzoni, Marina 10, 45, 48, 53, 63, 68, 202, 230, 238

Caesar, Gaius Iulius 207, 213
Campbell, Thomas 110
Canterbury Tales Project 219
Carlquist, Jonas 180
Carpenter, David 51
Cassirer, Ernst 116
CERL (Consortium of European Research Libraries) 4
Cerquiglini, Bernard 44, 45
Chalmers, David J. 107
Chaucer, Geoffrey 140, 141
Chernaik, Warren J. 28
Chernyk, Melanie 150
Chrétien de Troyes 65
Circulation of Knowledge and Learned Practices in the 17th-century Dutch Republic 94
Ciula, Arianna 59, 150

CLARIN (Common Language Resources and Technology Infrastructure) 3
Clark, Andy 107, 113
Clarke, Elizabeth 146
Codex Sinaiticus 174
codicology 5
Coleridge, Samuel T. 46
collaboratory 173
CollateX 90
Columella, L. Iuni Moderatii 205, 207
Contini, Gianfranco 48, 62, 63, 68
correspondence 183, 184, 185, 186, 187, 188, 189, 190, 192, 194, 195, 197, 198, 200
Cotticelli Kurras, Paola 68
co-worker 126, 127, 128, 129, 133
Crane, Gregory 159, 214, 218
Creative Commons 177
creole, methodological 87
critical apparatus 6, 10, 13, 45, 54, 63, 64, 65, 71, 74, 75, 76, 81, 82, 169, 180, 201, 202, 203, 204, 209, 212, 213, 214, 217, 218
critique génétique 45, 99, 114
Crompton, Constance 150
crowdsourcing 12, 30, 35, 36, 99, 100, 128
Cummings, James 75, 150
Cunningham, Ward 153
Czerwinski, Mary 86

Daalder, Joost 143
Dahlström, Mats 25, 34, 121, 122, 123, 162, 178
Daisne, Johan 49
Dalen-Oskam, Karina van 93
Damon, Cynthia 6, 13, 14, 45
DARIAH (Digital Research Infrastructure for the Arts and the Humanities) 3
data mining 56
Davidson, Elizabeth A. 7
Deegan, Marylin 28, 48, 50, 54, 61, 100, 123, 181
De Geest, Dirk 107

Dekker, Ronald H. 90
Deleuze, Gilles 98
DEMM (Digital Editing of Medieval Manuscripts) 2
Denbo, Michael 150
Dennett, Daniel C. 112, 113
De Robertis, Domenico 60, 61
Derrida, Jacques 97
Desenclos, Camille 13
DeZur, Kathryn 146
DHCommons 173
Dickson, Terra 150
Digital Archive 34, 49
Digital Byzantinist 161
Digital Classicist 147, 161, 165, 166
Digital Edition of the Old Church Slavonic Codex Suprasliensis 173
Digital Humanities Now 173
Digital Medievalist 147, 161, 219, 230
Digital Ramusio 78
Digital Scholarly Edition (DSE) xiii, 10, 12, 14, 21, 23, 26, 33, 51, 83, 84, 85, 90, 96, 98, 101, 102, 103, 104, 105, 106, 115, 118, 120, 121, 128, 162, 180, 183, 185, 186, 188, 237
Digital Scholarly Editions Initial Training Network. *See* DiXiT
Digital scriptorium 4
Digital Vercelli Book 225, 233
digitisation 26
DiNucci, Darcy 147
Di Paolo, Ezequiel A. 107
Di Pietro, Chiara 233
distant reading 56, 100
DiXiT (Digital Scholarly Editions Initial Training Network) x, 2
document 6, 11, 13, 19, 23, 24, 25, 26, 74, 104, 105, 114, 122, 127, 130, 131, 185
docuverse 98
Dolveck, Franz 210
Domesday Explorer 177
Donawerth, Jane 145
dossier génétique 49
Doubinsky, Claude 68

Douglas, Margaret 140, 141, 142, 146, 154
Dove, Linda L. 145
Drai-Zerbib, Véronique 236
Driscoll, Matthew James 45, 218
Drupal 157, 158, 227
DSE. *See* Digital Scholarly Edition
Du Bourg, Antoine 183, 186
Duggan, Hoyt N. 219
Duncker, Dorthe 121
DuRietz, Rolf E. 121, 122

Ebbinghaus, Ernst A. 67
Ecclesfield, Nigel 156
eCodices 4
editing
 critical editing 19, 20, 22, 38, 47, 49
 documentary editing 22
 genetic editing 22, 114
edition
 critical edition 20, 24, 46, 201
 documentary edition 104
 paradigmatic edition 52
 public edition 35
 reading edition 45
 social edition 35, 36, 80, 138
Edwards, Paul N. 101
Eggert, Paul 98, 125
Eisenstein, Elizabeth 43
eLaborate 90, 91, 92, 93, 95, 104
Electronic Beowulf 219, 231
Electronic Heliand Project 68, 73, 74
Elliot, T. S. 55
Elliott, Tom 200
Ellis, David 166
enactivism 107, 115
encoding 190, 192, 193, 194, 196, 199
endogenesis 109, 114, 115, 116, 118
ENRICH (European Networking Resources and Information Concerning Cultural Heritage) 4
EpiDoc 200
eReader 51
ETCL Research Group 80, 147, 151, 153, 154, 155

Euripides 213
European Science Foundation 1
exogenesis 109, 115, 118
Ezell, Margaret J. M. 145, 146, 159

Facebook 147, 222
facsimile 25, 27, 29, 30, 34, 38, 101, 149, 162, 163, 223, 228, 229
Falk, Rainer 13
Ferrari, Fulvio 64
Ferrer, Daniel 116
Finneran, Richard J. 53, 54
Fiormonte, Domenico 99
Fischer, Franz 2
Fitzpatrick, Kathleen 157, 158
Fitzroy, Mary Howard 140, 141
Flanders, Julia 41
Folsom, Ed 50
Foucault, Michel 98
Fox, Alistair 144
Foxwell, Agnes K. 138, 143
Foys, Martin K. 22
Fraistat, Neil 28, 41
Francis I, King of France 183
Franzini, Greta 12, 180, 181, 182, 186, 224, 238
Fritze, Christiane 2

Gabler, Hans Walter 25, 119, 121, 123, 124, 131, 162, 203
Galison, Peter 87
Gapenne, Olivier 107
Garnett, Alex 80, 147, 156, 157
Gärtner, Kurt 65
Gaudet, Chris 150
Gellhaus, Alex 109
Gendolla, Peter 60
genetic criticism. *See* critique génétique
Genette, Gérard 68, 71, 127, 140
Genette, Raymonde Debray 114
Gervais, Bertrand 128, 129
Geymonat, Mario 207
Ghersetti, Antonella 78
Gibson, Andrew 28, 150

Gibson, Jonathan 143
Girard, Hélène 184
Gold, Matthew K. 88
Gontarski, Stanley E. 115
Google Fusion Tables 170, 173
Google Sheet 167, 170
Gorman, Michael E. 87
Govindaraju, Venu 5
Grafton, Anthony 43
Graphic User Interface 85, 86, 102, 230
Greetham, David 25, 41, 42
Greg, Walter W. 42
Grésillon, Almuth 42
Guattari, Felix 98
GUI. *See* Graphic User Interface

Hannay, Margaret P. 145
Harrier, Richard C. 138, 141, 143
Haselkorn, Anne M. 145
Haswell, Eric 150
Hattfield, Richard 140
Haugen, Odd Einar 229
Hawking, Stephen 55
Hayles, Katherine N. 99
Heale, Elizabeth 138, 143, 150
Heiden, Serge 56
Heinsius, Nicolaas 209
Helm, Karl 67
Henry VIII 144
Herman, David 107, 108, 109
Herman, Peter C. 138
Heuvel, Charles van den 94, 97
Hirsch, Brett D. 2, 150
Hoccleve, Thomas 140
Hockey, Susan 84, 88, 100, 180
Holmes, Martin 150
Homer 41, 42
Howard, Henry 140
Howard, Thomas 140, 141
Howe, Christopher J. 7
Humanities, Arts, Science, and Technology Advanced Collaboratory 173

Hurlbut, Jesse 7
Hutto, Daniel D. 108, 113, 118
Huygens, Robert B. C. 67
Hyperstack edition of Saint Patrick's
    Confessio 103
hypertext 29, 44, 67, 73, 74, 78, 97, 98,
    99, 101, 102, 103, 104, 106, 129, 130,
    161, 179, 181, 230, 235

Ibsen, Henrik 130
Illetschko, Marcel 13
INKE Research Group 80, 147, 150
interdisciplinarity 7, 37, 84, 109, 163
interface 14, 85, 91, 95
interoperability 4, 7, 60, 74, 193, 196
intertextuality 11, 68, 98, 111, 112,
    113, 114, 115

Jakacki, Diane 150
Jannidis, Fotis 60, 75
Jenkins, Henry 28
Jenkins, Lekelia D. 87
Jessop, Martin 170
Jockers, Matthew L. 100
Joyce, James 99, 113, 115
Juxta 102

Kahler, Erich von 108
Kant, Immanuel 116
Kaptelinin, Victor 86
Karlsson, Lina 231
Kaster, Robert A. 206, 212, 218
Kenney, Edward J. 214, 216
Kenny, Julia 233
Kiernan, Kevin S. 219
Kirschenbaum, Matthew 87, 88, 130
knowledge site 114, 124, 125, 126,
    131, 132
Knyvett, Edmund 140
Kondrup, Johnny 121, 122, 123
Koolen, Corina 80, 147
Krippendorf, Klaus 167
Kristeva, Julia 98
Kwakkel, Erik 150

Lachmannian method 22, 44, 62, 76
Lancashire, Ian 165
Landow, George 97, 98, 99
Latour, Bruno 84
Lavagnino, John 46, 78, 79, 150, 173,
    174, 179
Lee, Anthony 140
Lee, Gwanhoo 85
Leitch, Cara 80, 147, 150
Lenz, Friedrich Walter 215
Lessing, Gothold Ephraim 121
Lethbridge, Emily 45
Leuf, Bo 153
Levallois, Clement 85
Lewalski, Barbara K. 145
linguistics
    computational linguisitics 56
    corpus linguistics 56
Loewenstein, David 144
Lowery, David 83
Loyen, André 210
Lucene 92, 93
Luiselli Fadda, Maria 68, 76
Lütjohann, Christian 210

Macé, Caroline 7, 164
Macrobius, Ambrosius Aurelius
    Theodosius 206, 207
Maegaard, Bente 95
Magee, Patrick 111
Mahony, Simon 2, 12, 147, 156
Malm, Linda 231
Mangen, Anne 130, 131
Mann, Thomas 99, 115
Manuntius, Aldus 43
Manuscriptorium 4
marginalia 11, 109, 110, 112, 114, 115,
    117, 180
Marotti, Arthur F. 139, 140, 144, 148,
    150
Martin, Robert C. 91
Masotti, Raffaele 233
MASTER project 4
Mays, J. C. C. 46

May, Steven W. 150
McCarty, Willard 28, 50, 88, 89, 123, 132
McGann, Jerome 12, 44, 45, 50, 57, 139, 140, 145, 148, 159, 220
McKenzie, D. F. 12, 44, 45, 139, 140, 145, 148
McKeown, J. C. 215, 216, 217
McKerrow, Ronald B. 42
McLeod, Alyssa Anne 150
McLuhan, Marshall 3, 58
media shift 124, 126, 128
Medieval/Modern Manuscript Studies in the Digital Age (MMSDA) 2
Meister, Christoph 84
Meli, Marcello 230
Menary, Richard 107
metadata 4, 8, 13, 34, 102, 103, 180, 186, 188, 189, 196, 197, 199
methodological pidgin 87
METS (Metadata Encoding and Transmission Standard) 181
Michelangelo. *See* Buonarroti, Michelangelo
Middell, Gregor 75
MMSDA. *See* Medieval/Modern Manuscript Studies in the Digital Age
Mogge, Dru 219
Mohr, Paul 210
Monastic Manuscript Project 165
Monella, Paolo 165, 212
Montaigne, Michel de 110, 111, 112
Moretti, Franco 87, 100
Most, Glenn W. 80
Moulton, Ian Frederick 146
Mueller, Janel 144
Muir, Bernard J. 220
Muir, Kenneth 138, 139, 143
multimedia 28
multimediality 60, 71
multimodality 60, 71
Murphy, Jessica 150
Myin, Erik 108, 113, 118

NeDiMAH (Network for Digital Methods in the Arts and Humanities) viii, x, xiii, 1, 2, 218
Nellmann, Eberhard 72
Nelson, Karen 145
Nelson, Theodor H. 97, 98
neo-Platonism 47
Network for Digital Methods in the Arts and Humanities. *See* NeDiMAH
Newman, Channa 68
Newton, Greg 150
Neyt, Vincent 117
Nichols, Stephen G. 45, 72
Nixon, Mark 109, 110
NLP (Natural Language Processing) 56
Nott, George Frederick 139, 143

O'Brien O'Keeffe, Katherine 121
OCR (Optical Character Recognition) 5, 6
O'Donnell, Daniel P. 75, 232
O'Donnell, James J. 28
O'Donoghue, Bernard 144
Ogrin, Matija 75
Okerson, Ann 219
Omeka 227
Ore, Espen 75, 164
Orlando Furioso Hypertext Project 177
Otlet, Paul 97
Ovidius, Publius Naso 204, 208, 209, 214, 215, 216

Pacheco, Anita 145
page 6, 44, 57, 91, 103, 114, 118, 122, 149
    page paradigm 9
Pakis, Valentine A. 66
palaeography 5
Paquette, Johanne 150
paradigm
    digital paradigm 9, 11, 27, 28, 31, 33, 38
    page paradigm 9

paratext 74, 140
Parzival-Projekt 71, 72, 73, 220
Pasanek, Bradley M. 94
Pasquali, Giorgio 63, 72
Payr, Sabine 83
Pedrotti, Marco 236
Peisistratus 41, 42
Pérez González, Carlos 61
Perseus Project 45
Peters, Keith 236
Petrarca, Francesco 109, 110, 111, 112
Petronius 203
Peursen, Willem Th. van 34
Pez, Bernhard 189
Pez, Hieronymus 189
philology
  digital philology 59
Phineas Fletcher's Sylva Poetica 174
Pierazzo, Elena 2, 5, 6, 10, 52, 57, 64, 75, 76, 80, 104, 114, 194, 218
Piers Plowman Electronic Archive 219
Pilling, John 110
PKP Research Group 80, 147
Plowright, Raina K. 87
Podracky, Jonathan 150
Poliziano, Agnolo 43
Porter, Dot 223, 225, 231, 237
Possen, David 133
post-structuralism 97
Powell, Daniel 150
Presner, Todd 155
Price, Kenneth M. 34, 50, 102, 162
Princeton Charrette Project 65
publication 29, 36, 54, 90, 146, 220
  digital publication 26, 33, 228
  fluid publication 29
  open access 15
  print publication 15, 51
  work-in-progress publication 51
Pugliese, Jacopo 233
Pusceddu, Cinzia 99, 165
Puttaswamy, Krishna P. N. 80

quantitative
  quantitative codicology 5
  quantitative method 5, 56, 85
Quentin, Henri 80
Quinn, Judy 45

Ramirez de Verger, Antonio 215
Ramsay, Stephen 100
Ramsey, William M. 107
Ramusio, Giovanni Battista 78, 79
Rasmussen, Krista Stinne Greve 11, 238
Ratha, N. K. 5
Ravasio, Pamela 86
Ravenek, Walter 95
Rayward, W. Boyd 97
reader 11, 45, 47, 48, 50, 51, 53, 54, 60, 64, 71, 98, 100, 120, 126, 127, 129, 130, 132, 133, 157, 173, 202, 208, 212
Reader 126
Reeve, Michael D. 203, 204, 212
Rehbein, Malte 2, 5
relationability 60, 67, 69
Remley, Paul 138, 141, 143, 150
representation 23
Reynolds, L. D. 203
Robinson, Peter 20, 21, 50, 98, 103, 104, 105, 125, 132, 163, 164, 180, 181, 213, 219, 220, 221, 225, 226, 227, 231, 237
Rodgers, Robert H. 206
Roelens, Xavier 49
Romano, Tim 220
Romantic Circles Electronic Editions 165
Roos, Richard 141
Rosselli Del Turco, Roberto 14, 75, 230, 233
Rossetti Archive 34, 50, 57
Rossetti, Dante Gabriel 50, 57
Rotunda Publications 165
Rowe, Katherine 150

Sahle, Patrick 2, 9, 21, 28, 31, 32, 34, 50, 61, 162, 163, 164, 165, 166, 169, 224, 231, 237, 238
Saibene, Maria Grazia 68
Sala, Alessandra 80
Schäfer, Jörgen 60
Schoenberg Database of Manuscripts 4, 172
Scholarly Digital Edition (SDE) 21, 33, 163, 224, 226, 227, 229, 230, 231, 232, 234, 235, 236, 237
Schomaker, Lambert 5
Schreibman, Susan 80, 84, 102, 128
science and technology studies 85
Sculley, D. 94
SDE. *See* Scholarly Digital Edition
SDE vs. DSE 33
Seaton, Ethel 141
Segre, Cesare 53, 63, 64
Seifert, Sabine 13
Seneca, Lucius Annaeus 111
Servius, Tullius 207, 208
SfarData 6
Shakespeare, William 55
Shannon-Weaver theory 46
Shelley-Godwin Archive 34
Shelton, Mary 138, 140, 141, 142, 143, 146, 154
Shillingsburg, Peter 7, 11, 28, 41, 46, 48, 49, 63, 81, 95, 96, 98, 101, 114, 119, 123, 125, 132, 213
Sidonius Apollinaris 210, 211
Siegenthaler, Eva 236
Siemens, Ray 9, 12, 80, 84, 88, 100, 102, 127, 128, 147, 150, 151, 158, 164
Simon, Herbert A. 83
single source principle 32
Smedt, M. de 99
Social Edition of the Devonshire Manuscript 137, 138, 139, 140, 141, 146, 147, 148, 149, 152, 153, 155, 158, 159
Söderlund, Petra 132
Southall, Raymond 138, 141

Spencer, Matthew 7
Sperberg-McQueen, C. Michael 52
Stadler, Peter 13
Stahl, Peter 65
Starza-Smith, Daniel 150
Steding, Sören A. 132, 133
Steinmetz, Stephanie 85
Stella, Francesco 59, 61, 68, 69
stemma codicum 14, 72, 76, 204, 210, 211
Stevens, John 144
Steward, John 107
Stewart, Henry 140
Stokes, Peter A. 2, 5, 8
Stolz, Michael 21, 61, 63, 71, 220
Stuart, Henry 141
Stussi, Alfredo 48, 50, 60, 61, 81
stylometry 56
Summit, Jennifer 150
Sutherland, Kathryn 28, 42, 48, 50, 54, 61, 100, 123, 181
Swift, Jonathan 112, 113

Tacitus, Publius Cornelius 217
Taeger, Burkhard 65, 66
Tandecki, Janusz 22
Tanselle, Thomas G. 121
Tapscott, Don 156
Tarrant, Richard J. 208, 218
TEI. *See* Text Encoding Initiative
Telma 186
Terras, Melissa 12, 180
text
  concept of text 30, 120
  fluid text 41, 99
  non-linear text 97
  one-text culture 46
text encoding 51, 234
Text Encoding Initiative 1, 8, 10, 13, 74, 75, 76, 82, 105, 114, 141, 151, 152, 153, 166, 169, 174, 175, 176, 177, 186, 189, 190, 191, 192, 193, 194, 195, 196, 197, 199, 200, 202, 213, 214, 216, 217, 218, 233

textual criticism 19, 20, 22, 24, 35, 47, 59, 64, 72, 78, 169
The European Association for Digital Humanities 173
The Humanities and Technology Camp 173
Thomas Aquinas 100
Thomson, Patricia 138, 139, 143
Thorburn, David 28
Thoutenhoofd, Ernst 34
Thumser, Matthias 22
Thynne, William 141
Timney, Meagan 80, 147
Timpanaro, Sebastiano 80
Tissier, Geoffrey 236
Tonkin, Emma 153
Touch Press 54
TRAME 4
transcription 8, 23, 24, 27, 29, 30, 31, 34, 35, 38, 69, 73, 75, 90, 91, 98, 100, 101, 104, 121, 140, 143, 149, 151, 152, 153, 180, 198, 213, 214, 229, 230, 232
transmedialization 32
transmission 211
  textual transmission 52, 53, 54, 55, 76, 78, 127, 179, 201, 203, 206
Travitsky, Betty S. 145
Trovato, Paolo 64
Tscherter, Vincent 86
Tudor 12, 138, 143, 144, 145, 146, 153
Twitter 147, 155, 158, 159, 166, 222

Uhlman, Anthony 115
Ullyot, Michael 150
Unsworth, John 84, 88, 121
Urtext 10, 20, 22, 25
user 54, 86, 100, 126, 129, 235

Valcárcel Martinez, Vitalino 61
Valla, Lorenzo 43
Vandendorpe, Christian 44
Van der Branden, Ron 49
Van Gogh, Vincent 101
Vanhoutte, Edward 48, 49, 97, 99, 121, 181

Van Hulle, Dirk 11, 49, 99, 110, 111, 117
Vázquez, Nila 64
Vegetius, Publius Flavius Renatus 204, 205, 209
Vervaeck, Bart 107
Vest, Charles V. 157
Virgilius, Publius Maro 207
Vitterhetssamfundet, Svenska 132
Vogeler, Georg 2

W3C (World Wide Web Consortium) 181, 234
Walker, Kim 145
Wall, Wendy 145
Walter, Axel E. 184
Wayback Machine 167
Web 2.0 147, 155, 157, 158
Weber, Carl-Maria von 187
Weber, Ingrid 150
Weel, Adrian van der 34
Weinreich, Uriel 64
Weller, Shane 117
Whitman Archive 34, 50
Widdows, Dominic 93
Wikibooks 12, 138, 147, 149, 151, 153, 154, 155, 156, 158, 159
Wikimedia 138, 149, 152, 153, 155, 156, 159
Wikipedia 20, 138, 152, 153, 155
Wikisource 152
Wilcox, Helen 145
William Blake Archive 34
Williams, Anthony D. 156
Wilson, Christo 80
Wing, Betsy 44
Wittek, Peter 95
Wittern, Christian 75
Wolf, Lior 5
Wolzogen, Hanna Delf von 13
work 123, 127, 131, 133
Wouters, Paul 85
Wurtz, Pascal 236
Wyatt, Thomas 138, 139, 140, 141, 143, 145

Xia, Weidong 85
XML (Extensible Markup Language)
 91, 105, 151, 152, 153, 169, 174, 175,
 176, 177, 180, 181, 188, 196, 213,
 214, 221, 232, 233, 234
XSLT (Extensible Stylesheet Language
 Transformation) 232, 233

Zangemeister, Karl 66
Zhao, Ben Y. 80
Zimmerman, Maaike 205
Zitner, Sheldon P. 143
Zotero Digital Humanities Group
 165
Zumthor, Paul 44, 63
Zundert, Joris van 10, 37, 85

This book need not end here...

At Open Book Publishers, we are changing the nature of the traditional academic book. The title you have just read will not be left on a library shelf, but will be accessed online by hundreds of readers each month across the globe. OBP publishes only the best academic work: each title passes through a rigorous peer-review process. We make all our books free to read online so that students, researchers and members of the public who can't afford a printed edition will have access to the same ideas. This book and additional content is available at:

https://www.openbookpublishers.com/isbn/9781783742387

Customise

Personalise your copy of this book or design new books using OBP and third-party material. Take chapters or whole books from our published list and make a special edition, a new anthology or an illuminating coursepack. Each customised edition will be produced as a paperback and a downloadable PDF. Find out more at:

https://www.openbookpublishers.com/section/59/1

Donate

If you enjoyed this book, and feel that research like this should be available to all readers, regardless of their income, please think about donating to us. We do not operate for profit and all donations, as with all other revenue we generate, will be used to finance new Open Access publications:

https://www.openbookpublishers.com/section/13/1/support-us

Like Open Book Publishers

Follow @OpenBookPublish

Read more at the Open Book Publishers **BLOG**

You may also be interested in:

**Digital Humanities Pedagogy:
Practices, Principles and Politics**
Edited by Brett D. Hirsch

https://www.openbookpublishers.com/product/161

**Text and Genre in Reconstruction:
Effects of Digitalization on Ideas, Behaviours,
Products and Institutions**
Edited by Willard McCarty

https://www.openbookpublishers.com/product/64

**From Dust to Digital: Ten Years of the
Endangered Archives Programme**
Edited by Maja Kominko

https://www.openbookpublishers.com/product/283

www.ingramcontent.com/pod-product-compliance
Lightning Source LLC
Chambersburg PA
CBHW050340230426
43663CB00010B/1926